THE MAN WHO INVENTED 'GENOCIDE'

The Public Career and Consequences of Raphael Lemkin

James J. Martin

1984
INSTITUTE FOR HISTORICAL REVIEW

The Man Who Invented 'Genocide'.
The Public Career and
Consequences of Raphael Lemkin
by James J. Martin

Copyright © 1984 by James J. Martin

Published by the
Institute for Historical Review
Post Office Box 1306
Torrance, California 90505 U.S.A.

Manufactured in the United States of America

First printing March 1984

Library of Congress Cataloging
in Publication Data:

Martin, James Joseph, 1916-
    The man who invented "genocide."

    Bibliography: p.
    Includes index.
    1. Genocide.   2. Lemkin, Raphael, 1900-1959.
3. Lawyers—United States—Biography. I. Title.
JX5414.M37   1984   341.7'7 [B]   64-6682
ISBN 0-939484-17-X
ISBN 0-939484-14-5 (pbk.)

Typesetting   Robin Schwarz
Proofreading   Claire Corlito
Cover Design   Tom Marcellus
Printing   Kingsport Press

"Historians are dangerous people. They are capable of upsetting everything. They must be directed."

— Nikita Khrushchev, quoted by Sergius Jacobsen, in a paper presented before a session of the American Historical Association in Washington, D.C., December 29, 1964, reproduced in U.S. Congress, Senate Committee on the Judiciary, *The Soviet Empire*. Report to the Subcommittee to Investigate the Administration of the Internal Security Act and other Internal Security Laws. 89th Congress, 1st. session, Washington, D.C.: U.S. Government Printing Office, 1965, p. 132.

JAMES J. MARTIN

TABLE OF CONTENTS

	1	*Introduction*
CHAPTER ONE	17	*The Man*
CHAPTER TWO	29	*Some Missing Historical Background*
CHAPTER THREE	115	*The Book: Some Observations*
CHAPTER FOUR	137	*Pièce De Résistance: 'Genocide'*
CHAPTER FIVE	167	*Success: The United Nations Organization Adopts 'Genocide' As A New International Crime*
CHAPTER SIX	193	*The Balance Sheet Of 'Genocide' Ratification: Raphael Lemkin's Victory In The UN And Failure In The U.S.A.*
CHAPTER SEVEN	255	*Postscript: The 1970 U.S. Senate Foreign Relations Sub-Committee Hearings On The Genocide Convention And Its Aftermath*
	287	*Conclusion*

APPENDICES

APPENDIX I	303	*The UN Circular: The Crime Of Genocide*
APPENDIX II	313	*The Statement Of Sen. Sam Irving On The Genocide Convention*
APPENDIX III	347	*Senate Bill 3155 On The Genocide Convention*
INDEX	353	

Introduction

LATE IN NOVEMBER, 1944, midway during what was prominently promoted by *Publishers' Weekly* as "Jewish Book Month" (November 10 - December 10), Columbia University Press was credited with quietly releasing, unaccompanied by the usual prestigious fanfare, a large (712 pp.) volume titled *Axis Rule in Occupied Europe: Laws of Occupation, Analysis of Government, Proposals for Redress.* Ultimately to become one of the most fateful works in the history of political thought in the 20th century, it was authored by an almost total obscurity, one Raphael Lemkin. Identified later as a refugee Polish Jew and lawyer holding a European doctorate, it took awhile before the credentials of the author and the significance of his work began to sink in. From internal evidence the book might just as well have been issued in 1942, or early 1943.

The publication auspices of his work went unnoticed by most but they were ominous: *Axis Rule* was directly sponsored by the Division of International Law Publications of the formidable warmonger foundation, the Carnegie Endowment for International Peace, staffed in part with some of the most influential and most implacable exponents for global war with Germany, well before it took place. After this war became a reality this organization had taken a leading position in the manufacture of postwar plans and schemes for rigging a world in harmony with and contributory to the interests of its prestigious sponsoring forces.

Starting with a vociferous accolade in the pages of the *New York Herald Tribune Weekly Book Review* on the last day of December, 1944, Lemkin was additionally reviewed with non-stop superlatives in a dozen other major periodicals in the USA, and in the London *Times Literary Supplement.*

There seemed to be some sense of mutual understanding in this orchestra of praise. The book was brought to the attention of the elite of the U.S. in all of the opinion-making sectors and likely regions from which the country's policy makers and enforcers might be likely to emanate. The reviewers glowed over this "indispensable" handbook for those who would be responsible for initiating "retributive justice" in Germany (Otto D. Tolischus in the *New York Times*), repeated in the *Christian Science Monitor,* which thought also that those who would "bear the responsibility for dealing with the Germans" would be unable to function properly without having it as their constant companion and referring to it continuously.

While Walter Millis burbled in the *Herald Tribune* about the author's "wide scholarship," echoed by Merle Fainsod in the *Harvard Law Review,* which latter reviewer identified Lemkin as "a noted Polish scholar and attorney," there was not a great deal of solid information available about him then, nor for some time thereafter. When Lemkin first surfaced in the U.S. was not revealed, but it had not been very long before his book. His major previously published work in the West was confined to two books, in French and Swedish, dealing with international law related to international money payments, foreign exchange and exchange rates, and associated banking laws around the world, a subject of great interest and importance to war refugees and emigres, an element always on the run, and one which was necessarily concerned with seeing to it that their money could be moved with them across the necessary national frontiers to the place where it might be most effectively employed. These books, *La règlementation des Paiements internationaux* (Paris, 1939) and *Valutareglering och Clearing* (Stockholm, 1941), were about all that one could refer to in seeking something of the author's credentials for writing such a book as *Axis Rule in Occupied Europe.*

There was forthcoming eventually a variety of tidbits of revelation as to his background and activities. It was obvious that his ponderous and expensive book would be confined to a small and select readership, and undoubtedly those eminent and influential figures in the U.S. who had collaborated in launching Lemkin and his fateful ideas wanted a wider acquaintance for him among the dominant left-liberal opinion-formers. Therefore the Stalinist-lining liberal weekly *The Nation* was elected to expose its then-nearly 40,000 subscribers and probably ten times as many readers to the core of his views and opinions.

In a long two-part article, "The Legal Case against Hitler" (February 24, 1945, pp. 205-207, and March 10, 1945, pp. 268-270),

Lemkin summarized his book, though not referring to his most portentous contribution, a new word, "genocide," until the closing remarks of the second part. At this point, in concluding his lengthy philippic, really an emotional legal opinion, against Hitler and the German leaders, whom he wanted arrested and tried before U.S. military courts *exclusively,* and stripped in advance of any possible plea that the proceedings were being conducted under *ex post facto* law, Lemkin uttered with grim hyperbolic judgment, "The Nazis have destroyed whole nations, a crime for which the present writer has coined the word 'genocide'—in analogy with homicide and fratricide." This was close to the same wording attending his first launching of the word "genocide," in the introduction of his book, dated November 15, 1943.

What some thought Lemkin presumably was referring to by this exaggeration was the German action resolving three of the rickety political creations of Versailles, Czecho-Slovakia, Poland and Yugoslavia, into their pre-1919 constituent parts, as best they could, with attention being paid especially to the unhappy minorities in all three, which had been forcibly welded together by the largely ignorant Big Three at Versailles, and ridden roughshod upon by their majority ethnic overseers, in a manner which by Lemkin's own theoretic imagination was itself clearly "genocidic." But since a major aim of the adversaries of the Germans in World War Two was the restoration to the best of their ability of the corrupt and unworkable European interim regime of 1919-1939, it was obvious that nothing even faintly breathing that such an order deserved dissolution was to be allowed expression in the 1943-1944 days. Others assumed that what Lemkin meant by the word "nation" was a racial, ethnic or cultural group which spilled across a number of national frontiers.

The editors of the *Nation* identified Lemkin as a former member of the International Office for the Unification of Criminal Law, a front of the League of Nations, but went into more revealing material regarding his more recent employment. Though it was not clear whether or not he had arrived in the U.S. before American belligerency in December, 1941, he had risen with celerity for a refugee immigrant who presumably had not been fluent in the English language, to judge from his publication record. He had already served as the "head consultant" to the Foreign Economic Administration of the Roosevelt war machine, an agency mainly concerned with the assignment and future ownership of the confiscated assets of the enemy. And he had just concluded a stint as lecturer before the School of Military Government located in Charlottesville, Virginia. This enclave was grooming those who would become the proconsuls of the coming American occupation of

Germany at war's end, and presumably for many decades thereafter. Hence Lemkin's pedigree made much more sense, and helped explain his lightning-like appearance and the wide dissemination of his views. What was in doubt was whether these latter were all his, or whether he was the mouthpiece through which the dominant forces behind the budding American Military Government, and the political and economic establishment it would front for, were launching their positions, blended with his so that a sophisticated product could be aimed to hit the public in one well-synchronized joint disquisition.

There were other odds and ends of significance concerning Lemkin which took awhile to surface, such as his membership in B'nai B'rith International. Another, which followed shortly upon his sudden enrollment among the forces seeking a vast blood purge in Germany, was his participation as an advisor to those representing the U.S. in the prosecution at Nuremberg of the principal defendants from the defeated German regime from the late summer of 1945 to the early fall of 1946. In the few weeks prior to the end of the war in Europe in the spring of 1945, however, no one was trying to pull together the many strands which had culminated in the publication of Lemkin's book and the loosing of his celebrated neologism, "genocide," which was to accelerate as a mischief-maker for over a generation after his passing, and which stood to be a plague in the area of international relations for a far longer time than that. In view of Lemkin's sponsorship and employment, however, there were grounds for suspecting that his name was a cover for the work of a high-powered committee.

In estimating the dependability of *Axis Rule in Occupied Europe,* during all the chorus of frenzied praise from American reviewers of all political persuasions, including the quarterly megaphone of the Council on Foreign Relations, *Foreign Affairs,* no one called attention to Lemkin's part of the book being mainly based on a compendium of second-hand and third-hand claims, allegations and insinuations. *Lemkin had actually witnessed nothing he reported,* especially that part of his work which pretended to be a reliable testimony to the extermination of part of Europe's Jews. His book had been preceded by many such allegations in the periodical and daily press of Germany's antagonists ever since 1941, if not 1936: contrary to some impressions conveyed long afterward, Lemkin was far from being the first to aver the annihilation of European Jewry via systematic, planned destruction. Nor did he stress this aspect among his many charges, or devote special attention to this in his extended *Nation* summary of his book, it might be pointed out.

As for his concept "genocide," especially anti-climactic is the immense appendix of about 400 pages of laws, rules, decrees, emergency regulations and promulgations of the Axis powers in occupied countries with which *Axis Rule* concludes, about 80% culled from sources published in 1940-1941. Not a whisper suggesting mass killing anywhere is to be found in this compilation, and the half dozen instances Lemkin specifically labels "genocide" among this bewildering collection of emergency edicts and ordinances are almost comic when compared to the apparition this word now coaxes forth. In fact, not a single instance can be found in the entire assemblage which provides for the putting to death of anyone except upon conviction for commission of specific offenses. A collection of less convincing and more irrelevant evidence in support of Lemkin's "genocide" charge could hardly ever have been made in the time admittedly spent preparing *Axis Rule.*

There is also some doubt as to the extensive impact Lemkin's book and legal stance had upon those who ended up in creating the International Military Tribunal at Nuremberg. His emphasis had been upon construing Hitler and his associates as "common criminals" who had to be prevented from adopting any defense based on the position that nothing with which they might be charged was covered by any existing law. As things turned out, Nuremberg took a direction away from Lemkin's proposals, which he acerbically criticized later on. Instead of becoming a purely U.S. military government proceeding, the trial became a device which more closely resembled a re-run of the infamous Moscow "purge" trials of 1936-1938, during which Stalin eliminated almost all of his most formidable rivals and potential adversaries. However, the disposition of the German defendants was given the cover of Anglo-American legalism and the imitation of a process run in accord with the traditional principles of justice long a part of Western culture.

Though "genocide," as such, did not specifically enter the lists as one of the six kinds of "crime" (though the word was used in the opening statement by the prosecution) handled before the bench at Nuremberg, the spirit of Lemkin's book and his new word lurked over the entire affair. But all did not share his general approach at all. One criticism was aimed at his proposal, which involved a lengthy and pretentious trial of the accused, designated as "war criminals" in "Allied" mass communications media and the pronouncements of their politicians for years, and inevitably facing conviction. One refugee legalist, the Hungarian Rustem Vambery, a particular darling of American left-liberals, supported in a very poorly concealed manner a disposition of the Hitler regime's top figures in the same manner as Communist murderers had liquidated Mussolini, an event which paralleled the publication of Lemkin's suggestions in the

Nation. Vambery certainly matched Lemkin in hatred for the Germans, but one could detect in his critique of Lemkin published a few weeks later that he considered Lemkin's formula little more than a slippery and evasive piece of inflammatory legal inventiveness.

There has probably not been a legal proceeding, genuine or sham, in the Christian era, where the outcome was so predictable as that which was followed by the hanging or jailing of the surviving apprehended top figures of Hitlerian National Socialism after the judgment at Nuremberg in October, 1946. Lemkin, a shadowy "advisor" to the American part of the prosecution, saved his expression of dissatisfaction with the outcome for later, but his hopes of derailing the dreaded evaluation of it all as an *ex post facto* procedure were sunk by Senator Robert A. Taft (R-Ohio), the sole American of any public stature who had the courage to condemn the Nuremberg verdicts as miscarriages of justice which Americans might some day come to rue. Taft's blunt evaluation on October 5, 1946 of Nuremberg as vengeance clothed in legal procedure and a violation of American legal principle in that the defendants were tried under *ex post facto* law, shook the American Establishment mightily, and led to the mobilization of a hysterical posse, a congregation of attackers and would-be rebutters of his position, from conservatives to Stalinist-liners; the entire American political spectrum was ranged against Taft, though most of these elements were really parts of a jelling basic Insider coalition which ultimately was to capture the nation and control much of the postwar world.

Few paid attention to Taft's return to the fray on October 8, when he once more denounced the pretentious *ad hoc* staging at Nuremberg, hailed by its supporters as a great advance in the establishment of new international law. Said Taft, "The whole plan of the Nuremberg and Tokyo trials was extremely unfortunate," going on to more specific criticism: "I did not criticize the courts for the convictions, but rather the whole novel and hypocritical procedure of the victors trying the vanquished for the crime of making war, under the form of judicial procedure." (Associated Press dispatch from Washington, published October 9, 1946). Many newspapers printed in the same issue containing Taft's second blast the nationally syndicated column by Paul Mallon, who boiled down the pretentious self-serving manifesto by the chief U.S. prosecutor at Nuremberg, Justice Robert H. Jackson, in the following manner: "Actually, about all Justice Jackson did was to make it a crime to lose a war."

The damage had been done: things were never the same again in the "war criminal" trial industry, though such spectacles were still going on over 35 years later, and are still a brisk enterprise, primarily in Germany. But the continued criticism of their basis has also

become a large and complicated affair. The feature of the early stage
of this after Taft was the condemnation of Nuremberg by the liberal
Supreme Court Justice, William O. Douglas, in his 1954 book *An
Almanac of Liberty* (New York: Doubleday, p. 96), in language
which almost suggested that Senator Taft had been his editor:

> No matter how many books are written or briefs filed, no matter
> how finely the lawyers analyze it, the crime for which the Nazis were
> tried had never been formalized as a crime with the definitiveness
> required by our legal standards . . . , nor outlawed with a death penalty
> by the international community. By our standards the crime arose
> under an *ex post facto* law . . . . Their guilt [sic] did not justify us in
> substituting power for principle.

However disappointing, Nuremberg did not spell the eclipse of
Lemkin; on the contrary, his star was just about to start a sensational
decade-long climb. To be sure, not everything that happened
smothered his presence and influence. The reviews of *Axis Rule* had
continued in the prestigious journals and papers all during the first
nine months of 1945, and this plus his employment in strategic posts
in U.S. government agencies relating to the wartime enemy surely
played a large part in recommending him to the entourage which
went forward to Germany to build the legal edifice at Nuremberg.
Paul Rassinier asserted, in his *Le Drame des Juifs Européens* (Paris,
1964, pp. 107-109), that *Axis Rule* was the most-talked-about work
in the corridors of the Nuremberg court in the late 1945-early 1946
time. Lemkin's book was cited in the process of the Nazi leader
Seyss-Inquart, and it was further linked with the Kasztner Report in
the effort to establish that the Nazis had exterminated all the
Hungarian Jews. And a new boost in importance for Lemkin was
about to ensue when in January, 1946 the famous Gerstein
"document," probably the most outrageous rigging by the elements
seeking to establish the mass extermination of European Jewry by
the Nazis, first surfaced. Now there was a tandem punch, Lemkin
cum Gerstein, to back the campaign to certify that this vast massacre
had been achieved by asphyxiating them to death in "gas chambers,"
in which the lethal agent was to change from time to time in the
accusation of the prosecution as each in turn became suspect or
untenable as the likely mass killer of such an immense number of
people in so short a time. How something so vast in scope as this
could produce no hard evidence is what may puzzle students of it in
the future.

    With the trial and obliteration of the Nazi leaders behind him,
and presumably with his long thirst for revenge at least partially
satisfied, Lemkin was free to go on to other things, and to take his
concept of "genocide" to the levels of international political

prominence he had originally advocated in his book. His authorship
of the term was still relatively obscured, and even the *New York
Times* did not credit its invention to him until October 21, 1945;
the *Times* created a category, "genocide," in its *Index* beginning with
the year 1947. But the sharp increase in the use of the term took
place in another arena, the halls of the United Nations Organization,
after its launching in April, 1945.

This new candidate for entry in the lists of international crimes
enjoyed subdued discussion until its possibilities began to dawn on
some of the world's submerged and subjected peoples, the "little
birds" whom Churchill in his magnanimity had suggested the big
powers, who were cast to run the UN as their private club, allow to
"sing a little" once in awhile, to give the world the illusion of the
UN's "democratic" basis. Though "genocide" had been useful in
the 1945-1946 time mainly to the aggrieved elements of European
Jewry and the long-range strategists of Zionism, it became obvious
to all with a sense of injury suffered in the past, or who sustained
new hurts or wrongs in the beginning years of the "golden postwar
future," that much could be done with such an omnibus fabrication
as "genocide." As a consequence of this warming to the subject on
the part of many who had not thought previously of their situation
in these terms, a new cockpit was about to be provided for the
exacerbation of grievances and disputes among nations.

So the "genocide" question slowly moved to another combat
zone, the halls of the new international organization superseding the
League of Nations. Thus it was in the deliberations of the UNO that
"genocide" took on its new trappings and gained its universal conno-
tation, with all using the word until it became a suffocating verbal
reflex, while tending to disagree to quite a degree on what its proper
definition should be. Ultimately a definition which tolerably satisfied
the main wranglers in the UN was hammered out into recognizable
shape, but with an annoying tendency for stipulations and reservations to be advanced by the representatives of this State or that one,
annoying especially to Raphael Lemkin, whose brainchild the word
was, and who thought that his definition should have been satisfactory to all and should have been allowed to exist unaltered in
perpetuity. In the end he was induced to share with others its
expanded "final" definition, but his mark remained on it most
prominently.

What took shape in the form of a UN draft genocide convention
were more elaborate extensions of what Lemkin had advanced in
the introduction to his book and in his *Nation* gloss on that. Simply
put, it declared that henceforth it would be an international crime
for a people or its leaders to destroy, *with deliberate intent,* national,

ethnic, racial or religious *groups* within that nation, or any other nation. Plainly omitted from this catalog were *political* and *economic* groups, an omission with very damaging future consequences. It was also evident that this draft convention did not condemn as international crimes massacres or exterminations *as such,* only those which could be established had been deliberately planned or intended as conscious policy. And though the vast majority which mulled- over this verbiage thought of the "group" in question as a *minority* most of the time, it left an interesting possibility for future rumination, as when the deliberately planned and intended annihilation was that of a *majority* by a *minority.*

The expansion of the concept of "genocide" and its much enhanced significance, now that it was about to graduate to the hard-core level of international politics, had various consequences. The more specific provisions had something to do with a wider acceptance of the entire matter, and a more popular sense of feeling that it was understood. But by the spelling-out of how "genocide" might now be construed, as well as the opportunities remaining due to what was omitted, and by the expansion of the scope of possibilities for the commission of "genocide," the scatter-gun and even random lodging of accusations of "genocide" was encouraged on the part of almost anyone who felt endangered by the consequences of the acts of others. From the beginning of the debates over the adoption of the draft convention the air in the UN was repeatedly rent with cries of the representative of one State or another, charging an element in his land, but usually that of an adjoining neighbor, with "genocide." What had happened was the achievement of fashionability of another ominous epithet added to the soiled and murky baggage of political terminology, one with seemingly endless consequences and almost unbounded scope for trouble-making potential.

The key to the post-Nuremberg propaganda associated with "genocide" and the agitation aroused mainly by Lemkin and his fellow enthusiasts in the corridors of the UN was the insistence on its primary definition as an *international* crime. This was essential to their grand strategy, which was to emphasize tirelessly the importance of separating the crime and those who committed it, or were thus charged, from any *national* protection, and to make possible a system of punishment far removed from where the violations supposedly took place, if necessary, and applied by people who did not have to be even remotely involved, if possible.

The fundamental aspect had to concern the neutralization and elimination of any resistance to the extradition of the accused to distant lands, to be judged by total strangers with a predisposition to

finding the accused guilty as charged, the latter in the manner of the
Soviet "judges" in the Moscow purge "trials" of 1936-1938. This
key proposition at the core of the entire business was knuckled
under to by many UN member countries, but it was the barrier to
ratification, in part, by the two super-powers to emerge from the
war. United States ratification of the Genocide Convention bogged
down, largely as a consequence of resistance to this provision and its
possible ramifications, and is now no closer than it was a quarter of
a century ago. Also, when the Soviet Union ratified it, they did so
with the reservation that no Soviet citizen would be subject to being
spirited abroad in the manner stipulated by the Lemkin school, and
Lemkin bitterly opposed accepting the Soviet ratification on that
basis.

It has been argued that the favorable momentum created by the
immense vaporings over the "genocide" question and its exploitation
in print and film provided a world opinion cover for the kidnapping
of Adolf Eichmann in Argentina and his spiriting to Israel, and his
subsequent "trial" and "execution." Critics were loud in asserting
that this was a demonstration of how genocidic proceedings might
work in the future, with the intimation that things might get somewhat worse than that. One can observe a noticeable cooling of world
interest in the matter from these times onward, 1960-1961, though
extraditions of people associated with Nazi Germany from other
parts of the world to face "war criminal" charges, almost exclusively
accusations of actions taken against Jews and Communists, have gone
on without respite (in the Soviet Union, trials and hangings go on
almost monthly to this day involving similar situations, though the
accused are charged with antipatriotic acts in behalf of the Germans,
against the Soviet Fatherland.)

However, there has been a steady sagging of practical achievement redounding to the credit of the "genocide" concept starting
around mid-1953, which requires a step backward in order to assess
the nature of the world situation developing after the Nuremberg
proceedings of 1946, down to the tapering-off after the first hyperthyroid exertions in behalf of this new wrinkle in world politics.

In his original proposition for the recognition of his newly-
invented political crime, Lemkin had been more concerned with its
political future than its etymological structure. In fact, the definition
of the word "genocide" underwent a succession of changes, altera-
tions, additions, polishings, expansions and broadenings, as its
potential began to be realized by those who were engaged in facilitating its passage through the meeting halls of the post-1946 United
Nations. For over five years, beginning in 1947, it promised to be a
matter of prime importance to the world, to large and small countries

alike. Then its aura dimmed rapidly, starting in mid-1953, never to rise to its former fashionability during the next quarter of a century. But, like a powerful explosive mine wrenched loose from its ocean floor moorings and now threatening everyone, bobbing about on the surface of the seas of the world, Lemkin's seemingly simple and clear-cut addition to world political language assumed a dark importance and reflected portentous possibilities far beyond what its creator had ever dreamed.

In the late 1970s, over a generation after "genocide" had made its quiet and unheralded entry into the world, it loomed as a likely instigator of a succession of bitter international disputes, probably, in several cases, beyond negotiation, and leading to situations likely to result in war. (Omitted from this general evaluation is a lengthy series of the most blatant and glaring internal massacres in a dozen African lands of a most obvious "genocidic" character as per Lemkin's recipes, but which his spiritual descendants have rarely had either the courage or energy to notice, let alone denounce.)

As for the United States, for over three decades unwilling under all regimes headed by both its major political parties even to ratify the Genocide Concention, nevertheless it remained a factor in domestic politics, a separate time bomb with its own promise for political discord, domestically, and possible resultant deep trouble.

From the start Lemkin showed his principal concern for procedure, allowing his new word to stand by itself, depending upon emotional and related factors to shore up his concept while he devoted major energy to getting something done about it. It was obvious in the climate of opinion prevailing late in 1944 that enough minds had been made up to promote the kind of action he thought necessary, momentarily directed at the immediate offenders, the Germans, who had "destroyed whole nations," his initial hyperbolical definition for the offense which they were charged with committing.

Lemkin's task was two-fold, as he laid it out in his book and his *Nation* articles. The first step he advocated was the swift adoption, "in the form of an international treaty, to be signed by the United Nations and the neutrals, in which 'genocide' would be placed on the list of international crimes, along with piracy, and trade in women, slaves and narcotics." (*Nation,* March 10, 1945, p. 270.)

But this was just for openers; having this new crime recognized, which for the moment was to be allowed to stand as the broadest acceptable or tolerable stipulation, the "destruction" of "whole nations," a second step had to be taken at once, or the establishment of this crime would never be followed on the stage of operational reality. Once accepted as a crime, it was likely that its commission would not result in anything other than pious hand-wringing and

mutters of rhetorical condemnation. The next step had to consist in
the devising of a system for its prompt punishment.

Said Lemkin, "The crime of genocide should be made extraditable." This meant that those charged with its commission,
presumably a considerable number of people at one time, since
"genocide" was a *group* crime against a *group,* which had taken place
in a specific spot, had to be made vulnerable to removal to some
other place for trial, and, presumably, conviction and disposal. It
could not be allowed that those of the same area where "genocide"
had occurred be the judges of the matter, and to take measures
within the context of their own legal processes. No one was to be
trusted in this matter; those accused had to be subjected to physical
removal to some other place if justice was to triumph and punishment properly meted out. Without agreement on the part of all
nationals of all national states that they were subject to indictment
and possible removal beyond the protection of their own laws, to a
location where they would be subject to procedures which might not
be even faintly similar to those with which they might be familiar,
then Lemkin's scheme for the swift and efficient handling of those
accused of "genocide" would never be realized.

Where a locus might be agreed upon, sufficiently remote from
the influence of all national states concerned to process a "genocide"
case, of course did not enter into the calculations of 1944. (Trial
before the International Court or a newly created branch thereof was
one contemporary suggestion.) As it turned out, given the fortuitous
situation resulting from German unconditional surrender, the conviction of the Nazi leaders in 1946 and their subsequent execution was
effected right in their own national State. But the chances of this
happening again did not appear to be very bright.

And when Eichmann was similarly disposed of, the situation was
also quite out of harmony with the theoretical suppositions related
to the "genocide" question which were under discussion in the late
1940s. To begin with, the "trial" of Eichmann involved a single
individual, which did not conform to the theory of "genocide" as a
group crime committed by many people, as the definition in the
Genocide Convention plainly intimated. Furthermore, the defendant
was kidnapped in and transported from one national State, where
the offense had not occurred, to another national State, which in this
case not only was not a real party to the affair, but had not even
existed when the acts for which he was tried, convicted and hanged
took place.

Whether Lemkin would have approved of the way Eichmann was
liquidated was beyond any powers of determining, since he had died
a year before the kidnapping took place. The chances are high that

he would have done so, in the light of all he wrote in 1943-1949, and in view of his long years of hectic crusading in the UN for the adoption of the Genocide Convention without the reservations and qualifications which in effect vitiated his original stipulations. Reasons could have been found to rationalize the reality that only a single individual was involved, though this act was in complete contradiction of his basic premise; "genocide" was a group offense against another group.

In one sense, Raphael Lemkin's new crime, and his new word for it, "genocide," achieved dizzying success. (The invention of new diseases by doctors is called "quackery"; there is no corresponding word for lawyers who invent new crimes.) Less than a decade after he first fabricated it, enough States represented in the United Nations Organization came to ratify the Convention which incorporated it as a new international crime, and most of them surrounded it with enabling legislation to make it the law of their lands as well. All this was achieved by 1951.

But victory and defeat are sometimes slippery abstractions, and Lemkin's triumph was darkened by one catastrophic frustration: the failure to persuade the representatives of the United States government to ratify the very same Genocide Convention, despite a program and an investment which appeared unstoppable. The drive to gain American endorsement collapsed in failure by the end of 1953. As a result a pall was cast on the entire "genocide" venture which has never been dispelled. No succeeding move to achieve this result ever was to do any better (the most recent foundered early in 1974), though none after this initial effort ever mustered such wide popular involvement, intense pressure, vast publicity and monetary investment.

Still, over 30 years after the UN had put the Genocide Convention into business, the impulse urging American ratification had not been entirely dissipated. Early in 1979 President James Carter twice issued eloquent calls to the country's legislature to ratify the document, even though there was a major discernible factor distinguishing the psychological climate of 1979 from that of 1949-1951. The nearly total loss of the global idealism found in many circles in the first postwar decade, and what then aroused certain sectors in the world, propelled by the most inflammatory war propaganda of all time, no longer could stir up much more than a twitch of concern in 1979.

To make matters worse for Lemkin's dream, his famous neologism had been vitiated by so much bad and incorrect usage contrary to the definition in the UN Convention incorporating it in its name that few knew it as anything but a synonym for a massacre by anyone any where, a situation which could not have drifted further from Lemkin's original intention.

Another complication had entered the picture, the concern for individual privileges, embodied in another UN document, the declaration concerned with "human rights," which now enjoyed widespread favor and savor, and which had eclipsed the Genocide Convention and its basic concept of *group* rights, and *group* responsibility for their violation.

The daily press has contributed an immense component to the erosion of the "genocide" concept by throwing the word around with unconscionable looseness and imprecision. This universal misuse has resulted in a continuous undermining of the sentiment of horror which Lemkin and his supporters counted on as a conditioning factor in their favor, and which they hoped the mention of the word would always evoke. All the while, the real massacres of millions, just during the time of the evolution of the legal entity of "genocide" in many parts of the world, followed by absolutely nothing, have greatly dulled the imaginations and capacity for experiencing indignation on the part of those who have grown to maturity who did not live in Lemkin's time and did not witness the events which stimulated him and his contemporaries and brought about their entire creation of the phenomenon of "genocide."

Not a single case among the many hundreds of charges of "genocide" after the judicial slaying of the leaders of Nazi Germany in 1946 has ever led to international prosecution and punishment. In fact, there has never been a solid consensus of UN member States in proceeding against any other State or group within that State in response to a "genocide" complaint lodged before their number. What has prevailed in the over thirty years since UN adoption of the Genocide Convention has consisted of a vague and unshared sentimentalism concerning the nature of "genocide," conceded to be an "unspeakable" crime, accompanied by a growing inability to define it accurately, even when using their own legal literature as a guidepost. When Raphael Lemkin and his collaborators embalmed the word in the form which the General Assembly accepted, the expectation prevailed that there would be prompt response and swift action in the event that a decision was reached in UN chambers that "genocide" had occurred somewhere. What has taken place has been a universal avoidance of any such determination and the total absence of the gathering of the physical resources necessary to pursue and punish those collectively charged with its commission, though these are mutually self-neutralizing. The inability to arrive at consensus guarantees paralysis of impulses to action.

There the matter stands at this moment. The likelihood of even less importance for Raphael Lemkin's imaginative and fanciful contribution to international criminal law in the future is extreme in terms of possibilities and probabilities.

Chapter One

THE MAN

RAPHAEL LEMKIN WAS BORN June 24, 1901 near the town of Bezwodene, in eastern Poland. His father was reputed to be a farmer, and his mother was described as a "brilliant intellectual." Eastern Poland was not part of an independent state in 1901, but a part of the western outer layer of Imperial Russia, which made Lemkin a Russian subject by birth. He said almost nothing about his youth for the record, and never related what he did as a young man during the tumultuous years of Russia's participation in the First World War. Nor did he ever say anything about participation in the violence and chaos which attended the collapse of Romanov Russia, the establishment of Bolshevism, and the fighting which absorbed Eastern Europe from the concluding months of the War into the early 1920s. From information supplied *Current Biography* nearly 50 years after his birth, it appears that Lemkin was studying abroad during his late adolescence, as well as in Poland itself. He was reputed to be able to speak 9 languages and read 14, and was a student in France, Italy and Germany, and specialized in philosophy in the Universities of Heidelberg, and of Lwow, in his native land. He was subsequently awarded doctorates at both these institutions. He was first employed following this as the secretary to the Court of Appeals in Warsaw, becoming Public Prosecutor of Warsaw in 1925.

So Raphael Lemkin began his public career in the newly created State of Poland, a product of the Versailles Treaty, which the American diplomat William C. Bullitt later was to characterize as "the stupidest document ever struck by the hand of man." Lemkin never had anything to say about the statecraft which led to the restoration of Poland as an autonomous state, the various military engagements with the Russians, Ukrainians, Lithuanians and Czechs, the wresting of Vilna from Lithuania, Galicia from the Ukraine, Teschen from Czecho-slovakia, and Danzig, and large parts of Silesia, Posen and West Prussia from the Germans. In view of Lemkin's hysteric concern for minorities during and after World War Two, it must have been a subject he was very familiar with, serving as a state functionary in the Poland of Jan Paderewski, General Joseph Pilsudski, Ignace Moscicki, Marshal Edward Smigly-Rydz and Col. Joseph Beck. Lemkin never discussed the boiling German, Ukrainian, Russian, Czech, Hungarian and Ruthenian minorities which the muddled chefs at Versailles brought together with the Poles in this political entity which never did achieve any significant degree of stability in the 20 years between the wars. A country consisting of about one-third unhappy national minorities, such as Poland of the 1920s and 1930s, as well as an additional large ethnic minority of some 3,000,000 Jews inhabiting all its regions, out of a total population of about 34,000,000 suggests a complex of problems sufficiently grave enough to baffle even the most wise of "statesmen." That it managed to endure 20 years impressed many.

Lemkin never indicated his political affiliations or possible party membership, a subject which excited a few of the curious later on, wondering how he had managed to stay viable through the riotous years of the 1920s, when the crashing of regimes and a constitutional crisis, and the subsequent military revolt and dictatorship of Pilsudski, created a maximum of insecurity for all office-holders and bureaucrats. To make things even more mysterious, Lemkin was a Jew, and the anti-Jewish sentiments which swept across Poland, especially in the 1930s, should have added a further ingredient of disorder and instability to his life. But somehow or other Lemkin remained on his feet.

Perhaps the reason for his miraculous survival, at least through the first ten years of his public career, can be credited to his involvement in the relatively non-partisan and matter-of-fact affairs of the League of Nations, the international political legacy of the War, and the treaties which brought the latter to a halt in 1921. But Lemkin also took part in the domestic affairs of Poland to a considerable degree, and enjoyed some prominence in the legal life of his homeland as well as representing it abroad. He later claimed to have represented Poland "at international conferences in many Western countries," and in 1929, four years after having become Warsaw's Public Prosecutor, he began a stint as Secretary to the Commission of the Laws of the Polish Republic, another prestigious Polish Establishment position. During this, in 1933, Lemkin represented

Poland at the League of Nations' Fifth International Conference for the Unification of Criminal Law, held in Madrid. It was here that he is supposed to have made his first proposal, entreating the League to draw up a treaty to ban "mass slaughter." But his original presentations to the Legal Council of the League at this 1933 gathering were 1) a document proposing the outlawing of "acts of barbarism and vandalism," as well as 2) a study of "terrorism," these subjects being far from identical with "mass slaughter," or the peculiar variations and special considerations of the latter, with which he became famous, 1944-1959.

It is necessary to direct attention at this early stage to one of the many grave deficiencies of Raphael Lemkin as a historian, though admittedly he was acting solely in his capacity as a prosecution attorney in placing on the agenda action which he thought commendable on his part, and an early identification of his main charge later on, "mass murder," though *ex post facto*, and, in view of contemporary sources and reports, utterly fallacious. In fact, were Lemkin to try to prove murder strictly on the basis of race, religion or ethnic origins, in 1933 or immediately prior to that, the assumption being that his League of Nations presentation in 1933 must have had *some* historical basis, he should have indicted the Poles of his native land, not the Germans whatever.

In 1931, two years before the election victory of Hitler's National Socialist Party and his accession to power in Germany, the New York *Times* reported scores of stories involving the killing and injuring of Jews in anti-Jewish pogroms and riots, and the closing of schools and universities, but all in *Poland,* not Germany. There were also such reports emanating in rather generous fashion from Rumania, Hungary and Austria. What came from German locations were stories almost on a daily basis in some months, for 1930-1933, of street fights between Communists and adherents to Hitler, in which the injuries and deaths were most frequently suffered by the *latter.* Germany was covered by a sizeable contingent of American foreign correspondents straining to report calamities suffered by resident Jews, but it was from the surrounding regions of Central Europe that such events were reported. In June, 1932 the stories of Communist-"Nazi" (the *Times* in 1932 enclosed this contraction in quotation marks) street fights and killings were almost a daily occurrence. But the accounts of the tribulations of Jews came from elsewhere in Europe.

The situation in Poland drew wide contemporary attention in the USA, and prior to Hitler's ascendance, the indignation of American Jews was vented on the Poles. Lemkin carefully skirted all this in his later incendiary accusations of Germans, as well as the

contemporary lethal combat in Palestine between Arabs and the
Zionist terrorist organization, Irgun (about which more later),
founded in 1931. Though the American press noted this Mideast
combat on a weekly basis, Lemkin later also preferred to omit
comment on it *in toto*. And he also failed entirely to report the
coming into existence in New York at the end of 1932 of an organization, the United Committee for the Struggle against Pogroms in
Poland, which sparked a major meeting in New York City of 31 of
the most prominent Jewish leaders in the land the last day of the
year. (New York *Times,* January 1, 1933, p. 11.)

A short time later Hitler won in Germany, President von
Hindenburg elevated him to Premier, and the reportage of assaults on
Jews switched around to dwell on the Germans (there were *sixteen*
separate stories dealing with the Jews in Germany on a single day in
the *Times* [March 29, 1933], for example). A few reporters had
qualifying observations to make: Miles Bouton of the Baltimore *Sun*
denied that the atrocity reports in March were correct, and even
Frederick T. Birchall of the New York *Times* suggested the situation
was far more moderate than some of his colleagues were alleging,
Stalinist supporters such as Lion Feuchtwanger especially being
among the hysteria-mongers. As early as March 20, 1933 Feuchtwanger was charging that a vast number of Jews had already been
slain, something no one else had been able to see. Even the preposterous and hastily-prepared *Brown Book of the Hitler Terror,*
entirely the work of a fierce Stalinist Comintern "front," the World
Committee for Victims of German Fascism, and directed out of Paris
by a dedicated and ardent Stalinist agent, Willi Muenzenberg, made
no such charges as Feuchtwanger's. Their specialty was Communists,
asserting that Hitler's supporters had murdered 250 of them, in the
main. (Albert Einstein innocently allowed his name to be used to
front for this mendacity in printed form, but later in the year
withdrew his sanction.) The first organization to protest Hitler in the
USA was the Communist Party, in a New York City demonstration
on April 4, 1933.

And when the concentration camp system was begun, the prevar-
ications grew by hyper-inflationary increments. James G. McDonald,
president of the American Foreign Policy Association, and an
implacable enemy of Hitler's regime, as well as an ardent Zionist, was
allowed to visit Dachau in the late summer of 1933, outside Munich
(the *Times* spelled it "Dukau"). He reported that the camp, originally
an abandoned former munitions factory, had been rebuilt by "300
Communists," and housed 2000 persons when he visited it. He could
find no evidence of violence or mistreatment, but did his very best
to suggest ominous sentiments of an intangible nature. McDonald

did not report that the average sentence to Dachau was for six months, and that it and other camps housed many ordinary felons, convicted in the German courts of the same kind of crimes committed by other people everywhere in the world. He also failed later to point out that political rights of prisoners were not suspended and that the inmates of the camps voted overwhelmingly for Hitler, as the *Times* reported (November 14, 1933, p. 13). It was the latter paper that also reported that thousands of these camp prisoners were released after the election, and also before Christmas, 1933 from several locations, including Bremen and Hamburg.

And contradicting Communist, and, later, Zionist fulminations suggesting "hordes" of people incarcerated by Hitler (this might have been a close estimation of those locked up by Stalin in the Soviet Union), the *Times* estimated (October 27, 1933, p. 11), that there were approximately 22,000 in the combined concentration camps in Germany. Who they were to begin with is also vastly different in the accounts filed by American contemporary observers on the scene. Edgar Ansel Mowrer, the dean of American reporters in Germany, president of both the Foreign Press Association *and* the Association of Foreign Correspondents in Berlin, declared in the *Times* (November 12, 1933, p. 3) that Jews were outnumbered 8-1 in the camps by others, including pacifists, Communists and many other categories of the repressed, with Jews likely in all categories, including that which consisted of devoted Stalinists. Since approximately half of the inmates in 1933 were released by the end of that year, Jews still locked up at that date who were not classed as some kind of *political* prisoner or ordinary criminal offender must have been a very tiny handful. Since we know from later evidence that the German Communists rapidly captured control of the *internal* management of the camps, and that Jewish Communists were known to rise to important jobs in that inside-camp management and administration, we have still another dimension utterly missing from Lemkin's view in trying to understand how he later came to the many ramifications of his invention, "genocide." Whatever he did, all of the preceding was not a part of his remonstrations before the League of Nations in 1933.

When Lemkin declared on p. xiii of his preface to his book *Axis Rule* that he had proposed before the Fifth International Conference for the Unification of Penal Law in Madrid in 1933 to the effect that an international treaty should be negotiated, declaring that attacks upon national, ethnic and religious groups should be made international crimes, and that the perpetrators of such crimes should not only be liable to trial in their own countries but, in the event of escape, should also be tried in the place of refuge, or else extradited to the country where the crime had been committed, it would appear that his position was almost entirely motivated by the rise of Hitler a few months before, and not by the other events he later claimed as his inspiration. And since he never ever mentioned Poland whatever as a source of part of that inspiration, he was guilty of the most towering and transparent hypocrisy, since, when it came to the attacks on Jews in the dozen years prior to Lemkin's innovative efforts, no land in the world even closely approximated his native Poland in the killing, injuring and the general cultural and social bedevilment of Jews.

Lemkin later claimed that the Polish government, headed by Moscicki, and with Col. Beck as foreign minister, disapproved of his efforts. Beck may have assessed Lemkin's performance at Madrid as hostile to Germany, a position the Polish regime was trying to avoid as it began its balancing-act among the French, with whom the Poles had an alliance (since February 19, 1921), the National Socialist regime of Adolf Hitler, with whom they wanted to be friendly, and the Soviet Union, with whom Beck signed, on May 5, 1934, an extension for ten more years of a non-aggression pact dating from July 25, 1932.

In any event, Lemkin separated from State service relative to League activities, and, presumably, from the Polish Foreign Office, and in 1935 began private legal practice in Warsaw, as well as continuing his work relating to Polish legal codification. In 1938 he was the editor of a 725-page book published in Krakow, titled *Prawo karne skarbowe,* this massive tome dealing almost exclusively with Polish internal revenue laws and tax evasion in that country, probably an aggravated matter as a consequence of all its unhappy minorities. The following year he got out, in an unlikely collaboration with Malcolm McDermott, a member of the North Carolina Bar and a faculty member of the Duke University Law School, in that state, a 95-page translation into English, titled *Polish Penal Code of 1932, and the Law of Minor Offenses,* issued simultaneously in the USA and England. It would appear that the major part of the work in the translation was by McDermott. But the important part of this relationship lay in the future, as will be seen.

Still another, and somewhat more substantial, scholarly effort by Lemkin made its appearance in print in 1939, this one in France, under the title *La Règlementation des Paiements internationaux,* a 422-page work devoted to a problem of growing importance and peculiar to emigres and refugees in the troubled and revolutionary world of Europe of the 1930s, that of getting their money out of one national State and into another, while probably crossing the frontiers of several others in doing so. The 1930s had seen a much graver aggravation to the world of international finance than even the World War had provoked, though in many ways these later irregularities were extrapolations of the collapse of the international gold standard and its relatively serene world-wide performance down to the end of summer, 1914. The regimes growing out of the war ending at various times between 1918 and 1921 had moved in a series of stages away from the regulation by gold and had adopted national money systems geared to local goals, managed currencies with equivalents in other moneys which were quite unstable, and sometimes invalid or unacceptable anywhere else, such as the Bolshevik Russian ruble, a purely internal currency. Coupled to this development was the consequence of incredible runaway hyper-inflation in some countries, and the appearance of regimes in this country or that which engaged not only in revolutionary money innovations and nationalistic finance which sometimes was accompanied by confiscation, but also the adoption of exchange controls and interference with trade and the sending of money out of the country which had the effect of virtually halting a large part of such transactions conducted legally.

Thus there had grown a brisk underground and extra-legal business in the smuggling of foreign currencies about the financial and commercial world, and a multitude of irregularities and unsymmetrical disformities in the economic life which characterized the welter of economic states of war being waged all over the international scene increasingly as the 1930s wore on, probably a greater cause of the war beginning in the late summer of 1939 than any other. Lemkin's was a contribution to trying to sort out this economic nightmare of interference in money flow and the payment of bills and obligations from one place to another quite a distance away. It was his major interest now, and one which he returned to repeatedly thereafter. He even was to diagnose the economic interference by a State in the economic life of its minorities or "groups" to be a stipulated sub-section of the great international crime he was to invent and name later on.

The nature of Raphael Lemkin's publications after ostensibly leaving Polish government service suggests that he remained at least informally a government functionary into the late 1930s. But he neglected to treat of this matter in an official way, despite the immense excitement of that period in Polish affairs. He made no mention of his attitude toward Polish adventurism as the Central Europe of Versailles began to crack apart in 1938, especially Polish gains at Lithuania's expense in March, 1938 and the taking of the Teschen province from Czecho-Slovakia in September of the same year. It would further have been illuminating to have heard him comment on the "imposing military parade" held in Warsaw on

November 11, 1938, when the most-cheered regiments were those having taken part in the Lithuanian and Czech exercises, according to the generous report on this celebration in the *New York Times* (November 12, 1938, p. 7.) This parade, celebrating the 20th anniversary of the reconstruction of the Polish state after the conclusion of World War I, was hailed in a broadcast speech by the Polish President, Moscicki, speaking from the occupied Teschen territory itself, during which he boasted that Poland had now "become one of the strongest European powers," according to the *Times,* while even the Polish Jewish paper *Nasz Przejlad* in a patriotic article on the parade had declared that "Poland's happiness is ours."

Lemkin never discussed publicly or officially what he was doing during the Polish-German diplomatic crisis of the late summer of 1939, though as a late member of the Polish government it could be assumed that he was obviously a partisan supporter of its policies. A few years later he gave indirect evidence of being an affronted Polish patriot as much as he did a Jew aggrieved at German programs hostile to Europe's Jews. But the outbreak of war between the Poles and Germans and the swiftness of the German invasion caught Lemkin in the same predicament as others. He did not refer to his actions in the years he was campaigning in behalf of his great crusade in the United Nations, but subsequently admitted that he joined Jewish civilian guerrilla fighters outside Warsaw, and engaged in such belligerent illegality well after the country's armed forces were immobilized and the territory jointly occupied by the German and Russian armies in September-October, 1939. He confessed to having suffered a leg wound in this fighting, and to have fled into the Polish forests with other guerrillas, which band presumably included a brother, where one sympathetic journalistic portraiture described him as living there "on potatoes and leaves for six months."

At various times Lemkin claimed that he and his brother Elias were the only survivors of a family estimated at one place at 40, at another 49, and at about 70 in still another, all the others being killed by the Germans, though he presumably told another journalist that an undetermined number of his family were killed by the Russians. This was more understandable, since the majority of the Lemkin clan resided in eastern Poland, which was not taken by the Nazis but by the Reds in the fall of 1939. There never was a clear picture of how many people were involved, or their precise fate, but in the 35 years after the end of World War Two, a myriad of survivors have traded on their experiences and claimed to have been the sole survivors of immense families, many of them allegedly 100 or more, all of whom were supposedly massacred in "death" camps or at random throughout the war, all innocent of having done anything to merit their fate. That Lemkin was honest enough to admit that he was a *franc-tireur* long after the cessation of formal hostilities in Poland, a form of behavior long condemned as illegal and grounds for summary execution upon apprehension, speaks well for him, and casts serious suspicion on the stories of unalloyed innocence related by many thousands of others of similar background in later years. Professional Zionists for years traded on their situation by avoiding identification with guerrilla warfare in Europe, 1939-1945, but subsequently there emerged a literature by a bolder element, boasting of unlimited and constant involvement in civilian armed combat with the German occupation army and those of its allies in 11 countries. That many lost their lives directly as a result of this situation was silently covered over at the conclusion of hostilities, at which time quite different narratives were substituted for any possible cries of triumph and boasts of bravery, daring and heroism. The conflict between the stories of innocent, helpless victims of tyranny and murder and the rival accounts of endless black market activities, money and refugee-smuggling, massive gun-running, continuous acts of sabotage numbering in the thousands daily, and the participation in countless armed combat situations with the German occupation troops, all these matters were left for much later times to sift gradually into the consciousness of the community, and quietly into historical record. In some cases it was 30 years before admission of wholesale and widespread participation in overt civilian guerrilla "resistance" warfare with the armed forces of Germany, by which time substantial advantages had been gained by the immediate post-war posing of the survivors as wronged and passive innocents. It was a circumstance which Lemkin did not profit from personally, but which he exploited substantially in advancing his innovations in international law. This theme will be investigated in other contexts subsequently.

How Lemkin was able to leave his native Poland in the early spring of 1940, traverse both the German and Russian occupied zones of that land into Lithuania, now involved in a special arrangement with the Soviet Union, which in turn was in a state of neutrality with Germany, was never described publicly. But it was undoubtedly a delicate undertaking, since the entire area traversed was occupied by one or another land unfriendly to Poles, including the Lithuanians, the two peoples having an ancient history of feuding with one another, and the interwar decades being a period of increasing tension and hostility between them. However, we find Lemkin able to make his way to the Baltic shore eventually, from which he was whisked off to neutral Sweden, across the Baltic Sea, patrolled constantly at both ends by the German and Russian navies, respectively.

This adventure was never spelled out, either, nor the complex of forces and factors making it possible ever explained.

Once in Sweden fortunate experiences immediately attended his arrival. Though most people in his circumstances would have been interned for the rest of the war, he was not. Instead, he was shortly involved in the academic scene once more, and in his year or so of presence established credentials with Stockholm University, at which he lectured on his special subject, international law pertaining to international payments, foreign exchange, and related international banking laws, in addition to the immensely complicated innovations which international warfare had forced upon all these activities, and on which he had published a large book in Paris the year before. His lectures on these subjects were published in Swedish in Stockholm in 1941 under the title *Valutareglering och Clearing.* It was not clear, however, whether the book appeared before his departure from Sweden on a long and presumably dangerous route across the Soviet Union, Japan and Canada, to turn up next in North Carolina, and to join the law school faculty of Duke University in short order, the location of his recent scholarly collaborator, Malcolm McDermott. This all seems to have been achieved in a matter of a few months in the late spring and early summer of 1941, a time of incredible international touchiness, and one is led to wonder at the apparatus which was able to bring all this about for the benefit of a single person, across successive national frontiers, several of which were in a state of extreme tenseness with one another, covering a trip of some 10,000 miles in the process. Who supplied the resources and assistance making this trek possible and how he obtained his visa remained unrevealed then and later, but the contacts with Duke University had surely proved fortunate. And it was at Duke that Lemkin was to prepare his real magisterial legal labor.

Barely installed, Lemkin was recruited to make a major address before the American Bar Association's annual meeting at Indianapolis, September 29-October 3, 1941, again on his favorite specialty, this one being titled "The Legal Framework of Totalitarian Control over Foreign Economies." With pro-war propaganda in the USA having been successful in saddling the general public with the fixation that Hitler Germany was "totalitarian," a description only of the Soviet Union, in reality, Lemkin's speech undoubtedly concentrated on the menacing practices of the Germans, thus acquainting the audience with the ways an *authoritarian* system functioned economically in relation to its neighbors and the rest of the world, while leaving the listeners as innocent of how a *totalitarian* order functioned as they were before. Most of them never did find out, and few know the difference to this day.

An extremely busy three years for Raphael Lemkin had begun. A succession of un-dramatic and unpublicized appointments in American wartime bureaus and government departments followed his joining the Duke University Law School, which found him flitting back and forth from Washington to Durham, N. C., during which time he served as an advisor to the Bureau of Economic Warfare and the War Department, and then serving as "head consultant" to the Foreign Economic Administration. Sandwiched among these was a vague appointment as a "foreign affairs" advisor, presumably to the State Department. Then came a stint as lecturer before the School of Military Government at Charlottesville, Virginia, educating the men who were to become the administrators of Germany during the period of American joint-occupation of defeated Germany. Other prestigious official appointments lay ahead, but these already described were his primary involvements during the time he was at work on a large and ultimately very fateful book.

He claimed that he had begun it in Sweden prior to departing for the USA via the famous "long march" across the top of the world and then traversing the entire length of the USA to North Carolina. It was not possible to figure out what part of it he completed there, though some of the German sources surely became accessible to him as a result of Sweden's neutrality in the war, and the consequent availability of the official publications, among other things, of both the warring coalitions. But in view of the large contingent which he acknowledged had helped him in the 24 to 30 months he worked on it in the United States, it would seem that he may have hardly got through a very sparse outline of the project, while the portion of the book he personally wrote appears to be entirely a product of his American residence, setting aside for the moment the possibility that some of it was done by co-workers. The major part of the compilation of laws comprising the latter two-thirds of the volume might have been begun while in Sweden, there being only a small fraction of these dating from after mid-1941. Published on November 25, 1944, Lemkin's massive (712 pages) tome, *Axis Rule In Occupied Europe,* published under the most respectable of the upper echelon of wartime Establishment auspices, served many purposes, but as far as its influence in the present moment is concerned, it served as the original launching pad for one of the most ominously portentous additions to world dictionaries in a very long time, "genocide."

Chapter Two

SOME MISSING
HISTORICAL BACKGROUND

AN EXAMINATION OF Raphael Lemkin's *Axis Rule In Occupied Europe* may be done under a number of misconceptions, which may as a result produce a wholly distorted view of what the book is all about, and lead to a succession of alarmingly faulty judgments on several subjects. The first mistake one is likely to make is to assume that the book is a work of history. In this category so much of the pertinent related information of the time it supposedly covers is not even mentioned that it soon incubates more confusion than it generates illumination.

The principal original obstacle to overcome is to realize that this work is not a narrative of a general sort but a narrow account with a preconceived conclusion, prepared in the form of a long legal brief. Therefore the evidence is carefully selected, for the purpose of blackening the accused, and setting up a situation in which the author's charge will be found valid and the accused, hopefully, found guilty as charged. The discovery that everything exculpatory is omitted and everything damaging to the author's client, the States at war with Germany and its Axis allies, is nowhere to be found, is disturbing only if one forgets what the limited goal of this account happens to be. Unfortunately, anyone assuming that this is a serious, "objective" literary labor is deceived from its very opening, and to base one's understanding of the subject and the broad outlines of the war which brought about what is detailed in this volume by how the subject is laid out here, is to come away with the plaintiffs' view alone, and a very murky, tangled conception of what their case is. In fact, after an exhaustive exploration of the entire contents of this hefty tome, it may seriously be questioned whether there is a case at all. If this were handled as a legal action in an American court under Anglo-Saxon legal procedures, the chances are high the whole "genocide" business would not survive the first hearing today.

Most of the historical material in this work, when not directly related to the legal documents collected in its final two-thirds, is so thin and dealt with in such offhand, cavalier fashion, that for one who lived through the time it reads like one were riffling through a stack of random snapshots, coming away with a few impressions but no understanding at all of what it was all about. The book further misleads in purporting to be an account of the occupation laws, procedures and administration of Germany and its allies in some 17 parts of Europe, substantiated almost entirely by reference to a collection of legal documents but not to any actual eyewitness reports of how life was really lived in such areas. In addition to this, though published late in 1944, there is almost nothing of note in it covering the time span after the end of 1941 or the early weeks of 1942. But the most annoying aspect of the book is its neglect of a decent account of the entire scope and background of the wartime drama, especially that part related to what kind of thinking grew out of the events of 1939-1944 and what all this has to do with the incendiary nature of the author's approach, and the social psychology influencing the opinions which he sought to have embalmed into law, for law is an idea, fundamentally. Therefore it has been considered essential to an examination of Lemkin's book at this time that it be preceded by a broad historical look at the time which the book spans, and at the important ideas engendered in it.

To begin with, the almost total failure of Lemkin to come to grips with the topic of the Jews, Poland and Soviet Russia disquieted no one and was discreetly avoided by all, preferring to allow Lemkin to concentrate on German sin and make his points on "genocide" uncluttered by the intense complications sure to have resulted from dealing with the subject broadly, historically, and honestly. By avoiding the controversy of the 1930s over the ultimate destiny of the European Jews, and by inventing and generalizing the legend that the Germans had killed most of them, Lemkin, and others engaged in this extensive propaganda ploy, dodged the entire question, while narrowing it.

One of the big issues even in the 1920s had concerned the controversy over whether the less-favored Jews of Eastern Europe would be better off under the socialism of the Soviet Union or the socialism of the rival but not-yet-arrived Zionism, with its goal of absorbing Palestine, since the end of World War One politically controlled by

Great Britain and physically and actually occupied by an overwhelming Arab majority.

Within a few years after the 1917 Balfour Declaration more or less committing the British to supporting an eventual Jewish home in Palestine, the more energetic and restless of the Zionists, mainly of Polish and some of Russian origins, began to exert considerable pressure upon Zionist organizations for the advancement of a "revisionist" program to ensure the eventual taking of Palestine. This involved a campaign of actual military operations against both the British, who took over Palestine after 1918 on a League of Nations "mandate," and the dominant demographic majority of resident Arabs. This was mainly the vision of the Russian Jew, Vladimir Jabotinsky, later to be referred to as the "Jewish Hitler" by those who resented his program. Actually, his proposal split Zionist organizations in the mid 1920s, being approved by the Order of the Sons of Zion but repudiated by the Zionist Organization of America in a resolution on June 28, 1926. At that time the ZOA not only castigated Jabotinsky but rebuked the Sons of Zion for endorsing it (New York *Times,* June 29, 1926, p. 12).

This hardly settled the matter. Jabotinsky's views grew in volume and dispersal in the next five years. (In 1962 the National Union Catalog of the Library of Congress listed 51 published works by Jabotinsky, all written before 1940, the year he died, mainly in Hebrew characters, but also in Polish, Russian, Spanish and English, and almost entirely devoted to some aspect of militant Zionism.) And in 1931 Jabotinsky formed the ominous organization named Irgun Z'vai Leumi, destined to dominate the Zionist terrorist activities in Palestine against both British and Arab opposition, and play a most significant part in eventual victory of Zionism in 1948, as well as supplying the new Zionist state of Israel with its most controversial leader in 1976, Menachem Begin.

However, in the meantime, in the aftermath of the 1926 confrontation over the issue of violence in establishing a future Zionist Jewish homeland in Palestine, the weight of numbers still supported the view that such a result had to come about by peaceable means. As late as April 16, 1945 U. S. Undersecretary of State Sumner Welles, in a speech before the vigorous Zionist New York City chapter of the Hadassah, declared flatly that a Jewish state in Palestine could never "be advanced by violence, or by the threat of force." (Part of his speech preprinted in *Nation,* May 5, 1945, p. 513.)

But this view had been increasingly made obsolete and largely irrelevant by the immense expansion of Irgun activities after 1931. One of its enterprises became an almost *verboten* subject of

discussion, its close workings with the anti-Jewish Hitler regime in
Germany after January, 1933. For over five years it was almost
unknown to learn of its establishment of offices in German cities to
recruit candidates for emigration (usually illegally) into British-run
Palestine, with the full cooperation of Hitler's regime, which not
only permitted this activity, but allowed Irgun people to bring in
unlimited amounts of foreign currency and escape the strict regulation of foreign exchange in Germany under the National Socialist
policies. But Irgun had such relations with other Central European
lands with anti-Jewish policies, too, including Rumania, Hungary and
Lemkin's own native Poland. Not a breath of this emerged in
Lemkin's *Axis Rule,* but, for that matter, not a word was entered
there as well on the ferocity of anti-Jewish public behavior in Poland
during the 1930s, far out-distancing such demonstrations in the rest
of Central Europe combined. That Polish Jews had taken front rank
in the Zionist impulse was not what angered Poles so much, as the
presence of so many Jews in high places in the adjoining Soviet
Union, since 1917, and the stiff controversy with the Soviets, exacer-
bated by a fierce war between the Reds and Poland off and on in the
three years after the end of World War One, which had sharpened a
nationalistic conflict.

The Poles occupied a precarious spot midway between Red
Russia and Germany, and had spent most of the previous centuries
divided between them. Maintaining independence from both was a
big problem, and the growing Polish bellicosity in the 1920s and
1930s had sharpened the conflict to the point where there developed
a Polish nationalism so hot that it spawned a large literature of
boastfulness, with Poles maintaining that they could defeat both the
Germans and the Soviets in the event of a future war involving all
three. As late as the outbreak of the Polish-German war in September,
1939 there were Polish statements to the effect that they would soon
be dictating peace to Hitler in Berlin. It was Leonard Mosley in his
book *On Borrowed Time* who remarked that when the Poles engaged
in saber-rattling, they did it with real sabers.

It can be seen that official Poland in the 1920s and 1930s was
not entranced by either the Marxist socialism of Lenin and Stalin to
the East, or by the visionary Zionist socialism which seeped from the
propaganda of Polish Jews most active in the advancement of a
future Zionist state. But as far as the Germans were concerned, at
least from 1918-1933, there did not seem to be much of any difficulty on this subject. The Jews of Germany were only a sixth as
numerous as those of Poland, in a total population almost three
times that of Poland, about 1%, in actuality, where they were
roughly 10% of the Polish population. So Polish relations were

somewhat better with Germany, and continued to be so even after the German revolution of 1933 and the emergence of Hitler as the controlling force. Lemkin, as a Polish government functionary between 1925 and 1935, knew all that. He also must have been intimately familiar with the increasing difficulty of Jews in Poland under Pilsudski, Moscicki, Smigly-Rydz and Josef Beck. His book does not even faintly allude to this historical background. That Poland eventually got to be so unpleasant for Polish Jews that many tens of thousands of them migrated to Germany, finding that living under Hitler and the anti-Jewish Nuremberg Laws of 1935 was quite preferable to living in the Polish "Republic" which employed Raphael Lemkin, must have pained him greatly.

So in advancing his grotesquely distorted vision of "genocide" Lemkin had a great deal to conceal concerning the record of his own land, Poland, as well eventually of all the countries at war with Germany in 1944. When Lemkin charged the Germans with being the world's most prominent and persistent "genocidists," he was guilty of intellectual dishonesty of a staggering magnitude. His long history of "genocide," which he declared a few times was in the making, might have been written with the Germans meriting hardly more than a footnote. And had his wartime account been a dispassionate historical survey, incorporating the deeds of the Russians, Americans, British, French, Belgians and others of the precious "Allies," instead of being simply a primitive propaganda twisting of a few months' duration of wartime German actions, as well as those of *their* allies, there is grave doubt that Lemkin's new crime would have been considered seriously for more than an hour by his patrons and subsidizers, and his chances of publication by the lush and opulent Carnegie *apparat* so microscopic as to raise doubts almost beyond measurement.

There was another important development in this very complicated picture, however. This was the increasing combat among Jews, especially as the 1930s wore on, as to whether there would be a better future for the downtrodden portion of the Jewish community in a socialist Soviet Union, or a socialist future Zionist State. This divided many sharply, and continued to do so even after the creation of Israel in 1948, and, in actuality, right down to the present moment. Behind the upheaval in Soviet-Jewish relations in the last 30 years has been this fundamental confrontation. It was very hot in the decade before Lemkin's book was published, but again we have an important matter of world affairs which he swept under the rug entirely. As both a Jew and a Polish government functionary and obvious Polish patriot, the matter must have disturbed Lemkin profoundly, personally, but publicly he never admitted it existed until he joined in Jewish charges of "genocide" against Stalin in 1950.

As a result of this problem, we find that those Jews who denounced Polish atrocities versus their resident Jews were almost entirely Marxist-oriented, either being involved with the Communist Party in several places, or allied to them in the many Marxist-leaning "liberal" pro-Soviet Popular-Front "transmission belts," as CP power-figures were known to refer to them. For the most part, the strictly Zionist Jews somewhat under-emphasized this ongoing event in Poland, probably the result of cordial relations between the Polish government and Irgun, which had a substantial recruiting office in Warsaw, sifting over Poland's unhappy Jews for the youngest and most fanatic in favor of a Zionist Palestine.

There is a very rich literature concerning the treatment of Jews in Poland in the decade or more prior to war between Poland and Germany, September 1, 1939. There is space for only a small representation of it here.

One may for example take a representative year, 1931, using only the Scripture of American liberalism, the New York *Times,* as a source. In the *Index* of that newspaper for that year alone it takes an entire column in tiny agate type just to *list* the stories published on violent Polish-Jewish affairs: the steady outpouring of reports from the scene on anti-Jewish riots, the closed schools and universities resulting from these, and the killing and injuring of Jews, reported nationwide by the end of that year, supplemented by similar stories from Rumania, Hungary and Austria. Using this paper as a guide, one would have to report that Jews had less trouble in Germany than anywhere else in Central or Eastern Europe, even though the level of domestic strife had increased somewhat there as well as everywhere else. (One may recall an address of Adolf Hitler in the city of Brunswick on October 18, 1931 in which he declared that only his National Socialist party could restore "law and order" in Germany. This was a front-page story in the New York *Times* for the following day, and it is listed in the *Index* of that paper, for that year, but it is almost impossible to find an edition of the *Times* filed anywhere from which it has not been deleted. Perhaps those responsible would prefer other things from those distant times to become as invisible, such as the editorial in the *Times* almost a calendar year later [October 9, 1932], which yawned that Hitler had become a "bore.")

An especially serious outbreak of anti-Jewish rioting occurred in Poland in 1936-1937. The American liberal weeklies, the *Nation* and the *New Republic,* with significant pro-Soviet Jews in their organizations, both editorially condemned the riots and killing of Jews. The *New Republic* denounced it all as "a blot on the name of the Polish

Republic," while that of the *Nation* (May 22, 1937, p. 578), was somewhat more abusive of Poland. Albert Allen, writing in *The Fight,* monthly organ of the American League Against War and Fascism, a frankly pro-Soviet propaganda organization, and one with many pro-Soviet Jews in its membership, devoted a whole article to the affair, titled "Polish Pogroms" (July, 1937, pp. 10-11, 26), in which he asserted, "In no country has anti-Semitism been so sustained and devastating as Poland." This, after 4½ years of Hitler in Germany. In December, 1937 there was formed as a protest group against what was happening to Jews in Poland, the Writers Committee to Aid Polish Jews. And on April 2, 1938 the *Nation* published a long article on the subject by William Zukerman, a pro-Soviet Jew, who observed in rather blunt terms,

> For the last two years the Jews have suffered almost incessant physical assaults and pogroms . . . . This outburst of anti-Semitic bestiality has no equal in Europe, not even in Nazi Germany, where despite the vicious propaganda . . . and the cruel anti-Jewish decrees of the regime, the people have not degraded themselves by a single anti-Jewish pogrom.

Six years later Zukerman, still arguing vehemently against the flood of Zionist promoters of migration to Palestine, and with the war behind everyone, restated this view:

> For Nazi anti-Semitism, with all its beastliness and savagery, was primarily political, a means to an end. The anti-Semitism of pre-war Poland was pathological; it was nationalism become abnormal, almost mad. The physical attacks on the Jews in the streets, parks and public places, the daily beatings of Jewish students, men and women alike, in the universities and high schools of Poland had no parallel even in Nazi Germany. (*New Masses,* Feb. 19, 1946)

There is a large supporting literature reflecting the same kind of narrative supplied by Zukerman, and hardly confined to papers read by a small intellectual coterie. In contrast, *Time,* read by many millions in the USA and world-wide, on November 10, 1941 (p. 31), reproduced a portion of a piece read over the air from Germany by George Axelsson of the New York *Times,* which concluded, in summarizing the attitude of Germans at large to their remaining Jews (by then less than 200,000 in the rough statistical estimates of some observers), "In public places or in contacts as a fellow-worker in factories the German working man seems to treat the Jew as an equal." And Alex Dreier, head of National Broadcasting Company's Berlin desk, and the last American radio man to leave Germany, in a magazine article which seems to have been written while on route back to the USA in the end of 1941, stated without qualification,

"During my entire stay in Germany I never saw a German civilian participate in an attack on a Jew." However, Dreier, expelled on November 15, 1941 along with Howard K. Smith of the Columbia Broadcasting System, probably in retaliation for the expulsion of Manfred Zapp of the German DNB news bureau from New York City earlier, was one of the first Americans to turn over the rumor that the Germans were already murdering vast numbers of Jews. In an article appearing in the +4 million circulation *American Magazine* in April, 1942, which the editors probably had as early as Christmas, 1941, Dreier, whose radio, and subsequent movie and television career was to go on for over 40 more years, claimed that in mid-November, 1941,

> When I left Berlin, as many as 2,000 Jews were being transported in trucks to Poland every day. In Switzerland I heard reliable reports that hundreds were being gassed to death *en route.*

So, at this early date, Polish and other propaganda yarns of mass murder by gassing were already well under way, and it might be pointed out that such rumors as these were as valid "proof" of what was going on as were the somewhat tardier Zionist booklets Raphael Lemkin used as his documentation of similar accusations three years later. (By Dreier's calculations, there should not have been a Jew left in all Germany by the end of January, 1942 at the latest, though their presence in much larger numbers than commonly assumed had to await the end of the war to be verified.)

Raphael Lemkin, a resident citizen and functionary of Poland while this was going on down to the spring of 1940, must have seen many cases such as these persons described in American publications. But he never uttered a word about it in *Axis Rule,* nor publicly or officially called attention to it afterward, in the dozen years he lived after the establishment of Communist Poland, during which Jews rose to high places in the regime, despite the later distaste of Nikita Khrushchev for their prominence. Therefore his selecting out of Germany in 1947 as the land *par excellence* in the world for "genocidic" behavior over the years was a grave distortion of political realities.

By the time Zukerman had once more called to public memory the serious predicament of Polish Jewry in the 1930s in his 1946 *New Masses* essay, Communist and Zionist positions and policies regarding Poland's Jews had gone through a succession of coolings and heatings. A peak of estrangement had occurred during the diplomatic crises of 1938 and 1939. During the former year the Polish government, by cancelling the passports of Jews who had fled Poland for Nazi Germany, precipitated the German abrogation of the visas on these passports and rendering the holders a class of "stateless" persons, leading to tenseness which was capped by the sensational assassination in the German embassy in Paris of the 3rd secretary, Ernst vom Rath, by the young Polish Jew, Herschel Grynszpan, allegedly an act resulting from his resentment at the Germans preparing to deport his parents back to Poland from Nazi Germany. This led to the demonstrations against Jews in Germany which were so massively exploited by Zionist and other propaganda organizations in November, 1938, and were still being utilized in behalf of Zionist goals 45 years later. Though it is hard to attribute directly a single Jewish death to this 15 hours of property destruction on November 10, 1938, it is a source of wonder why this has been selected by Zionists for such massive attention, and not the many pogroms against Jews in Poland before and after, which killed a great many Jews.

The start of the Second World War involving Germany and Poland in September, 1939 after the collapse of the negotiations concerning the Danzig question between the two lands did not appreciably change things, since Communist Russia and Hitler Germany had concluded a diplomatic understanding in August just prior to hostilities, so Soviet neutrality between September 1939 and June 1941 did not lessen repeated Communist commentary on Polish treatment of Jews in the 1930s era. Furthermore, the occupation of over half of Poland by the armed forces of the Soviet Union in October 1939 and the adoption of a repressive policy of their own toward Poles, Jews and non-Jews alike, also had a major part in the downplaying of what was happening. The confusion was maximized by this absence of a common front on the issue and it became a matter of taking sides as far as which of the two occupying lands were injuring Jews the most.

The diplomatic understanding between Germany and Russia on August 23, 1939 produced a momentary attack of sanity in America relative to foreign affairs, and in particular had the effect of cooling the ardor of the tens of thousands of vociferous partisans of Stalinism to such an extent that there occurred an unprecedented wave of psychiatric breakdowns among these well-to-do and mainly upper middle class admirers of Bolshevik Communism, later referred to hastily by Malcolm Cowley, one of the directing voices of the *New Republic,* in 1943. The temporary political neutrality among what are known in these times as the "limousine liberals" was just that, however; it was to be followed by an even more lunatic decade, that of 1941-1950. But in this short hiatus between the pro-Sovietism of 1919-1939 and that of 1941-1950, there was a momentary confusion on the correct line to adopt *re* the Jews of Central and Eastern Europe.

Typical of this was the essay by Howard Daniels, an Australian engaged in European refugee work, in the *Nation* for January 27, 1940 (pp. 92-94), titled "Mass Murder in Poland." Only 4 months after the end of the German-Polish war, this was about the first piece in America alleging that massacres of Polish people, especially Jews, had begun. The indigestible aspect of Daniels' piece in establishing his thesis was that he apparently was spending his time on the Soviet side of the demarcation line separating the two main occupying powers in Poland (Lithuania, Czecho-Slovakia and Hungary had also grabbed parts of the dismembered Polish state too). Daniels declared that Poland's 3,000,000 Jews had been roughly divided into 1½ million apiece under the Reds and the Germans. In the new Communist government the Russians established in their eastern more-than-a-half of Poland, Jews were rising to top posts there as they had in Moscow more than 20 years before. As to the German disposition of their 1½ million Jews, Daniels told two contradictory stories; he alleged that the Germans were trying to 1) "exterminate" theirs in ways he was not too clear in laying out, while at the same time he charged that they were 2) encouraging a mass exodus of Jews from their side to the Soviet side of the demarcation line of the occupation, a move which he said the Reds were trying to halt. However, in an attempt to be "balanced," Daniels told America's liberal elite that orthodox religious and Zionist-inclined Jews in both the German and Russian zones were about as badly treated.

With the outbreak of the German-Russian phase of the European war on June 22, 1941 the propaganda situation regarding the welfare of Red Russia in America returned to the period preceding August 23, 1939, with this difference in respect to the Polish Jews: now there began a concerted campaign of defamation of the Germans by both Communists and Zionists, and a joint propaganda accusing the Germans only of massacring the Polish Jews welled up from both centers in a flood, continuing for over 40 years, despite a number of ruptures later on in the fabric of Soviet-Zionist amicability. Though it had long been agreed that millions of Poles, including Menachem Begin, had been moved into parts of the Soviet Union far beyond the Ural Mountains into Central Asia and Siberia by the Red Army, there was a heavy concentration on German behavior toward Polish Jews, with some conflict between Polish non-Jews and Jews who had managed to flee to England and there create one of the pathetic little rump governments-in-exile so assiduously attended by Winston Churchill's British war regime.

Within six weeks of the June 22, 1941 outbreak of war in Poland between the Germans and Russians, this Polish refugee government had issued, in the French language, a *White Book* accusing the

Germans of gassing Poles. (*Time,* August 4, 1941, pp. 27-28.) As can be seen, this allegation preceded the spreading of a second or third hand charge of the same nature by the American radio commentator, Alex Dreier, by about four months. It is principally of significance in that it pointed out the road things would proceed upon until the attainment of the destination at Nuremberg.

By about this same time the big guns of Zionism in the USA were starting to be heard, propelled only part of the way by the talk of mass murder of Jews in Eastern Europe, in Germany, or in the other regions occupied by Axis armies. It will be seen that Lemkin almost entirely ignored the domestic German side of the matter, being obsessed with the *international* aspect of it apparently, in the early stages of his campaign, though he also argued almost from the beginning about making "genocide" offenses international in scope and extraditable no matter where they were committed. An important speech on November 22, 1941 in Boston by Rabbi Joshua Loth Liebman before the Junior Hadassah, the young womens' Zionist organization of America, was especially noteworthy as an indication that there was a goal behind all the charges now being wholesaled about the world. Said Rabbi Liebman, of Temple Israel,

> The Jewish people will say, "we were the first victims. We seek indemnity for the millions of our people sent across the face of the earth in refrigerated cars to die, for all the children who perished on barbed wires trying to cross inhospitable frontiers, and for all concentration camp martyrs . . . . We shall say to democracy that we are ready to share its poverty but never to bear persecution again. We have the right to ask in the name of the ideals for which democracy is suffering air raids and bombings, a little piece of earth. Call it Palestine. Let our people find an end to homelessness."

The allegation of the mass-murder of millions of Jews had been well-seated even before the USA became a formal belligerent in the war on December 7, 1941, and it became more and more obvious that Zionism's prize goal of Palestine was what lay just beyond the propaganda charges; the mass death of Europe's Jews was not an allegation supposedly serving a purpose in aiding the winning of the war by Germany's enemies. It was being formed into the moral foundation of the future state of Israel. But the promotion of the charge was now a joint effort of Soviet Communism and world Zionism, and their differing goals in doing so became incidental.

There is no worthwhile examination of the joint exploitation of the charge of the Axis annihilation of Europe's Jews by Moscow and Tel Aviv, 1941-1946, but the existence of a degree of cordiality lacking down to September, 1939, if not June, 1941, surely helped out, and some coordination of respective claims prevailed for sure after America and Russia were for the first time war "allies." When the chief Rabbinate of Palestine proclaimed December 2, 1942 as a day of prayer, fasting and mourning among all the Jews of the world in behalf of the already-claimed murdered millions, the New York *Times'* supporting editorial (December 2, 1942, p. 24), claimed that "Of Germany's 200,000 Jews in 1939 all but 40,000 have been deported or have perished," while going on to assert that "according to evidence in the hands of the [U.S.] State Department," "an order of Adolf Hitler demanding the extermination of all Jews in all territories controlled by Germany" was known to exist. Researchers nearly 40 years later were still searching for that order, or information leading to anyone who might have ever seen it at any time.

What this entire episode represented in reality was a well-coordinated and orchestrated propaganda assault, carried out in a three-pronged operation from London, Washington and New York, involving the machinery and spokesmen of the Polish Goverment in Exile, the U.S. State Department and at least eight cooperating Zionist organizations located in Britain and the U.S.A. And it was all achieved between November 24 and 27, 1942.

A London dispatch to the *New York Times* published November 26 quoted extensively from a statement by Dr. Ignacy Szwarcbart (two days later spelled Schwarzbart), a Jewish member of the Polish National Council representing the refugee government in London, that nearly one-third of Poland's pre-war 3,000,000 Jews had "perished" in the first three years of German occupation. He attributed the majority of the deaths to "executions by mass-murder and gassing," as well as by the "organized spreading of diseases." (This latter was also a favorite charge of the Stalinists against the Japanese after the end of the Pacific War.)

Dr. Schwarzbart claimed the Germans had two separate ghettoes in the Polish city of Lublin to process the Jews for destruction, as well as a special center in Belzec where mass electrocutions were conducted, the Jews being stripped naked and pushed into a large room under the pretext of being given a bath, only to discover they were standing upon a sheet metal floor. When the electric current was turned on, the occupants, *in toto,* according to Dr. Schwarzbart, died "instantaneously." They were then buried in large numbers in vast common graves, excavated by "a large digging machine" "installed nearby." Dr. Schwartzbart also bore a message from the British section of the World Jewish Congress to the effect that Norway's 2800 Jews had been all sent into forced labor in northern Norway or to Poland.

Immediately following this was an even longer story based on a report filed by Rabbi Stephen S. Wise, which he claimed was based on a conference between him and the State Department on November 24. The highlight of this meeting was his hearing that State had possession of a copy of an order by Hitler himself calling for "the immediate extirpation of all Jews in German-occupied Europe." This was backed by "affidavits obtained by the State Department from Jewish sources of information in free countries" (but not from Jews in the occupied lands) that atrocities of the vilest sort in immense numbers were taking place constantly. Said the *Times:*

> Rabbi Wise said the State Department documents included affidavits from "reliable persons who knew" of such atrocities as turning Jewish bodies into fats and soap and lubricants, and the latest Nazi method of killing Jews by having doctors (sic) inject air bubbles into their veins. He said the earlier gassing with prussic acid had been found too expensive.

Rabbi Wise declared that leaders of Jewish organizations, including the American Jewish Committee, the American Jewish Congress, the American Jewish Labor Committee, the World Jewish Congress, B'nai B'rith, the Synagogue Council of America and Agudath Harabonim, were convinced of the "authenticity" of all this material.

As if by coincidence, the Finance Minister of the Polish Government in Exile also happened to be in New York City, despite the desperate dangers of Atlantic crossings in that grim war year of 1942. In an interview with the press, Dr. Henryk Strasburger, at the Waldorf Astoria Hotel November 27, reiterated most of the material emanating from London and Washington, with decorations. Not only were 1,000,000 Polish Jews already massacred, but 400,000 non-Jewish Poles had suffered the same fate, half of the latter in the "human slaughter houses" created in Poland by the Germans, and the remaining 200,000 "murdered by other means."

But this was just a start. There apparently were even larger numbers not included in this 1,400,000 who had been exterminated; "innumerable (sic) others" had been "scientifically starved to death or allowed to die of disease." Dr. Strasburger claimed that all this loss of life had been determined by consulting "official figures of the Polish Government."

According to Dr. Strasburger, elaborating a bit on these horrifying matters, the first German "slaughterhouse" had been created in Kaunas, the capital of Lithuania, which they had taken from the retreating Red Army at the end of June, 1941. The second of these installations went up in Belzec, some 60 miles from the Polish city of Lwow (Lemberg), in southeastern Poland (since 1945 a part of the Soviet Union). It was in the latter "where electrocution and lethal gas chambers were being used."

At the luncheon which followed this interview, given in honor of
this celebrated guest by the Central Eastern European Planning
Board, he demonstrated that he came not only to bring tidings of
almost unimaginable atrocities, but also to make some suggestions
for the post-war political map of that area of Europe, which presumably had the approval of all the powers which had obviously sanc-
tioned this auspicious visit to the U.S.A. Dr. Strasburger suggested
that some kind of regional organization take place of all the states of
Central and Eastern Europe "extending from the Baltic to the
Aegean and Adriatic," presumably the hodge-podge of states created
at Versailles between Russia and Germany, and prior to September,
1939 firmly in the Anglo-French orbit. It did not look like the latter
kind of organization would come back, and the "new" thinking was
along lines of some regional association of not-yet-explained dimensions. Dr. Strasburger, dwelling on their small size and individual
weaknesses being attractions to being "subjugated by the great
European powers," declared their salvation lay in a federation, an
idea which had been batted around for a long time under various
auspices, and now undergoing a revival of currency. And its future
was bright, for, as Dr. Strasburger declared, the people living in this
"parallelogram" had "common characteristics" and were "the children of freedom and democracy." It was a pity that Dr. Strasburger
and the other seers of this Planning Board did not seem to anticipate
in the slightest that the whole region would in two and a half years
be enjoying the Stalinist brand of "freedom and democracy."

But insofar as the matter at hand was concerned, Strasburger's
performance meshed smoothly with all the parts of this operation.
That same day (November 27, 1942) the Polish National Council in
London, during a special meeting, restated the claims of vast Polish
loss of life under the circumstances already described by Schwarzbart
in London and Rabbi Wise and Dr. Strasburger in New York. With
Mikolajczyk presiding, the press heard Schwarzbart testify a second
time in support of the allegations, seconded solemnly by another
Polish Jewish socialist, one Zygielboim. This set the stage for the
December protests and the formulation of the wartime United
Nations pronouncement.

By this time a major collapse of German arms in south-western
Russia was portending, starting in the third week of November. The
evening of November 29, 1942 a large gathering was held in Carnegie
Hall in New York City under the auspices of the Committee of
Jewish Writers and Artists, at which speakers praised the "victorious
advance of the Russian armies," and urged Russian and American
Jews "to cooperate in the solution of the Jewish post-war problems,"
as the New York *Times* reported the event (November 30, 1942,

p. 3.) The highlight of the meeting was the reading of a personal message from Chaim Weizmann, president of the World Zionist Organization and of the Jewish Agency in Palestine: "Dr. Weizmann said the advance of Russia's armies 'brings us step by step nearer to the hour of liberation for those whom Hitler has sworn to exterminate; every hamlet retaken from the Nazi invaders, every village reconquered, reduces the unprecedented plight of the people under the heel of those evil forces.' "

This was a puzzling declaration by Weizmann. It was not possible to determine from it whether he believed that those rescued in the Russian hamlets and villages were Jews or non-Jews, and, if the former, why they were still there and not "exterminated," as Weizmann declared Hitler had "sworn" to do. If James N. Rosenberg, honorary chairman of the Jewish Joint Distribution Committee, was right, then the returning Red Army conquerors could hardly have been finding *Polish* Jews in the regions adjoining Stalingrad. In a statement he made in 1942, widely circulated by Stalinist publicists, and still being repeated nearly a year and a half after the end of the war, the Stalinist regime had pretty well cleared the region of such. In the *New Masses* for September 24, 1946 (p. 14), Rosenberg was quoted as saying in 1942,

> Of some 1,750,000 Jews who succeeded in escaping from the Axis . . . about 1,600,000 were evacuated by the Soviet Government from Eastern Poland and subsequently occupied Soviet territory and transported far into the Russian interior and beyond the Urals. About 150,000 others managed to reach Palestine, the United States, and other countries beyond the seas.

Several times the last figure he gave were known to have reached the USA even while the war was going on, hence this 150,000 total managing to reach points outside Russia was gravely understated, thus suggesting that his figure for those relocating in the Soviet Union somewhere was also an understatement. But these were times for the wildest of amateur demographic statistics being bruited about, with no possibility of a decent scientific census being conducted in the vast area subjected to martial chaos. Therefore the specialists in what today are designated as "ball park estimates" enjoyed a veritable golden era, requiring long periods of study of those who sought to make any of them make any sense, whether gravely exaggerated or understated. The International Labor Office's *Displacement of Population in Europe* (1943, p. 59), declared that more than 1,000,000 people were deported from Poland to the Soviet Union in the 1939-1941 period, but this did not tell anyone much of anything, and this sub-rosa Communist front may have been even more seriously reducing the actual total. Nowhere were there any credible reports on the numbers who lost their lives in Communist-occupied Poland *prior* to the moving of so many of them into the Soviet Union. Considerable numbers appear to have remained in Poland, Jews and non-Jews alike, if the voluminous Zionist literature on the conduct of *franc-tireur* civilian warfare and sabotage, and that of the Germans reporting on it all, can be believed. From such works as the American Jewish Congress' publication *They Chose Life* (1973) it would appear that the majority of Jews who spent the war in a "resistance" underground against the Germans did so mainly in the regions of what had been pre-war Poland.

Therefore, when Raphael Lemkin in his short chapter in *Axis Rule* on "genocide" made his sole charge of systematic mass murder against the Germans, of Jews, and also non-Jewish Poles and Russians, he was already well behind a stream of similar accusations dating back for many months. It was in a 12-line sub-paragraph, and he cited for his documentary support of this charge a quotation from the December 17, 1942 "Joint Declaration by Members of the United Nations," issued simultaneously that day in London and New York, and then published on the first page of the first number of volume 3 of the *United Nations Review* (1943). In this declaration, gathered together from reports filed by a dozen or more of the enemies of the Axis, but depending heavily on allegations of the governments in exile, the Jews of Europe were said to be being moved to Eastern Europe, where they were being "worked to death," or "deliberately massacred in mass executions." There was no indication of the method being used, and nothing was said of "gas chambers," leaving the reader to imagine how this was being achieved. The other source Lemkin cited, along with this wartime UN declaration, was a Zionist propaganda work prepared by the Institute of Jewish Affairs of both the American and the World Jewish Congress, titled *Hitler's Ten-Year War on the Jews*,[1] published in New York in 1943. This source maintained that the Jewish loss of life directly traceable to German mass murder was 1,702,500 persons, presumably all disposed of by the end of 1942. However, one can see the relative venerability of these charges, well after several others advanced previously. That they antedated mention in the introduction of Lemkin's book by ten months, and mention in the rest of his book by nearly two years, should serve to deflate Lemkin's reputation as the first person to asseverate that Axis-occupied Europe was the site where European Jewry was being systematically annihilated in mass executions.

Why Lemkin chose to use these two sources to support his late 1943 (and unpublished until late 1944) charges of mass murder of

Europe's Jews as a calculated and planned policy is not clear. There were others, just as sensational, all made available at around the same time, early December, 1942. That there may have been specific reasons for this chorus of similar cries has already been suggested. When Rabbi Liebman made his dramatic Zionist speech in Boston in late November, 1941, threatening the world with a very large Jewish "reparations" bill at any coming peace treaty, and suggesting that Jews would be happy with a "little piece of earth" "call it Palestine," there did not seem to be the likelihood of a settlement of the European war anywhere in the near future, with German arms successful everywhere. But by late 1942, it was another story. The impending catastrophe facing the German armed forces in the Stalingrad region of southwestern Russia suggested that the fortunes of war were shifting, and though "victory" appeared to be still very distant, it became obvious that postwar claims might just as well be advanced at the earliest opportunity, and, in harmony with past actions, a convincing accompaniment to claims for redress had often been allegations of grievous wrongs suffered. Atrocity propaganda had far more than the search for sentimental understanding as its objective; it was the smokescreen cover for demands for something far more substantial than that.

As already pointed out, organized Zionism had already made a dramatic splash in late November and early December, 1942. But there were others. The most important of these we have seen consisted of charges launched by Rabbi Stephen S. Wise, toward the end of the first week of December, 1942, and antedating the formal charge made by the wartime United Nations by a week. Based on alleged statistics supposedly prepared in the Polish "underground" by one of the earliest of the exponents calling for the destruction of Germany, a Polish Jew, Henryk Strasburger, the Wise report drew mixed reactions in the US, and two of the editorial reactions are reproduced here for their contrasting effect. The Communist *New Masses* editorial, "Poland's Jews," (December 8, 1942, p. 21), accepted it without question:

> One of the most fiendish of all the ghastly reports from Hitler-dominated Europe is the news that 1,000,000 Jews—nearly a third of Poland's Jewish population—have been systematically murdered by the Nazis. Another million Polish Jews are now menaced by starvation and the lack of medical supplies. Mass electrocutions and gassing have become common, and, because it is less expensive the bestial fascists are now turning to a new method—the injection of air bubbles in the bloodstream. Dr. Stephen S. Wise has amplified this information with affidavits from reliable Washington sources that the Nazis were offering fifty reichsmarks for corpses which are converted into soaps, fats, fertilizers and lubricants.

Responding to the same press release, the editors of the venerable *Christian Century*, the weekly organ of American Protestantism most widely respected in the US, observed ("Horror Stories from Poland," December 9, 1942, pp. 1518-19):

> We question whether any good purpose is served by the publication of such charges as Dr. Stephen S. Wise gave to the press last week. . . . Dr. Wise's figures on the number of Jews killed differ radically from those given out on the same day by the Polish Government in Exile. Whereas Dr. Wise says that Hitler ordered all Jews in Nazi-controlled Europe killed by the end of this year, the exiled Polish government claims only that orders have been issued for the extermination of half the Jews in Poland by the end of this year and that 250,000 have already been killed up to the end of September . . . . Dr. Strasburger, whose "underground" figures are used to support Rabbi Wise's charges, is the same Polish leader who is campaigning in this country for the complete destruction of Germany . . . . Dr. Wise's allegation that Hitler is paying $20 each for Jewish corpses to be "processed" into soap fats and fertilizer is unpleasantly reminiscent of the "cadaver factory" lie which was one of the propaganda triumphs of the First World War.

The editors of the *Christian Century* indeed had good memories and had learned the revisionist exposes following the First World War well. The hoary British lie of the German cadaver factories had been admitted by General Charteris as early as 1925, and other British propaganda figures had deflated many others, which had served to inflame neutral American sensibilities, 1914-1918. But this was a new war, being fought and paid for (but not led) by a new generation. Lord Northcliffe, the mastermind of World War One propaganda, had remarked that the only people more gullible than Americans were the Chinese, but it seemed to the *Christian Century* that the children of those who fought and believed in the First were showing even less reserve and thought while engaged in the Second, even believing the same discredited mendacity a second time around.

An important aspect of the situation at the end of 1942 was the resumed unity of Communist and Zionist propaganda versus Germany, and the essential agreement on the substance especially of the atrocity campaign. The Communists had to forget or suppress their earlier positions in doing so, and, by admitting the latest Zionist allegations, had to admit, though only by default, that they had lied when they claimed to have spirited 1½-2 million Polish Jews to safety, in order to have Zionist claims that more than a million had been murdered by the Nazis and another million threatened with death, make sense. However, this was not done, and both stories flourished side by side well into 1943 and beyond. In fact, in 1943 the Institute for Jewish Affairs book *Hitler's Ten-Year War on the*

Jews, quoted the Stalinist figure on removal of Jews to the Soviet Union, even managing to raise it a little (1,800,000) without disputing or refuting it (p. 300). But the highest total in this department was not claimed until after the end of the war. One of the most popular departments in the family weekly magazine *Collier's,* with nearly three million subscribers and probably five times that many total readership, was Freling Foster's "Keeping Up With the World," a page devoted to short news bits in abbreviated paragraphs. In the issue for June 9, 1945 (p. 6) Foster revealed, "Russia has 5,800,000 Jews, 41% of the present Jewish population of the world, of whom 2,200,000 have migrated to the Soviet Union since 1939 to escape the Nazis." There was no later disclaimer of this declaration nor did Foster indicate his source.

But this kind of material was coursing along with quite contradictory competition. The very next month one could read Meyer Levin, later to be famed for his part in creating one of the stage versions of the Anne Frank story, assert in *The Nation* that "Seven million Jews were slaughtered for being Jews." Levin, in Paris when he wrote this, was aware that Jews were disappearing for quite different reasons as well. "Those who have concluded that being a Jew is not worth the price are constantly slipping away from the community," he observed ruefully; "Day after day in the *Journal Officiel* one finds columns of notices of Cohens and Levys who have changed their names to Dumont and Bontemps." (Levin, "What's Left of the Jews," *Nation* [July 28, 1945], pp. 74-76).

A few years later, such contradictions were quickly buried.[2] Now a still different change in the realities of world politics made attractive a return to the support of such views once more. With the defeat of the Germans before Stalingrad, it was not hard to project their coming general collapse, especially now that the USA was in the war and its prodigious war production beginning to make an impact. December, 1942 seemed to be the time to get prepared for the political realities sure to become evident, hence the rash of atrocity propaganda charges, all amply provided for in the publicity department. But, like the New York *Times's* claim that an order from Hitler outlining the extermination of Europe's Jews was in the hands of the State Department, the new "evidence" on the German processing of dead Jews for soap and fertilizer, supposedly based on "affidavits from reliable Washington sources," proved to be fully as difficult to pin down, eventually joining the other elusive wartime propagandistic ectoplasm once its purpose had been served. As Norman Angell had observed well before the outbreak of this new war, people acted, not on the basis of facts, but on the basis of their *opinion* about facts. In this case, action was to come about on the basis of opinions of non-facts. The latter has always been the main-stay of effective atrocity propaganda, and it is a matter of opinion whether the Reds or Zionists outdid the other in publicization of alarming excesses. The brief period of Soviet reserve on atrocity propaganda, 1939-1941, was followed by the most incendiary of such charges made by themselves. About two weeks before the USA became a formal belligerent in December, 1941, the Communist foreign minister, V. M. Molotov, made an allegation broadcast to the world, accusing the Germans of starving their Red prisoners of war, cutting off their hands, gouging out their eyes, ripping open their stomachs, raping all the women in their advance across eastern Poland and western Russia, and stripping the wounded naked to die of exposure. In the US, *Time* magazine, probably a psychic belliger-ent before even the lands which eventually became engaged in the fighting, sympathetically reproduced Molotov's charges in their issue the week before the Pearl Harbor attack (December 1, 1941, p. 26.)

The joining of Soviet and Zionist propaganda campaigns relating to charges of German mass murder of Jews was not a difficult aspect of all this, an enterprise in which the major anti-German countries and the governments-in-exile all joined, leading to the famous December 17, 1942 declaration which turned out to be one of Lemkin's two principal sources in taking part in spreading this story himself in *Axis Rule*. His failure to update his book, allowing it to appear as a product of the period ending, at latest, the end of 1942, also lost him the opportunity to use a stream of later works dwelling on even more exaggerated aspects of these early atrocity statements. The prize omission from his book was the sensational supplementa-tion resulting from the capture by the Red Army late in August, 1944 of the first German concentration camp to fall into "Allied" hands in the course of the war to that moment, Maidanek, in Poland. The stories which swamped the West after this brought to the mind of some the trusting and naive reportage of Eve Curie in her book of the previous year, *Journey Among Warriors*. Though she was not quite as vivacious a fellow traveler as André Gide a decade before, her clever total-war propaganda had served as a sturdy vehicle for lengthy Soviet atrocity stories, which she said she believed because all the people she questioned about them gave her "the same version of the facts and swore they were true." Such innocence concerning the disciplinary lock step of the Communist Party may have been the order of the day in 1943, but it should have served as warning to some when the Red propaganda publicity machine managed the Maidanek affair, succeeding in outdoing rivals in the purveying of such material, and perhaps stealing a lap on Zionist exploiters of similar content.

The USA first learned of it in any broad manner via the pages of *Time* magazine, which printed a direct translation of the event from a Moscow Communist newspaper, the story having been written by a Red war correspondent, one Roman Karmen ("Vernichtslungslager," August 21, 1944, pp. 36-37). This "first eyewitness description of a Nazi extermination camp," as *Time* billed it, set the standard for many more to follow it. Karmen claimed the camp contained five crematoria, adjoining several gas chambers, where people were killed 250 at a time, by chlorine gas. The crematoria were supposed to have disposed of 1400 people a day, and the ashes were alleged to have been shipped back to Germany in large cans, to be used as fertilizer. Karmen claimed "more than half a million" persons had been exterminated at Maidanek.

Without permitting any hiatus during which someone else might enter and complicate the scene, the Red promotional drive to publicize Maidanek continued shortly after the big splash made in their behalf by *Time*. Two new fronts promptly appeared, the Soviet-Polish Atrocities Investigation Commission, and the Polish Committee of National Liberation, the latter the Stalin-backed Red government based in Lublin, not far from Maidanek, and which opposed the London-backed exile remnant, stripped of its real leadership after the mysterious death of Gen. Sikorski in an air crash in July 1943, on a return flight to London from Gibraltar.

The "Atrocities Investigation Commission" rounded up some 30 Western journalists, who had been dutifully reporting the Russo-German war in the East from their hotel rooms and lobbies in Moscow, and conducted them through a guided tour of Maidanek a few days after Karmen's story was published in the USA in translation. In this party was the New York *Times*'s W. H. Lawrence, and various veteran pro-Red figures including Edgar Snow and Maurice Hindus, virtual Stalinist public relations officers in the American press. These three and others poured a cascade of print upon American readers, amplifying the Red atrocity claims, and adding various embellishments of their own. It was "the atrocity story of the year," as the *Christian Century* described it, though once more calling attention to this "corpse factory" tale as too suspiciously parallel to the discredited version loosed in World War One to be believed. Lawrence reported Maidanek to be "a verifiable River Rouge for the production of death," repeating what he was told by the Red tour guides that the deceased had been asphyxiated by gas and their bodies cremated in huge furnaces. Claims were now made that the Germans had killed 18,000 people a day, though the expanded capacity of the crematoria, to 1900 from 1400, still could not have come within a small percentage of taking care of all these dead bodies. The death toll, a half million according to Karmen a few days before, was now boosted to 1½ million; Both Lawrence and Hindus repeated this figure in American dispatches. The evidence advanced by the Reds to support this claim was a warehouse, 150 feet long, which contained clothing and other apparel supposedly worn by the victims prior to their massacre. Hindus claimed it contained among other things 820,000 pair of shoes. Snow, citing other figures which he said came from the Red Polish government in nearby Lublin, supported their claims to having found the ashes of 1,000,000 (though all these ashes were supposed to have been shipped to Germany for fertilizer) at Maidanek, and that by this time, into the second week of September, 1944, the Red authorities had uncovered the ashes of some 4,000,000 more at the captured camp at Treblinka and three other German camps in Poland; the taking of Auschwitz, or Oswiecim, lay four months into the future. Snow's piece to the *Saturday Evening Post* ("How the Nazi Butchers Wasted Nothing," October 28, 1944, pp. 18-19, 96) was datelined "Maidanek, Poland," and was accompanied by official Soviet photos of an incinerator, the pile of shoes, and of cans supposedly containing the ashes of the dead, but strangely enough there was no photo then, or later, of a gas chamber.

The editors paralleled Snow's gracious piece of pro-Red promotional material with an angry boxed editorial titled "This Is Why There Must Be No Soft Peace." So part of the motivation for this stunning account was laid bare; the Morgenthau and other plans for the reduction of Germany to a veritable goat pasture were being hurled around the USA by press and radio, and this was very strong supporting material for such plans. There appeared to be another, however, serving Soviet purposes in Poland, not concerning Germany. The Warsaw rebellion against the Germans had taken place at about the time these camp revelations had begun, and the Polish exile government in London, experiencing the anguish of being sold out by their Anglo-American benefactors, had reacted bitterly upon the defeat of the Warsaw uprising by the Germans, claiming that the Red Army had stopped their advance on the city within artillery range, allowing the Germans to suppress the Polish revolt and kill 250,000 Warsaw residents. The London Poles claimed they had inspired the Warsaw rebellion, and that the Russians had allowed it to suffer defeat so as to enhance the fortunes of the Communist Poles based in Lublin, whose leaders had made the Maidanek charges, conducted the Western journalists through the facilities there, succeeded in grabbing the main headlines in the Western newspapers, while relegating the Warsaw recriminations to a subordinate status. The only American correspondent taking part in this memorable first guided tour of a German concentration camp captured by the Reds in

Poland who sensed the political realities behind all this sensational propaganda was Richard Lauterbach, *Time* and *Life* Russian correspondent, who sent in his report from Krakow in "liberated Poland." He alleged the 1½ millions killed in Maidanek were dispatched by the German Gestapo, but at least allowed a restrained description of the new political scenery, especially the slow drift of Poland west of the Curzon Line into the orbit of the Stalinist PCNL. It was obvious the Soviet exploitation of the concentration camps and the sensational charges they were lodging concerning the massacre of 1,500,000 in just one of them, which defied any logistical comprehension of such an action, had solid political, not sentimental, objectives behind it.

In all this there was no mention of Jews, and from that time to this, there have been discrepancies in the Zionist and strictly Communist accounts of the German concentration camps in Poland. The Zionists have claimed the casualties to have been suffered mainly by Jews, with the Communist stories sometimes failing to mention Jews as victims except in a fleeting moment here and there in their narratives.

But support for the Jewish version was gathering in the wings of this "death camp" panorama. It may be recalled that Zionist and Zionist-sympathizer sources in 1942 and early 1943 claimed that the US State Department and unnamed "Washington officials" had been the support for claims of official German plans for the mass death of Jews in German-occupied Europe. But there had never been an official American affidavit reinforcing Zionist claims in those times and none had occurred thereafter, despite the growing volume of the assertions and the magnitude of the alleged actions. Finally, one of these took place.

As *Newsweek* (December 4, 1944, p. 59) put it, "Last week, for the first time, an American governmental agency, the War Refugee Board, officially backed up European charges of mass executions by the Germans." The timing, it can be seen, was very close to the publication day of *Axis Rule,* November 25, and once more gave circumstantial evidence of coordination of different drives concerning a matter of mutual interest, the lodging of atrocity stories with the public, but aimed at somewhat different levels. *Newsweek* went on to identify the War Refugee Board as largely an agency reflecting the views and goals of Treasury Secretary Henry Morgenthau, whose published plan for the reduction of Germany to a pastoral colony of its enemies was really a formula for turning Central Europe into a festering Stalinist satrapy. This new gambit appeared to be tailored to an assault on the American public's sensibilities in order to get the sanction to achieve his aims in Germany, as well as those of many allied to him, politically and psychically.

Newsweek went on to support the WRB's claim that the Germans had massacred 1,500,000 to 1,765,000 people at Brzeznia in south-western Poland, and for the first time rang in the soon-to-be far more ominous location of Oswiecim (Auschwitz), where only another 1,500,000 were alleged to have been disposed of systematically. The evidence for all this? "Stories told by two refugee Slovak Jews and one Polish officer who had been at the camps," *Newsweek* declared, in summarizing the WRB report. How these "witnesses" would have held up under just the typical cross-examination one has become accustomed to observe in American courts can only be imagined, as accusation was equivalent to conviction in the wartime atmosphere of late 1944, a kangaroo court circumstance which was to prevail for the rest of the 1940s in the famed "war crimes" trials of Nuremberg, Manila and Tokyo, though developed in Russia in 1943, where the prototypes of these judicial lynchings were first paraded before the world.[3]

In sketching the outlines of the atrocities story down to the moment of the publication of Raphael Lemkin's book, one must be aware that several related matters were intertwined with it in almost inseparable fashion, and the complications they all produced can not be understood without at least a minimum effort at describing them as events taking place while the numbers-game of atrocity claims and the conflicting narratives on refugee and emigre preservation and deliverance were reaching the record.

Among these related themes, one must note as the obverse side of the stories dealing with alleged German extermination of the Jews in their grip the threat, prediction, or recommendation that the Germans also be annihilated. That these were threats, in the main, dodges the fact that there was at least a self-fulfilling potential there, and what happened to the Germans between 1945 and 1950 must also be kept in mind as a continuing effort to sort out statistics relative to Jews is being made. The reluctance for those who were neither Communists nor Jews to substantiate the claims of German mass-murder of occupied Europe's Jews is not so much squeamishness but tied into other developments, primarily the slowly developing concept of "war crimes," which became entwined in the general theme of atrocities, leading to promotion of calls for retaliation against the Germans in the form of massacre of large numbers of *them,* upon the achievement of war gains and the establishment of favorable circumstances permitting such political reprisals. Soviet as well as Zionist political goals loomed large in this atrocity-reprisal propaganda. One may argue that the loss of life due to German atrocities as alleged, 1940-1945, *had* to be established as true in order to vindicate the programs inflicted upon the Germans,

1945-1950. With very few exceptions, the flood of postwar plans insofar as they concerned the future of the Germans, from 1942 on, especially, emphasized incredibly ferocious impositions upon a future conquered Germany, though the immediate postwar political realities resulted in the softening of several of the recommendations, some of which will be taken up shortly.

We find another aspect entering into the narrative concerning Jewish refugees and emigres fleeing the Germans, as to their eventual destination, the claims by American and other Western lands for providing ultimate shelter. It was wartime policy on all sides of the "Allied" establishment to soft-pedal this matter, to conceal America as the refuge for Jews in general, later to blossom into a propaganda in which whole books were produced alleging that the USA for all practical purposes refused entry to all but a handful. In all the refugee-Jew drama the class nature of the problem was almost always reduced to a bare murmur, even though it was a rare Jew of means who experienced a German concentration camp (one recalls the special case of the interned French former Premier, Leon Blum, 2 years at Buchenwald, where he had his own private house and servant), while there were continuous but discreetly buried stories the entire war of those with money and friends abroad achieving passage out of Europe with minimum discomfort.

A case in point is the report filed from Lisbon, Portugal on August 7, 1944 by the correspondent for the U.S.A.'s leading weekly organ of Protestant Christianity, *The Christian Century,* José Shercliff. Published in the issue for September 27, 1944, p. 1113, Shercliff was comparing the appearance of two groups of Jews recently arriving in Lisbon, one from Hungary and another party of 153, from North Africa, the latter bedraggled and in seemingly dire straits;

> "Different indeed is their case from that of the wealthy Hungarian Jewish families who arrived here last month and are living luxuriously in one of Portugal's most pleasant health resorts, awaiting the end of the war. Fifteen hundred more of these wealthy Hungarian Jews are expected in Spain. General Franco has granted them entry visas, and the German authorities are sending them there in a special train."

And still another, and most important, related theme was that of the Stalinist-inspired-and-led, and mainly British financed and supplied, "resistance," "underground," civilian guerrilla warfare against the Germans in eleven countries, boasted about in millions of words during and especially after the war, in which Jews participated most disproportionately to their ratio in the European population. The rules of land warfare which govern the conduct of the U.S.

Army provides for draconian prohibitions against such practices in combat in which they are involved, and provides ferocious means of suppression for those caught in such endeavors, about which more will be developed later on in this study. But the Germans were expected to put up with these mass violations of martial conduct (also lacking the sanction of the Hague Conventions of 1899 and 1907), and after the war were subject to vicious reprisals, especially by the Soviet Reds, for having tried to suppress it. The world press pullulated all during the war in stentorian bawls of praise at the exploits of this forbidden civilian armed enterprise in the lands occupied by the Germans, and had the hypocritical effrontery to urge the execution of all German military commanders who had attempted to put it down. (The "Allies" who righteously supported this had their own innings trying to combat this kind of Communist warfare in their long series of wars in Africa and Asia, 1950-1975.)

Some attention to specific details of the foregoing few issues is now in order.

Ben Hecht, the novelist and playwright-screen writer who was to become a belated Zionist of the most fierce, if not feral, views, declared in his book *1001 Afternoons in New York* (Viking, 1941), that the Germans were destined to become "the persecuted, cringing race of tomorrow," doomed to be the Jews of the future, as a consequence of their reputation between 1933 and that moment. Hecht was the spokesman here for a view and position among Jews respective to the Germans which frequently went well beyond what the latter were known to maintain toward Jews. However, it should be pointed out that demands for the annihilation of the German people were no exclusive property of Jews, by any means, then or later. But there were some memorable gestures in this propaganda, a few of those, 1941-1945, worthy of noting here.

The most spectacular and all-encompassing appeared in the spring of 1941, so savage that a publication front was invented to launch it into existence. In its famous report of 1936 on Jews in America, *Fortune* magazine, while correctly decrying the erroneous views among many Americans exaggerating Jewish economic power in banking and heavy industry, declared without qualification that Jewish ownership of the taste-making and taste-influencing media in America amounted at least to 50%, which obviously included publishing. However, none of the major companies known to have Jewish ownership, management and editorial direction cared to have anything to do with this work, *Germany Must Perish!* The author, Theodore Newman Kaufman, was identified by *Time* magazine as a 31-year-old New York Jew, and his sponsor, Argyle Press, of Newark, N.J., was apparently his own firm. But he apparently had powerful friends, able to influence *Time,* which almost never admitted the existence of privately printed books, let alone reviewing them, into devoting long and favorable commentary on this one. Kaufman's book was essentially a plea for the sterilizing of the entire population of Germany, but concentrating especially on that part within the age brackets most likely to produce offspring. This would guarantee the gradual extinction of the German ethnic strain.

Kaufman's scheme obviously awaited the total and unconditional defeat of the German state in war (how he would have prevented the escape all over the world, upon impending military defeat, of maybe millions of Germans, thus guaranteeing their survival as a genetic strain, he did not explain very clearly), and who would fill this large vacant spot in the middle of Europe apparently did not bother him very much, either. But it was a memorable tactical suggestion, even if a strategic catastrophe for the world of incredible dimensions. Its implementation of course was the critical matter related to it all; in the spring of 1941, it did not appear to be one of the most likely things to happen right away.

But it was something to ponder, especially when a journal with millions of readers such as *Time* took it seriously as a possible policy suggestion. Not quite in its class, but showing much the same sentiments, were the recommendations of the exquisitely Germanophobic University of Chicago history professor, Bernadotte Schmitt. Speaking before the 21st annual meeting of the National Council for the Social Studies the last week of November, 1941, in Indianapolis, a speech also given generous space by *Time,* Prof. Schmitt, a non-Jew of Alsatian extraction, urged that the first essential was the "complete and overwhelming military defeat of Germany, to be accomplished if possible on German soil." Thereafter, said Schmitt, Germany was to be reduced to an "agricultural economy," which he said was what the Germans were trying to impose on the rest of Europe, a policy which he calculated would reduce Europe's 80 million Germans by 30 million, apparently as a consequence of mass starvation added on to vast loss of life suffered while undergoing military annihilation. As Schmitt analyzed the European situation,

> Since there are only 45 million Britons, 45 million Italians, 40 million Frenchmen, and 30 million Poles, as opposed to 80 million Germans, the equilibrium of Europe would be more stable if there were only 50 million Germans.

Schmitt, the leader for over a decade in producing historical works placing near-total responsibility for the First World War on Imperial Germany, was noted by a few to have omitted all mention of Stalinist Russia, closely approximating the combined population of Western Europe, and Schmitt never mentioned or considered how many Soviet Communists were too many Soviet Communists for Europe's welfare and "equilibrium." Those who thought Schmitt the epitome of demographic wisdom in 1941 had the 40 years after "victory" in 1945 to mull over and ruminate upon the consequences.

It will be seen then that the ancestors of the celebrated Morgenthau Plan were numerous. Few followed precisely in the footsteps of Kaufman and Schmitt, and many were somewhat more detailed and specific as to what they wanted wreaked on the Germans. Furthermore, they came from an ever-widening spectrum of opinion-making, but generally were equally savage. In the meantime the statistical guesses and generalizations on the status of Europe's Jews continued, one of the most quoted and "respectable" appearing the week the USA became a formal belligerent in the war in December, 1941. Released by the Institute of Jewish Affairs of the American Jewish Committee, *Jews in Nazi Europe* was crammed with absorbing numbers. In this 151-page report, it was stated that the Jews of Germany, considered to be 760,000 in 1933, were now down to 250,000. Of Poland's 3,000,000 some 300,000 were now declared to have died, though it was not specified as to what proportion of the deaths were attributed to the Germans and the Russians in their respective zones. This covered the September, 1939-September, 1941 period, and was considered five times the normal death rate. It was further estimated that between 1933 and 1940, 1,000,000 Jews had fled Europe, 330,000 to Russia, and another 300,000 had fled Nazi-occupied western Poland, destination not given. About 150,000 were declared to have gone to England, France, Belgium and the Netherlands from Germany and areas east, 135,000 to the USA, 116,000 to South America, whose Jewish population was said to have gone up 30%, and finally 110,000 to Palestine. Privately, surveyors of this calculation considered it grossly understated and miscounted, Stalinists having already claimed that six times as many Jews had already found a haven in the Soviet than the AJC claimed had fled there. According to a United Press report dated November 6, a month before, there were only 120,000 Jews remaining in Germany, less than half which the AJC report claimed. And a number of related discrepancies could be found by almost anyone with the diligence to note them down and possessing the ability to count.

It is of course true that in a war the military outcome is of primary consideration. But it is still an agency by way of which subsequent policy is established and carried out, and there is never a war so mindless that some kind of political objective does not lie under its surface somewhere. Or, policy may constantly be being formed anew while the fighting is going on, or modified by what takes place during such fighting, during which time those doing the fighting may be making excuses to themselves why they are at war and what they hope to achieve at its end which would be better than what was prevailing when it started.

In the second World War, quite a bit of the matters just mentioned took shape in 1942, a year of German domination of Western Europe and deep penetration into Western Russia to the gates of the Soviet's major cities. The enemies of Germany had to be content with superiority at the fringes of this action, and largely strategic moves which mainly led to the spreading of the war, stretching out the manpower and resources of the opposition more thinly, and preparing the landscape for a contest of attrition in which their vastly superior manpower, resources and industrial might would bring eventual Axis defeat.

Insofar as the war in the West was concerned, therefore, barring the air bombing of Germany and its surrounding controlled areas from strategic bases in Britain, and an occasional catastrophic sally like Dieppe (turned later by astute propaganda into a successful venture, in the same way the utter disastrous defeat-retreat known as Dunkirk in the spring of 1940 emerged a little later on as a miraculous success), 1942 might be known as the Year of the Illegal Civilian Warrior. And the efforts of the Germans to repress and destroy such civilian military enterprise in occupied Europe had a large part to play in the deepening propaganda campaign against them, the *franctireurs* turned into heroes by the Allied propagandists, their successes, fueled by Allied money and guns, praised to the skies, and their defeats mourned at vast public ceremonies, followed by dire threats of future reprisals and generous programs of punitive campaigns and copious executions. This element of novelty soon added its coils and tendrils to the general theme of atrocities and related actions concerning Jewish repressions, complexities which aided the maturation of the entire "war crimes" morality-play acted out before the entire war, in the years immediately following cessation of hostilities.

But it was in the East that the far greater participation in the war by civilians prevailed, also highly praised by the still mainly inactive West, a war which involved very many Jews, even if it was not common for this to be reported at the time. Ultimately this was a source of great pride to Zionists, who simultaneously boasted of their prowess in this illegal enterprise, while justifying it as action in the face of sure "extermination," (a very large number took no part in it and managed to avoid "extermination," too, it seems), and wailing at the fate of those caught at it and executed. It may never be known how many of these civilian guerrillas lost their lives in actual combat with German army units, or were captured and shot thereafter, who traded in on postwar reassessments and emerged as victims of the "death camps," or were calculated as lost in other activities than the ones in which they were really in. Raphael Lemkin himself later capitalized on his six months as a civilian guerrilla well after Poland had capitulated, and the accounts of others with similar records and experiences are legion. Later Zionist bibliographies described the participants in this irregular combat only as "martyrs" and "heroes." And as a result of the curious juxtaposition brought about by ex post facto "legal" innovations at Nuremberg and elsewhere, the German enemy and its allies being declared "criminal," the actions of its opponents, no matter how contradictory to the Hague Conventions dealing with the rules of land warfare they were, emerged as the real legal entity in it all. In the histories of no other war than that of 1941-1945 are the illegal and irregular guerrilla participants memorialized so gloriously, with the possible exception of the phase of the Napoleonic wars associated with the French occupation of Spain.

Harold Callender, a well-respected correspondent to the New York *Times,* in pieces published on December 21 and 22, 1942, related that the so-called "partisan movement" in France was anything but spontaneous, a widely believed fable, but organized by the Stalinists beginning in June, 1941 with the outbreak of the Russo-German phase of the European War. But it enjoyed its greatest success in the East, and surely involved a large number of civilians who either scorned the chance to move to safer areas or were forced to remain as auxiliaries of the Red Army. In Poland they became most active after German forces swept past them, and certainly involved people who were not in any kind of concentration camp. An Associated Press story published in the USA on January 10, 1942 and derived from British radio, announced that "A little war" was "going on along the Warsaw-Lublin railway," that guerrillas had "interrupted all traffic," and that they had shot German officers in Lublin. A similar procedure had been under way in France some months before, where the Germans had responded to the murders of some of their officers by "underground" gunmen by holding French responsible. An editorial in the *Christian Century* on November 5, 1941 (p. 1359) had deplored this practice, remarking, "The likelihood in the matter . . . is that the assassins are probably French Communists, whose first allegiance is not to France but to Russia." (That many of them were not even *French* Communists but a Stalinist underground originating in several other countries, awaited later recognition.) And a book in 1942, *Europe in Revolt* (Macmillan, 1942), by a former Berlin and Vienna editor, Rene Kraus, went into melodramatic description of this underground "resistance," a source of nagging annoyance to the German occupation, even if its totality was extremely exaggerated in terms of total numbers. On the strength of this innovation, regardless of its real scope, German roundup of suspects, including all the foreign Jews they could find in France, got under way. A new element was being prepared for the concentration camps, as well as a new episode in the atrocity story library.

It can be seen, then, that in the first year of war between Stalin and Hitler, the Red underground in all the countries occupied by the German armies had aggravated them continuously in a series of assassinations of their soldiers and officers from France across Poland, and German tempers were getting raw. Then came the bombing of the car bearing the chief administrator of German-occupied Czecho-Slovakia, Gen. Reinhard Heydrich, in a Prague suburb on May 27, 1942, causing wounds from which he died a few days later. The two assassins were flown into Europe by the British and airdropped near their target, from which they worked with a few members of the pathetically small Czech underground, all cooperating with the tiny knot of emigre Czech politicians constituting the government-in-exile headed by Edouard Benes. It may be debated for a long time what Benes hoped to gain by this unsupported lethal gesture, other than trying at the time to make points with Stalin by showing him that the Czechs were not entirely the most passive land occupied by the Germans, which they were in reality without a doubt.

The eventual death of all the conspirators in a shoot-out with German police and soldiery in Prague a few days later was followed in June by a fierce reprisal, the chief event of which was the demolition of the Czech town of Lidice by the Germans and the shooting of its male inhabitants as a reprisal for having served as a shelter for the assassins.

As far as this study is concerned, however, the principal consequences of this event, as ill-advised as it appeared to be then and which judgment has not changed much since then, was the beginning of the first major propaganda calling for prosecution of the entire German leadership as "war criminals." Benes submitted to the "Allies" a request that in the event of victory, they hang all the top Nazi leadership for Lidice, and a vast propaganda exploitation of Lidice spread across the "Allied" political front. In the USA a Lidice Lives Committee was formed, with the formidable Germanophobe, Clifton Fadiman, as its executive chairman, its nominal chairman being ex-Ambassador to the Soviet Union, the millionaire Joseph E. Davies, author of the fulsomely fawning book *Mission to Moscow,* so pro-Communist that it even embarrassed Communists. This committee sought in the summer of 1942 to persuade 31 towns in the USA, one for each of the "United Nations" at war with the Axis, to change their names to Lidice in memoriam of the town destroyed by the Germans on June 10. By the fall they had succeeded in achieving two: the town of San Geronimo in Mexico on August 30, and, earlier, on July 12, a real estate development near Joliet, Illinois, incorporated as a new town named Lidice. The Fadiman-Davies Committee was still seeking no. 3 in October, 1942.

However, the exploitation of the drama of Lidice went far beyond such maneuvers. Americans in particular were led to believe that the Heydrich murder was symptomatic of widespread unrest against the Hitler regime in Germany itself, and that the underground civilian "resistance" was truly formidable, all of which was pure invention. But it gave many people the impression it was true, and thus encouraged them to believe the war would terminate somewhat sooner than realities suggested, and thus also stimulating the sentiment that proceedings against the enemy's leadership were worth contemplating as a serious, practical matter. Zionist leaders were quick to take advantage of the improved climate in the propaganda war this all provoked, as well. The World Jewish Congress, formed in 1936, and meeting in London late in June, 1942, put the number of Jews put to death by the Nazis at a round one million.

By October, 1942, the machinery had been set in motion in England, Russia and the USA to fabricate a device for postwar handling of "war crimes" and "war criminals," the Heydrich-Lidice drama having been steadily exploited. When it was announced that Lord Simon, the British Lord Chancellor, and Roosevelt, had jointly put into at least shadowy form a United Nations Court of Justice to "try all criminals-of-war after the war," Stalin and his Foreign Minister, Molotov, countered by proposing to set it up at once and start operations immediately "by trying, and hanging, Nazi Arch-Criminal Rudolf Hess," as *Time* phrased it.

There was no reported opposition to this, and in retrospect it was a remarkable preview of the Nuremberg stagings insofar as they reflected the Moscow purge-trial trappings which assumed guilt and the sentence prior to courtroom proceedings. *Time* sympathized with Stalin's unhappiness which grew from the report that the British Foreign Office had changed Hess's status from that of prisoner of State to that of prisoner of war, this cloaking him with the protection provided by the 1929 Geneva Convention respecting the treatment of prisoners of war. But this did not restrain US Rep. Emanuel Celler from issuing a supporting bellow in behalf of Stalin, "Shoot Hess Now!" which was launched in the Communist weekly, *New Masses,* but which went far beyond Hess, Rep. Celler calling also for punitive action against all known German, Italian and Japanese leaders, and against the members of their political organizations, for their Jewish persecutions. Rep. Celler named many individuals not in Allied hands whom he thought should be executed, and praised the Soviet Union for beginning a general investigation in Russia to provide substance for an eventual massive retaliation of the sort he so ardently desired.

When Hitler, also in October, 1942, took all this talk of coming mass executions of Axis leaders and followers alike seriously, and delivered a speech in which he declared that they were fighting so hard because they knew that they would either win the war or be "exterminated" at its conclusion, it provoked denials of various kinds, typical of which was that by David Lawrence, editor of the *U.S. News* weekly magazine, who scoffed,

> Has the President of the United States or the Prime Minister of Great Britain ever said anything to indicate that we intend to exterminate the German Nation? Hitler knows very well that the Democracies, while punishing him and all the Nazi Party criminals [sic], will not suffer innocent people to be harmed. Hitler knows that the Christian spirit that he despises still flows through the veins of his adversaries.

Compared to this perfumed rhetorical eyewash, Hitler was a fairly precise prognosticator, as events were to turn out.

Thus, what had been mainly vaguely expressed sentimental opinions began to take firm outlines in the latter half of 1942, urged on by the spectacular succession of events in Central Europe in May-June, at a time when "Allied" performance in the military field was at a standstill and when words were the only effective weapons making an impact. But the consequences of Lidice were not all there was to the blossoming of talk of atrocities and "war crimes" reprisals. Among the Soviet functionaries, an independent strain of related talk had somewhat proceeded prior to this. When the warmly pro-Soviet book, *Moscow War Diary,* by Alexander Werth, was published, early in the spring, and well before Lidice, this dependable pro-Stalinist transmission belt had placed his stamp of approval on a statement by S. A. Lozovsky, the head of Stalin's puppet labor union front, the Profintern, that it would be a good thing to kill the entire membership of Hitler's National Socialist Party; in the light of this, Stalin's recommendation toward the end of the war that only 50,000 German military officers be murdered was comparatively mild.

But one way or another, the momentum accelerated, and all involved began to join in magnifying the problem in public display. Jews in 29 countries set aside December 2, 1942 as a day of fasting and public mourning "in protest against Nazi murder of their people,"

Newsweek reported, with work stopping in New York City for 15 minutes at 10 a.m. that day, "while half a million Jews prayed that the killers be brought to retribution after the war." Shortly after that the British Ministry of Economic Warfare, inexplicably, entered this part of the picture by serving as a sounding board for new Zionist claims that another half million Jews had been sent to Eastern Europe, and that the death toll of Jews in Poland and occupied Russia, added to those deceased since the start of the war in September, 1939, now stood at 2,000,000. This set the stage for the famous United Nations announcement at the end of December, 1942 on the part of the three main adversaries of the Germans plus their eight satellite governments-in-exile in London, plus the rump French National Committee there headed by Gen. Charles de Gaulle, wherein they solemnly pledged themselves "to punish this bestial policy of cold-blooded extermination" after the war. This propaganda release, read before the House of Commons in London by Foreign Secretary Anthony Eden and broadcast to the world in 23 languages, was to be one of the two pieces of "evidence" cited by Raphael Lemkin nearly two years later as support for his charge of "genocide." By that time Lidice was mainly forgotten by most, but its subliminal impact, reinforced by many new and more sensational claims, was firmly in place in the popular mind.

With the mouthpieces of the wartime United Nations now in the atrocities steeplechase on a formal basis, even though their soothsayers had not yet agreed on what a "war crime" or a "war criminal" was, it was time to analyze what the various stands on the subject consisted of, what some of the loudest voices were for, and to have in mind what the exploiters of alleged German atrocities were trying to achieve. The hard-core Germanophobes seemed satisfied with a retaliatory program which smashed Germany flat, killed as many of its populace as possible, cut up and redistributed its territory, and reduced its survivors forever to as mean a livelihood as possible. A British variation of this impulse seemed motivated by the hope that Germany would be rendered impotent as an economic competitor indefinitely as a result of this draconian program.

As for the Soviet Reds, their version of political biology appeared to be satisfied with the dispatch of specific German leaders considered most unlikely recruits in a new Communist order, though they deplored the wrecking of German productive facilities and major real estate, expecting to be the residuary legatees of much of it after war's end. Those with Polish dreams of restitution contemplated mainly being put back into the State business, though most of them began to realize as 1943 went by that this would have to be done at heavy German territorial expense, the Stalinist regime making it more and more evident by the week that they fully expected to retake the large region in the East back into the Russian State. Jews were to be found in all these, as well as purely Zionist goals. and the exploitation of atrocities fitted in well with some sectors of their Haganah underground, which long believed that the way to get Palestine was through desperate action resulting in the "martyrdom" of many Jews, in order to win world sympathy, which was considered a far more potent assist than unaided efforts on their own. The purely revenge-seekers were to be found among them, for sure, though most of them were in literary and political circles; the rabbinate in general expressed little if any of such emotions. There were as many non-Jews as Jews urging a Carthaginian settlement for Germany, and sometimes exceeding the latter in issuing savage recommendations. The UN declaration at the end of 1942 stimulated the expansion of the atrocity tale among all, however, and the accusations began to get more reckless, it now being sensed that reasonable proof was less and less likely to be required to substantiate them. The momentum of favorable public sympathy was with them, and working it for all it was worth was the order of the day.

A remaining objective worth mentioning in the atrocities-counter-extermination propaganda obviously is simply that of strengthening domestic pro-war sentiments and activity, an old goal in all wars, and probably the main one in the dissemination of this kind of atrocity material in the war of 1914-1918. This seems to be evident in the release of the book *Is Germany Incurable?* (Philadelphia, Lippincott, 1943.) The author was allegedly a psychiatrist, Richard Brickner, and his message could also have been useful to the elements favoring the extermination notions of Kaufman two years earlier. A panel of six supporting psychiatrists was recruited to support Brickner's thesis, which would have been more plainly understood had he transposed the first two words of his title and eliminated the interrogation point at its end. But he and his defending cast were subject to a withering deflation by the liberal historian, Harry Elmer Barnes, who in turn was bitterly assailed by a veritable posse of Brickner's supporters assembled by Norman Cousins, editor of the *Saturday Review of Literature,* including Cecil Brown, Henry Steele Commager, Carl van Doren, Clifton Fadiman, William L. Shirer and Rex Todhunter Stout, the bitter controversy going on into late October, 1943. But probably the only effect the book really had was suggested well before it all began, by Gregory Zilboorg, M.D., five months earlier:

> As a sign of the times, Dr. Brickner's book may be passed over with some forbearance. We are at war with Hitler, and anything that makes the populace hate the Germans is grist to the bloody mill of this global

struggle. Machiavellian propaganda may appear unsavory to the over-sensitive, but in the midst of battle anything that keeps the heat of hate at the level of its white glow is welcome to the combatant.

One may argue that, granting Brickner's book could be inter-preted as mainly a contribution to "Allied" wartime propaganda in a war still at its peak, his message had a large and dark undertone which lent itself to long time exploitation, as a support for postwar vengeance, and as an aid for attitudinal poisoning for an immense period of time. The main objection to the Zilboorg interpretation of Brickner's book insofar as its intent was concerned is that there is no shut-off spigot to hate, and its consequences can spread to millions and last for generations, once loosed, for whatever reason. The main hate campaigns of both World Wars were so skillfully and universally projected that large residues of them are still at large, and surface frequently at moments when aspects of these wars are recalled, for whatever reason. That wartime hate campaigns interfered with the re-establishment of peace is most palpable, a matter explored by Francis Neilson, Member of Parliament in 1914 when the First World War began, and a citizen of the USA since the early 1920s, in his booklet, *Hate, The Enemy of Peace,* issued in 1944, when the road back from a hate position was already quite untraversible.

The post-Lidice months saw the various aspects of the atrocity propaganda campaign and the proposals for fierce punishment of the Germans swirling around in a veritable tornado of words, with the usual sensational and contradictory reports sailing through the air, helping to keep a maximum of unsettled conditions for students to try to understand. Stories that Jews were being *sent* to Germany to help the severe labor shortage, and employed elsewhere by the German army in labor battalions, began to disappear and to be replaced by new accounts of their mass murder. *Newsweek* had pub-lished short reports on the deportation of Jews from Slovakia to Germany for employment at various wartime tasks, and on January 18, 1943 (p. 10) this same source reported, "Hungarian newspapers have lately carried scores of death notices of Jews killed on the Russian front, though they aren't permitted in the army. Serving in labor groups, they were caught behind the lines by the swift Russian advances."

But paralleling these were allegations of continuing mass murders in Poland and renewed charges of practices repeating those of 1914-1918. The *New Republic* (January 18, 1943, p. 65) claimed as authority the "Socialist underground" in Poland for informing them that the Nazis were "using the bodies of their Jewish victims to make soap and fertilizer in a factory at Siedlce" (by Maidanek time, it has been seen, this activity was supposed to have happened in Germany proper). Shortly after the *Christian Century* repeated from the London socialist paper *New Statesman & Nation* a summary of an "official" report from the London Polish government that "the people actually engaged in murdering the Jews in Eastern Europe are a special corps of Lithuanians, Latvians and White Russians, " and not Germans at all.

Not so palatable to Socialists outside the Soviet bloc and Poland, however, was a bit of jarring news a month later that two well-known Polish Jewish Socialists, Victor Alter and Henryk Ehrlich, had been put to death by the Soviet authorities, sometime before December, 1942, when this news was first supplied to William Green, head of the American Federation of Labor, by Maxim Litvinov, one time Red foreign minister. It did not become generally known until this act was denounced in an official report by the London Polish government published on March 8, 1943. Arrested in 1939 when the Reds took over a large part of Poland, they had been released in June, 1941, only to be re-arrested in Kuibyshev, the temporary capital of the Soviet Union, in December of that year, and subsequently executed on a charge of having aided the war fortunes of the Nazi invaders, a most unlikely course of action. The remarkable thing about its propaganda effect in the USA was the tiny stir this event created; the American Socialist leader Norman Thomas was one of the few to protest it. It was interesting to compare the immense outcry in 1924 when another distant Socialist hero, Matteotti, was killed upon orders of Benito Mussolini in Italy, something which was never proven, but a subject for outraged comments for over 50 years after. The Ehrlich-Alter killings by the Soviet government, freely admitted, produced nothing of this kind in America. But it did provide an unsettling situation in the complex of Polish-English-American-Russian relations which set the stage for a far worse circumstance the following month of April, 1943, and was further to complicate the entire atrocity picture.

In the early spring of 1943 one of the most active of "Allied" war correspondent-journalists, Alice Leone Moats, published her book, *Blind Date with Mars.* It contained one of the very few reports on the Poles deported to eastern Russia and Siberia by the Reds after October, 1939, and amnestied in part after June, 1941 and the start of the fighting with the Germans. She was impressed by their miserable physical condition upon seeing them arrive in European Russia, and she was about the only Western journalist to comment, "no trace could be found of over five thousand [Polish] officers and fourteen generals" among the returnees; it was her estimate that the Soviet regime had incarcerated 2,000,000 Poles.

A few days after her book appeared, the answer to her specula-
tion was supplied by the publicity and propaganda agencies of the
Hitler regime, which announced the discovery of mass graves in the
Katyn forest, near Smolensk in western Russia, containing the bodies
of many thousands of Polish officers. In the *Newsweek* report (May
3, 1943, pp. 42, 46), it was quoted from the official German news
agency, DNB, that these mass murders were the work of four OGPU
(=NKVD=MVD=KGB) Jewish commissars, Lev Rybak, Abraham
Borisovich, Pavel Brodninsky and Chaim Feinberg. The reaction by
the Polish government-in-exile in London headed by General
Wladislaw Sikorski was to ask for an investigation of this by the
International Red Cross, which led to a furious attack from Stalin
and the breaking of diplomatic relations between the London Poles
and Moscow. It is possible the non-communist Polish cause had been
slipping in "Allied" esteem and sentiments as Stalin's military star
had been rising in Eastern Europe. The Katyn Forest matter signalled
its precipitate decline, also timed with the near-simultaneous "Allied"
success in North Africa, and the sharp rise in the feeling that the war
was definitely heading for an "Allied" victory, which meant heavy
repair of all diplomatic and political fences and lines of communications, and that meant in particular the avoidance of antagonism of
Stalin.

The official American slant on Katyn seemed to be supplied by
Elmer Davis, head of the main US war propaganda bureau, the Office
of War Information. Since Stalin was an "ally," it was understandable that Roosevelt regime spokesmen would take a view critical of
German charges and supportive of Communist denials, and counter-
charges against the Germans, though the area where the killings had
taken place was not in German hands when they had taken place, by
evidence supplied from the dated materials such as correspondence
exhumed with the dead.

On the radio Davis repeated the skepticism demonstrated by
American fellow travelers with the Reds, and the press almost
unanimously followed his lead. The more voluble of the Red apolo-
gists in the USA simply turned the accusation around and charged
the Germans with trying to cover up an act of their own. The scrambling of the nation's major newspapers to minimize the seriousness of
Stalin's break with the London Poles was a pathetic sight, and they
were all prostrated by the thought of the exploitation of this affair by
German propaganda. *Newsweek* called it "One of the most tragic
disputes to haunt the relations between the United Nations," and the
Christian Century called it a "major defeat" for Anglo-American
diplomacy. But the *Nation* brushed it off as a "Nazi trap" and a
"bulls-eye for Goebbels," the German propaganda minister. William

L. Shirer in the New York *Herald Tribune* also stated it was a German propaganda fake, that the Germans had done it, and that they were simply trying to exploit the already strained Russo-Polish political climate. The *Nation's* counterpart liberal weekly, the *New Republic,* responded to the event with spinal-cord swiftness, denouncing the whole matter as a "crude and outrageous provocation" of the Soviet Union by Hitler, and undermining all the good deeds the Reds had performed to enhance Polish security. The *NR* editors fiercely reproved Sikorski's group, attacked them for challenging the previous Red claims to eastern Polish territory, and hoped Roosevelt and Churchill would heal the split, and help bring about a new Polish government "that could work with Russia," and still not be a Red "puppet," a repetition of an endless and futile liberal dream which was not abandoned for decades. They concluded by regretting that the Poles were so independent and not "like the Czech leaders," whose eager pro-Soviet tenor they much appreciated. A week later (May 17, 1943, pp. 651-652), the *NR* editors returned to the tack of six or seven years earlier, suddenly re-discovering that Poland had been "under a dictatorship for years," after almost four years of endlessly bellowing about Poland being a "raped democracy." Now, they saw Poland as a land "in many respects" "as illiberal as the Nazis themselves." The reaction of the London Sikorski Poles to Katyn was grounds for the "Allies" now to move away from them, and make provisions for the Poles in the postwar period to be guaranteed the opportunity "to set up whatever government they wish" at the end of the war.

Time accepted the Communist stand on Katyn also, and agreed it was a German disguise for their own prior atrocity. It also regretted the Poles had "fed the flames of anti-Soviet suspicion" by asking for the Red Cross investigation. In nearly two pages of commentary, *Time* warmly sympathized with the Reds, yearned for "definite Anglo-Russo-American postwar understandings," supported Anglo-American efforts to squelch the Poles, backed Red claims to eastern Poland and saw this in no way as evidence Stalin was trying to create a Red Poland.

Time's companion publication, *Life,* adopted a similar view, called Katyn a German action, not Russian, and denounced the Poles as "the most chip-shouldered chauvinists in Europe," a return to the Popular Front-fellow traveler estimate of 1934-39. Sikorski's call for the Red Cross to look into the matter *Life* called "stupid," and the London Poles simply "ultranationalists," and especially chiding Sikorski for failing to "win Russian confidence," "almost the first duty of any Polish government that wants to survive." Furthermore, said *Life,* it was "healthy" to be reminded that Stalin's regime was not influenced by public opinion, that the Atlantic Charter was "not an adequate United States foreign policy," and might even be a "dangerous policy," "if it makes us forget that the behavior of all nations is still controlled by their selfish interests." Since the major aspect of US self-interest lay with Russia, then American diplomats had better not "get too huffy in backing the Poles." It was instructive to see how the Katyn affair so quickly put the torch to the bales of purple words Luce's American Century press had written in worship of moral and ethical abstractions since 1939.

Most of the followup stories directed to the many millions of American readers of the major circulation magazines and papers a week after the first reports were solidly with Stalin against Sikorski and the Poles. *Newsweek* (May 10, 1943, pp. 29-30), varied slightly from the general consensus, coming to the Soviet side, and scolding the Poles for having believed even for a moment that the Germans might be right, though it was believed a matter for concern that Moscow might recognize the Communist Polish puppet entourage in Russia, the so-called Union of Polish Patriots, headed by Wanda Vassilevskaya, wife of Alexander Korneichuk, Soviet Vice Commissar for Foreign Affairs, Ukrainian, "popular" playwright, and supporter of Bolshevik annexation of the Ukraine.

One can see that Katyn was important, probably the only genuine mass atrocity of World War Two which was accompanied by evidence in the form of a large number of deliberately murdered dead (even the Reds when they exploited Maidanek 15 months later showed no pictures of the dead they claimed had been massacred there[4]. One can also see that whether the Reds had done it or not, or despite efforts to establish the simple facts, all was quickly buried under hysterical evaluations of it in terms of Western pro-Communist political future relations. Only the *Saturday Evening Post*, about a month after the first revelations concerning Katyn had been made, showed a distaste for converting the entire matter into a political sentiment display. Irked by the universal press and radio dismissal of the Polish charges of the murder of their officer corps by the Reds as mere Nazi propaganda, the *Post* editors remarked acidly,

> The forgers of public opinion in London and Washington, who first censored the dispute altogether and then tried to sell us the notion that it was all a figment of Doctor Goebbels' imagination, have done a poor service to international realism.

One might argue that little "international realism" was capable of surviving in an atmosphere such as prevailed in wartime London and Washington, but the determination to exculpate Stalin's regime from all responsibility for the Katyn Forest massacre ranked close to the top of all Western "Allies" political objectives the rest of 1943. One may fairly date the determination to bring about a Stalinist-Red puppet Poland with the Katyn imbroglio. The venom toward Poland rose sharply in the English language press, and Red blinders tended to be worn most of the time by political opinion makers the rest of the war. One of the more succinct admonishments to the London Poles to cultivate Stalin came from one of the more articulate pro-Soviet transmission belts in London, the *New Statesman & Nation:*

> To imagine as some Poles apparently do, that they can rely on the United States or Great Britain to guarantee their frontiers or maintain their security, if they are at odds with their far more powerful neighbor, is to move politics into the atmosphere of cloud-cuckoo land.

This paper was one of those which thought it toweringly sagacious statesmanship for Britain to have promised to support the Poles with assistance should they get in trouble with the Germans in March 1939 by breaking off negotiations for the settlement of outstanding differences, but their turnabout now was not evidence of newly acquired wisdom and realism, nor a manifestation that *they* had emerged from "cloud-cuckoo land"; the paper had simply moved into a more secure Soviet province of that hypothetical territory.[5]

The fuss created by General Sikorski and his London Poles over Katyn was still swirling when he was killed in the mysterious crash of the plane bearing him back to London from Gibraltar on July 4, 1943. *Time* thought it had spoken the last word on him and Katyn in its issue of the 12th (p. 36) when it reiterated its conviction that the death of the Polish officers in Russia was simply a wild Nazi "propaganda claim," and it was very unhappy he and his fellow Poles believed it had happened. With the British Foreign Office and Eden on the Red side of this controversy, having just exerted great pressure on Sikorski to appease Stalin, the magazine thought it surely was on the side of the angels *re* Katyn, and that it would soon blow over. Thirty-five years later Katyn was still a hot issue. It is significant for our immediate purposes however to observe that Raphael Lemkin discreetly skirted the entire subject in his lopsided concern with "genocide" in his book.

The immense flap over the Katyn forest massacres and the enormous embarrassment they caused the directors of war propaganda among the "Allies" because of the pall of suspicion cast over the Stalin regime as the possible guilty party in these murders (long since proved) did not cause much delay or disruption in the pumping out of new calls for the obliteration of Germany and its people in harmony with the numerous suggestions of this sort after the Lidice affair. Some of them were uncannily close to what was to happen, while others were not much more that gaseous fulminations of political refugees and emigres.

The professoriat made their contributions to this vicious collection, one of the most incendiary being that of the University of Chicago Germanophobe, Bernadotte Schmitt, whose suggestion for the starvation of 30,000,000 Germans had been made before an audience of approving educators in 1941. With a couple of years to think things over, Schmitt went a little beyond his earlier suggestion in a University of Chicago Public Policy Pamphlet (No. 38) which began to get around in the early summer of 1943, *What Shall We Do with Germany?* Schmitt got right down to business, urging as severe a treatment as could be applied. He declared his program was "based on the conviction that the Germans are not like Frenchmen or Britishers or Americans but possess certain national traits which make them impervious to reason, generosity or even fair play," a discovery which should have been quite a surprise to the scores of millions of Americans of German descent, though none of them were known to have protested this vicious slur. Schmitt urged the utter military wrecking of Germany by armies meeting in Berlin from all directions, the dismemberment and carrying away of the entire industry in the country, followed by intense punitive actions on a vast scale, "in the hope that the sadistic traits of the Germans may be restrained"; "Let us make life difficult and unpleasant for them," Schmitt cooed in conclusion.

On the heels of this came a small book by Emil Ludwig, *How to Treat the Germans* (Willard, 1943), which he supplemented by a long article in the 3,000,000 circulation family magazine, *Collier's,* "How to Treat Defeated Germany." It included most of the more ferocious recommendations of others, but included a grim suggestion for the walling off of Germans from the rest of the world, a policy of total non-fraternization, supported by "a law," which he thought "should forbid any German to pass the frontiers of his country." He urged that the occupiers import "hundreds of intellectuals," to replace German teachers, and that education and communications be placed 100% in the hands of non-Germans. He also called for the cutting of Germany into two countries, and for the punishing of "scores of thousands" of its people, though he did not recommend the material looting of the land, so dear to others.

An eerie volume was produced at about the same time by Professor Max Radin of the Law School of the University of California at Berkeley, *The Day of Reckoning* (Knopf). It was an imaginary work purporting to be a report of a trial of Hitler and his six most prominent lieutenants, held in 1945 following an Allied victory. This uncanny outline of what was to happen three years later (less Hitler) received enthusiastic reviews (in Radin's futuristic account the defendants were found guilty and executed too), though only the scope of the Nuremberg proceedings was not anticipated. Prof. Radin's professorial colleague, at Harvard Law School, Sheldon Glueck, also gave indications that the legal lights in several regions were at work on the same project in 1943, as was Lemkin; Glueck's later treatise on "war criminals," well before Nuremberg, "Punishing the War Criminals," was given a thorough advance exposure in the *New Republic* in which he revealed "Proof of guilt is now being assembled and prepared," and felt comforted that the "Allies" had already agreed that "offenders" were to be tried "at the scene of their crimes and under the laws of the victims' countries." This was a clear indication Prof. Glueck would approve of the upcoming first trial run of "war crimes" proceedings, the kangaroo court sessions the Stalinists would shortly stage at Kharkov.

The real season for what-shall-we-do-with-Germany books was to be 1944, but 1943 still had a few to loose, including Paul Einzig's *Can We Win the Peace?* (Macmillan), another hard-peace, deindustrialize-Germany recipe. But the work which fascinated especially the liberals and which received far more interest and attention was Heinz Pol's *The Hidden Enemy* (Julian Messner.) Pol, a Jewish refugee and former "editor" variously in Berlin and Vienna whose pseudonym faintly disguised his original name, Pollack, was essentially fronting a Marxist proposal, intended partially to head off the popularity of the mindless Carthaginian destruction schemes of the likes of ancient professional Germanophobes such as Britain's Lord Vansittart, about which more later. Pol, more in tune with Stalinist desires for maintaining a unified Red German state instead of a fragmented Germany, kept the focus on the class angle. His target for annihilation consisted of the military, economic and aristrocratic elite, to be "purged" in the manner of the somewhat similar elements during the French Revolution. He thought at some propitious moment the "Allies" might cooperatively launch a mighty "Great Purge" of Germans by other Germans, killing off "about five hundred thousand Nazi leaders and other members of the elite," and then develop another elite, but one which was cleansed of German "imperialist" tendencies. Whereupon Germany could proceed onward effortlessly to "the final success of the retarded democratic revolution," by which he undoubtedly meant the victory of Stalinist-Leninist Communism which had been so rudely interrupted by Hitler. Among the enthusiastic reviews of Pol's book was the venerated Reinhold Niebuhr, at the bottom of almost anything suggested for new policy in Germany since 1934 which promised to involve something which might be described as "democratic collectivism." Niebuhr had months before in the *Nation* expressed the view that Stalin would undoubtedly oppose dismemberment of Germany, a policy which Niebuhr found "ominously favored by certain circles in both Anglo-Saxon countries." But in the case of the aftermath of such a bloodletting as Pol suggested, Niebuhr was not too sure Stalin would let it go to a logical conclusion; he and his social democrat liberal allies were worried that Stalin might even make a deal and come to terms with a Junker residuary legatee of the Nazis. But the job Pol wanted to see done obviously was one which only the Communists could do; Hans W. Weigert, reviewing the book for the *Saturday Review of Literature,* (September 25, 1943, p. 6), detected this in the book, and flatly stated that the initiative for the effecting of such a program as that of Pol would have to come from Moscow. Nevertheless, the romantic aspect of a grandiose nation-wide murder spree wiping out everyone at the top in Germany enchanted most of the reviewers; Fadiman in the *New Yorker* (September 4, 1943, pp. 75, 77), spoke for the majority in decreeing that Pol's book should be "compulsory reading" for all Americans.

The Katyn revelations acted as a mild damper on atrocity propaganda from "Allied" directions for a short time, but the predicament of Jews in Nazi-occupied regions remained a subject for wide comment despite it all, and quite aside from all the ferocious plans and recommendations for the obliteration of Germany and its populace after the war (much of this feral talk fitted in well with the increasing mass bombing of German cities by strategic air forces based in England; some of the grimmest calls for annihilating Germany came at the time of the fire-bombing of Hamburg, one of the most frightful events in the history of modern warfare.)

At the peak of the first major wave of recommendations for the elimination of Germany from the map, a frequent correspondent to the *New Republic* felt constrained to remind the editors that

> not one religious Jew, not one rabbi, has ever debased himself to such ignominious nonsense as to propose the "total obliteration" or the total sterilization of the whole German people. That was left to such "intellectuals" as Westbrook Pegler, Quentin Reynolds and even Ernest Hemingway, following the irresponsible Nathan [sic] Kaufman, who rendered inestimable service to Mr. Goebbels.

The reference to non-Jews who had issued calls for the disappearance of Germany from the world was telling, and soon to be well-outmatched, since the notables referred to had relieved themselves of these hate effusions in 1942.

The release of provoking Zionist tracts emphasizing the atrocity theme early in 1943 was matched by a parallel propaganda of a more positive sort, and fed into a drive for refugee relief which had very mixed results. In New York, two massive spectacles were staged in Madison Square Garden, one directed by the famous showman, Billy Rose, a pageant titled "We Will Never Die," intended in part to "mourn" the 2,000,000 Jews now alleged to have died in Axis-controlled Europe. On the political side among the "Allies," there was a report that in response to a British note, Secretary of State Cordell Hull had proposed an Anglo-American conference to be held in Ottawa, Canada, to consider more "havens" for Nazi "victims" fleeing Europe, an indication people were still able to get out. In the accompanying report to the press on their refugee relief work as of mid-spring, 1942, Britain was credited with taking 100,000 persons and parts of its Empire another 120,000. As for the US, a total of 547,775 visas had been issued between 1935 and June 30, 1942 to the "victims of persecution" by the Hitler regime. As this conference on the refugee question, now set for Bermuda in April, approached, many of these same statistics were repeated, but the British total of actual people of refugee-evacuee-internee status from Axis Europe being maintained in Britain, its colonies and Palestine, was listed as 682,710. It was remarked in closing that the British Dominions had separate totals which obviously upped this figure considerably, but they were not released.

American figures continued to issue from official sources, but their tardiness and mixed categories made any precise summing-up difficult. Kurt R. Grossman, writing in the *Nation* (December 11, 1943, p. 691) declared,

> Of the 314,715 aliens who, in conformity with a Presidential proclamation, registered in February, 1942, as enemy aliens of German origin, the greatest number are refugees who were forced to leave the homeland by the cruel treatment meted out to them. The majority are Jews.

Grossman of course had no figures on those who did *not* register, the implication of his account being that there was a substantial number here as well. No one complained about Grossman's estimate of this aspect of Government statistics. But Zionist agencies sharply contested Assistant Secretary of State Breckinridge Long's figures, announced before a meeting of the House Committee on Refugees at about the same time in December, when he declared that between 1933 and 1943 over 500,000 refugees had been admitted to the US, and giving the impression that most of them had been Jews.

The reason for this challenge becomes clear when one tries even on a superficial scale to assess the situation in the labyrinth the refugee statistics had become. The Communist, Zionist and Anglo-

American West claims were irreconcilable. The Soviet Union claimed they had taken at least 1,800,000 Jews from Poland into their interior regions. This figure was agreed to by the Institute for Jewish Affairs of the American Jewish Congress, as late as in their report on the status of Jews in Nazi-occupied Europe of September, 1943. The *New Republic* quoted the IJA report as declaring that only 180,000 other Jews had "emigrated to other lands." But the combined Anglo-American claims to admission of refugees went well beyond a million, combined, and these were just the *official* figures; they made no provisions for those who might have entered the USA, the United Kingdom, including its colonies, dominions and mandated territories, such as Palestine, *illegally*. Since illegal migration about Europe was a very substantial affair, it was reasonable to presume that it was just as big an enterprise elsewhere. And, of course, nothing was said of emigration of European refugees to such places as the Orient, South America, South Africa, and many other lands not in the war zones or in German hands. For the IJA-AJC statisticians to insist that only 180,000 Jews had gone elsewhere in the world other than the Soviet Union required non-Jews and non-Stalinists to conclude that less than one in ten of the Europeans fleeing Hitler Germany and its allies was a Jew.

Nevertheless, the Zionist publicists stubbornly adhered to the estimate that of Europe's 8,300,000 Jews when Hitler had come into power in 1933, ten years and a half later, only 3,000,000 were left; the Axis powers had murdered 3,000,000 and roughly 2,000,000 had emigrated, only 180,000 of these to other regions than Soviet Russia. That this IJA-AJC report late in 1943 contradicted their report of December 1941 was the most obvious import of the new statement on world Jewish population. In the December, 1941 publication, it was admitted that nearly 350,000 Jews had fled to the United States, South America and Palestine alone, before the USA was even in the war. Now this figure was drastically reduced, with a new total of about *half* that figure for *the entire world* outside the orbit of Josef Stalin.

Late 1943 was too hyperthyroid a time to engage in a sober and dispassionate sifting of all these incredible demographic assertions. But it was obvious that a great many people were being declared dead who were very much alive; they continued to grow in number as the allegations of the murdered millions steadily escalated in the next 3 years. American journals dutifully repeated the latest IJA-AJC claims, including the insistence that of the 2,000,000 Jews who had migrated from occupied Europe, nine-tenths of them had gone to Russia, presumably swelling Russia's Jewish population to 5,000,000, all "heroically fighting Hitler in the Soviet Union," as the Communist weekly *New Masses* blared ("Toward Jewish Unity," September 14, 1943, p. 6). A month later this journal repeated the earlier figure and identified the origin of the new residents in the Soviet State: "The Soviet Government has admitted 1,800,000 Polish Jews and is looking after their well being." No Zionist organ is known to have complained about this, since it conformed with the identical figure they had published seven weeks earlier. In harmony with their return to prominence in the wartime statistical steeplechase, Communists added their measure to expanded atrocity stories as the summer of 1943 wore on and Katyn drew less and less attention. On August 17, the *New Masses* announced, "Two distinguished Russian-Jewish visitors to our country recently made the terrible announcement that, according to Soviet Intelligence, the Jews of Germany have by now been completely exterminated." Thus a new source of information had been supplied: Jewish agents of the Soviet spy system, though all they did was re-affirm what the Soviet transmission belt Lion Feuchtwanger had insisted as far back as 1936. But the Communist literary weekly could not resist making the Soviet point once more on the destination of Poland's refugee Jews. In a reproach to Ben Hecht and other Jewish publicists who had taken a belated interest in creating refugee assistance fronts, the latest being the Emergency Committee to Save the Jewish People of Europe, the editors acidly commented, "It is understandable that one who has so recently discovered the Jewish problem as Ben Hecht should be ignorant of the fact that 1,800,000 Jewish refugees from Hitler have been rescued by the Soviet Union—more than the rest of the world combined." (Editorial, "Key Hole Outlook," *New Masses*, November 30, 1943, p. 4.)

A chilling preview of the point toward which the mountains of atrocity propaganda beckoned was provided by the Stalin regime in December, 1943, not long after the famous Teheran conference among Roosevelt, Churchill and Stalin, where some of the most fateful decisions were made which contributed to the disorder of Europe for the following generation. The first execution of "war criminals" for "war crimes" took place *before* the United Nations Commission for the Investigation of War Crimes, in full flight in London the week before Christmas, 1943, had even been able to come up with a definition of what a "war criminal" was. [This did not bother the respondents to a British Gallup Poll, who favored shooting same outright (40%) torturing them (15%), and trying them (15%)].

Though the bacchanalia at the British Embassy in Teheran where Stalin and others helped Churchill celebrate Churchill's 69th birthday with from 35 to 50 alcoholic toasts and what *Time* called "the

most spectacular meal since the Last Supper," did not seem to deal
with the subject beyond the strange exchange among the famed participants as to an acceptable number of German officers who should
be shot on capture. The grim business of executing "war criminals"
was to start in the Soviet city of Kharkov not long after. Four people
who confessed to everything as charged, in what looked like a left-
over Stalin purge trial of the 1936-1938 time, were promptly hanged
publicly in that city before an audience of 50,000. For the first time
during the entire war the Anglo-American reportorial corps in
Moscow were permitted to see something happen, never having been
on the scene of a single event in the war in Russia anywhere before
that moment. A belated report (by six months) of the Kharkov hangings was made by *Time's* Moscow bureau head for 1943-1944,
Richard E. Lauterbach ("How the Russians Try Nazi Criminals,"
Harper's Magazine, June, 1945, pp. 658-664), which, though he tried
to decorate it with positive trappings, still came out as little more
than a judicial execution ceremony. Nuremberg and most of what
else followed subsequently were little more than minor variations on
a similar lethal theme.

For a few (only the editors of the Catholic liberal weekly
Commonweal were greatly disturbed by the Kharkov proceedings;
e.g., December 31, 1943, p. 267), it was a chance to get back to
earth once more, after having forgotten what "justice" consisted of
in Red Russia, under the pressure of thinking nice thoughts about an
"ally" during wartime. One might have remembered the preposterous
column filed from Russia by Bill Downs, *Newsweek's* Moscow correspondent ("Red Justice," June 7, 1943, pp. 57-58), with its incredible
commentary on the prison labor camps, which made them almost
sound as though they might be fun to be in. A curious *Collier's* main
editorial a few days before Kharkov ("Our Russian Ally," December
18, 1943, p. 86) echoed Downs and others trying to sell Americans
on the genial institutional transformation taking place in the homeland of our Red "ally," though they had broken step a mite by a
gentle reference to the "still large and reportedly brutal concentration camps" with their "ten to twelve million guests." It is no
wonder the postwar totals of those who spent the war in Hitler's
camps had to be escalated upward in such prodigious manner, having
somehow to be made imposing and formidable enough to balance off
admissions such as this. In any case, Kharkov was a reminder to those
who might have swallowed *Collier's* and their own belief that Stalin
was moving the Soviet toward "something resembling our own and
Great Britain's democracy" that there were a few things in which the
wartime trio of partners were not quite exactly in unison. It took
Nuremberg and after to reveal how much more the USA and Britain

had moved in the Soviet's direction when it came to "justice." The Kharkov hangings took place almost a year before Raphael Lemkin's book was published; they aroused no reaction from him.

As 1944 began, it was obvious that there would be no rational settlement of this war, that it might terminate in a hysterical maelstrom of massacre and destruction which would make that ending in 1918 seem orderly by comparison. The tireless exploitation of atrocity propaganda by the Western "Allies," the Jewish massacre charges and dire predictions of coming vengeance were just elements in the total picture. The Reds, not so consistent and not as prominent on the atrocity ferris wheel, soon became steady riders. Partially to offset Katyn, and partly to profit from increased good fortunes in the war and the opportunistic gains accruing therefrom, the Soviet for a time took the lead. The Kharkov public hangings of "war criminals" gave them a temporary jump on the others, encouraging sustained actions and charges down to Maidanek, in August, 1944, as we have seen, which predicted the somewhat more sensational exploitation of Auschwitz (Oswiecim), early in 1945. In the West the lawyers recruited for the purpose went about it in a slightly different manner, with the fabricating of "war crimes" preceding the actual dispatch of the people accused of committing them. It was obvious that the Axis efforts to dislodge the status quo of 1919-1939 would rank high in the indictment, a clear case of "aggression," by the indictment being prepared, though those who flung this word around could no more define it than they ever had been able to, and would be as helpless later on trying to do it. It grew increasingly evident that indictment in the propaganda of their enemies sealed the fate of the Axis leaders, and their trials, mainly in the Moscow and Kharkov manner, were to be mainly public spectacles seeking to establish *how* guilty they were. As the year wore on, Stalinist atrocity charges seemed to be lodged against nearly everyone, and it became increasingly difficult especially in wartime America, after the Moscow, Cairo and Teheran conferences, to deny a particle of their validity. Neutrality on the subject had to be avoided because of the large literature already on the record here on Red atrocities against Poland and Finland, 1939-1941, and against tens of millions of their own citizens, still not a proper subject for any Communist-savoring American liberal, or among their old friends among the opulent.

The apparent test for American "principles" came in January, 1944 when the Reds lodged atrocity claims against the Finns, fortuitous allies of the Germans, on the grounds of maltreatment of Communist prisoners. This caused a few pained smiles in American circles, since the Bolshevik regime was not even a signatory to the Geneva Convention respecting treatment of prisoners of war, dating to 1929, and had acquired the reputation for being the most outrageous of all regimes when it came to maltreatment of their prisoners of war. It is to the credit of the Finns they rejected the Red charge, and they made the unusual plea of asking a nominal enemy, the US, to send journalists or other investigators to Karelia to investigate the legitimacy of the Red accusations. Obviously, the wartime regime of Franklin D. Roosevelt could not ruffle Stalin's feathers by complying with such a request; the Red charge had to be substantiated, by default.

At about the same time as the accusation of Finnish abuse of Red prisoners the Red propaganda machine played a master card against the Germans, in some ways a Katyn-in-reverse, and well promoted in America by such ardent friends of Stalinism as Jerome Davis, for the millions of middle class American readers of *Collier's*, and one destined to become a perennial, still dredged up, but mainly later by Zionists. This was Babi Yar. The original account seems to have been broadcast by Communist Germans holed up in Moscow, their radio story, later published, accompanied by the usual Sovfoto pictures, which might have been taken any place in view of the willingness to accept anything from Russia now commonplace in American mass communications of the more affluent connections. According to Davis' account as strained through the German Communists' allegation, the German army, ten days after capturing Kiev, had gathered the city's Jews together, placed them under arrest, following which "the universal belief [*sic*] is that they were shot in a mammoth ravine called Babi-Yar." The method of massacre later changed, some even believing the dead were buried alive, but the Communists conducted no exhumations here, as the Germans had at Katyn. There was nothing but self-serving statements to back the claims, though there were rumors the dead were victims of the Red Army in its retreat in 1941, when its "scorched earth" policy required the destruction of vast property holdings. A long-kept secret was the Russian civilian resistance to this, and the many small battles fought between them and their own army, accompanied by immense loss of life, all of which was blamed on the Germans, though it is unlikely the latter could have brought all this about, logistically, in view of what they had in manpower and materials when the region had been invaded. Davis was conducted to the site twice by Red propaganda officials, though it was never decided how many dead were there or how they had been killed. Later Zionist publicists went well beyond the original Red promotion of Babi-Yar,[6] and it is an established tale in the surviving Zionist version of the war in the East. Babi-Yar was probably what was in the mind of the fierce Zionist publicist, William B. Ziff, when he published the following a little later in 1944 in his book *The Gentlemen Talk of Peace* (Chicago: Ziff-Davis) (pp. 373-374):

> Millions of unoffending people have been butchered, in a continuous pogrom . . . . They have been tortured, degraded, burned, robbed, gassed and machine-gunned in whole community batches. Many were buried in mass graves before they died. Eyewitnesses (*sic*) state that the earth trembled in the convulsions of their last agonized breathing.

Babi-Yar was the obverse of Katyn in the propaganda field, but the Reds missed an advantage in failing to excavate the premises and conduct a body count. Belief replaced evidence here.

The exploitation of Babi-Yar not only reminded some of the Katyn story, it was promoted just a short time before the Reds ran their version of Katyn by the world, having re-captured the Smolensk region and the grim location near it which had become universally known as a result of German publicity in 1943. The first week of February, 1944 the Red Army conducted a guided tour of the captured site themselves, showing it off to 19 persons, one of whom was the daughter of W. Averell Harriman, one of the opulent Americans reputed for his gentle attitude toward Stalinism, and known far and wide as Roosevelt's Kremlin trouble-shooter, in a class almost beyond Harry Hopkins. Seeking to unpin themselves from the blame for Katyn, and to re-pin it on the Germans, this latest episode in this grisly serial did not come off entirely to their satisfaction. *Time* for one was now not quite as convinced of German guilt as they had been 10 months earlier, but editorial hesitancy was effectively compensated for by their Moscow correspondent Lauterbach, who was well-satisfied that the Reds had proved they were innocent ("Day in the Forest," *Time*, February 7, 1944, pp. 27-28).

From Jewish quarters the atrocity stories and the totals of the murdered millions continued to come and grow. A late entry in 1943 and generously broadcast in the first half of 1944 was *The Black Book of Polish Jewry*, a 343-page work decorated by 60 pictures, issued by a refugee Communist Jewish publishing house from Poland, Roy Publishers. *Time* described it as "an account of the Nazis' systematic extermination of the Polish Jews", and claimed it was based on sources provided by various Jewish entities, the Polish government in exile, and even the German government (January 10, 1944, p. 78.) The *Nation* (May 20, 1944, p. 604), called it the "appalling story" of the reduction, "through starvation, epidemics, and wholesale slaughter" of two-thirds of the Polish Jewish community, which in this work was claimed to have consisted of 3,250,000 persons in 1939. And I.F. Stone (Isidor Feinstein), writing in the same journal three weeks later ("For the Jews—Life or Death?" June

10, 1944, pp. 670-671), became the first to assert the new high
claim of total lives lost, with his declaration, "Between 4,000,000
and 5,000,000 European Jews have been killed since August, 1942,
when the Nazi extermination campaign began." Stone apparently
neglected to correlate his claims with those made in past years, and
overlooking that Communist and Zionist sources in December, 1942,
just four months after Stone asserted the extermination program
began, already charged the Germans with exterminating 1,000,000
Polish Jews, something that hardly could have happened just
between the months of August and December, 1942. But it was
another interesting contribution to the immense conflicting stew of
statistical claims of alleged Jewish loss of life at German hands.
Stone's figure went well beyond anything repeated by Raphael
Lemkin five months later. All ignored the embarrassing job of
explaining how such programs were logistically possible.

Punctuating the extermination stories from the East were the
continuing escape stories from the West. Barely two months before
D-Day (June 6, 1944) *Newsweek* published still another account of
Jews escaping from France with the connivance of German officials
bribed by the placing of large sums of money to their credit in
Swedish or Swiss banks, for which they acquired exit visas from
German-occupied northern France to Portugal (French Jews readily
escaped from Vichy France as a matter of course, with or without
the assistance of the Vichy officialdom.) Concluding its short
account of the above procedure, *Newsweek* remarked, "Thousands
of Jews have bought freedom in this fashion." ("Unhappy Paris,"
April 3, 1944, pp. 40-41.)

Particularly puzzling was the publication in London by the
Jewish Socialist publisher Victor Gollancz, known the world over for
his series issued under the banner of the Left Book Club, of a work
titled *Escape From Berlin*, by a Jewess named Catherine Klein. She
spent the period from the fall of 1939 to the fall of 1942 in Berlin,
prevented from emigrating, she said, by a new law passed by the
Nazis after the war had begun forbidding "non-Aryans" from leaving
Germany if they were under 46 years of age and engaged in a job
involving war work. She managed to make her exit via Switzerland
and was in England, presumably, when her book was published. The
reviewer in the *Times Literary Supplement* (March 4, 1944, p. 112),
concluded, "It was the deliberate humiliation of people of her race
that weighed most on the author's mind." This variation from the
extermination claim contributed a strange obbligato to the prevailing main theme of this wartime propaganda concerto.

However, it was obvious that these many separate themes had
political overtones. And the world growing out of the objectives of

drastic punishment and repression of the Germans and vastly enhanced Stalinist power and influence over all Central and Eastern Europe did not seem to include provisions for the returned economic and socio-cultural power of other elements displaced by Hitlerian policies and programs. Though the constant publicization of atrocity tales seemed to point in that direction, on the large political plane, Stalinist Communism appeared to be locked in as the main eventual gainer. The principal area of non-agreement appeared to be only the eventual disposition of Germany itself, as will be seen. But it was obvious that a war which appeared to have started out in September, 1939 to preserve the political status quo ordained at Versailles had resulted in a situation making its survival even in the most drastically reduced condition quite impossible. When Pierre Laval predicted in the summer of 1940 that Britain would not return to the Continent regardless of what now happened, he proved to be an incisive prognosticator.[7]

In the sobering-off period following the bacchanalia of Stalin, Churchill and Roosevelt at Teheran, Dec. 2-7, 1943 the Red press made it a little more obvious what could be expected as the new map of Central and Eastern Europe. The Red newspaper *War and the Working Class* at year's end bluntly declared that the Baltic states of Esthonia, Lithuania and Latvia would not be a question any longer and that the matter was "closed"; they were to be a part of the Soviet Union "by their own choice." Furthermore, no governments would be permitted in Poland and Czecho-Slovakia which were not "friendly" to the USSR. *Time* put this together with the comment in the London *Economist* decrying South African leader Jan Christiaan Smuts' prophecy that Europe would be straddled by Russia and with Britain playing second fiddle to the USA as a result of its impoverishment by "victory," as indicating that "it reflected a feeling that Britain *must* make the best of the new Europe and the new world, find hope and safety with the USSR and the U.S." ("In the Afterglow," *Time,* January 3, 1944, pp. 31-32.)

Time reassured the British that they need have no fears about Soviet revolutionary expansion; after all, the nationalistic verses sung by those celebrating Stalin's 64th birthday were evidence that the Soviets had abandoned "world revolution." But that obviously did not mean determination to make all the neighborhood as Red as Moscow. A week later *Time* gloated over the predicament of the Hungarians, being both anti-Slav and anti-Red, lying in the path of Stalin's armies now. And a few weeks later it had much the same to say as the Red Army approached Czecho-Slovakia's frontiers. *Time* devoted its cover story March 27, 1944 to Jan Masaryk, the refugee government's foreign minister, and his simple trust and faith in the

Reds saving the Czechs forever from "Teutonic agression," as well as his compliance with Churchill, as opposed to the refusal of Sikorski and the Poles earlier, in conceding to coming Stalinist "leadership" of Central Europe. In fact, said *Time*, in their portrait of this far-seeing Czech "statesman" and his predictions of an era of pleasant and fruitful relations with Red Russia, as a result of all this, "The Czech Communists with headquarters in Moscow and a branch office in London, seemed to have a good chance to enter the [Czech] Government," once Masaryk and his cadre were able to return to Prague. (When the Communists splattered Masaryk on the pavement outside his office in Prague four years later, the wartime hallucinators and their parrotted call for "coalition with the Communists" got another demonstration of how such unions worked out under the pressure of the Stalinist dynamic.)

It was increasingly evident in the last nine months of 1944 that the main strains of the atrocity propaganda and the hate campaign waged against the Germans had far more than Jewish revenge as its goal. A smashed, impoverished, depopulated and hacked-up Germany was an immense achievement in the advancement of a Red Europe, possibly including Germany itself, and lapping at the frontiers of France and Italy, which, with proper "assistance" and the return from Moscow of their opulently-living Red bosses, Maurice Thorez and Palmiro Togliatti, might be expected to become Stalinized, in turn. A tough anti-Red Germany was the only conceivable obstacle to this grand design, and the many different impulses for wrecking such a Germany all worked for European Stalinization, whether they were conscious of this or not. The purely mindless Germanophobes, mostly concentrated in America and Britain, exerted powerful influence toward such a consequence. It was chill comfort to watch them rub their chins in rueful contemplation of their handiwork a year or two afterward. And the muted bellow of Churchill at Westminster College in Fulton, Missouri in March, 1946 announcing the preliminary dimensions of the Cold War versus Stalin, and stealing Goebbels' expression, "iron curtain," to describe what he had worked so hard in company with Stalin to achieve, 1943-1945, was a vainglorious gesture in trying to recoup the unretrievable. It was the task of a generation of liars in mass communications to sell to the English world Churchill's utter debacle as a great "victory," and the wrecking of a possibly tolerable world as the "saving of civilization."

The grotesque and slanderous slur notwithstanding, when the multi-million circulation *Collier's* magazine declared in their inflammatory editorial "Apes with Machine Guns" (March 11, 1944, p. 82) that "This is a war between humans and subhumans for mastery of the earth," they symbolized the self-defeating content of "Allied" hate propaganda. It typified the kind of totalitarian milieu the more grim of the *revanchistes* wanted to work in, one which they eventually got, including the desired objective of legalizing the illegal and the declaring of the legitimate "criminal," an ideological turning of the European arena on its head which made the destruction, massacres and deportation of millions and the kangaroo court hanging of enemy leaders all acquire the patina of quasi-legality, a foundation on which the politics of Europe were built and were still continuing over 35 years afterward. At the core of its first stirrings was far more Stalinist than Zionist inspiration, as will be seen in the Pucheu and Carretta cases, the prototypes of what procedures were to be employed against Laval, Petain, Tiso, Mussolini, Quisling, and the luminaries done to death following the process of Nuremberg, Manila and Tokyo, and thousands of the lesser known in the years following.

A brief examination of the differences which prevailed among the American, Soviet and British planners for dealing with the vanquished Germans, once attained, is called for, as well as a look at the purely propagandistic suggestions for action which got the widest attention.

The drive to put a Carthaginian finish to Germany, as has been seen, began well before the plan proposed by Treasury Secretary Henry Morgenthau, first aired at the September, 1944 Quebec Conference of Roosevelt and Churchill (Raphael Lemkin's *Axis Rule* had been in manuscript a full year by then), and subsequently discussed at great length and with much heat for months thereafter. Though underlings of Morgenthau later tried to ascribe its origins to Gen. Dwight D. Eisenhower (see Fred Smith, "The Rise and Fall of the Morgenthau Plan," *The United Nations Magazine,* Vol. I, No. 2 (March, 1947), pp. 32-37), the ideas in it and several others were circulating widely prior to September, 1944. The fulminations of Rex Stout and his hand-picked posse of 17 writers associated with the Writers War Board were familiar fodder to ideologists, far more drastic than those of Reinhold Niebuhr and his Council for a Democratic Germany, the latter also being somewhat closer to notions loose in Soviet Russia on this subject. Stout's group was more interested in destruction and annihilation than in political realities likely to prevail at war's end, which affronted others not connected with either the WWB or the CDG. Stout even drew a fiery reproach from the editors of the *Christian Century* three months before the Quebec meeting ("Hate-Mongers Attack Policy of Decency," June 14, 1944, p. 716), throwing in an additional personal dig at Stout, "an author of detective fiction who has been charged with earlier Communist connections." But there was nothing seemingly related to Communist views in his Germany-must-be-destroyed line, quite out of harmony at that moment with what was emanating from Moscow.

In actuality, the Administration launched a semi-official posting of its views on German settlement positions when Under-secretary for State Sumner Welles' book *Time for Decision* was published in mid-summer, 1944. Norman Thomas, reviewing it at length and with substantial precision in the Catholic weekly *Commonweal* (July 28, 1944, pp. 354-356), was one of the very few in the land to criticize Welles for his proposals for carving up Germany into 3 states (which is what happened, eastern Germany being attached to Poland and *central* Germany becoming "East" Germany), settling Poland on Soviet terms, supporting the idea of immense population transfers, the assignment of Eastern Poland to Russia, and the clearing of East Prussia of Germans and the attachment of it to Poland. Thomas considered Welles a naive bumpkin with respect to Communist Russia, compared to himself, and remarked that if Welles's experience with the Reds was as broad as his, "he would see in Communism, still completely controlled by Stalin, a far graver potential threat to the peace and harmony of Europe than anything that can be done by a defeated and hated German General Staff." Thomas was sure that Welles's grandiose complicated menage of regional and world organizations, liberally buttered with "blind appeasement of Stalin," would never usher in the millennium, and was already convinced the "peace" was already lost; the persistence of conscription and heavy armament by the big powers after the war would be proof of that. But on Welles and his German policy recommendations, Thomas really unloaded:

> No people as a people is bad enough for the fate Mr. Welles would bring upon the Germans, and no people, not even the Big Three nations, could they be assured indefinitely of the leadership of Mr. Welles's hero, Franklin Delano Roosevelt, along with Churchill and Stalin can or will successfully play the role of God of wrath, modified by the formulae of this book. Mutual forgiveness is a requisite of statesmanship.

But play the "God of Wrath" the Roosevelt entourage certainly did, though they had peripheral advice from others who wanted far worse to be wreaked upon Germany, and Japan as well. The Morgenthau formula for turning Germany into a goat pasture was advanced in parallel fashion for Japan in the Far East. An insider in the war regime writing under the pseudonym "Pacificus" for the *Nation* (October 14, 1944, pp. 436-437) credited Stanley K. Hornbeck, chief of the Far East desk in the State Department, as the principal voice who "favored the transformation of Japan into an agricultural country incapable of waging modern war." An even more drastic proposal, however, and probably the finest prescription for an eventual Communist Asia, was the suggested plan of the liberal military "expert," Major George Fielding Eliot, in the mass-reader (probably 15,000,000) picture magazine *Look* for January 23, 1945 (p. 74), "Let's Destroy Japan." It was a program that made the Morgenthau plan for Germany read like a Germanophile design by comparison; it would be hard to find anything to compare with it for incipient political unreality and unsurpassed disaster. In many ways the ferocity of Maj. Eliot was the logical consequence of over three and a half years of unprecedented propaganda savagery which started with Roosevelt's "day of infamy" incitatory exhortations and ended with the atom bombing of Hiroshima and Nagasaki, during which the Japanese enemy was reduced over and over to the level even of non-mammalians. In fact his recommendations were a slightly expanded version seen as early as 1942 in the book by the Columbia University pedagogue, Nathaniel Peffer. In his *Basis for Peace in the Far East* (New York: Harper, 1942), Prof. Peffer anticipated the bloodthirstiness of Maj. Eliot by urging the bombing, burning and machine-gunning of Japan "into total destruction" "for its pedagogic effect." This prompted the *New Republic* editor and reviewer, Malcolm Cowley, to murmur, "It seems to me that only an essentially mild and bookish author would recommend wholesale massacre as an educational measure or a healing drug." (*New Republic* [December 21, 1942], pp. 830-831.)

Still another indication of Administration views on a grim solution for Germany was that revealed by the *Newsweek* columnist Ernest K. Lindley ("Planning Postwar Germany: Behind the Scenes," October 2, 1944, p. 44), considered a direct pipeline for the White House into mass communication. His summary of the ferocious plan for the looting and destruction of Germany after "victory" contained not one hostile or critical word.

But Lindley's *Newsweek* fellow-columnist and former top New Deal brain, Raymond Moley, went Lindley and the others one better later in his "Punishing War Criminals," (December 11, 1944, p. 112), largely a spirited and warmly approving review of the tigerish book *War Criminals,* by Harvard Law's Prof. Glueck. Moley concluded his accolade with a brief disquisition which sounded as though it had been cribbed in spirit from a Moscow 1936 purge prosecutor:

> It may be that the difficulty in making plans is the reconciliation of the legal principles of Soviet Russia, of Continental criminal law, and of Anglo-American law. Russia, quite justifiably, is suspicious of Anglo-American law, with its protections for accused persons, and is proceeding with trials in her own territories in her own way. In setting up international machinery, we shall have to cut through a good deal of our

own juristic tradition, but this is a case where new conditions must make new law.

No one could have been more in harmony with this view than Raphael Lemkin, and Nuremberg saw just such a recommendation bear fruit, though in reality it was simply the ancient racket of *ex post facto* reinvoked again, even if done this time with exquisite hypocrisy and a mushroom cloud of wordy obscurantism carrying it well past any previous employment, but casting a drab and dreary pall over the substance of Anglo-American legal tradition and cultural foundations from which they have not yet begun to emerge.

To be sure, payoff time was approaching. After the millions of words of wearying, boresome rhetoric about ending "Nazi tyranny," Churchill had now announced that it no longer was an "ideological" war, a signal to the Germanophobes that they could now wage open season on Germans *in toto,* without the delicate and dishonest distinctions that the previous years of propaganda had required (but few Anglo-American socialists, Marxist-Leninist-Stalinist or not, had uttered any words of horror about the millions of fellow German Marxists maimed, slaughtered and rendered homeless in the industrial parts of Germany's 70 largest cities under obliteration-saturation bombing). Now the situation called for the material accounts to be brought up to date, though all this required some attention to the political consequences of the destruction and the mass looting being scheduled, along with the depopulation, mass transfers and further massacres planned.

One of the logical elements to undertake this assessment was *U.S. News,* its columns traditionally directed to the business-financial-commercial-industrial part of the American community. Seven weeks before the initial promotion of Morgenthau's ideas the editors of *USN* ("After Germany Falls," August 4, 1944, pp. 14-15), began to agonize on the already-widely recommended schemes to 1) hack Germany into several states; 2) disarm it totally; 3) occupy it indefinitely; 4) turn over its soldiers as prisoner-of-war slave labor to Russia indefinitely; 5) transfer several parts of its territory to its neighbors; 6) strip it of its industry; 7) saddle it with many billions of dollars in reparations, and 8) execute its financial, political and industrial leaders as "war criminals." Their problem was to rationalize all this, which they firmly approved of, but at the same time hoped to achieve while continuing to preserve Germany as a good customer for British goods and preventing the Germans from ever maneuvering itself into "a balance of power game between Russia on one side and the Western Allies on the other." However, as they kept thinking about this through the Quebec conference, and toting up some of the likely consequences of agreeing with the Morgenthau and Vansittart bellowers for a crushed Germany to be forced to stew in its own wreckage, misery and starvation for generations, some of them were even then convinced that this promise of sustained vengeance could not be realized except for a very short time (it was to last most of the next five years at near-maximum strength). The editors, in a sobered reconsideration (September 29, 1944, p. 8), called to mind that

> Germany, in normal times, accounts for half of Europe's trade. An impoverished Germany, one on a sitdown strike, would mean a depressed Europe . . . A healthy Europe, with a sick Germany in the middle, isn't a type of setup that can be brought about easily. So, chances are that if the economic going gets rough in postwar, ways will be found to permit Germany to seek prosperity again, that today's attitudes will undergo a rather sharp change.

The only thing wrong with this evaluation was that it took a lot longer for it to be realized than the editors expected. The turnaround was complicated by the looting, massacre and territorial loppings and the legal lynching of its wartime political elite in harmony with Soviet political biology carried out by the Anglo-Americans. Only when Stalin looked like the logical inheritor of all of Germany as a result of this stupidity did the latter begin their reconsideration.

Editor Lawrence, upon further rumination over the wisdom of announcing to the Germans of coming programs for dismembering Germany, dismantling Ruhr industry, dispatching millions of Germans to serve as Russian slave labor, and the whole fantasy of the Morgenthau contingent for the pastoralization of Germany, thought of it only as a strategic blunder by Roosevelt and Churchill ranking with almost any other in history. Undoubtedly Lawrence did not oppose all this, but thought the "Allies" should have kept quiet about it, and advanced instead a formula for getting the Germans to abandon Hitler and promising the Germans "a constructive program of economic opportunity for the German people." (Editorial, "Prolonging the War," October 6, 1944, pp. 32-33.) (*U.S. News* believed that the real driving force behind the proposal and planning for the de-industrialization of Germany was Harry Hopkins and a "working group" close to him, and that statements on the subject by Morgenthau, Hull and Stimson were "window dressing." October 6, 1944, p. 68.)

A very small, muted strain of criticism of these impulses did exist in the US, probably best exemplified by the main theme in the early wartime book authored by ex-President Herbert C. Hoover and Hugh Gibson, *The Problems of a Lasting Peace,* treated as a news event by

Time (July 6, 1942, p. 14). Its strong case against a dismembered Germany, already being talked about by stentorian Germanophobes then, was couched in the homily, "We can have peace or we can have revenge, but we can't have both," which the two distinguished authors extended later in a four-part series in *Collier's* in June, 1943. The following month, addressing a conference at Princeton, N.J., under the auspices of the Commission on International Justice and Good Will of the Federal Council of Churches, of which he was chairman, John Foster Dulles warned against "the demand for vengeance on whole peoples," which he admitted growing, and disparaged another strong view gaining ground: "a great military force is being increasingly looked upon as the only assurance of future peace, and a new Holy Alliance is envisaged to dominate the world by its might." (*Christian Century,* July 21, 1943, p. 852.)

To be sure, though its readership was largely confined to a segment of American Protestantism's clergy and influential lay figures, the *CC,* under the editorship of Charles Clayton Morrison, did act as an influence against some of the headlong totalitarian drives of the liberal war machine headed by Roosevelt, but they could hardly stem it. Again a marked minority, on the Morgenthau Plan, it could not repel the spreading of responsibility for it internationally:

> As a matter of fact, his [Morgenthau's] plan comes directly from the Postwar Policy Group of Conservative Peers and Members of Parliament —the controlling body of Mr. Churchill's own Tory Party, which has just issued its second memoranda on war aims. (*Christian Century,* "British Tories Discover an American Spokesman," October 4, 1944, p. 1125.)

But all British subjects hardly were in accord with the Morgenthau Plan, regardless of a bi-partisan majority in favor of it there, as they were here. A lengthy and very ill-tempered blast at it came from Maj. Gen. J.F.C. Fuller, inexplicably also a wartime *Newsweek* columnist, on war topics mostly, and probably the most out-of-place writer anywhere in the world during the Second World War. Gen. Fuller in a full page denunciation was mainly concerned with what this "stupid" piece of political warfare had done to stiffen German resistance and extend the war and its loss of life and destruction. Timed with a major "Allied" military breakthrough, to tell the Germans the Rhineland would be excised and assigned to France, that Brandenburg and Silesia would be given to Poland, and East Prussia to Russia, that the Ruhr would be internationalized, that all Germans would be subject to forced "reeducation," their leaders killed or sterilized, and "80,000,000 Germans crammed into a country which could not support half this number," was a lapse in political acumen Gen. Fuller did not believe possible. Said he in conclusion:

> It raised the devil and this time the devil became a German. Though [Gen.] Eisenhower said, "We come as conquerors but not as oppressors," the politicians shouted: "We come as obliterators and hangmen." What would you Americans and we English have done had we stood in Germany's shoes? We should have done what she has done—set our backs to the wall of the Rhine and have fought like the devil." Fuller, "The Devill Is Raysed Up," *Newsweek* (October 30, 1944), p. 38.

The unofficial "advisers" on policy toward Germany after "victory" were in a class well beyond Morgenthau or any of the other official contributors. In some ways they supplemented Morgenthau, but their main difference lay in killing; the plans being promoted involved far too few German deaths for them. William B. Ziff's *The Gentlemen Talk of Peace* (Macmillan), issued four months before the Morgenthau proposals were being mulled over after Quebec, was reviewed at some length by the New York *Herald Tribune*'s foreign news specialist, Joseph Barnes, who remarked that in the part of the book dealing with Germany, Ziff "makes the plan attributed to Mr. Morgenthau seem, in comparison, the benevolence of some kindly old gentleman." Ziff wanted the Ruhr amputated from Germany, all its factories dismantled and removed, all the officers and the entire Nazi Party down to its smallest functionaries exiled to Madagascar, all German universities closed, its army and police totally eliminated, and all political rights expunged. Ziff wanted Germany to have zero industry, no access to any raw materials from outside its severely reduced homeland, with Russia to have everything to the Oder River, and all Germans to be permitted to work only on farms or as forced work groups all over Europe.

It was Ziff who published the lawyer Louis Nizer's book, *What To Do With Germany*, via his own publishing house, Ziff-Davis, on January 31, 1944. Nizer specialized in mass murder recommendations, several hundred thousand carefully engineered killings of Germans in several areas of German society. Nizer's book had the endorsement of Vice President Henry Wallace and Senators Harry Truman and Claude Pepper.

A variation on Nizer's theme came from the famous director of American propaganda in the First World War, George Creel. Creel surfaced in October, 1943 with a lengthy article in *Collier's* ("Revenge in Poland," October 30, 1943, pp. 11, 69-71), a hyperthyroid accolade to civilian guerrillas and their illegal war against the German occupation in Poland, a type of activity condemned in the bluntest and most severe language if conducted against Americans in the

Army Field Manual FM 27-10, "The Law of Land Warfare." Creel
was overwhelmed with joy at its being employed against the Germans.
His anonymous communicant claimed to have killed 800 German
soldiers by June, 1943, and his band were supposed to have destroyed
17 German trains, as part of a very long catalog of destruction and
death, as well as boasting of shooting many "collaborationists," all
"dangerous," by which were probably meant non-Stalinists. Creel's
informant closed by confiding that, despite Nazi actions against
Jews, he and his co-workers had "managed to rescue a fair percentage
of rabbis and intellectual leaders," and had them "safely hidden."

Creel's book, *War Criminals and Punishment* (McBride, 1944),
contained several themes found in later proposals, which he later
expanded upon in a long series of over 50 portraits of German
leaders and their "principal stooges" among other Axis allies, accompanied by ferocious caricature cartoon drawings of the men involved,
which virtually reduced them to insects, by one Sam Berman, though
even he did not approach the concentrated hate in such efforts
attained by Arthur Szyk. Creel closed the series with an article reinforcing the line in his book, urging the shooting of Hitler and others
upon capture, without any trials, the others before military tribunals
and dispatched with verve and swiftness, and above all avoiding any
of the folderol related to civilian courts. In this way Creel believed it
would be possible to put them all to death with a minimum of
expense of energy. Creel hailed the Bolshevik Kharkov trials and
their swift executions, and thought the US was committed to follow
their example.

The theme that the solution of the German "question" might
require the killing of the entire German population or the carrying of
all of them off to permanent captivity in other lands was a recurrent
one in the wartime discussions, especially in the US liberal press.
These fates were not considered an impossibility. On occasion there
were persons who identified themselves with such views but generally
moderated the number they wanted murdered. *Look* magazine,
another publication of an opulent American family which frequently
went well beyond the threadbare Communist press in pushing Stalinist views on world politics in particular, took up this theme in
pressing against anyone in the US favoring anything but a very hard
"peace" at war's end. One essay was supplied by a refugee long
savored by the liberal weeklies, Max Werner, who, in his "We Can
Keep Germany Beaten," (September 19, 1944, p. 74), adopted the
political biology line of the Stalinists; his secret formula was simply
to kill the entire leadership of the land. "The *Who's Who* and the
Social Register of the Third Reich must be destroyed." Werner
followed the Red line in another recommendation. He was against

partition of the country, and thought that all that had to be done was the killing of "a few hundred thousand real war criminals," after which the country could be turned over to "whatever progressive, democratic and anti-fascist forces there are inside Germany." This of course was another recipe for a Soviet Germany. But it was bound to contain too many Germans for a real exterminator along the lines of the Soviet Jew and journalistic hack, Ilya Ehrenburg. *Look* gave Ehrenburg his head in a revolting hate concerto which was studded with remarks such as "I have enough hate in me to last several life-times," with his main message being, "Kill Germans!" ("The Breath of a Child," September 19, 1944, pp. 50-51.)

If these people were too emotional and febrile for the calmly-measured intellectual view, there was always the *doyen* of Germano-phobia, Britain's Lord Vansittart, who never had taken kindly to the propaganda which had always referred to the enemy as "Nazis". Vansittart's enemy was the entire German people for as far back as anyone wanted to consider, and a string of one-barrel crackpot books dwelled on this simple theme like a one-note symphony. On the occasion of the release of the Morgenthau Plan, Vansittart got access to a large American audience with his counter-proposals, which, again, like several of those which have been examined here, made Morgenthau on Germany seem pale and mild. *Newsweek* arranged a kind of public debate between him and the widely read American columnist, Dorothy Thompson, a pre-Pearl Harbor war monger of the very first stripe, but steadily relenting in her molten zeal as the war coursed on and the consequences of what she had so wildly favored began to enter her consciousness. What appalled her the most about Vansittart's abominable but skin-deep hate reflexes was the utter lack of any political awareness whatever. She interpreted his program as the surest method of keeping any German from "conver-sion to liberal democracy," and a guarantee of the capture of Germany by Stalinism, internally, "and the closest possible collabor-ation with Russia," on the international political level. Her ideal was the "neutralization" of Germany, drawn into an international organization, and "policed" by it. The other alternatives she saw were "the Soviet Union encroaching permanently into Germany" or of Germany becoming "an economic and political colony of the Anglo-Americans." It was the peak of irony for her two "alterna-tives" to become policy simultaneously and to continue with various sophisticated complications for over a generation afterward. Vansittart angered the propaganda maestros unduly by stubbornly insisting, in his efforts to deal with the Germans as Germans and not as "Nazis" and non-Nazis, that "The number of Germans in concen-tration camps has been grotesquely inflated and the majority of them were not political prisoners," his point being that Hitler never had any real political opposition after 1933 (Vansittart, "The Vansittart Case," *Newsweek,* October 9, 1944, p. 108). (Whether this was an astute guess on Vansittart's part or whether it was based on his access to intelligence reports establishing it as a fact is not known, but it was true that German nationals were a relatively small minority in the camp system in the closing year of the war. What Vansittart did not know or did not care to state was their immense influence in running the camps from the inside, especially if they were members of the German Communist Party.)[8]

Vansittart's undermining of both Stalinists and Zionists, the principal elements responsible for the "grotesque inflation" of the numbers in German concentration camps, was an interesting variation entered into the vengeance-for-Germany steeplechase, though it should be evident by now that there was a multitude of entrants here, with much mixed motivations as well as some interested only in senseless destruction, massacre, misery and desolation. But in all of it, the Soviet deviation from most of these schemes was quite obvious. Even Stalin's proposal at Teheran that 50,000 German army officers be shot was modest compared to a dozen or more suggested massacres of hundreds of thousands to millions of Germans in all social categories; only his own mouthpiece Ehrenburg was in their class.

As far back as September, 1943 Louis Fischer, the *Nation's* fervently pro-Bolshevik correspondent from 1922 on, though much exercised by the 1939 Hitler-Stalin pact, had suggested, in an *Atlantic Monthly* piece, "What Shall We Do with Germany?" (September, 1943, pp. 46-50), and had contemplated the possibility of the Soviet forces occupying Berlin and most of Germany first. Then he quickly drew back, dwelling on the possibly preferable situation growing from Americans succeeding in this. He did not consider the likelihood of all the "Allies" (except China) arriving there all at about the same time. But it can be seen that a Soviet Germany was in the minds of some observers all the time.

One of the most sophisticated was Shirer, who, in his New York *Herald Tribune* column devoted to the "propaganda front," revealed himself as one of the most polished and finished Germanophobes of those claiming English as their native tongue. Where a Vansittart, a Nizer, a Kaufman or a Hecht would explode like a flame thrower in some vast, uncontrolled booklength outburst, Shirer, the master propagandist, disguised as a propaganda analyzer, dealt out the hate-the-Germans in steady corrosive drippings; his May 7, 1944 column was a classic example. By now Shirer was well past the "Nazis" stage; all Germans were his hate objects now. Where he showed real skill however was in his earnest parenthetical entreaties to look favorably on the spread of "socialism" in Europe upon the downfall of the Hitler regime, a process he saw spreading rapidly, and with unqualified approval, after the war was over, in a book titled *End of a Berlin Diary.* This kind of supporter was undoubtedly far more difficult to decipher for the ordinary reader than the explicit Soviet sympathizers. (Shirer never defined his ground rules in his propaganda "analysis" column. It seemed to be based on the conclusion that what he wrote was true, that Hitler's adversaries did not deal in it, and that what the military enemy in Europe, and his critics in America, said, were all lies.)

But the Morgenthau Plan, since it had the obvious trappings of official approval, smoked out the concealed supporters of the Stalinist vision for postwar Europe. The most magisterial was a record six-column editorial in the *Nation,* "A Plan For Germany," (October 7, 1944, pp. 395-397), presumably written by its editor in chief, Freda Kirchwey. In its firm hostility to the Morgenthau recipe, especially that of wrecking German industry, she stressed the "economic consequences" of this, and managed to sound like Lawrence in the businessman-oriented *U.S. News.* Stressing Germany's importance as "the heart of the economy of Central Europe," she pointed out that "to destroy German industry is to weaken still further an economic structure already demoralized by years of war." Furthermore, she declared,

> It is clear that Russia will support no scheme for the dismemberment of Germany or the destruction of German industry. Only the other day, Tass, official Russian news agency, bluntly said that "projects of this kind have not been and are not considered by the [Soviet] European Advisory Commission." We have had many indications that the Soviet government expects German industry to contribute heavily to the restoration of Russia. As much as two years ago the Russians expressed doubt as to the wisdom of the demolition air attacks on German industrial plants. Their own air force has carried out no such destructive raids.

This did not demonstrate Soviet moral superiority but it surely made evident their light-year political strategy superiority to Roosevelt and Churchill. A generation after the war the Soviet Union still was able to draw interest on the political capital they banked with the Germans by abstaining from such "Allied" atrocities as Hamburg and Dresden, let alone Berlin, the most strategically bombed city of all.

On the subject of personal reprisals, one might say there was a distinct advantage to the Soviet approach of "class guilt," and the political biology of eliminating those whom it could not by any conception imagine might become adjuncts to a Red German future.

Samuel Grafton, a New York *Post* columnist and nationally syndicated writer during the war, supported this approach, as opposed to
the Anglo-Saxon theories of "individual guilt," even though by their
obliteration bombing the latter demonstrated a collective theory of
responsibility for the "Nazi tyranny" which went far beyond the
views of the Soviets. There was not much individual discrimination in
a policy which showered phosphorus incendiaries and ton-weight
explosives on an entire city, massacring women and children by the
many thousands night after night. Eventually it might be argued that
the Anglo-Saxon view expanded to include both individual *and*
collective "guilt," enjoying the prosecution of specific "war criminals"
and whole populations via "denazification" at the same time.

The master demonstration of likely Stalinist plans for postwar
Germany came directly from Moscow via the transmission to the
Saturday Evening Post early in December, 1944 by its solidly established correspondent Edgar Snow, as reliable a barometer and
semaphore-waver interpreting Soviet views as anyone active during
World War II. Snow told American readers of the nearly 3,500,000-
subscriber *SEP* that the "real foundation" of Europe had been "laid
in Moscow" that past summer, while the other "Allies" were dazzling
themselves with such things as founding the "United Nations" at
Dumbarton Oaks (August 21-September 27, 1944). Snow claimed
the future of Poland, Czecho-Slovakia, Rumania, Bulgaria and
Finland was hammered out there, and probably the future of a large
part of Germany as well. He reported a conversation with Edward
Boleslaw Osubka-Morawski, chairman of the Polish Liberation Committee, who told him while he was in re-captured Poland that
Poland's boundaries were already settled; "Our frontier on the West
will follow the Neisse River over to the Oder, and then northward to
the Baltic. It will jog a little to the west to include the port of
Stettin," the Polish Communist puppet told him. Snow was not sure
FDR and Churchill would agree entirely, but since Churchill had
already indicated that the Poles would have to yield territory in the
East, they could be expected to get compensation elsewhere. As
things worked out, Snow had been told what largely eventuated.
Snow also quoted Soviet newspapers which printed a story that
called for a division of Germany into three zones, and the city of
Berlin to be divided into three parts; the Russians were to have one-
third of the city, East Germany and East Prussia, Poland was to get
Silesia, and the Soviet Union were to have the services of 10,000,000
German workers for ten years, as well as extracting a $300 billion
reparations payment from the Germans. Snow further commented
on Stalin keeping alive and vigorous in Moscow the collection of
German Communists and Socialists arranged under the "Free

Germany Committee," which was committed to full support of Soviet policy. They had accepted "in principle," he said, the Soviet view on the origin of the war, as well as declaring their intention upon assuming power in Germany at war's end the intention to pay off the German war reparations, to punish all war criminals, expropriate "culpable" landlords and industrialists, liberate all political prisoners, abolish all discriminatory racial laws, and to establish "freedom of religion" and of peasant and working class economic and political organizations. In conclusion Snow remarked, probably unnecessarily, "Friendship and cooperation with Soviet Russia is, of course, a fundamental pledge." (Snow, "What Russia Wants to Do to Germany," *Saturday Evening Post,* December 2, 1944, pp. 19, 87-88.)

If affairs in Eastern and Central Europe were moving in a steady, measured pace toward a Stalinist finish, accompanied by a thorough permeation of the entire region by the psychological approach to everything characteristic of a true totalitarian outlook such as only the Stalinist world view was, it might be noted that in 1944, as Stalin's Western "Allies" began to take control of the fringe areas formerly in German hands, something close to a Stalinist finish was becoming evident there as well. The harvest of years of atrocity propaganda and revenge proposals was about to begin, and solutions not much different from what were being imposed in Red-controlled Europe were being employed in places where their influence was obviously far less evident, though in one sense just as real.

One impressive incident indicating things to come concerned the apprehension in North Africa early in 1944 of Pierre Pucheu, the Vichy government's Secretary of State for Industrial Production, and one time Secretary of the famous combine of French iron and steel makers, the Comite des Forges. The makeshift regime of Gen. Charles de Gaulle, propped up by Churchill since their flight to London in the spring of 1940, and given the illusion of being what they were not, namely, a representative of more than just a scattering of Frenchmen, took the responsibility for the "trial" of Pucheu. The chief witnesses against Pucheu were three Communists from the "French" underground guerrilla resistance, another illegal and furtive force working in full defiance of the Hague Conventions and with full support from Churchill's war regime. These three persons declared that Pucheu had been condemned to death by something they called the "Council of Resistance," and demanded that de Gaulle's kangaroo court follow out their action, Pucheu being scheduled for conviction and execution for having had Communists shot while a functionary of the Petain regime in the southern half of France. The prosecution's case was feeble in the extreme, and Pucheu deeply embarrassed it by reminding them that in 1941, some

90% of the French people recognized the legitimacy of the Vichy regime, that it had been accorded diplomatic recognition by other lands, including the USSR and the USA, that the de Gaulle Prosecutor himself, Maj. Gen. Pierre Weiss, had supported Petain, Pucheu's boss, and that the Judge, Verin, had taken the oath of allegiance to Vichy. Gen. Henri Geraud, the real chief of state in North Africa, had refused to come to Algiers for the affair, and was against the trial on the grounds that all the documents necessary to conduct an honest proceeding were in France, where they were not accessible to the court, the Germans still being in control there, and the Allied invasion still ten weeks away. But one was able to see in the doom of Pucheu the prototype of a long, long string of similar processes supervised or winked at by the "Allies," while simultaneously intoning imprecations about the lawlessness of the enemy and assembling catalogs of pseudo-evidence such as was soon to be seen in the likes of Raphael Lemkin's *Axis Rule in Occupied Europe.* Pucheu never had a chance.

In truth, there were no elements within the war regimes of either the USA or England which were averse to such proceedings, nor did they frown on the employment of a certain amount of quite naked violence in the "liberated" areas such as North Africa and the half of Italy retaken from the Germans. After the many thousands of pages published, thundering at the "fascists," it may be that it was felt that tolerating a few token assassinations, murders, "executions" (Communist murders were usually described as "executions," and continue to be so identified 40 years later), and lynchings, seemed necessary to vindicate all the tough talk when the talkers were impotent as a consequence of military realities. An electrifying example of this was seen in October, 1944 when a Communist mob broke into a Rome courtroom where a Pucheu-type "trial" was being conducted, kidnapped the defendant, Donato Carretta, the one time director of the Regina Coeli prison in Rome, and drowned him in the Tiber, then hanging him by the heels outside the prison, a grisly barbarism which was to be repeated following the Communist murder of Mussolini six months later. The Pucheu and Carretta incidents indicated that despite all the reverent talk about law, legality and related beatitudes, the Western powers were rather closely attuned to the spirit of Kharkov. A little tremor took place in Henry Luce's plutocratic American Century press after Carretta's lynching, and his picture magazine, the +1,000,000 circulation *Life,* devoted 2 full pages of photos related to it, accompanied by a slightly queasy editorial ("Danger Ahead?" October 9, 1944, pp. 36-37). A few of his people could see tens of thousands of such murders coming in a dozen countries, whether soiled by the camouflage of a corrupt legal proceeding or not. The published comments by the New York *Times's* Anne O'Hare McCormick, and *Life's* own correspondents from overseas, John Osborne, Percy Knauth and Charles Christian Wertenbaker, frankly faced the strong likelihood of a great many more of such farces as the Pucheu "trial," and the Carretta lynching, in the future, all an unofficial adjunct to homeland Soviet political biology, and all promising the same ultimate result, the advancement of Stalinist political settlements in one land after another. Wertenbaker was convinced France would soon go Communist after a sufficiently prolonged campaign of obliterating possible enemies of Communism; McCormick described the already bitter street battles in Italy between their Reds and the Christian Democrats. The only one convinced that Communism would not prevail was Knauth, in Bulgaria. He was sure there would be no big upheaval there. "Communism never has been and never will be strong in Bulgaria," Knauth assured the *Life* readership and its ownership. It was a rare foreign correspondent who was ever more wrong that Knauth.

When Knauth's observations were compared with another correspondent, such as R.H. Markham, writing in the *Christian Century* a short while later (Markham, "The 'New Order' in Bulgaria," August 15, 1945, pp. 931-933), one might have been inclined to think the former was describing another country or perhaps another planet. Markham, fluent in Bulgarian, and with over 40 years' intimate knowledge of the country through literature and residence, described the post-"liberation" in Bulgaria as run by "a Communist-led and Communist-saturated regime," whose idol was "the swaggering, pistol-toting Partisan," and installing a system of "justice" "as new as Tiglath-pileser" (a reference to the 8th century B.C. Assyrian monarch notorious for killing his captives). Markham, commenting on these Stalinists "taking sound movies of their mass executions and sending them all over Russia," concluded that what they were applying was "pure lynch law," and that "the courts were simply a device through which the Communists are wiping out their political opponents." It was a story to be told hundreds of times from a dozen countries from mid-1945 onward.

Actually, while Rome's "resistance" Reds were lynching Carretta and mauling his body, Communists in France, Belgium, Luxembourg and Holland were having a similar field day in the wake of the advancing Anglo-American armies, to the frontiers of Germany, shooting and jailing their enemies, mutilating or disfiguring them in various ways and marching them through the streets carrying degrading signs about their necks and being announced by their Red captors as having been "traitors." The apparent "treason" of such people had been against Stalin or his underground representatives in these countries during German occupation, far more than it had been against their various homelands. Through the months of September, October and November 1944 this massacre continued, slowing down momentarily in France as the befuddled Gaullists who had come into power after arriving on the scene in the wagons of the Anglo-Americans began to realize what a snakepit they were supervising, and started to curb the more hysteric excesses of their Stalinist "underground" allies.

On November 25, 1944, the day Raphael Lemkin's book *Axis Rule* was published, the *Nation* published a furious editorial written by its editor, Freda Kirchwey, who apparently was conceiving herself as some kind of 20th century Madame Defarge, denouncing the Gaullists for disarming the "Communist-led" "Patriotic Guard," and for muffling slightly the murderous proclivities of the Red-led "resistance" "partisans," and the Maquis. Such pressure was also exerted against these Stalinist civilian illegal auxiliaries in Belgium. Kirchwey expostulated, "Allied policy is not likely to be wise enough to recognize that the revolution in Western Europe must be allowed to run its course," a euphemistic phrasing for the 1917-type Red massacres spreading across French-speaking Europe. (Kirchwey, "De Gaulle and the Resistance," November 25, 1944, pp. 632-633.) A little over three weeks later, *Newsweek's* lead foreign affairs story was titled "France Sated with Bloodletting: Moderates Move to Halt Purge." (December 18, 1944, p. 52.) This deserved the prize for premature story of the year; the bloodletting had barely begun, and it was to run on for years. What it was like to get caught in it was graphically described by Sisley Huddleston, one time foreign correspondent from France for four major London newspapers, who spent the war in Vichy France or Monaco, owned a home in Normandy, and was subsequently caught in the Red roundup, in his books *Terreur 1944* and *France: The Tragic Years.* Months of political killings followed at an even accelerated pace. *Newsweek* remarked that "spokesmen for the resistance movement" howled in the Consultative Assembly, France's makeshift emergency legislature, for many more; "They asked for heads, and, amid ringing cheers, named the heads that they wanted to roll." And the real power at the time, the Anglo-American authorities, stood by and let it happen, discommoded now and then when the Red underground, still armed, occasionally did a little sniping at men in American army uniforms as well, and engaged American guards of supply depots in minor skirmishes while trying to raid and loot these facilities.

We are now at the threshold of the historical moment when the book *Axis Rule in Occupied Europe* was published. The foregoing consists of a brief gathering together of pertinent information aiding the understanding of the total situation surrounding its issuance, and placing in the record many matters the author, Raphael Lemkin, chose to omit, for which there may have been a great many reasons. Since his book gave the illusion of being a factual account of a very large undertaking, but, as will be seen was simply a grandiose legal brief, which traditionally does not include material injurious to the case it purports to establish, this historical survey is for the purpose of calling attention to pertinent facts, opinions and events necessary to the establishment of a clear view of the total situation. James Forrestal, the USA's first Secretary of Defense, had a statement printed, framed, and hung in various offices of the Pentagon, which read, "A man's judgment is no better than the information on which it is based." This preceding historical outline is presented in that spirit.

---

(1) Two of the latest-dated sources cited most often by Lemkin were small books titled *Hitler's Ten-Year War on the Jews* and *Starvation Over Europe (Made in Germany)*, both issued in 1943. These were published without attribution other than indication of their publisher, the Institute of Jewish Affairs of the American Jewish Congress and the World Jewish Congress. Since they were the backup for some of his most serious accusations and charges, one might have thought Lemkin would have made an effort to determine who had written them, while choosing to be a transmission belt for two of the most influential Zionist organizations anywhere. But this he did not do. A brief re-examination of this matter is in order, mainly to investigate how reliable any dependency upon them was justified, especially the precise figures they contained as to the number of Jews deliberately put to death in Europe by the beginning of 1943, statistics Lemkin quoted without the faintest reservation whatever.

In view of two different men claiming to have written these books, it is of some importance to memorialize briefly the careers of both of them, Zorach Warhaftig, and Boris Shub, since subsequently they were hardly obscure or inconsequential. And since reference sources made a point of mentioning that both books were based on "research" directly credited to Warhaftig, it is worthy to attempt to establish its relevance and credibility, as well as its pertinence.

Warhaftig, another Warsaw lawyer like Lemkin and Begin, was born in that city on February 2, 1906 and after obtaining a law degree from the University of Warsaw, began a career in law in that city which stretched from 1923 to 1939. (This made him a practicing lawyer at age 17 according to the biographical sketch in *Who's Who in World Jewry 1965* [New York: David McKay, 1965], p. 1018). He had early connections with the international Zionist movement, and served as Vice Chairman of the Central Palestine Office in Warsaw from 1936 until the involvement of Poland in war with Germany in September, 1939. His sketch omits the years 1939-43 but this gap was bridged in the book by Marvin Tokayer and Mary Swartz, *The Fugu Plan* (New York and London: Paddington Press, 1979).

Like many others, Warhaftig fled Poland for Lithuania in 1939 as did Begin, who was arrested there by the Soviet N.K.V.D. and ultimately sent to a Siberian work camp, as he relates in his book *White Nights* (1957.) So neither of these two important Zionist functionaries (Begin was head of the Betar youth) ever spent a moment in German custody.

Tokayer and Swartz detail the heavy migration of Polish Jews into Lithuania and Russian-occupied Eastern Poland from September, 1939 on, noting extensive refugee settlements in Bialystok and especially Vilna. From 1940 on a vast movement of these same people began to the Far East via the Soviet Union and on into Siberia, thence to Manchuria, North China and increasingly to Japan. Most traveled on passports with transit visas to the latter country; Tokayer and Swartz relate that in one 15-day period, August 18-September 1, 1940 the Japanese consul in Kovno, Lithuania issued 6,000 transit visas to Jews alone. (Many religious Jews wanted no part of residence in the Soviet Union or its now-occupied Polish and Baltic areas, and these were the people Warhaftig was principally interested in.) The trip to the Far East took 11-12 days by rail via the Trans-Siberian railroad trains, from Lithuania to Moscow, first, then to Vladivostok, and from there several directions, into Manchuria, North China, and, increasingly, Japan, where sizable contingents located in Tokyo and Kobe, particularly.

Warhaftig became one of these himself, leaving Vilna and arriving in Kobe in October, 1940. As a member, prior to this trip, of the executive board of the World Jewish Congress, and also with influential connections in the Jewish Joint Distribution Committee and the Jewish Agency as well as the Union of Orthodox Rabbis, he was soon active in getting yeshiva scholars either to Palestine or the West, as he had been in Central Europe working with these Zionist organizations in getting them to Palestine or East to the Pacific.

After arriving in Kobe, Warhaftig went to Yokohama, and in the winter of 1940-41 succeeded in getting visas for hundreds of orthodox Polish Jews to Japan from the Soviet Union on the promise to get them ultimately to Palestine. Most made the same trip from Lithuania to Moscow and thence to Japan from Vladivostok, exclusively on Japanese ships. Many went to Shanghai, now occupied by the Japanese, after reaching Japan, after the plan to get them to the West via visas to the Dutch colony of Curacao fell through, because the World Jewish Congress refused to back Warhaftig up, according to Tokayer and Swartz (*The Fugu Plan*, p. 174.)

Warhaftig then devoted his energies to getting Polish Jews in Japan to Shanghai, his negotiations having the support of the Joint Distribution Committee. By June, 1941 there were already 17,000 in Shanghai. Warhaftig's Committee for Assistance of Jewish Refugees succeeded in getting several thousand more to China from Japan.

The details of Warhaftig's success in entering the U.S.A. personally in mid-1941 are not known, though Tokayer and Swartz tell a peculiar story of his being rebuffed by the State Department about others, refusing to grant visas to Jews with relatives still in "enemy-overrun territory" (Tokayer and Swartz, p. 188.) (The U.S. was not yet in the war in mid-1941.) However, he seemed to be quite successful in getting an American visa himself, apparently leaving Japan a short time after the Russo-German phase of World War Two erupted June 22, 1941.

The beginning of Warhaftig's employment as Deputy Director of the World Jewish Congress' Institute of Jewish Affairs In New York City is not precisely dated, but well before 1943, the publication date of the two books referred to above. It thus can be seen that he was not in the Central European war zones for nearly four years prior to the issuance of these books, both pointedly related to "research" attributed only to him.

At this point Warhaftig's career crossed over that of Boris Shub. The latter, a graduate of the University of Michigan and Columbia University Law School, went to work as an editor for the Institute of Jewish Affairs, then located at 330 West 42nd Street in New York City, at just about the time Warhaftig arrived in the U.S.A. to become its Deputy Director. Shub's father David was well known in New York journalism, the principal editorial writer for the Social Democrat Menshevik *Jewish Daily Forward,* and later after the war even better known for a widely circulated biography of Lenin (1948). But this was son Boris's first job of significance, and it was later given very little attention or promotion. Only a reader of reference works was to learn of his involvement in the production of the two books, *Hitler's Ten-Year War on the Jews* and *Starvation Over Europe (Made in Germany.)*

Both Warhaftig and the younger Shub were to claim credit for writing these works but the bibliographical references credited them to Shub. In his sketch in *Who's Who in World Jewry* Warhaftig claimed authorship of *Starvation Over Europe,* a one hundred page work, but in the *Library of Congress and National Union Catalog Author Lists, 1942-1962* (Detroit: Gale Research Co., 1970), Vol. 124, p. 320, it is plainly stated that this book was "Written by Boris Shub on the basis of research of Z. Warhaftig." *The Cumulative Book Index 1943-1948,* p. 1198, also credits this book to Shub. As for *Hitler's Ten-Year War,* which Warhaftig did not claim, the *Cumulative Book Index 1943-1948,* p. 2067, identified Shub as its *editor,* this time, but once more working with Warhaftig's materials.

Shub died quite prematurely on April 21, 1965 at age 52. In the column-long obituary in the New York *Times* for the same day (p. 45), it was also stated that he had written these two books. The general invalidity of much of these works, essentially a pair of Germanophobe tracts written from a specific self-serving posture, never bothered Raphael Lemkin. He cited them with aplomb as the soundest of factual conclusions. That Warhaftig's absence from the scene most of the last four years of the period they purported to cover undermined them critically was a most obvious factor, but this was a matter not up for consideration. What he could have possibly known except at second, third or fourth hand about German affairs or the state of the food situation in Central Europe while in Kobe, Japan or in New York City 1940-1943 must have been extremely limited. In the interest of history instead of Zionist propaganda Warhaftig might have performed a service by writing a history of the Polish experience of Jews in the 20 years following the creation of the Polish state in 1920. This was something he knew something about, having lived there throughout the two decades in question. Instead the world got these two distorted polemics, wrought into English style by Boris Shub from what was quaintly described as "research" by a deeply-committed functionary of a number of major Zionist organizations. And the convoluted partisan misrepresentations they advertised entered the traffic of Lemkin's brief without the slightest reservation or modification.

(2) The simultaneous use or issuance of contradictory propaganda material on this question dates back to well before the war, and suggests differing auspices behind the release of such materials, and differing objectives. An example is the book *The Yellow Spot* (New York: Knight Publications, and London: Victor Gollancz, 1936), and issued in Paris the same year in a German edition, *Der Gelbe Fleck*. The subtitle is the revealing aspect. That of the English language edition is *The Outlawing of Half a Million Human Beings*, while that of the German edition is *die Ausrottung von 500,000 deutschen Juden (The Extermination of 500,000 German Jews)*. There is obviously several light years of difference in these two conditions. The English language version was prepared in England and its authors identified only as "a group of investigators." The book strains to demonstrate the worst imaginable situation facing the Jewish community in Germany under the impact of National Socialist legal impositions, but ends up making quite deflated admissions. It can find only a hundred Jews among the 2000 persons imprisoned at Dachau, in the 1930s, the symbol of extremity in concentration camps all over the world (those of Stalinist Russia in those days are virtually never mentioned), and its closing sub-section relates widespread German ignoring of impositions against Jews, and articles "testifying to German sympathy and humanity" toward Jews "in the entire press of Hitler Germany." (*Yellow Spot*, p. 287.)

On the other hand the German language edition of this book, published in Paris in 1936 also, by Editions du Carrefour, bears a special foreword by Lion Feuchtwanger which is not to be found in the London and New York editions. Feuchtwanger reiterates in slightly different language the lurid claim in the subtitle (" . . . die systematische Vernichtung [*sic*] einer halb Million hochzivilisierter Europaer.") (*Gelbe Fleck*, foreword, p. 5.) This suggests that the promotion of the German language edition was mainly a ploy of the Stalinist Comintern (their operation in Paris in 1936-1938 was formidable), even if the English language editions suppressed mention of Stalinism as a factor in German political repression of Jews. In 1936 and 1937 Feuchtwanger was the editor in Moscow of a German language Communist literary magazine, *Das Wort*, and followed the Stalinist line with precision. His book *Moscow 1937* (New York: Viking, 1937) was scathingly denounced by liberal critic Edmund Wilson (Wilson, "Russia: Escape from Propaganda," *The Nation* [November 13, 1937], pp. 530-535), while Feuchtwanger's servile literary chores for Stalin were excoriated by anti-Stalinist leftist Dwight MacDonald in the March, 1941 issue of *Common Sense*, the powerful monthly edited by Selden Rodman and Alfred M. Bingham.

The failure of Feuchtwanger to acknowledge assisting with the preparation of the book *The Yellow Spot* is not due to any delicate reservations he may have entertained about involving himself with outrageous propaganda excesses. Three years earlier he had been very generous in alleging that a vast number of Jews had been slain in Germany as early as the beginning of the Hitler regime (New York *Times*, March 21, 1933, p. 11), though this catalog of atrocities was denied as having happened by Miles Bouton of the Baltimore *Sun*, 4 days later. However, when the New York *Times* reported later in the year (November 3, 1933, p. 9) that the Central Organization of German Jewry instructed German Jews to support the Hitler regime's foreign policy, and that Interior Minister Frick had issued orders against molesting Jews at the polls, such news stood little chance of being given credence as against the incendiary Comintern propaganda of massive slaughter of Jews in Germany in 1933. The *Times* compounded the already-complex situation four days later (November 7, 1933, p. 15) by quoting that consummate combination of Protestant theologian and social democrat Marxist ideologue, Reinhold Niebuhr, as saying that "Hitlerism" represented the first organization of the middle class in modern times. (Niebuhr actually expected a leftist revolt short of pure Stalinism to overthrow Hitler and his party sometime in 1934 or 1935.) In any event, the idea of anything as conservative and law-and-order-oriented as the German middle class endorsing mass murder as envisioned in Feuchtwanger's imagination simply did not make sense as German politics were construed in 1933.

(3) An inkling as to how most of the many 'war crimes' trials in a dozen post-1944 European countries, and in cowed, subdued satellite-client West Germany would have resulted, had they been conducted in the United States, can be divined from what happened in a New Jersey court in May, 1973.

It involved a hearing prior to the granting of U.S. citizenship to one Isydor Pilcewicz, a Polish Jew by origin and a veteran of a German concentration camp at Alem, near Hannover. He had subsequently emigrated to Israel, where he was a citizen from 1957 to 1962, and thereafter became an immigrant into the U.S.A.

Pilcewicz's worthiness for citizenship here was challenged by Polish and other survivors of this same camp who had emigrated to the U.S. and had also become naturalized citizens. The objection had actually been made in 1972 when this matter first came before the Immigration and Naturalization Service. The principal witness against Pilcewicz was one Abraham List, 41 years old, who swore that Pilcewicz, a barracks leader at Alem, "selected at random" by the German overseers of the camp, had murdered List's cousin and 20 other persons by beating them to death.

After listening to this testimony, Passaic County District Court Judge Thomas R. Rumana, in Paterson, N. J., dismissed the allegations against the citizenship candidate Pilcewicz as "incoherent hearsay," and in his five-page decision, observed that there was "not one direct observation" of Pilcewicz having killed anyone at Alem. Slightly incensed that anyone would dare to lie in his court, Judge Rumana called attention to three major discrepancies between List's testimony in 1972 before the INS and that which he had just made. A full account of this was printed in the New York *Times*, May 25, 1973, p. 78, col. 7.

(4) The failure on the part of the Polish Communist and Soviet regimes from 1945 on to match the Germans in undertaking mass exhumations a la Katyn seems to indicate they missed a propaganda coup, in view of the widely claimed mass executions of Jews in far greater numbers than were represented by Polish army officers at Katyn. Max Weinreich, in his *Hitler's Professors* (New York: Yiddish Scientific Institute, 1946), pp. 164-165, charged the killing of Jews by the tens of thousands at a time at Vilna, Kaunas, Riga, Minsk, "and countless towns of the area," including a mass grave of 20,000 Jews murdered in fields near the town of Konin, in central Poland. This latter he reported from a Yiddish weekly published in Lodz, maybe 70 kilometres southeast of the site.

Nothing whatever in the manner of Katyn was ever undertaken here, or, if so, publicity to such was non-existent.

(5) Early in 1971 the definitive work on the Katyn Forest massacre by Louis FitzGibbon was published almost simultaneously in England (London: Tom Stacy Ltd.) and the U.S.A. (New York: Scribners), titled *Katyn: A Crime Without Parallel*. It aroused much comment internationally, and calls for even another inquiry into it all, this one from the British Parliament.

In between the second (April) and third (October) printings of FitzGibbon's book there was released a strange story bearing on the Katyn account from a location previously maintaining total silence upon it all. On July 22, 1971 the widely circulated Israeli newspaper *Ma'ariv* published a long account attributed to one Abraham Vidra, a 64-year-old retired building construction employee, both a former Polish citizen and one time resident in the Soviet Union. The reason for this much-belated relation could not be determined, but it did contribute to the gathering of opinion invidious to the Stalinist contentions concerning responsibility for the Katyn slayings.

According to Vidra he had concealed what he knew about it for thirty years because of a promise he had made to a Jewish officer in the Red Army at the time. Vidra claimed he had been arrested by Soviet authorities "for Zionist activities" in Poland (the same experience of Menachem Begin), and had ended up interned in the large prison camp at Starobielsk, in the eastern Ukraine. This was the same camp where some four to five thousand Polish army officers had also been imprisoned by the Red Army.

Vidra's details clashed with known facts to the contrary as to what befell these Polish soldiers. He claimed ten thousand of them were at Starobielsk when less than half that number had been there. That they were moved out while he was there quite likely took place, but they were not the men subsequently systematically murdered and buried at Katyn; no one knows for sure the fate of the Starobielsk prisoners. Approximately 4,000 of these men had been sent to Starobielsk, another 6,500 to a second camp at Ostashkov, and 4,500 more to a third, Kozielsk. It was the contingent of these prisoners of war at Kozielsk which had been transported to Katyn and then murdered, in successive groups of about 300 at a time.

For the rest of Vidra's story we are dependent upon him solely for its veracity. But his dating of the departure of the Polish officers from the camp at Starobielsk also clashes with verified data to the contrary; he maintained these men were taken away at the end of 1940, when it is known they were removed starting in April of that year, and a few maybe as early as the end of 1939.

Vidra declared that these men were assembled in three groups for dispatching beyond Starobielsk, and that it was at the time the third and last group was about to make their departure that he made the acquaintance of and became friends with one Joshua Sorokin, a Soviet Jew and a major in the Red Army, who was in charge of the camp supplies and had been detailed to supervise this final shipping out of the Poles from Starobielsk. Sorokin apparently accompanied them, for Vidra spoke of his return, following which, on a trip to a nearby village, speaking Yiddish to one another when alone, Sorokin allegedly told him the Poles had been shot in the forest near Smolensk, though Katyn was not specifically mentioned as the place despite its location in that area. It was during this conversation that Vidra said that Major Sorokin, "badly shaken," claimed he had been an eyewitness to this mass murder; "What my eyes saw, the world will never believe," is how Vidra quoted the Soviet officer. Vidra went on to tell the *Ma'ariv* reporter that Sorokin made him promise not to reveal what he had been told for 30 years, which the former assured him would remain a secret for that much time.

Vidra then recalled that he had been transferred in February, 1941 to Talitza, in the Ural Mountains, where his new job was to help "break in" the new prisoners. It was there that he encountered among the new arrivals two Soviet lieutenants, whose names he remembered as Alexander Suslov and Samyun Tichonov. They drew attention because "they behaved in a peculiar way, unlike the other inmates," and no one knew why they were imprisoned at Talitza. He had orders to keep these two men away from the others in the prison camp "Because they were not quite all right," and concluded they had suffered nervous breakdowns.

The most dramatic part of Vidra's narrative was his claim that on one occasion, Lt. Suslov had broken down and told him that he and Lt. Tichonov had actually taken part in the shooting of these men, though some of the details are not corroborated by what has long been learned of what happened at Katyn. Suslov according to Vidra asserted that some of the Red soldiers ordered to kill the Poles refused to do so and committed suicide instead, throwing themselves into the mass grave. At the Katyn exhumation in 1943, no bodies of any Soviet personnel were recorded as found there, something which would have caused an immense sensation had it been done.

Vidra concluded by recalling that he met Major Sorokin again, after the war during which the latter had lost a leg. Now discharged from the Red Army, Sorokin implored Vidra again not to reveal his secret, though by now it is apparent Vidra had learned of it independently as a result of his reported experience at Talitza. Vidra, on the verge of emigrating to Israel, renewed his promise.

His explanation of why he was now telling this story was not especially convincing, though its timing may have had something to do with worsening Soviet-Israeli relations. So whether it was a pure invention, a very flawed and partially erroneous effort to capitalize on the Katyn sensation of the moment, or a description of still another mass murder of Polish officers (the fate of some 10,000 others is still a mystery) may never be known. In a conversation between this writer and FitzGibbon in Los Angeles in September, 1979 the latter expressed grave doubts as to the veracity of the entire Vidra account. (The *Ma'ariv* story entered the wire service traffic worldwide and was made available to newspapers in the U.S.A. via Associated Press. The account on which this summary is based was published in the Colorado Springs *Gazette Telegraph* for Thursday, July 22, 1971, p. 5-A.)

(6) Despite the close relationship of the exploitation of Babi Yar to that of Katyn, the Soviet propaganda agencies, so finely tuned to all opportunities to utilize atrocity stories for world consumption, one of their major industries for two generations, never undertook an exhumation of the Babi Yar site in an effort to wire down decisively the allegations made about the immense number of massacred Jews buried there. Ultimately the figure grew to fifty times as

many dead at Babi Yar as at Katyn but all there has ensued has been recrimina-
tory exchanges as to the nature of the dead. Eventually spokesmen for the Jews
of the area trimmed down their claims. In the late 1940s charges that 75,000
to 100,000 were shot there were common, an example of this being the
Ukrainian Jewish poet Savva Golovanivski's verse about Babi Yar in 1949. But
some years later when Prof. Salo Baron of Columbia University wrote his *The
Russian Jew Under Tsars and Soviets* (New York: Macmillan, 1964), he reduced
these larger figures to precisely 33,771 (p. 325.)

This was a remarkable achievement, seeing that neither an exhumation nor
any kind of body count had ever been made to determine what the situation
was. But larger figures persisted, and actually grew. When the city of Denver
permitted the creation of a memorial Babi Yar Park out of unused municipal
land in September, 1981, (formally dedicated October 2, 1983), it was preceded
that spring by a promotional piece written by a San Francisco writer named
Andrew Sorokowski published in the Denver *Post* for April 23, 1981. He
claimed that Babi Yar was a site for burial by the Germans of repeated massacres
amounting to 200,000 people. In this total he allowed the now accepted 33,700
allegedly killed on Monday and Tuesday, September 29-30, 1941 but asserted,
"over the next two years, another 66,000 Jews were rounded up in Kiev, taken
to Babi Yar and shot." The other hundred thousand killed and buried there
according to that writer were non-Jews.

(7) "They [the English] will not win the war. I have no ill-will toward them,
        but England's day has passed. No matter what happens now, she will lose
her empire. Tomorrow she will have become a Holland. She will not gain a
foothold in Europe again. She left it forever when she reembarked from
Dunkirk. She did not want to divide the world with Germany and the world is
going to get away from her. Everything that doesn't end up by being Russian
will be American." — Pierre Laval, quoted by Paul Morand, Chief of the French
Mission in London for Economic Warfare, on his return to France, in a conversation with Laval, President of the Petain government, at Vichy, in August, 1940.
France During the German Occupation, 1940-1944 (3 vols., Stanford, California:
The Hoover Institution, 1957), Doc. No. 144, Vol. III, p. 1336.

Philip W. Whitcomb, an American journalist, was almost continuously in
residence in France from mid-June, 1940 until the declaration of war between
Germany and the USA early in December, 1941, and then in Vichy France from
mid-1942 to the end of that year. In detention-custody of the French and then
German authorities, until early 1944, and returning to France after the Allied
invasion in June, 1944 as the Baltimore *Sun* European correspondent, Whitcomb
translated the entire work which was issued in 1957 as *France During The
German Occupation, 1940-1944*. In his own essay, vol, 3, pp. 1603-1610,
Whitcomb emphasized that no more than 50,000-60,000 Frenchmen left France
during the entire period of the German occupation, fewer than had customarily
left the country in peace time. (p. 1607). Even after the American invasion of
French North Africa and the German occupation of Vichy France, the total
number of French who left France amounted to "perhaps an eighth of one per
cent of the population." Not included in this of course is the number of French
military prisoners taken by the Germans in the war in the spring of 1940,

amounting to about 2 million, held as prisoners of war in Germany, and reduced to half that by negotiation between the German government and that of the Vichy regime, during the 1940-44 period.

To a considerable number of outsiders, at least, Laval was a better Frenchman than de Gaulle. At least he remained at home, and tried his best to make the lot of his people under German domination more endurable and worthwhile. It was much easier to run away, as did one seventh of one per cent of all Frenchmen, and make loud noises and threatening gestures from afar. It took far more courage to stay home and face the music. His removal from power and destruction at the end of the war cannot be described other than callous judicial murder. His "trial" was a despicable evasion of the very elementary concepts of justice, howled at by a screaming and gesturing "jury" picked from the tiny knot of returned French political ideologues, undoubtedly most of them working under the strictest Stalinist discipline; the description by the American journalist Whitcomb in the closing pages of the third volume of *France Under The German Occupation* is not easy to forget. Whitcomb called special attention to Laval being 4 times Premier of France, and 18 times heading one or another ministry in the French government in his political career. (It was Laval's daughter Josée who first turned on the light in the torch held by the figure in the Statue of Liberty.)

An example of "justice" under Charles de Gaulle: Laval was tried before the following "jury" as stipulated by a law signed by de Gaulle; 12 jurors and 12 substitutes were required to be chosen from the 80 people who voted against the establishment of the Petain regime on July 10, 1940 (569 had voted FOR the Petain regime at that time.) Another 12 jurors and 12 substitutes had to be chosen from persons who were deported to Germany, 1940-44.

These 48 jurors sat in raised galleries on both sides of the courtroom and continuously shouted "violent abuse" at Petain, Laval and other accused and witnesses during the trial, according to Whitcomb, a witness to it all as the Baltimore *Sun*'s European correspondent present at the proceedings. *France During The German Occupation*, vol. 3, p. 1610.

Paul Saurin, member of the Chamber of Deputies representing Oran, in North Africa, in his deposition included in *France During the German Occupation*, vol. II, pp. 690-709, pointed out that de Gaulle had created in Algeria three concentration camps to house his political enemies once Roosevelt and Churchill had approved his installation in North Africa. Further, a few days after the "liberation" of Paris in August, 1944, de Gaulle started flying into Paris various persons he had incarcerated in Algeria for lodgment in the prison at Fresnes. Included, who were treated as common felons, were Flandin, former President of the Council of Ministers, Peyrouton, a former French Ambassador and Governor-General of Algeria, and Boisson, former Governor General of French West Africa. As Saurin concluded sardonically, "The elegance of the deed gives the measure of the man who ordered it."

(8) There have been accounts of the Communists running the German concentration camp at Buchenwald from the inside stretching from Paul Rassinier, who was an inmate there himself for fifteen months, 1944-45, to the head of "Allied" psychological warfare, R.H.S. Crossman, and well beyond. It is very

likely that there was a Stalinist *apparat* well entrenched in every German camp from the very beginning, for that matter, starting with the 300 Stalinist Germans who built Dachau from an expanded abandoned World War I munitions factory in 1933 (see story by James G. McDonald, president of the American Foreign Policy Association, on a personal visit to Dachau in the summer of 1933, published in the New York *Times,* September 11, 1933, p. 9.) But it is part of our fairy tale education that this aspect of it be suppressed, and other features be emphasized, to maximize the effect of atrocity tales, which always have far more ultimate political clout.

One of the more detailed accounts of this above phenomenon largely escaped notice in the scrambling panic of the approaching Cold War in the fall of 1946. It appeared in the October, 1946 issue of the magazine *American Mercury* (pp. 397-404) during the editorship of Lawrence E. Spivak, known ultimately to millions for his part in radio and television programs as a testy interrogator of government and other guests on information shows. This account was written by Colonel Donald B. Robinson, identified as "Chief Historian of the American Military Government in Germany," and was titled "Communist Atrocities at Buchenwald."

Buchenwald was taken by American troops on April 11, 1945, though in years subsequent to this "liberation" it was turned over to the Stalinist Red Army, who proceeded to convert it into a concentration camp again to house *their* enemies, which was discussed by this writer in a review of an American edition of the works of Rassinier in the newspaper *Spotlight* for October 8, 1978. What was discovered of Stalinist management of Buchenwald was learned during the period of American tenure of control there, however.

Col. Robinson summarized the findings of an Army report which he said "first crossed my desk when I was on duty at General Eisenhower's Supreme Headquarters." This report stated that some 300 prisoners, a cadre formed from all its members from the Communist Party in Buchenwald, had seized control of the camp self-government set up by the Germans (*Häftlingsführung*) early in 1942. This underground organization proceeded to dominate the 60,000 inmates until the end of the war, and, Col. Robinson declared, "It was stated categorically by the Army report" that "the Communist trusties were directly responsible for a large part of the brutalities committed at Buchenwald."

Said Col. Robinson of the report, further, "It appeared that the prisoners who agreed with the Communists ate; those who didn't starved to death." According to the report, "The most important Communist stronghold at Buchenwald was the Labor Office. There it was that inmates were given work assignments or selected for transport to places like the dreaded Dora camp at Mittelbau," a location of especially hard labor. This was precisely what happened to Rassinier, an implacable anti-Stalinist though himself a socialist and pacifist.

The camp hospital, according to the report, was another Stalinist fort; "Its staff was composed almost 100% of German Communists," and, as Col. Robinson quoted from it, "Hospital facilities were largely devoted to caring for members of the [German] Communist Party. All scarce drugs were reserved for Communist patients, and hospital food was available for members of the

Party." As for the others, "Anti-Communists, when they became ill, were left largely without care."

"Another of the Communist citadels," as Col. Robinson called it, was "the Food Supply organization." Quoting again from the report, he read, "Favorite groups received reasonable rations while others were brought to the starvation level." It was further asserted by the report that this same operation had previously confiscated thousands of French Red Cross parcels sent to French prisoners, and that KPD "block chiefs" got them.

A fourth Red bastion within Buchenwald was, the report went on, "The Property Room, called *Effectenkammer*", "also under Communist control." Col. Robinson claimed that fleeing German guards took such things as money and gold, but that KPD trusties took everything else; "The day Buchenwald was liberated, the [U.S.] Army intelligence men were astounded to note that the 300 surviving German Communists were dressed like 'prosperous business men,' " the latter three words quoted from the report.

Col. Robinson detailed two threats to German KPD control of Buchenwald. Early in 1943 several large groups of Poles were sent there from Auschwitz, Army intelligence learned; "They had occupied the same ruling position" there, and "attempted to capture the same sort of control in their new home." But, he went on, "The German Communists were too well entrenched," and smashed this effort by having many of the Poles executed.

The second threat occurred a few months later "when large groups of French and Belgian prisoners" were sent to Buchenwald; "Because of their Western outlook, these too represented a menace to the German Communist rule." And as a result, "Almost all of the first convoys were shipped immediately to the dreaded Dora Camp." Neither Col. Robinson nor the report he was quoting from, apparently, discussed the struggle within Buchenwald between the Communists and the common felons, a large number, according to Rassinier, convicted of serious crimes common around the world. These men however were fiercely loyal to Germany as opposed to the Communists, whose basic political affections lay with Stalin in Moscow.

Probably what most surprised American intelligence operatives who put this report together from which Col. Robinson read was learning that the KPD underground in Buchenwald had maintained careful contact with the Communists outside; even at the height of Hitler's war with the USSR, Germany and German-occupied Europe crawled with an immense legion of Stalinist adherents. Camp inmates received steady orders and information from them. There were many French, Dutch and Spanish Communists at Buchenwald as well, and said the report, "A vast underground system of councils and meetings was built up to integrate them." But the Party discipline seemed to impress most of all: "From Buchenwald an inmate went out regularly to establish contacts with a Communist courier bringing news and instructions. Bound by his loyalty to the Party, the contact man never made use of his opportunity to escape personally."

For those whose only scrap of knowledge of Buchenwald was the famous photograph by Margaret Bourke-White of the small party of inmates staring out through a barbed wire fence, obviously staged, and looking remarkably well and utterly lacking in emaciation, this story might have enabled a few things to fit together for the first time, but not much, apparently. Wondrous are the uses of

left wing photographs. One of the very few in the land who recognized what was
being done by this campaign of atrocity photographs and films was the liberal
literary and film critic, James Agee, author of *Let Us Now Praise Famous Men*
(Boston: Houghton, Mifflin, 1941). Almost alone in the country brave enough
to resent the brainwash, Agee protested in his column in the super-warrior left-
wing Germanophobe and pro-Stalinist *Nation,* itself an almost incredible event
(Agee, "Films," *Nation* [May 19, 1945], p. 579):

> The recently released films which show Nazi atrocities are only part
> of what is rather clearly an ordered and successful effort to condition
> the people of this country against interfering with, or even questioning,
> an extremely hard peace against the people of Germany. The simple
> method is to show things more frightful than most American citizens
> have otherwise seen, and to pin the guilt for these atrocities on the
> whole German people.
>
> I cannot get my thoughts in order yet, to write what I think needs
> writing, about such propaganda and the general reaction to it. But I do
> want to go on record against it as I believe many other people would
> like to, before our voices become undistinguishable among those of the
> many confused or timid or villainous people who are likely after awhile,
> when the shock wears off—and when it is safe or even stylish—to come
> somewhat to their senses.

Agee went on in this vein for some time, an act of intellectual courage really
unmatched in that moment. That few had caught up with him nearly 40 years
later testifies to the thoroughness of the work of the multitude of mindbending
adversaries he correctly recognized right at the moment it was starting to
materialize.

Close corroboration of Colonel Robinson from another American Army
officer on the situation in still another German camp "liberated" by the U.S.
Army came 20 years later. Ellis E. Spackman, Chief of Counter-Intelligence
Arrests and Detentions for the U.S. Seventh Army, was involved in upper-level
operations attending the taking over of Dachau, near Munich. Writing in the San
Bernardino (Calif.) *Sun-Telegram* for March 13, 1966, Spackman, at that time a
professor of history at San Bernardino Valley College, stated the following:
"When we liberated Dachau, we found the nationalities represented in the
following order: Poles, 9,082; Russians, 4,258; French, 3,918; Jews, 2,539;
Italians, 2,184; Germans, 1,173; and scattered prisoners from 34 other countries,
making a total of 31,432."

Though Spackman at that time believed the extermination legends just as
much as the next as a received opinion, he could not explain these tens of thousands of living prisoners. But he did support, independently, Rassinier and
Robinson, in all major details as to the complexion of Dachau and how it was
run. He quoted Prof. Albert Kervyn, of the economics department of the University of Louvain in Belgium, himself a Dachau prisoner for a time, who declared,
"The SS [German concentration camp guards] rarely murdered anyone." Prof.
Kervyn described almost all violent deaths as resulting from the workings of the
inside organization of the camp.

The actual camp commandant was identified by Spackman as a former Soviet Red Army officer of Armenian extraction named Melazarian, responsible to a German superior. Melazarian was nearly beaten to death by the prisoners upon the arrival of the Americans, and then, said Spackman, "shot and killed by our troops." His replacement, "elected by the prisoners," was a German Communist, Oscar Mueller, whom Spackman said the U.S. forces consulted. Prof. Kervyn had told Spackman that among the mainly political prisoners, mostly Communists of many national varieties, were "several hundred" desperate felons, who "were mostly murderers serving life sentences." Many of these held "posts of authority over their fellow prisoners," he told Spackman, with one in every 30 prisoners being part of the internal camp "self-government" (*Häftlings-führung*) (the Germans simply did not have the manpower to staff these camps with anything but a thin managerial cadre.) These prisoner-bureaucrats, Communists or common criminals, alike controlled the distribution of food, the operation of the prison hospital and all health services, and the very important work-assignment details; incurring the displeasure of the Reds, as happened to Rassinier at Buchenwald, meant assignment to a very bad job.

Spackman, still inclined to blame the Germans for all the "monstrous cruelties" that took place, in the face of this information and testimony, had to admit that "the prisoners were the actual instruments that inflicted the barbarities on their fellow prisoners." This was precisely what Rassinier described as what happened at Buchenwald, and independently supported by the U.S. Army historian, Colonel Robinson.

There is an interesting recent source on Dachau, in the British periodical *After the Battle,* No. 27, February 15, 1980. In the article "Dachau," (pp. 1-33), by Andrew Mollo there is a strange mixture of immediate postwar style propaganda incendiary verbiage and very subdued rational talk associated with much later and cooler estimations. Mollo, seemingly obsessed with the topic of American Army massacres of surrendered German prisoners of war at the scene, to which he devoted an unexpectedly large part of his illustrated piece (the photographs are exceptional), managed to escape mention of the subject of "Communists" entirely other than in a reference to the very early origins of the Dachau camp. However, he does corroborate the census figure cited by Spackman, even though he omits mention of the prisoner of war status of most of the men found by the "liberators." Though mouthing the expectable and conventional talk of the "horrors" of the camp at the moment of its capture, Mollo then goes on to say (p. 15), "While the bulk of the inmates were lean and hungry but otherwise in reasonable condition," there were "huts crammed with ill and dying prisoners suffering from tuberculosis and typhus." Mollo's account of who was in charge at Dachau differs completely from Spackman's, while quoting from its surrendered officer in charge (p. 13), that the able-bodied amounted to about 93% of the total. Mollo also skirted *very* warily the once-trumpeted "gas chamber" subject.

When it comes to memoirs and commentaries from the concentration camp ex-prisoners themselves in the earliest times of their "liberation," one is struck by their paucity, despite the scores upon scores of thousands turned loose. One is additionally impressed by their self-serving, sometimes almost to a revolting proportion, and their incredible contradictions which suggest in many cases the most bald-faced mendacity. Among the earliest there are many from Stalinists, which mainly have the frank quality of avoiding the braying of "innocence," a characteristic of the majority particularly of the last two decades, though there are exceptions. One is impressed by the ingenuous quality of the statement by the Parisian, Sim Kessel, on how he ended up in Auschwitz: "When I was arrested on July 14, 1942, I had just crossed the demarcation line [between Vichy France and German occupied France] carrying a suitcase loaded with automatic pistols" (Kessel, *Hanged at Auschwitz* [New York: Stein and Day, 1972], p. 16). Various others, though just a tiny knot of the total, admit the cause of their arrest as spying for Stalinism, participating in armed civilian ambush warfare against German troops in behalf of some Red campaign some-where, and other enterprises of this nature.

What is exceptionally scarce is a reminiscence by an ex-prisoner of his part in the camp management, though there is a general conclusion that one in every 30 of the incarcerated had a job running the camp. One of the earliest of a mere handful of such revelations was broadcast nationally in the U.S.A. less than two months after war's end in 1945, in the pages of then-600,000-circulation *Newsweek*. It was reported by the magazine's Stockholm correspondent and involved an interview with a youthful national of Norway only 21 years old, though the reason for his imprisonment was never revealed in this account. It involved his stay at Auschwitz, which was rapidly overtaking Dachau, Buchenwald and Belsen, all in Germany, as the symbolic center for concentration camp horror stories. It went this way:

> The story was told to me by a 21-year-old Norwegian student, Erling Bauck, who has just returned to Stockholm en route to his native Oslo, after spending three years at Auschwitz concentration camp. Bauck admits he was one of the "trusties." He says that none of the horror stories told about Nazi concentration camps was exaggerated, but he himself landed by chance, and otherwise, in a position where he had his own shoe shiner at his service, another man to mend his socks, a third to do his laundry, and so forth. He obtained clean bed sheets, smoked fat Havana cigars, and procured a watch, fountain pen and other articles. The ordinary fare, consisting of a quart of cabbage soup and a half pound of stale blackish bread, he disdained.
>
> The reason for Bauck's favored position was that he managed to get put in charge of the Elite Guard canteen. He diverted to his own use cigarettes, brandy and other merchandise destined for the Elite Guard trade. With these he paid for his privileges and favors.
>
> Bauck was not the only one to enjoy these privileges—out of 16,000 internees in Auschwitz, some 500 were in key positions where they were not only enjoying material favors, but were safe from gas chambers and crematories. These 500 formed a camarilla preying on newcomers who were promptly stripped, upon arrival, of watches, rings, jewelry, food, parcels, and so forth on the pretext that they were making a contribution to a nonexistent underground welfare fund for internees. The plunder permitted camp racketeers to obtain anything they wished by means of barter. For lads who could pay in kind, there were movies, cabarets, concerts, and brothels.

The remainder of Bauck's story as reported second hand included all the expectable reiterations of yarns about what went on at Auschwitz, though none of this had any relation to Bauck personally and consisted mainly of repetition of other peoples' allegations. Bauck's politics were never mentioned, nor the reason for his having taken five months to get from Poland to Sweden, the Auschwitz camp having been "liberated" by the Red Army in January. What Rassinier was to explain in his book *Le Mensonge d'Ulysse* (five editions, 1948 to 1961) as the appetite for ever more sensational stories from camp veterans led to later multiplications of Bauck's statement of the Auschwitz camp population by twenty and the number of daily deaths and cremations by forty. But the reportage of his story was an interesting momentary breach in the iron curtain of unrelieved monolithic atrocity tales beginning to accumulate in these early post war months, a literature which was to grow large enough to fill a reasonably-sized library in days ahead. For the full account of Bauck's relation see "Luxury in a Horror Camp: Nazi Pets Led Fuller Life," *Newsweek* (June 25, 1945), p. 50.

Chapter Three

THE BOOK: SOME OBSERVATIONS

1. GENERAL

THOUGH RAPHAEL LEMKIN'S NAME graced the title page of *Axis Rule in Occupied Europe* as author, a formidable contingent of aides helped him prepare it. His acknowledgment of copious help from some three dozen other people in a variety of important and strategic locations is sufficient evidence for assuming that the book might have been the product of a committee. Its atrocious organization helps to build that suspicion. Though the book, when examined with care for a length of time, appears to be intended as a vehicle for launching the new crime invented by the author, and the word describing it, "genocide," the structure of the book is grounds for believing that it was put together by several people at different times. Instead of giving signs of being a continuous intellectual project, it suggests instead as a consequence of abrupt changes in direction and style that persons other than the author either introduced interpolations or suggested them to the author. Since English was not his native tongue, and, being in the USA a bare two years before it was finished, the assumption could also be made that he received substantial help in English formulation, syntax and style.

Axis Rule is neither a dispassionate historical treatment of the subject nor a serious work in public affairs bearing objectively upon related matters of international law. It is prepared as a narrow legal brief, with profound prejudice in behalf of the author's patrons and hosts, and structured in such a way as to give at all times the absolutely worst possible emphasis or interpretation to the story of

the German administration of the area of Europe under their control
and that of their five associated states, covering some 17 regions,
further broken down into 21 sub-regions.

The latter two-thirds of the book consist of 400 pages of verbatim reproductions in English translation of close to 350 Axis laws,
decrees, emergency promulgations, field orders, occupation edicts,
regulations and military stipulations, mainly culled from a battery of
German language sources, but derived from many related official
printed sources as well. It is assumed that the author had a point to
make in filling so much of this ponderous and largely-unreadable
volume with all this legal baggage. The prosaic case built upon this
material loses in impressiveness as one goes through this work, so it is
no wonder that the ineptness of the support is livened up by adroit
and skillful insertion at strategic points of the most transparent of
incendiary propaganda, derived from handouts of obvious self-
serving organizations or even more partisan-leaning political forces
representing the rump governments-in-exile from the Continent
lodged under their protectors in England and the USA. More will be
said about this shortly. Thus, Lemkin's "evidence" for "massacres"
and the like derive exclusively from the latter agencies and organizations, not from any legal evidence as posted. Many of these wartime
institutions are themselves reporters of third and fourth hand
rumors, gossip and outright inventions, and are never backed up by
statutory or other documentary evidence anywhere. Despite sensational accusations concerning mass killing of Jews, for instance,
repeated in nearly every instance from Zionist fronts in England and
America, Lemkin's citation of "genocide legislation" in his massive
appendix of Axis laws deal with subjects so trivial and matter of fact
that they almost provide comic relief when compared with the earlier
dramatic charges. The concluding part of this chapter will deal with
this.

Lemkin, installed as a professor in the Duke University Law
School in mid-1941, shortly after his arrival in the USA following his
trip across half the world, ceased to be even remotely a direct
observer of what he detailed in *Axis Rule* with that date, and may
have ceased to be such well before that. His presence in the USA for
2½ years prior to the publication of his book subtracts from the
impression circulated around from the end of 1944 that his findings
had some fresh and on-the-spot pertinence. An examination of the
book reveals exactly the opposite. Knowledge of where he was at the
time the most recent material in the book eventuated reinforces the
belief that the laws which bulk out most of the book might have
been collected in a wide variety of places, and compilers employed
by the Carnegie Foundation and utilizing the law library resources at

the convenience of the US government's many wartime administrative branches might have put together most of this book without Lemkin having much of anything to do with it at all.

It is quite probable that not a single reviewer of the book ever bothered to read the collection of legal citations which pack the latter two-thirds of the volume, and, if any part was consulted, it was most likely to be the propagandistic text which constituted the front one-third. Why the book was not updated, containing, when issued late in November, 1944, only a few scraps of substance going past early 1942, is puzzling. Most of the sources used to that point were available in the USA, a neutral from the fall of 1939 to December 7, 1941, almost the entire time span covered by Lemkin. A number of law libraries took these Axis legal compendiums on a routine basis prior to *de facto* belligerence, and some may have trickled into the country for some time after that. But the narrative and statements for the period after that are supported almost entirely by wild and generalized imputations and rhetorical arraignments, which may have become easier to believe as the evidence in support of them became increasingly more difficult, if not impossible, to find. But in the end, all of this mattered little; it was Lemkin's colorful new word, in reality an ugly hybrid neologism, which, despite its slippery and evasive definition, along with his tardy repetition of the yarns of mass killing of Jews in German-occupied Central Europe, survived even in the consciousness of the "experts."

From the internal evidence it is plain to see that the Carnegie Foundation's decision to publish Lemkin's book was determined, not by reverent concern for the ethereal nature of blue-white pure international law, but by the prevalence of Allied arms. Successes of the latter in the summer of 1944 undoubtedly were a mighty stimulus to the somewhat stagnated postwar planners for Germany. It was surely intended to provide assistance for the latter, not as a report on how Germany and its associated powers were running occupied Europe for the previous three years. Since very little of the book's substance went past the end of 1942, it was nearly worthless for the above purpose, little more than a memorandum, and an extremely fragmentary one, full of vast holes and memorable for its lack of real content.

Axis Rule was fatally flawed from its basic conception, an attempt to infer from a collection of carefully selected laws and promulgations how Axis Europe actually functioned, the assumption being that Lemkin had in mind relating an operational situation. But what he did was analogous to an effort to explain the actions and behavior of a living organism while having nothing to base this upon except skeletal remains. Lemkin did not quote from a single person living under Axis occupation in the time span he covered; surely one could have expected the US government or other members of the wartime United Nations to supply him with someone who had actually been there and could report on the reality, and not its simulation. Quoting a wartime enemy except in a hostile way undoubtedly was out of the question, but Lemkin never even bothered to cite or interview any representative of a neutral land, whose people were familiar with the workings of occupied Europe in many details, and could have supplied important facts on daily life. Compared to actual observers, Lemkin was as reliable as to what was going on as if he were working from the dark side of the moon. What he succeeded in doing was the fashioning of an account of Axis-occupied Europe cut from the whole cloth of United Nations propaganda, and one courses through his heavy tome to the end without learning more than a tidbit or two about what he presumably had undertaken to relate.

Lemkin's preface was signed and dated November 15, 1943, from "Duke University, North Carolina and Washington, D.C.," which also served to describe his shuttle back and forth in the book's preparation. Why it should have sat over a year before publication, and been supplemented with little or nothing in the interim, other than citations from various propaganda briefings and inflammatory pressure group handouts, is somewhat mysterious. When one considers the battery of assistants the author had from the massive legal libraries of the Library of Congress, the Carnegie Foundation and Duke University, plus at least four interested Government bureaus, it was indubitably a mouse-sized portfolio of additions to the book which was made during the year it existed in near-finished shape, let alone the sparse addenda appended for the year *previous* to that.

It may be that Lemkin's work was not thought worth publishing, until the great military breakthroughs of summer, 1944. One gets this impression from another quarter, the book's foreword. Its author, George A. Finch, was director of the International Law Section of the Carnegie Foundation, and it was dated August 18, 1944, as the Anglo-American armies were making their way into the environs of Paris. The apparent galvanization of the Carnegie apparatus into action was not marked by any special inspiration in Finch's appendage to Lemkin's work, however. There has rarely been a volume led off by a fugleman's preliminary as lame and irrelevant as that of Finch's to Lemkin. The only legal precedent he could come up with to back Lemkin's case against what the Germans and their allies had allegedly done in occupied Europe was a pronouncement by President William McKinley at the time of the Spanish-American War in 1898 (Finch might have emulated Telford Taylor and started back at the Napoleonic wars), and a passing reference to the Hague Conventions of 1899 and 1907. (The very selective employment of the Hague agreements against the Axis and the sophisticated evasion of these same agreements when brought up in relation to the behavior of Germany's enemies will be examined briefly later. And it did not even seem to graze Finch's consciousness that the noble Ally, Stalinist Russia, was not a signatory to the 1899 and 1907 Hague Conventions, let alone the 1929 Geneva Convention on war prisoners.)

In still another sense, *Axis Rule*'s publication seemed to be coordinated with that of the War Refugee Board's booklet, *German Extermination Camps: Auschwitz and Birkenau,* which also appeared in November, 1944. The WRB, largely masterminded by the US Secretary of Treasury, Henry Morgenthau, was in some respects the coordinator of harsh postwar plans for the Germans, and was surely interested in mobilizing everything toward that objective that could be dredged up. The above-titled work was almost entirely based on Stalinist propaganda allegations. Though *Axis Rule* fell far short of Morgenthau's *Germany Is Our Problem* (Harper, 1945), out a short time later, it contained material useful to the presumptuous Nuremberg proceedings subsequently. So, if things did not seem to suggest other than that the war might last a very long time at about the moment *Axis Rule* was finished in 1943, encouraging the Carnegie post-warriors to feel that it had to be sat on for a long time before the emergence of circumstances indicating it might be a useful and practical political tool, the dramatic turnaround in late summer, 1944 gave to Lemkin's book an utterly different aspect. Lemkin's additional presence at the incubation cell in Charlottesville, Virginia for America's budding governors of occupied Germany, upcoming, lent additional circumstantial evidence to the re-evaluation of his work. His presence here and his work as a close functionary with at least two and possibly four other government bureaus concerned with the future settlement of accounts with the Germans, and with possible ties to several others, made hash of Lemkin's posing in subsequent years as a lonely "private man," carrying on his campaigns in single-handed isolation.

Axis Rule in Occupied Europe gives evidence of having started out to be one thing, and later being converted into quite another. It commences as an expansion on Lemkin's previous surveys published in France and Sweden on international finance, international payments, foreign exchange controls, currency and money regulations, and similar prosaic matters, incorporating much commentary on the technical legal administration of that part of Europe in German hands as a result of the war beginning in September, 1939 and extending through the end of 1941, but with sharply reduced attention to such and most other subjects after that date. Suddenly, after eight chapters and some 70 pages of this, Lemkin inserts his prize contribution, "genocide," a chapter unrelated to most of the foregoing material. His book now becomes a launching pad for this neologism, and the study promptly veers away from the legal evidence adduced to support his economic theorizing and assertions, soon venturing into the purple dimensions of hysteria. With the abandonment of documentation there is also the abrupt switch to dependence on third and even fourth hand, in some instances, propaganda allegations. As will be seen, the legal support for his omnibus charge of "genocide" is exceedingly sparse and notably limp, and in a few instances, in the view of some observers, almost comic. There is virtually no relationship between the legal evidence advanced and the charges made when one takes up the major accusation, deliberate and intentional massacre and extermination of the Jewish population of Europe by the regime of Adolf Hitler. The citation of laws or decrees which are disadvantageous to the personal safety of Jews, or result in unfair impositions on Jewish freedom and economic power is not supporting evidence for charges of official, intentional total physical annihilation. The attempt to support horrendous mass murder accusations with *ex-parte* propaganda handouts from the most palpable of self-serving agencies represents a sensational departure, and the minor parenthetical additions, which give the impression of afterthoughts, neither help his cause, and the entire "genocide" presentation seems to have no part in the central theme of the book. If one casts this in the structure of a legal proceeding, in an American court, Lemkin's "evidence" for much of what he inserts in *Axis Rule* would have stood about as long as it took a judge to expend the breath to throw it out.

It would appear that *Axis Rule* is at least two projects, 1) the collection of legal documents which fill the 400 pages comprising the third part of it, and which seems to have been done first, and then 2) the first two parts, the remaining third of the study, for which Lemkin took credit. But it soon becomes obvious that it is in no way a history of the rule of portions of Europe occupied by the Germans, Italians and their allies. Its lop-sided concentration upon the years 1940-1941 detracts heavily from its pretended role of reporting on the nature of the governing of this large area, 1939-1944, and the effort to supply missing dimensions by liberal borrowing from propaganda made by the adversaries of the occupiers serves to undermine the legal approach to the subject. Perhaps it is realized at some point in preparing the work how inadequate the legal emphasis is in trying to describe a total situation. If Lemkin and his cited emergency legal evidence is to be believed, and taken seriously as a true representation of life in Axis Europe, most of the area would have long before starved, and war production would have ceased well before the book was published.

There was a vast difference between what took place and the conception of reality filtered through Lemkin's legalisms. The assumption that these edicts and promulgations represented a faithful picture of what went on implied sustained enforcement, and obedience. Omitted in all cases were emendations indicating possible amendment, alteration, supplementation, repeal, failure to enforce, deliberate administrative neglect, replacement and other possible operational conditions, such as wholesale neglect, or defiance, or evasion. The impression is allowed to stand that what he had gathered had the permanence of Hammurabi's Code. That much of Axis Europe was adjusted to the new situations growing out of the war was evident from its ability to take on the world in a global war; no regime based on fear and compulsion alone could have performed like that, but it is Lemkin's objective in part to suggest this as its only dynamic, and as such contributes to a comprehensive misunderstanding of the enemy and a failure of realization of the real source of his strength. An examination of the grave misconceptions of a specific nature and the historical distortions in *Axis Rule* may now take place, along with a preliminary investigation of some of the socio-political theory and philosophy which attended Lemkin's conception of minorities in a world of national states, without which his central and enduring construct, "genocide," will remain largely incomprehensible.

2. SPECIFIC

Raphael Lemkin's *Axis Rule in Occupied Europe* is far more remarkable for what it left out than for what it contained. Purporting to be a serious work of history and public affairs set in a legal framework and bearing upon deep matters of international law, it turned out to be mainly a piece of muddy partisan war propaganda; the hook buried in it is still stuck deeply in the world's neck. A proper confrontation of *Axis Rule* as a historical work might require a labor of equal size insofar as it would involve a challenge of its first 264 pages. The mixture of fact, rumor, gossip, references to malicious unfounded propaganda and sheer unadorned mendacity is singular and arresting, probably owing to the complexity of the force that admittedly worked on the book, which surely had something to do with its irregularly-paced and multi-faceted structure. Some of its deficiencies as a historical study will now be undertaken.

For the most part, it is quite impossible for one to discern how the Germans administered the regions of Europe under their control, operationally, from a study of the preliminary chapters of Lemkin's *Axis Rule*. Since it was a view from afar, based almost entirely on a collection of the statutes, decrees and promulgations of the Hitler military occupation, derived from books and related printed sources, plus wild propagandistic handouts from narrow interest groups hostile to or at war with the Germans, there was little if any real substance to it as might be reported by an actual observer or participant with personal experience under it. War conditions prevented such an on-the-spot report, for the most part, from what might be called a detached source. The result was that this encouraged the substitution of the very worst possible interpretation in every case of what appeared to be the situation, aggravated by asides and innuendoes which had no authority in fact, and which in cases were often inventions, the latter the most likely where the matter was the most grave. In the over 400 pages of the legal documents applying to occupied Europe originating with the Germans and their allies, Lemkin did not find a single one which had even the faintest positive quality to it. All were blackly malicious tools to bring about the demise of all and the obliteration of everything. The combination of his allegations and the extrapolations on his guesswork as to how things *might* be taking place resulted in a conclusion that the entire region was one immense seething chaos. But the fact of continued German warfare on two immense fronts against a very large part of the world in opposition obviously was in contradiction to this. Were conditions as drastic as Lemkin alleged, it is hard to imagine how any regime might have been able to continue sustained combat against overwhelming manpower and material odds. Lemkin was not even restrained or moderated by such neutral studies and reports as had been issued in the lands of Germany's adversaries, in which a small amount of understanding could be gleaned with sustained study, though it is unlikely that anything not basically hostile would have been allowed to see publication in England or America, and thus policy propped up Lemkin's basic contentions.

The existence of a law or decree at some time in the past was taken as absolute evidence that it had been enforced to the letter, and had never been repealed, abandoned, or replaced by something else quite different in content, after the immediate emergency which had provoked its appearance in the first place had passed. Though he had up to four years to verify if any of the foregoing had followed something done, 1939-1941, for example, there is virtually nothing of the sort to be found in the catalog bringing up the rear two-thirds of *Axis Rule,* and it did not seem that Lemkin's numerous helpers were able to assist him in such a project. The application of such standards to the criminal and civil law code of any nation would have left any scholar on the globe speechless or in substantial shock, at discovering what bottomless evil such a legal code authorized. But it must be kept in mind that in this study it was Lemkin's apparent basic assumption that a *law* and *evidence of its enforcement* were the same thing.

So with the exception of a handful of sporadic citations, we really can learn little more than nothing about how the Axis "ruled" Europe down to six months before the end of World War II in Raphael Lemkin's book. In generalizing on its legal content, nearly 70% of the legal documents are found to be emergency decrees and proclamations from the years 1940 and 1941, *ad hoc* material resembling what has been common to wars since antiquity, and hardly evidence of some peculiar sinisterness. A further breakdown of these along subject lines reveals that 80% of all the collection deal with money, property, exchange rates, conditions of employment, labor and compensation, transfer of ownership, international exchange rates and their control, and many related matter-of-fact regulations of the dullest and most prosaic sort, accompanied by related stipulations regarding citizenship and mobility, in Axis-occupied countries, and regions of countries.

Especially arresting is the contrast between the brief passages in Lemkin's book where almost as asides the gravest charges of outrageous massacres are made, and his recommendations for future action against mainly the Germans, assuming their eventual defeat, especially in the conclusions of Chapters V, VI and IX. Over three-fourths of his advice is along the lines of instituting a system of economic "restitution," and not the innovating of courts and trials for the defeated; only after the publication of his book do we see Lemkin branching out into this uncharted region of "war crimes" and their punishment. Even in his preface (*Axis Rule*, p. xii), presumably written after everything else had been structured for publication, his proposals for postwar "redress" centered mainly about the creation of "machinery for the restoration of property," via an "international property restitution agency," supporting "national property restitution agencies" in each interested country, and other "property restitution tribunals, both national and international." In view of the many billions of dollars of damage caused by Anglo-American bombing of cities in Germany and of German-occupied areas, one may have wondered how Lemkin proposed to bring about "restitution" in such matters (Germany's enemies also owned much property in Germany prior to hostilities). But the startling thing in all this was the utter absence of any recommendations for arrest and trial for all those people who had to be involved in the mass killing of millions of Jews and others, in view of his brief repetition of stories of such events. The disparity between the accusations and the proposals for bringing the accused to justice induces a conclusion that the insertion of the mass murder charges was a late afterthought, in view of its fundamental collision with the rest of the Lemkin study. To make sense, his book should have concluded with a ringing call for legal tribunals to try these alleged mass murderers. But his study neglects this *in toto,* and concerns itself only with restoring property taken from the enemies of the German war regime in the lands it occupied. Perhaps this is why Lemkin was recruited immediately after his book's appearance to dwell on this entirely neglected subject, in the *Nation* and other magazines.

The discrepancy between the two vastly contrasting aspects of his book called for something of the sort which engaged his attention thereafter. Part of the restitution problem hinged on the mass murder charges. If as many had been annihilated as the sources Lemkin repeated had charged, it would have been an insuperable task to restore their property to them or their survivors, assuming there were any of them, hence a large part of his book would be irrelevant. The issue had to be transferred from the property considerations, which dominated Lemkin's book, to the massacre allegations, which actually took up a tiny fraction of one per cent of his published labors. There is obviously an immense difference between losing one's bank account and being arbitrarily put to death. That is essentially the two basic charges being made in Lemkin's thick book, the former at least superficially and faintly supported with legal documents, the latter inserted in the former almost as an aside, and backed up by nothing except propaganda fulminations of various self-serving political forces in opposition.

In a firm but spirited defense of the behavior of the State of Israel in Palestine for over 30 years, George W. Ball, Undersecretary of State under Presidents John F. Kennedy and Lyndon B. Johnson, 1961-1966, U.S. Permanent Representative to the United Nations, 1968, and in 1978 the senior managing director of the massive banking house of Lehman Brothers Kuhn, Loeb, Inc., declared, in an article in the October, 1978 *Harper's* magazine, "A benign military occupation is a contradiction in terms." This declaration is not just totalitarian-liberal hypocrisy intended as a defense of a favored regime somewhere, but a recognition of a fact of life, seen in the history of military operations for millennia. It is of fundamental importance in this study of Raphael Lemkin and his work, which concerns German behavior as an occupying power, and relates as well to Lemkin's theory of war and the structure of international law relating to the conduct of war. In view of his repeated charges against the Germans of violations of the 1907 Annex to the Hague Convention involving the regulations spelled out therein "respecting the laws and customs of war on land," it is necessary also to examine these insofar as they apply to all belligerents, and to note how selectively Lemkin employs them. In the course of this examination, quotations from the American and British (but not the Soviet) codes relating to the law of land warfare, identical in harmony with the Hague Convention, will also be made, to imphasize the glaring double standard Lemkin utilized in fabricating his case against the Axis powers.

Lemkin's theory of war seemed to be derived from a stage operetta, but was by his admission based on what he called the "Rousseau-Portalis Doctrine," which reputedly consisted of the dogma that "war is directed against sovereigns and armies, not against subjects and civilians." In his updating of this 18th century romantic concept, Lemkin's revision read, "war is conducted against States and armed forces, and not against their populations."

Both Lemkin and his Carnegie editors fell silent here, resulting in one of the few instances where a concession was made to his possible international law specialist readers. Though it was reasonable to assume that one conventionally educated through high school might recognize the first of these two figures as the controversial philosopher of the pre-French Revolution, Jean Jacques Rousseau, maybe not more than a dozen or more Americans would have been familiar with the second, Jean Etienne Marie de Portalis (1746-1807), the French jurist and political figure prominent in the early years of the Napoleonic era, and probably the most important of the four who were responsible for producing the Civil Code of Napoleonic Law, published in 1801. Where Lemkin and presumably his guide George Finch let down the readers of *Axis Rule* was not so much the failure to identify the creators of the "Rousseau-Portalis Doctrine," but the utter absence of any source citation whatever which might be followed up to see where Lemkin had derived this exotic dictum relating to the conduct of warfare.

It can be argued that an even worse lapse on Lemkin's part while essaying forth as a theorist of war was one of historical omission. Surely anyone with just more than a schoolboy's knowledge of history would reflect upon the times of Rousseau and Portalis just a bit further along and recall the career of Napoleon Bonaparte, for whom Portalis himself labored, as we have seen above. One can hardly say that Napoleon paid much attention if any at all to that "Rousseau-Portalis Doctrine," so seemingly formidable when condensed for us by Lemkin. So we can assume that the famed

fabricators of this theory of war were entirely engrossed in some
other era of history, perhaps since the time of Charlemagne, but
certainly not of their own day. For on the very heels of their reputed
pronouncement of their belief in the desirability of the restricted
nature of war came the grim Little Corporal, than whom no one
more personifies the arrival of the era of unlimited warfare, as the
famed British strategist, General J.F.C. Fuller, was to put it.

Leaving aside for the moment comment on the incredible naivete
of this postulate, one might have been inclined to wonder where
Lemkin spent World War One, as well as to speculate what he
thought the enemy should be in a *civil* war, such as the Bolshevik
revolution which raged in part in his own area of origin, 1917-1922,
the spate of wars *that* was followed by with its neighbors, as well as
what had gone on in areas of the Far East since the early 1920s. No
one had fought a war which scrupulously avoided the civilian population as far back as anyone could remember, even if some localized
18th century wars had perhaps just grazed civilians because of their
sharply curtailed geographical limitations and short duration. But
such constraints were not to be found in the 1899 and 1907 Hague
Conventions, and it was a wondrous development that Lemkin
should have essayed forth to sell such an idea in the sophisticated
world of 1943-1944. One might have been aroused to admiration of
his incredible innocence, or his polished internalization of the hypocrisy of his patrons, whose strict avoidance of conducting a war
against civilians included at that moment an attack on the civilian
population of much of Western and Central Europe via obliteration
bombing of many scores of cities, and having killed scores of
hundreds of thousands of them at the time Lemkin was announcing
this pious concept of war. Lemkin's attribution to the Germans of
waging a unique "total war" out of harmony with the "Rousseau-
Portalis Doctrine" was quaintly ludicrous, to be sure, and in retrospect one might be led to wonder how the Carnegie Foundation
sophisticates allowed it to appear in his book, not only in view of
the "Allied" strategic bombing of millions of civilians in cities far
behind the war lines, but also in view of their conduct of unrestricted
submarine warfare in the Pacific, which cost three times as many
enemy civilian lives as those of combat forces. But of such brash
hypocrisy is modern war propaganda made.

Actually, Lemkin's analysis did not fit any land at all in the West
in which the Germans were involved, least of all France, Holland,
Denmark, Norway, Belgium or even Czecho-Slovakia. But if German
armed forces were at war "against peoples" in the case of Poland,
Yugoslavia or Stalinist Russia, it was demonstrable that this was so
because these "peoples" were in wholesale armed civilian warfare

against them. And this requires a substantial digression, in order to make plain the ground rules whereby armed civilians are a recognized belligerent according to both the Hague Conventions as well as the rules of land warfare even of the major Western powers at war with the Axis.

Since Raphael Lemkin's *Axis Rule in Occupied Europe* is intended to be taken seriously as a study in international law, and is studded from end to end with the verbiage of legalism, it may be helpful to refer to some law here, in an effort to keep the lanes of understanding clear, and to make it possible in part to keep track of Lemkin's arguments and to divine overall what he is talking about.

In order for civilians to be recognized as part of the formal armed forces of a belligerent land, they had to comply with four plain stipulations, spelled out in the very first article of the Hague Convention of July 29, 1899, and repeated verbatim in the first article in the Annex to the Hague Convention of October 18, 1907, ratified by all the principal powers involved in World War Two except Soviet Russia (but by the Czar's government, before them). These were:

1. To be commanded by a person responsible for his subordinates;

2. To have a fixed distinctive emblem recognizable at a distance;

3. To carry arms openly;

4. To conduct their operations in accordance with the laws and customs of war.

In the case of a territory which was about to be invaded and was not yet occupied, the Hague Conventions recognized as a legitimate part of that country's armed forces the inhabitants of such, "spontaneously" taking up arms, to be recognized as belligerents only "if they carry arms openly," and fought according to the laws and customs of war, even if not having time to comply with the other two stipulations. Under these circumstances, such civilians were entitled to be treated like the uniformed troops of their country and to be accorded the status of prisoners of war if captured.

In the U.S. Department of the Army Field Manual FM27-10, *The Law of Land Warfare,* Chapter 3, "Prisoners of War," Section I, "Persons Entitled to be Treated as Prisoners of War," the four above stipulations of the Hague Conventions are repeated verbatim in Paragraph 61, with considerable elaboration following on treatment of prisoners of war. It is evident from this that those who fail to observe these requirements are not recognized as legitimate belligerents, and, in Section II, "Persons Not Entitled to be Treated as Prisoners of War," the Manual FM27-10 spells out who they are in paragraphs

80, 81 and 82 of this section, and what shall happen to them if apprehended, as follows:

80. Individuals Not of Armed Forces Who Engage in Hostilities

Persons, such as guerrillas and partisans, who take up arms and commit hostile acts without having complied with the conditions prescribed by the laws of war for recognition as belligerents (see Paragraph 61 herein), are, when captured by the injured party, not entitled to be treated as prisoners of war and may be tried and sentenced to execution or imprisonment.

81. Individuals Not of Armed Forces Who Commit Hostile Acts

Persons who, without having complied with the conditions prescribed by the laws of war for recognition as belligerents (see Paragraph 61 herein), commit hostile acts about or behind the lines of the enemy are not to be treated as prisoners of war and may be tried and sentenced to execution or imprisonment . . . .

82. Penalties for the Foregoing

Persons in the foregoing categories who have attempted, committed, or conspired to commit hostile or belligerent acts are subject to the extreme penalty of death because of the danger inherent in their conduct. Lesser penalties may, however, be imposed.

As to what the American Army was taught to expect from a defeated and occupied country insofar as its civilian populace was concerned, we may turn in this same Manual FM27-10, to Chapter Six, "Occupation," Section VIII, "Security of the Occupant: Penal Legislation and Procedure," Paragraph 432, "Enforcement of Obedience":

Subject to the restrictions imposed by international law, the occupant can demand and enforce from the inhabitants of occupied territory such obedience as may be necessary for the security of its forces, for the maintenance of law and order, and for the proper administration of the country. It is the duty of the inhabitants to carry on their ordinary peaceful pursuits, to behave in an absolutely peaceful manner, to take no part whatever in the hostilities carried on, to refrain from all injurious acts toward the troops or in respect to their operations, and to render strict obedience to the orders of the occupant.

In the edition of the British *Manual of Military Law* which was in circulation during World War Two, in Chapter XIV, "The Law and Usages of War on Land," Paragraph 442 specifically identifies the behavior also described in the US *The Law of Land Warfare*, Paragraphs

80 and 81, as a "war crime." The paragraph reads as follows (note especially *ii*):

> War crimes may be divided into four different classes:
>
> (*i*) Violations of the recognized rules of warfare by members of the armed forces.
>
> (*ii*) Illegitimate hostilities in arms committed by individuals who are not members of the armed forces.
>
> (*iii*) Espionage and war treason.
>
> (*iv*) Marauding.

It may be seen therefore that during the Second World War, participation in armed combat by civilians, except under narrowly defined terms and circumstances as spelled out in the Hague Conventions, was considered by the Anglo-American armed forces, for sure, a very serious offense, punishable by death, as such enterprise by *franc-tireurs* had always been in the past. That it was also held in the same light by the armed forces of the other countries involved in the war, including those of the enemy lands, can be assumed. We may now get back to the underpinning of Raphael Lemkin's main allegations in *Axis Rule,* with occasional references back to the materials quoted above as various pertinent aspects come into view. Since his book is primarily about a military *occupation,* that of the Germans, such an account should deal with two main topics: the behavior of the occupiers, or "occupants," to use the terminology of the Hague Conventions, and *also* the occupied. Since the book tells us virtually nothing about the behavior of the occupied, it has been construed here as necessary to describe the objective theoretical conditions relating to occupied people and their lands as found in the rules of land warfare. It is also necessary to spend some time on the behavior of the occupied populace, since it often has a serious effect on the behavior of the occupants. This dimension is also missing for the most part from Lemkin's survey, allowing one to assume that all actions by the Axis powers in occupation were initiated without inspiration or instigation resulting from the actions taken by the occupied, or the result of wholly capricious acts upon a wholly passive, inert, and unresponsive populace. The latter calls to mind a remarkable bit of narrative by August von Knieriem, the defense counsel for one of the defendants in the second round of Nuremberg trials, largely staged by the U.S. Army, and masterminded by the ineffable Telford Taylor, who over 35 years later was still going about the USA delivering lectures on what a great job he and his associates had done. In his book on these, *The Nuremberg Trials*

(Chicago: Regnery, 1959), von Knieriem related at one point (p. 358) the following:

> Partisan activity was of tremendous scope. According to the testimony of the Chief of the General Staff of the [German] Army, the interruptions of railway traffic caused by partisans amounted to 1,200 to 1,600 a day. To these were added raids on shelters, vehicles, and small units, acts of sabotage against cables, bridges, broadcasting stations, and air-fields; acts of violence against the peaceful population —all in all, several thousand war crimes per day. [Pantaleimon K.] Ponomarenko himself, the leader of the Russian partisans, has stated in a publication that 500,000 Germans were killed in guerrilla warfare.

A quarter of a century after the end of World War II there developed in countries outside the Soviet orbit a literature which sought to reduce drastically the scope and membership of the Soviet partisan effort, 1939-1945. This partially coincided with an effort which began mainly in the early 1970s to eliminate previous mention of the vast movement of Central European Jews to the Soviet Union after 1939. Since there already existed various bibliographies which mentioned immense Jewish participation in these partisan activities, it created a problem for this new historical enterprise. And the latter had no effect on the Soviet sources which imperturbably promoted their own version, conceivably superior to that of distantly-located long-ex-post-facto efforts to dismantle the Soviet accounts.

Though William B. Ziff, in his long and boastful account of Jewish military prowess (Ziff, "The Jew as Soldier, Strategist and Military Advisor," in Dagobert D. Runes, ed., *The Hebrew Impact on Western Civilization* [New York: Citadel Press, 1951], pp. 240-312), noticeably avoided mention of the Jewish component in both the Soviet Red Army and its civilian partisan auxiliaries, and concentrated mainly on performance in Poland and adjoining regions, the Soviet chroniclers have not. One of the more remarkable commentaries was that by Professor Joseph Braginsky in the lavishly illustrated English language magazine *Soviet Life* ("Jews in the USSR—Equals Among Equals," June, 1973, p. 49):

> It is in the Soviet Union that the Jews have found their real motherland; they proved their loyalty by fighting together with the other Soviet peoples against fascist Germany. Almost 340,000 Jews were awarded orders and medals for valor and labor achievement during the war years. The title of Hero of the Soviet Union was conferred on 117, and Hero of Socialist Labor on 71.

In actuality, far from representing an outside figure on the performance of partisans in Soviet service in World War II, Ponomarenko's was one of the more conservative, when compared, for instance, to the declarations found scattered throughout the semi-official six-volume *History of the Great Patriotic War of the Soviet Union* (1960-1963). Citing from page 281 of volume VI of this work as his source, the Soviet historian Grigory Deborin stated,

> In the Great Patriotic War Soviet partisans killed, wounded or captured 1,500,000 Nazi soldiers, occupation officials and collaborationists . . . . (Deborin, *Secrets of the Second World War* [Moscow, USSR: Progress Publishers, 1971], p. 211.)

The essence of the problem was succinctly captured in two brief news stories on page two of the New York *Times* for February 29, 1944. The first, a United Press story datelined Moscow related, "Three hundred thousand Germans have been killed, 3,000 enemy trains derailed and almost 1,200 Nazi tanks and armored cars destroyed by Soviet partisan bands in the last two years, the magazine *Bolshevik,* organ of the Central Committee of the Communist Party, reported today [Feb. 28]. Among the German troops killed were thirty generals, and about 6,300 officers and 1,500 pilots, *Bolshevik* said. In addition, the partisans blew up 3,200 railroad and highway bridges and destroyed 474 planes, 378 guns, 618 cars, 1,400 trucks and 895 ammunition dumps."

The second, a few inches away, was an Associated Press story datelined from London, and was a digest of a Moscow radio broadcast heard in England. It alleged that the German occupation forces had "tortured to death, shot, or poisoned in murder vans" more than 195,000 Soviet citizens during the occupation of the city of Kiev, in the southwestern USSR, since late 1941. (Some thought this was the beginning of the famed Babi Yar atrocity story.)

The likelihood that both these reports might have been grave exaggerations is not the point, knowing of Soviet willingness to supply their English and American "allies" with some of their most eagerly sought reading, atrocity stories and accounts claiming near-total destruction of their enemy, both of which often approached the absurd. What these two stories represented from a legal point of view, which Lemkin understood very well, was the conflict between an army fighting simultaneously against a massive civilian component and the excesses resulting from the saturation spread of such a confrontation. The traditional extreme distaste for soldiers to engage civilians in armed combat needs no development here, it being no different in the war of 1939-1945 than at any other time before or since. But the immense encouragement of such a situation especially in the last four years of the war in Europe created an irretrievable circumstance. The enemies of Germany enjoyed a schizoid field day in simultaneously teaching their own troops to deal with civilian combatants with maximum severity while bawling at the top of their lungs in approval of the same behavior in the lands occupied by the Germans. Lemkin, writing a book about an occupation, both in title and content, managed to avoid coming to grips with this paradox. His mustering of "law" in contexts where it did his case good was expectable, but in those areas where it would certainly have not performed this service his negligence was characteristic of all the self-serving expositions of the wartime masquerading as examinations of "law" or legal situations. That the winning "Allies" were to brush the entire matter aside after the war and to try to escape coming to terms with the problem by such preposterous operations as declaring *ex post facto* that a large part of their defeated enemy were just "criminals" simply made impossible a kind of rough *quid pro quo* eventuating.

That all the "victors" were to engage in brutal and grievously defeating experiences of their own in later years with the very same kind of ugly armed conflict with civilians all over Asia and Africa was fully merited. Nothing has approached in futile sadness *their* explanations of wholesale ineptness in dealing with this problem in a dozen wars, all of which have been lost. The dishonest gloating over the predicament of the Germans, 1941-1945, in their unsuccessful coping with the phenomenon of illegal civilian participation in war has not abated, however, despite the manuals of law governing their fighting forces still including the most ferocious prescriptions for dealing with potential civilian adversaries in any new conflicts likely to eventuate. The tribute to compound hypocrisy is impressive.

The various Nuremberg tribunals staffed with Germany's conquerors may have decided well in advance that all acts committed by Germany's enemies were irrelevant to the matter at hand in running their incredible kangaroo court proceedings, but the fact still stands that what has been described above were *still* war crimes of a sort, or at least punishable offenses as construed by the Hague Conventions and the American and British Armies, rulebooks of land warfare. Raphael Lemkin should have discussed this factor at length in his book, but barely mentioned this illegal warfare, a strange omission on the part of a lawyer with pretenses to being a great world international legal mind. When he did bring it up it was in the context of a denunciation of the Germans for trying to suppress it, and he came close to incorporating the suppression of these infractions under his omnibus legal construct of "genocide."

Lemkin said nothing about it in *Axis Rule,* but in biographical information furnished *Current Biography* half a dozen years later, he claimed to have been a civilian *franc-tireur* himself against the Germans in Poland for six months, sustaining a wound, and ultimately being spirited off to Sweden as described elsewhere. Thus he was himself engaged in activities not protected by the Hague Conventions, and subject to execution had he been captured. However, Lemkin interpreted the Hague Conventions in a special way. Even though a country's military forces had been defeated and the country occupied, as long as any civilian continued to oppose the enemy, the land could be viewed as not yet completely subdued, and he insisted that they were covered by the Hague rules applying to land warfare (*Axis Rule*, pp. 248-249.) He thus turned the Hague rules on their head, and in the case of the Germans in Serbia, he insisted the Germans were in violation of them in trying to assert their authority on a country side Lemkin insisted was never subjugated.

What Lemkin left out was the part played by Stalin and Churchill in supplying the fresh insertion of guerrillas and weaponry, keeping the irregular "partisan" war going. Lemkin in his selective indignation blended several kinds of different things and facts when it came to this subject, conveniently neglecting to admit that most of this guerrilla activity was induced after a period of relative quiet, especially following the entry of the Soviet Union into the war late in June, 1941. Thus Lemkin looked upon all civilian warfare against the Germans everywhere in the German-occupied regions as some form of bona fide local patriotic resistance, regardless of its clash with the Hague rules, and surely was in clear violation of the stipulations spelled out in both the British and American armies' published rulebooks on land warfare.

A recent effort to incorporate the changes in the laws of warfare as reflected in the four Geneva Conventions of August 12, 1949 is to be found in *International Law — The Conduct of Armed Conflict and Air Operations* (Judge Advocate General Activities, Air Force Pamphlet AFP 110-31, Washington, D.C.: Department of the Air Force, 1976). This "pamphlet" is a thick double-column manual corresponding to the Department of the Army's Field Manual FM 27-10, but including much spongy commentary which is heavily interlarded with Allied World War Two and Nuremberg-era propaganda, seeking to evade or excuse Allied ignoring or violating of the Hague Agreements, while justifying the post-May, 1945 course of action taken against the defeated enemy. It is a substantially unconvincing account. The effort to make sense out of the 1949 Geneva Conventions, especially those parts dealing with the suggested innovations involving the presence of a neutral country in each of the belligerents, seeking to oversee enforcement of the provisions of the

Conventions with respect to civilians, is especially feeble. The recognition that these 1949 additions to the laws of warfare have gravely extended possible civilian participation in the event of new wars is made in a hesitating manner (p. 11-2), belatedly recognizing the German problems with such irregulars by complaining of the "liberation" and "informal partisan" "armies" participating against the Americans in Vietnam. The air of rigid righteousness toward the Germans, insisting on their toleration of such vicious participants in the 1939-1945 war, which was universal among Allied propagandists, is quite lacking now in this querulous commentary after having experienced it themselves for a change.

The ambivalent beauties of guerrilla warfare and the sinuosities of its possible legal interpretations did not reach their peak in terms of hypocritical adaptation regardless of the resulting situation until after the war, and the insertion in the August 12, 1949 Geneva Convention regarding the "rights" of populations of occupied countries of a strict prohibition against the "mass forcible transfers" of people from the occupied country to any other country whatever (see Paragraph 382 of Section III, "Rights of the Population of Occupied Territory," in Chapter 6 of the Army Field Manual, *The Law of Land Warfare,* "Occupation".) Technically, since the adoption of this most recent Geneva Convention, land armies theoretically must fight around and through civilian populaces, and risking in the process an algebraic-ratio increase in the possibilities of sustaining grievous guerrilla-caused casualties. That this results in vastly increased dangers to the occupied civilians and encourages a form of warfare which largely fails to discriminate between or among any of the people in its path few if any care to discuss, only part of which became evident in the Vietnam War. One consequence of this was the famous synthetic case forged against Lt. William Calley of the U.S. Army, surely one of the high-water examples of supersaturated hypocrisy ever strung together by shamefully devious and malicious forces anywhere. But this matter did not exist in World War Two, and mass deportation of civilians as a precaution against possible future hostile and lethal behavior was undertaken by both sides. Lemkin conveniently chose to dwell exclusively upon such action by the Axis enemy, seeking to create the impression it was unique and exclusive with them.

In making so prominent a point as he did in charging the Germans with making war on the "people," instead of the State and armies of an enemy, Lemkin had to skirt very widely the matter of massive civilian involvement, to the number of hundreds of thousands, counting the entire war zones. His smothering of attention to the illegality of *franc-tireur* resistance in many areas, and concentrating on regions where the issue had not been decided, created a vast gray area where the legal status of it all might be debated indefinitely. This made it possible for him to fling the cloak of immunity from reprisal upon these participants in the war for thousands of acts every day of everything from common sabotage and gun-running to the gunning down of German soldiery. The expostulation against repression of this and the attempt to pillory such attempts as reprehensible, and, in turn, illegal, provided generous support from such a legalist as Lemkin to Stalinist and (even before that) to Maoist politics by default if not by intent. Lemkin gave no evidence of recognizing that Stalinist patriotism imbued and dominated very large parts of "resistance" fighters in every country occupied by German forces, especially after June, 1941.

This in turn had a direct bearing on Lemkin's views of minorities and war, and his casual assumption that they could bear arms as civilians against an uniformed enemy, but suffer no consequences of defeat. In the case of Jews, presumably according to his outlook, an entire minority might make war on an enemy such as the German forces, take their lives at will or when able to do so, as *franc-tireurs,* and engage in boundless sabotage and assistance to the enemies of the Germans, without having to consider the consequences. The interlock between the various elements involved in guerrilla warfare, whatever may have been their differing motives and intentions and objectives in so engaging, presents different problems in trying to resolve them while analyzing the basic approach of Lemkin in his legalizing of the entire situation. The minority question will be dealt with exhaustively in due course, but it cannot be separated in true isolation from all the other factors involved in the war. When we see Lemkin listing as reprehensible a German order for the control of guerrilla activity against German soldiers in Serbia in the fall of 1941, singling it out for special mention under "anti-guerrilla legislation," one not only can see his attitude toward military affairs and the same kind of international law he was to bring up repeatedly against the Germans, but one can also see this in the context of the entire war and know why he did this.

In building his case against the Germans, Lemkin had to be very selective about international law violation. A sign of his partisanship on the subject was his inclusion as a special appendix to his book only those articles of the 1907 Annex to the Hague Convention (Nos. 41-55) which applied to occupation. As a violator of the very first one himself, by admission later on, it did not suit his case to include the forty articles prior to those he cited, of which his partisans and protagonists had surely broken at least Nos. 22 and 25 by their strategic air war against German cities, admitted after the war to be a matter of policy and not of simple retaliation or reprisal, as the wartime propaganda departments encouraged the Allied populaces to believe. In the same way that concentration camps established by the Axis drew Lemkin's heated denunciation while avoiding all mention of the same institution in Britain, France, the USA and particularly the USSR, he found it possible to cite the 1907 Hague Convention repeatedly in allegations of German violation thereof, while failing to notice any breaking of its articles on the part of his patrons. How irrelevant Lemkin's hosts thought the Hague Rules were awaited war's end and the termination of the Nuremberg trials. When Telford Taylor, in his final report to the Secretary of the U.S. Army on these trials, reaffirmed his response to counsel for the defense when they cited Allied breaking of the Hague Rules by blandly asserting they were obsolete, in his declaration, "Many of the provisions of the Hague Convention regarding unlawful means of combat were antiquarian," (von Knieriem, *Nuremberg Trials,* pp. 443-444), Lemkin is not known to have uttered a public rebuke of Taylor. By that time the Hague Rules had served Lemkin's and the prosecution's purpose; it was perfectly all right now to dismiss them as "antiquarian," another step in the outrageous process of using laws two ways, applicable to German behavior but irrelevant when an attempt was made to make them stand in the case of charges of violation by their accusers. That they were a veritable nuisance by then to the Allied prosecution was quite obvious.

There are several subjects and sub-topics, including Raphael Lemkin's social and political philosophy and his concept of the relations of the parts of a social system to one another, his strange total silence on favored countries such as Poland and the Soviet Union, the concentration camp issue, the problems of Europe's Jewry, among others, which cannot be treated separately, since they have been woven into his overall major issue of "genocide" to the point where they are part of an inseparable garment, and must be examined and discussed in this total situation. For that reason, it is incumbent upon us to move to that aspect of his work, which despite the structure of his book eventually became its central issue, *malgré lui.* From that day to this, the word "genocide" calls to mind its inventor, Raphael Lemkin.

Chapter Four

PIÈCE DE RÉSISTANCE: 'GENOCIDE'

genocide, *n.* Extermination of a national or racial group as a planned move; coined by Dr. Raphael Lemkin, 1944 [sic]. *The American College Dictionary* (1958 ed.), p. 506.

Mass murder of a race, people, or minority group for political [sic] reasons or the like. *The New Century Dictionary of the English Language* (1959), vol. I, p. 645.

The deliberate and systematic destruction of a racial, political [sic], or cultural group. *Webster's Seventh New Collegiate Dictionary* (1965), p. 348.

The systematic, planned annihilation of a racial, political [sic] or cultural group. *The American Heritage Dictionary of the English Language* (1969), p. 550.

Decimation or extermination of a racial, ethnic, religious or nationality group *by a more powerful co-occupant of a territory.* Prof. Donald J. Bogue (University of Chicago), in *Encyclopedia International* (New York: Grolier, Inc., 1972), vol. 7, p. 503. (Emphasis added.)

Acts committed with intent to destroy in whole or in part a national, ethnical, racial or religious group. (Definition in Article 2 of the United Nations Genocide Convention, in 1973 UN publication *The Crime of Genocide.*)

There is universal agreement that Raphael Lemkin invented the word "genocide," as well as most of the many definitions of the manifestations of this new crime which took shape over the succeeding decade. What is not clear is precisely when he came up with this idea. The word first appears in the preface he wrote for his book *Axis Rule in Occupied Europe,* which was dated November 15, 1943, but which was not published for over a year after that. Whether he brought the word over with him from Poland or Sweden or whether he conceived it in the USA we do not know from official evidence. His first elucidation is as follows:

> The practice of extermination of nations and ethnic groups as carried out by the invaders is called by the author "genocide," a term derived from the Greek word *genos* (tribe, race) and the Latin *cide* (by way of analogy, see homocide [sic], fratricide) . . . . (*Axis Rule,* preface, p. *xi.*)

Ignoring that there was no analogy, the latter two words being entirely Latin in root, not a hybrid of Greek and Latin, and that "homicide" was misspelled, we are dealing with the first instance in print of one of the most fateful etymological inventions of all time. And we are about to see, upon very little additional examination, a tactic used many times by Lemkin, the mixing of various categories of facts and the blending of things which do not mean the same thing whatever, thus producing a mélange almost defying subsequent analysis.

Lemkin came up with a modification of his original definition of "genocide" on page 78 of his Chapter IX, "Genocide," as follows: "By 'genocide' we mean the destruction of a nation or ethnic group," further clarified in this manner: "Genocide has two phases: one, destruction of the national pattern of the oppressed group; the other, the imposition of the national pattern of the oppressor," adding this final elaboration on his theme: "Denationalization was the word used in the past to describe the destruction of a national pattern."

One observes at once a basic contradictory collision between these two definitions. In the first, Lemkin defines "genocide" as the *extermination* of a "nation" or "ethnic group." In the second he defines "genocide" as the *destruction* of one of these two, and its replacement, in terms of its "national pattern," by that of this element's "oppressor." Now—if a people are *exterminated,* one can hardly have anything left to transform into something else. The nature or sense of definition #2 is that the *destruction* is not physical in the sense of killing everyone, or even *anyone,* but of imposing a totally different cultural identity upon them, which is most obviously several light years away from the total obliteration of the physical people. Lemkin could not make up his mind which of these two states or situations he wanted recognized as "genocide," and, with some help, later on, and after processing through the word mills at the United Nations, came up with a definition incorporating *both* of them. As a result, he and his supporters were able to enjoy the luxury of considering both total extermination and fundamental cultural transformation of a living group to be possible, *seriatim*. And to this day the exponents of "genocide" cannot decide which of these they want to be understood as the true understanding of their verbalism. The former has become the vulgar conception.

Lemkin is the source of additional confusion in his employment of the word "nation." In the first three pages of his chapter "Genocide," he is content to use the word in the conventional sense, a distinct people occupying a specific piece of territory, and roughly equivalent to a national state, or country. But in later use in the chapter (p. 91), what he meant by "nation" was a recognizable minority residing in any national state. Hence, in his preface and later in his discourse in the liberal weekly *The Nation*, he proceeds to blend the two, speaking of the Axis powers and their "destruction of entire nations," hyperbolic legalistic showboating and propagandistic dramaturgy which really had no relation to what some thought he meant, the dissolution of the Versailles Treaty synthetic states of Poland, Czecho-Slovakia and Yugoslavia, the latter two primarily by the German recognition of the new states of Slovakia and Croatia, respectively. But the confusion he was to cause here was to encourage additional misunderstanding later on as well.

On still another issue, Lemkin left a legacy of indecision, his failure to make it conclusive as to how he construed the commission of the new crime of "genocide" to be indictable. In a rambling and confused discourse comprising the last five pages of his short chapter on "genocide" in *Axis Rule*, he drifted and swayed back and forth as to whether it would be conceived as an individual or collective offense. This he did not resolve until later, when his new crime began to run into competition with the postwar UN Declaration of Human Rights, by which time Lemkin was set on "genocide" being construed as a *collective* crime against a *group*, and presumably also *committed* by a group, a view which was calculated to provide a pesky problem for future prosecutors, unless in a Communist country where such proceedings were commonplace.

Before going any further, it might be profitable to go at once to Lemkin's ponderous 400 pages of Axis laws which brought up most of the rear section of his three-pound book, to see what he and his numerous coterie of helpers had found in support of this arresting new legal proposition. Scattered about this mass of mainly dull and unreadable legal and quasi-legal documentation were decrees and orders which Lemkin specifically arranged under the heading

"Genocide Legislation." They comprise *in toto* about three per cent of the entire collection, counting those specifically designated as such plus those additionally referred to in his text, which seem to be afterthoughts, prepared after the collection had been formally put together. There is as a result of this lack of coordination between the text and the documentary section a difficulty in locating the actual law he cites in his text, a half-dozen of them appearing in sections which are not designated as "Genocide Legislation." There appear to be only six of the latter, as well.

The first of these "genocidal" laws (pp. 399-402) consist of the 1st, 2nd and 6th orders designated as "measures against Jews" issued by the German Chief of Military Administration in Occupied France on September 27 and October 18, 1940 and February 7, 1942. The first called for the registration of all Jews residing in Occupied France, and forbade those who had fled elsewhere from coming back. It also required that all profit-making businesses owned by Jews in Occupied France to be designated as such. The second was an expansion of the first insofar as it dealt with the subject of required registration of Jewish-owned business enterprises. The sixth established a 8p.m. – 6a.m. curfew for Jews, as well as a prohibition against Jews moving from their residences as of February 7, 1942 to some other location. Violation of these orders involved fines and imprisonment if violators were detected and convicted.

The second "genocidal" law (pp. 440-443) was an order of August 6, 1940 by the German Chief of Civil Administration in Luxembourg, which stipulated that the *official* language of the country insofar as it was used in the judicial and educational system, as well as *official* publications of all kinds, was to be German; this was spelled out in another order of September 14, 1940. In this same "genocide" section was an order of January 31, 1941 requiring Luxembourg nationals and aliens alike to adopt a Germanic *first* name, while "recommending" that they Germanicize their family name as well if it was not already a Germanic one. The final item in this section was a decree of January 20, 1941 requiring the registration in Luxembourg of all persons engaged in the enterprises of painting, architecture, design and drawing, music, literature and the theatre, on pain of being forbidden to work in these fields should they be detected failing to register.

The third listing of a "genocidal law" (p. 504), a peculiar one which, along with that which was listed next, will be commented upon subsequently, was an order signed by Adolf Hitler himself, along with General Keitel and Hitler's deputy Lammers, on July 28, 1942, which provided for a wide scale of economic benefits which would accrue to Norwegian and Dutch women who became mothers of children fathered by German occupation soldiers. Such subsidies were intended, according to the language of the order, to remove "any disadvantage from the mothers and promoting the development of the children."

Lemkin's fourth category of "Genocide Legislation" (pp. 552-555) was along the lines of the above, an order of October 29, 1941 signed by Hans Frank, the Governor General of Poland, making it possible for a person of German origin but not possessing German nationality, though residing in Poland, to obtain a certificate which would document his German origin, and another order signed by Frank on March 10, 1942 establishing a grant of child subsidy to families of Germans resident in the Polish Government General (a vast area of southern Poland occupied by the Germans but not intended for German annexation). The family, to qualify for this small subsidy, had to have at least three minor children already.

The last section of "genocide legislation" (pp. 625-627) were three laws put into effect in the new state of Croatia, seceded from Yugoslavia, signed by its chief of state, Dr. Ante Pavelic. One nullified any legal business transaction between Jews, or between Jews and others, made within two months of the proclamation of the independence of the State of Croatia, *if* its value exceeded 100,000 dinars, unless it had been approved by the Croatian Minister of Justice. The second prohibited the use of the Cyrillic alphabet in Croatia, and the third conferred Croatian nationality only on persons of "Aryan origin" and who had furthermore not participated in activities hostile to the establishment of the "independent State of Croatia."

In his text, which preceded the legal documents, and obviously from the context of the former, written after the latter were collected, there are further references to "genocide" laws which Lemkin did not mark specifically as such, one on p. 139 referring to laws in Czecho-Slovakia authorizing the repressing of guerrilla resistance warfare and presumably involving German cultural smothering of Czech nationalistic expressions, mainly of a musical and literary nature, and on page 143 an extensive charge against the Croatians for "genocide" against the Jews, though no deaths of anyone were mentioned, but concentrating on deprivation of citizenship, prohibition against practice of certain professions, introduction of forced labor and also deportations.

Lemkin on pp. 196 and 213 again referred to the laws in Luxembourg and Norway involving attempted official Germanicization in some limited areas in the former and the support for the children of German soldier-fathers in the latter, followed (p. 236) by praise for Red guerrilla activity in the USSR and the indirect identification of the suppression of this as "genocide."

As an afterthought Lemkin threw in another "Genocide Legislation" section (p. 601), an order signed by the German commander in
occupied Serbia of December 22, 1941, which established the death
penalty for anyone apprehended *sheltering* Jews or hiding them, but
mentioning no penalties applicable to Jews themselves in this case.
Almost all of this order applied to Jewish property, not to their
persons, calling for the registration of all property, as well as con-
tracts involving the purchase of or barter for Jewish assets on the
part of non-Jews. The earlier part of the order seemed to be directed
against the concealment of Jews returned as guerrilla fighters, which
hardly was uncommon.

And bringing up the tail end of this curious assemblage of "genocidic" legislation, as designated by Lemkin, was a statement in his
text (p. 249) to the effect that "genocidal" measures had been inflicted upon Jews in Serbia in addition by passage of a law which
apparently deprived some Jews of making a livelihood by specifically
forbidding them to practice "professions." Lemkin's reference was to
p. 596 of the legal documents, which turned out to be an order
signed by "The Military Commander in Serbia," dated May 21, 1941,
which stated: "Jews and gypsies or persons married to Jews and
gypsies shall not be admitted to the operation" of "cabarets,
vaudeville houses, and similar places of entertainment." These were
the "professions" from which they were barred.

It may be observed that the foregoing is an incredibly minuscule
and almost comically petty bag of evidence to support so horrendous
and grim an allegation as that of Raphael Lemkin, which would be
both true and at the same time in many ways a grave understatement.
But it was never Lemkin's evidence which made such an impact on
the world at the conclusion of the war ending in 1945 and for a
decade and a half thereafter. It was his rhetoric and his success in
United Nations politicking during that time. That his charges of mass
murder and related sentiments took up a microscopically small
fraction of one per cent of his literary labors in behalf of the
Carnegie Foundation is a point worth making, but the promotional
machine behind what he had to say weighs exceedingly more in consequence than the quality or substance of all his literary effort many
times compounded. Nevertheless a somewhat longer look at his work
is called for, and when placed against the backdrop of the evidence
set forth in support of his thesis, it will be easier to estimate its
psychological and philosophical sources as well as its unstated
premises and submerged objectives.

In order to get at the real impact of Lemkin's product one must
re-work much history of the war time, and deal with his efforts as

largely a part of the psychological war propaganda being waged against the Axis. That his real evidence in support of his allegations is pitifully sparse has to be examined parallel with the impact of his prestigious supporters and patrons, who were always far more concerned with appearances than they were with realities. One might hope that something as formidable as "genocide" was to become might have had a somewhat more substantial basis, but this has not been the first thing of its kind whose reputation for substance has grown in an inverse ratio to the facts capable of being mobilized in its support.

It is hard to get at the dimensions of Lemkin's concept of "genocide" by trying to wade through his hazy and wandering prose, heavily emotional and sentimental at one point, coldly and distantly abstract at another. The more he proceeds, the more obsessive becomes his fascination with his new word, which he ends up applying to almost everything he can observe in Axis operations in occupied Europe. At the same time his brain child is sprawling in all directions, as he attempted a more or less succinct definition for the crime it was supposed to describe, there is a tendency for his subject to get away from him. Soon one is only incidentally involved in trying to understand Axis rule in occupied Europe. That he and his associates eventually emerged, after many years of polishing, with an omnibus prohibition against many things which were lumped together as "genocide" does not strike all as remarkable, since its vagueness in many ways contributed to its increasing obsolescence in the real world as its emotional apparition aspect grew in international imaginations. But "genocide" persists as an appellation mainly employed to describe something going on in someone else's country.

Probably more important than Raphael Lemkin's legal theorizing and rationalizing was his political and social philosophy. To come up with something like "genocide" required a particular way of looking at the world. The political and social thinking behind his views of minorities required him to envisage them as always basically passive and lacking initiative. They are always lying there, inert, and doing nothing to warrant their being assaulted by ravening majorities. They start nothing, and are indeed theorized as too feeble or too innocent to begin action resulting in discomfort, or danger, possibly, to majorities. Hence Lemkin sees them in a permanent moral glow, always the sinned-against, always the victims of glowering majorities, who in turn are always acting in a criminal manner when they attempt any curtailment of minority action.

Lemkin is not very lucid where he tries to establish the basis of "genocide." His tireless reiteration that its nature is conspirational, and that the acts are so self-evidentially injurious to a minority, that they have to be intended and deliberate, is not overwhelmingly convincing. His lightfooted traipsing into the minefield of motivation had aspects of a pseudo-Freudian analysis, but his legal thinking tends to invade from all directions, with too much of the prosecuting attorney's tendency to find the allegation equal to proof despite any diminution of impact resulting from paucity of evidence.

Though Lemkin seems to hide what he has in mind by concentrating on the real or likely tribulations of "groups," from the context of his work one knows he is thinking of minority groups. His examples from history, which he somewhat later advanced as the plausible reason for his becoming concerned about "genocide," all involve tiny enclaves of people, and their predicament usually a consequence of the unfortunate outcome of a war somewhere. He does not seem ever to have conceived of a minority becoming involved in as bad if not worse crimes than those he charged to or alleged against majorities. An unstated aspect of Lemkin appears to be that minorities have a blank check to go forth and dispose of majorities in whatever cause they may care to concern themselves with, and are not to be considered to be acting "genocidically" when so engaged. The omission of *political* and *economic* categories in his list of genocidically-endangered "groups," a reality in the definition of the crime of "genocide" to this day, gives an indication of that kind of thinking. (It can be seen of course that these omissions have gravely undermined the "genocide" concept over the years, and at the same time have provided sophisticated elements anywhere a loophole whereby they can escape the charge of "genocide" quite easily by construing their unwanted minority group or groups as *political* adversaries acting as a subversive element within the body politic in behalf of a foreign enemy, and subjected to annihilation for *that* reason and not for racial, religious, ethnic or cultural factors.)

In view of the above, Lemkin's claimed inspiration for his "genocide" crusade deserves a brief span of attention here. There is little doubt that it was mainly a subjective reaction to the world history of roughly the previous decade to publication of his book, though, in posting his historical examples of "genocide," his very selective presentation totally overlooked that it was all a very ancient matter. He shunned antiquity as a rich source of the events which he claimed shocked him so at the moment, and neglected in its entirety the record in the Old Testament, taken as indisputable fact by Judaic and Christian believers alike, which related, sometimes in a boastful way, of a lengthy string of combat among peoples in which the vanquished were massacred to the very last person; in the modern world Lemkin would never have been able to find anything faintly comparable to that. But establishing the venerability of "genocide" was not his first priority objective.

The examples which he did give as having inspired him to go forth on his global joust with "genocide" were extremely limited, though with passing time and the increasing fashionability of his campaign, the number of examples grew. But they persisted in being tiny enclaves whose unfortunate fate was related to the momentary incidents relating mainly to defeat in local wars. There were no mentions of long-standing racial or socio-cultural collisions, only catastrophic momentary events, which lend no credence to his thesis, since a basic condition of his concept, "genocide," the *deliberate, planned intent* of such efforts at eliminating a "group," was exceedingly hard to believe when the subject involved very brief time spans; deliberate planning takes time.

Missing entirely from his catalog of these grievous events which he claimed shook him so profoundly were things like the Irish experience at English hands for three centuries in their own country, during which enough of the elements of what Lemkin had styled "genocide" had taken place to make possible a multi-volume work by him had he chosen this subject, but it does not appear that anything of this magnitude even grazed his consciousness, of course. The middle of World War II was not the time to bring up facts like this, with America deeply wrapped in embrace with England in their global battle. The circumstances of world politics encouraged the exclusive concentration on details which could be propped up at the door of the enemy, or to the citing of events so obscure and so distantly located that even historians could be counted on not to know what he was talking about, such as his agonizing over the "600 Christian Assyrians" allegedly murdered in Iraq circa 1933. This memorialization of "genocide" in the past could be counted on to stir nearly no one in the West, since the fraction of people who had ever heard of it must surely have been so small that an electron microscope of our own day might have been hard-pressed even to detect it.[1]

One factor in neglecting things like the three-century subjection of the Irish may have been Lemkin's fixation on minorities. He seemed by default to see nothing wrong in "genocide" being waged by minorities against majorities, which is how he could have interpreted the English presence in Ireland. Had the USA been Lemkin's adversary instead of his host and refuge, protector and benefactor, one can imagine the bonanza he could have created for himself out of the history of the English colonists and their descendants with respect to the Indian tribes from 1607 onward. The Indian experience at the hands of the Spanish also called for memorialization.

But this was carefully omitted as well. A very recent event had occurred, however, in view of Lemkin's rage at mass deportations at the hands of the Germans and their allies (he carefully dodged Stalin's mass deportation of half a million Volga Germans a short time earlier as well): the Roosevelt regime had deported the entire Japanese ethnic minority from the U.S. Pacific Coast over two years prior to the publication of his book. But no population transfers unless undertaken by the Germans made Lemkin's catalog of dishonor as peripheral "genocidic" operations (it goes without saying that Lemkin did not breathe a word about the millions of his fellow countrymen Poles moved into Siberia and Central Asia by Stalin, 1939-1941; this would surely have poisoned his rather clear picture of one-sided sin.)

All in all, what Lemkin cited as his principal motivation leading to his grim invention in international law was indeed sparse and flimsy in content, but what might be likely to stir a pettifogger turning over the lesser debris of history. However, if one keeps firmly in mind that Lemkin's big book was a narrow and partisan legal brief and not history except by the most wondrous stretching of the imagination, it can be understood why most of the real examples which might be cited to help launch his exotic concept, "genocide," which he could have dredged up from the past, were totally neglected. But, having cited a few very minor diversionary ones, he was fair game for criticism in omitting the important ones, conceding that mentioning these would have irreparably tarnished the patina of innocent righteousness painted over his patrons and protagonists.

Raphael Lemkin's confusing, scatter-gun posting of his "genocide" case is extremely hard to follow, since bits and pieces of it are to be found all over his book (and made even worse by his emendations in the following few years.) Any sustained attempt to criticize this doctrine should be an effort similar in structure and length to that originally propounded. Since he managed to locate, even with a large battery of assistants using some of America's most comprehensive law library collections, almost nothing to support his most inflammatory accusations, the evidence he had to fall back on in his documentary section is disappointing in the extreme. If there was a point in reproducing 400 pages of prosaic legalistic dullness such as he chose to do, with the apparent warm and approving sanction of his opulent and influential publisher, it remains thoroughly hidden to this day. But, having found no documentation to support the incendiary charges of "extermination" advanced right from the start against Germany and its partners, this presumably encouraged even more pronounced dependence on agitational propaganda published by a variety of the adversaries of the Axis, almost all of it originating from sources which reported nothing first hand, and published immense distances from the scene where it allegedly was transpiring. Lemkin's repeating of these sensational examples of *agit-prop* without a qualm or qualification is what made him a celebrity, and a quotable source to the present moment. If one trembles at contemplating going on trial for one's life, let us say, before a court conducted by the likes of a Raphael Lemkin, fear and trepidation would surely be a proper reaction.

One should keep in mind that Lemkin's *Axis Rule in Occupied Europe* was ostensibly being sold by the author and his promoters as the prelude to a memorable and lasting gesture in the extension of international law, even though, as has been pointed out, the contrast between his alarming charges, and the recommendations he advanced for "redress" at the conclusion of this rhetoric, resembled that between something being declaimed in stentorian tones before the Court of International Justice, and the droning conclusions of a referee before a small-claims court or a child-support case. But, being something related to what was presumed ultimately to apply to all, as law is considered to be, his brief should have dealt with his new sin of "genocide" in a broad historical manner, not simply as a specious attack on a hostile side in a global war. For that reason, what Lemkin left out often says more about the situation than what he elected to include.

In later years, critics of Lemkin and his "genocide" case assumed that his book was primarily a tour de force emphasizing Jewish grievances. Nothing could be further from the fact, once one has examined this volume closely. Despite basing most of his charge of universal massacre of European Jewry on a Zionist propaganda booklet published nearly two years before his own book, this was actually done in a footnote, and seems to have been pasted on to his original work as a virtual appendix. Through most of the book, Lemkin reflects far more the emotional and sentimental embodiment of the affronted and outraged Polish patriot. This especially shimmers through when he is concerned directly with matters involving Poland. The substantial deletions and/or omissions from his picture of European political history in *Axis Rule* are understood in the context of the wartime realities, but in more than incidentals also relating in a silent manner to two decades of pre-war affairs.

A few of these embarrassing facts have been alluded to, above, in the context of events transpiring during the war. The score of years prior to the war perhaps deserve even lengthier scrutiny for happenings which might have made Lemkin's book a sturdier and more dependable guide in the fabrication of the legal construct of "genocide."

One peculiarity connected with the ponderous buildup by

Lemkin of his concept of "genocide" was his delicate avoidance of
the slightest criticism of Communist Russia in *Axis Rule,* and in
everything else he wrote subsequently on this subject, until the outbreak of the Korean War (1950). There is no record of a word of
reproach from Lemkin in the 20 years between the beginning of his
legal career in Poland and the publication of *Axis Rule* of any Soviet
leader or ruler of any sort. Nor is there the faintest breath of protest
or complaint about the unbelievable volume of "genocide" carried
out in the Soviet slave-labor camps, the only real "death camps" of
the 1920-1945 era, both European and Asian, down to the German-
Polish war of September, 1939, or during the rest of the war. Though
a towering literature on the subject had piled up in the quarter of a
century before the appearance of *Axis Rule,* Lemkin seemed to be
totally innocent of it, and found absolutely nothing to get excited
about concerning this massive area of "genocidal" enterprise.
Lemkin's discovery elsewhere of "mass murder" and "genocide"
only in 1933 has a particularly false ring to it, in view of what he was
able almost at first hand to see going on in the Soviet Union for a
decade and a half before, let alone what he was able, as a direct
witness, to observe what was happening to his fellow Jews in Poland
from Versailles onward, to and beyond 1933. Lemkin never got
around to attack Polish "genocide" on its Jews, even after a Red
regime took over the country in 1944-45. If Jews may have had
special status in Bolshevik beginnings, Lemkin did not detect the
winds of change in the Soviet Union, 1936-1939, when Jews in great
numbers became the victims of Soviet policy, even though they were
not designated as such but as "counter-revolutionary wreckers,"
"enemies of the Soviet State," "Trotskyites," "saboteurs of socialism" and a long list of other *political* slogans, as they went before the
firing squads and into the slave labor camps in record numbers in the
era of the purge trials. Lemkin should have realized at that time the
ease with which unwanted minorities may be dispatched, without
even momentarily referring to their ethnic, racial, cultural or national
status, by designation of being a *political* adversary.

The key to understanding most of this is the realization that
Axis Rule was first of all a war propaganda tract, and in view of the
Soviet Union being an "ally" of Lemkin's champion and protector,
it is to be understood that the book could contain no criticism of
Bolshevik "genocide" going back to fifteen years before the rise of
Hitler to power in Germany. The suppression of the national aspira-
tions and tendencies of the USSR's many "republics," and the fate
of the three Baltic states and Finland, 1939-1941, at Soviet hands,
draw not a word, but Lemkin's rhetoric elsewhere in his book clearly
and unmistakably identifies them as victims of "genocide," by

default, even if it is considered utterly out of the question to bring it up. This was simply another instance where the suppression of a substantial swatch of history was necessary to enhance his case. As a protestor of "genocide," Lemkin was probably the most selective in the objects of his indignation of all who have ever mouthed the verbal reflex since he invented it.

If Lemkin suppressed all comment on the Stalinist record among the Soviet "republics," and the Red record in the Baltic states and Finland, he was additionally close-mouthed about the Red Army and Soviet political agencies in Eastern Poland, 1939-1941. Though Comintern publications and their plutocratic echo-chambers in the American press repeatedly commented during the war on the massive population transfers from the Eastern 60% of Poland into Siberia and other Soviet regions, including, it was alleged, almost all of Poland's Jews living in this region, this series of events is avoided by Lemkin in its entirety. Being the area of Poland of which Lemkin was a native made this silence doubly mysterious. There had already emerged a considerable literature, part of it by escaped Poles, on the Soviet concentration camps created to hold them in 1939 and after, but this is one kind of wartime writing by Poles to which no reference is made in *Axis Rule.* Only German changes in the population disposition in Poland appear in Lemkin's book, treated as a horrendous crime defying description; the much larger and somewhat more severe population disruptions by the Reds in Poland escaped mention.

Not a great deal about the Germans in Western Russia appears in *Axis Rule,* but the best face possible is placed on the Soviet part in it. It is a little awkward to see Lemkin seethe over the creation by the Germans of one-party states in Axis Europe, though his skill at utterly ignoring the prodigiously larger one-party state of Stalin, and the virtual one-party state of Poland prior to 1939 and wartime defeat, by which Lemkin himself was employed for a time, is an impressive part of his self-service disguised as factual reportage of the wartime European political scene. In his Chapter XXV on the Soviet, Lemkin had a 12-line sub-paragraph, titled "Genocide and 'Resistance' " (pp. 236-237). In this 6½ page chapter on the German occupation of the western regions, he reversed history twice, charging that the Red guerrilla "resistance" was a reaction to German "mass executions," a faithful echo of Communist political propaganda. He also blamed the "scorched-earth policy" in Russia on the German armies, when from the beginning even the major printed sources in the West ran scores of articles vociferously crediting the Red Army with this program of destroying Russian towns and farms in their retreat in 1941, and completely suppressing the story of the savage fighting between Russian farmers and civilians and their own

army as a result of such practices and procedures, these Russians
being outraged at having their homes and means of subsistence
destroyed by the retreating Communist armed forces. It took over 35
years for information on this amazing narrative to make its way into
the pages of Western journals.

Lemkin's free admission that large numbers of other Soviet
civilians had been engaged in "constant guerrilla fighting" against the
Germans since June, 1941, indicated the true relationship of this
war, that the German effort to suppress it followed Red initiative,
not the other way around. And, like all wartime propagandists,
Lemkin made not the slightest effort to distinguish between the civilians who were killed as a result of illegal civilian participation in the
war, those who for a time qualified to be considered *bona fide*
auxiliaries of the Red Army, and those who were simply caught in
the cross-fire between the rival armed forces; any dead Soviet civilian
was automatically charged off as a victim of German "mass-murder."
Further, in Chapter XXV, Lemkin wrote hesitantly if not reluctantly
about the German efforts to liquidate communism and to restore
private property in such areas as they managed to occupy and run
for a time in Russia. His main effort was devoted to illustrating
German weaknesses and failures at this, concluding that they were
not genuine and were simply gestures along the lines of dressing up a
"propaganda slogan" (pp. 232-235). Soviet orthodoxy should have
been grateful for this.

Though he scattered references and stray material identified with
his new crime, "genocide," throughout the portion of the book that
he wrote, Raphael Lemkin devoted the totality of Chapter IX to this
subject as well, which did not help things in some respects, and
requires much use of his index to locate many other related items
found elsewhere, as well as careful reading without this assistance.

In this chapter, Lemkin broke down "genocide" into eight categories, which may have seemed puzzling to those who had already
accepted the definition he had loosed early in his preface, *extermination*. Here, as has been mentioned in another context, he advanced a
rival definition, "the destruction of a nation or an ethnic group,"
both the latter meaning the same thing upon noting his further elucidation on "nation." The eight-fold listing was as follows: 1) Political;
2) Social; 3) Cultural; 4) Economic; 5) Biological; 6) Physical;
7) Religious; 8) Moral. As things turned out, most of the discussion
of all these sub-divisions tended to approach the insubstantial, and it
was No. 6, physical "genocide," which turned out to be almost his
only suit, and the one he was to push beyond any of the others, to
the degree that today it is nearly all that "genocide" is conventionally thought to be. It is also the count of Lemkin's omnibus charge

which he was able to support the least, and present the weakest and poorest evidence to clinch. It is ironic that it was the only portion of his allegation which really took hold. In actuality, his entire case backing the charge of "physical genocide" rested on a 12-line subsection, in which his total evidence consisted of the repetition of somewhat early accusations made in pamphlets issued by wartime propaganda agencies, and self-serving propaganda fronts.

Before getting to that, some attention might be accorded the matters brought up in other subdivisions of the general charge. It is rare that a construct so bold and expansive has been made on the basis of so few facts, but 1944-1945 was a time when this was possible to a greater degree than at any time since 1917-1918, and well beyond the situation which one may confront since then. Since this was a wide-range anti-German offensive, at its core, few who encountered his crusade had to be convinced of much in wartime, even though he got around to lodging similar accusations against some French, the Italians, Croats, Slovaks, Hungarians and Bulgarians as well. Lemkin's stretching of his tenuous "evidence" to support his sensational case most reviewers of his book found quite convincing, and no one bothered to consider the sources which he cited to back up his most extravagant assertions. That he frequently re-directed attention from his voluminous compendium of Axis occupation laws and the like, mainly of 1940-1941, which hardly reinforced him anywhere, to the more meaty but far less factual incendiary allegations in 1942-1943 propaganda booklets issued by the Polish government in exile in London, and the equally intemperate releases of Zionist organizations in New York, is understandable. Without them, his weak and unsupportable thesis would have been transparent even to his well-wishers. The wilder, broader and more shocking the accusations and declarations, the less likely there was to be any source, evidence or support for it, which had no palpable effect on his credibility. But in a significant manner it set the tone and direction of the future Nuremberg trials, where witnesses were remarkable for their absence and where "evidence" consisted almost entirely in loaded affidavits, of which in one sense Lemkin's entire book was an example.

One of the difficulties in following Lemkin's case results from the ease with which he swung in and out, following minor complaints by filing on their heels the most unusual and sweeping assertions, with the reliability of the documentation declining in direct ratio to the comprehensiveness of the assertion. One cannot for instance determine whether it is the saddened former League of Nations protagonist or the incensed Polish patriot speaking when Lemkin registers such outrage at the German efforts to re-Germanize the regions torn from them after 1918, and their refusal to accept the Versailles *dictat* as on a par with the Mosaic tablets.

When, for instance, Lemkin charged (*Axis Rule*, p. 81) that the Germans were carrying out a "genocidal" policy of revamping the Continent by seeking to replace the entire population of occupied Europe with Germans, there being nothing in his massive collection of Axis occupation laws even faintly approaching confirmation of such a policy, he fell back for verification support for his declaration upon Hitler's *Mein Kampf,* Alfred Rosenberg's *Myth of the Twentieth Century*, and other early post-World War One rhetoric of this sort, along with quotations from the sinister pre-World War II gossip of such German political losers in the 1930's as Hermann Rauschning, a particular darling of Allied propaganda-makers. This was not very substantial material to run by the readers in his try to establish that the Germans were elaborating a "system designed to destroy nations according to a previously prepared plan." (Allied investigation after hostilities ceased could not establish that the Germans had any coherent plan for dealing with even Central Europe.) The absence of anything tangible, factual or historical in the sense of having happened in wartime Europe did not bother Lemkin. Of course there were the population transfers and deportations from one area to another, the removals almost always being described as for the purpose of providing forced labor somewhere, or to make openings for German settlers. German actions as motivated by the continuous armed attacks on their troops by civilian guerrillas and acts of sabotage taking place by the thousands daily did not enter Lemkin's analysis of German policy. But German settlers even in parts of occupied Poland which had long been German prior to 1918 was "genocide" as well (*Axis Rule,* p. 83.)

At one point Lemkin could not make up his mind, charging the Germans with waging a "war of extermination" (*Axis Rule,* p. 80), which implied a general destruction of everyone was taking place, majorities as well as minorities. It was implicit in Lemkin's stipulations involving his many-faceted concept of "genocide" that a war could no longer be fought to obtain territory, in the time-honored manner of warfare over the millennia, since the capture of enemy land and the removal of its population, to be replaced by that of the victor, was a "crime." This was "genocide," plain and simple, at least in November, 1944, applying to the Germans and their allies. It was just one of the many aspects of *Axis Rule* which was to be turned inside out and stood on its head when the adversaries of the Axis were victorious. The expulsions of the Germans from their eastern territories and from the Sudetenland of Czecho-Slovakia were never referred to by Lemkin in 1945-46 and after as "genocide." Reviews of his book were still being published when the vast population transfers and the verified mass killings of German minorities were occurring in the regions wrenched from Germany after 1918 and where Lemkin had been so furious about their re-conversion to parts of the German Reich, "political genocide" in his language of 1944. What it had been in 1918 he offered no appellation for.

It may seem ludicrously anti-climactic, after a general charge that the Germans were achieving the extermination of occupied Europe's non-German population, that Lemkin should take up a succession of other Axis policies which obviously had nothing to do with extermination. Why interferences in the cultural, economic, religious and moral aspects of the life of a people already dead needed to be examined did not strike Lemkin's protagonists as redundant, but take place it did, following in his book the omnibus accusations of bringing about the de-population of occupied Europe. Probably this could be charged off to the incompetence of the Carnegie editors.

It will be recalled that attention has already been given to Lemkin's special pains taken in designating the German replacement of French by German in the official language of public communications and some schools in Luxembourg (and also Lorraine), as "cultural genocide." (Arthur Koestler in his *The Thirteenth Tribe* (1977) remarked, almost as a matter-of-fact aside, about conquerors replacing the local language with theirs for thousands of years, but in 1940-1941, it was a novel "crime" which Lemkin apparently had never heard of until committed by the Germans.) He was to take this matter far beyond this point now, charging that German "cultural genocide" in Poland had proceeded to the point where all Polish national monuments had been destroyed, and that their libraries, archives, museums and art galleries had all been stripped and pillaged. The basis for this allegation was the Polish government-in-exile's propaganda *White Book* (New York: Greystone Press, 1942.) In the same "cultural genocide" category Lemkin claimed in Poland, the young were being channeled exclusively into trade schools, and excluded *in toto* from liberal arts studies (*Axis Rule,* pp. 84-85). In the department of "religious genocide," also in Poland, Lemkin dropped the casual charge that the Germans had sought the extirpation of the Roman Catholic Church, and had already largely achieved this through the "systematic pillage and destruction of church property and persecution of the clergy." That this was being done by an occupier which was traditionally half-Roman Catholic itself should have been news to many, and should surely have aroused much interest in the Vatican. That Lemkin's Carnegie sponsors made no editorial investigation of this and many other sensational charges like it, supported by nothing at all of a documentary nature, probably says more about them than it does about Lemkin. One thing was certain, however: the ponderous collection of Axis occupation law gathered in the last 400 pages of *Axis Rule in Occupied Europe* said nothing about it. Probably there was no real reason for Lemkin to abide by any canons of restraint or moderation relating to his former homeland; here the Carnegie people seemed to have given him his head. After charging early in his book (p. 22), repeated from pp. 7-8 of No. 69 of the *Polish Fortnightly Review*, that the Germans had murdered some 500,000 people in the Warsaw ghetto by February, 1943 if not earlier, under the direction of the German police chief and State Secretary for Security in the Government General of Poland, W. F. Krüger, using three methods of mass annihilation, "death by gas in special chambers, electrocution, and in the so-called death trains by the action of quick-lime," anything else Lemkin might say about the Germans in Poland was bound to be outlandishly anti-climactic. The charge of mere destruction of church property on the heels of this incredible mass murder claim was surely a first-rank curiosity; one wondered to where his sense of priorities had departed after reading this pair of disparate irregularities. (The *Polish Fortnightly Review* was a propaganda organ of the Polish government-in-exile, published in London since 1940. The people it represented never had anything substantial to say about Polish government or affairs in Poland again.)

Since the preponderant part of *Axis Rule* is an inveighing against Axis occupation *economic* policy, and since 80% of the Axis laws and rules deal with restriction of movement on the part of populations in occupied areas, employment, ability to transmit funds internationally, business ownership and opportunities, professional limitations, labor and wages, and a score of related matters, there seemed to be no real reason for Lemkin to expand upon Axis "economic genocide." The whole book was a long compendium complaining of this. But there is a short section with this title anyway. The banking practices of the Germans in Poland are specifically identified as "economic genocide" (pp. 85-86) supported by earlier additional claims (p. 63) the Germans were guilty of extortion in gains made in clearing or trade relations, for which latter Lemkin cited as his source a very detached and precious one: the British Ministry of Economic Warfare, in a report gleaned from the New York *Times* (October 29, 1943, p. 3, col. 8.) This, about the latest source to be cited in a book to come out 13 months later, had already, unconsciously, no doubt, been directly contradicted in a story in *Business Week*, the authoritative American weekly (March 13, 1943, p. 48). Regretting that the Anglo-American "Allies," in their course across North Africa (to be repeated later in Sicily and southern Italy), brought with them and bequeathed upon *their* occupied peoples an ionospheric-high inflation, the editors suggested they had something to learn from the Germans, who kept the German mark at par with local currencies, or even set it slightly below the local money; "The U. S. and British have yet to learn what the Germans have taught; occupation is made easier if money rates are unchanged or altered in favor of the local people." But, of course, one must keep in mind George Ball's apologia for Israel 35 years later, that a mild and genial military occupation is unknown in history. It is strange that there should have been such contradictory sources relating to occupation monetary policies. Allied war propagandists generally peddled exactly the reverse of the real situation, depending heavily on a work by one Ernst Feilchenfeld, *The International Economic Law of Belligerent Occupation*, also published by Lemkin's publisher, the Carnegie Endowment, in 1942, which elaborated on the story of alleged German looting of occupied lands by over-valuation of the German mark. Feilchenfeld also happened to be Lemkin's principal dependent source on this subject. We find in Lemkin's section on "economic genocide" the same contradictory problem faced earlier in his discourse on the general topic, where he followed his bland declaration that the occupied populaces had been exterminated with supplementary commentary on their ensuing cultural and religious "genocidal" difficulties. In the economic category, after more than once declaring millions to have been the victims of mass murder, he proposed an elaborate set of schemes for monetary recompense for the deprivations they had suffered. But all these workers, forced or otherwise, could hardly have been put to death while simultaneously being seriously considered as beneficiaries of massive restitution. In the latter case we find in the postwar period the "liberators" following Lemkin's recommendations, virtually the only action in close harmony with his suggested restitution institutional innovations. How many persons who were beneficiaries of this policy who actually went to work in the German wartime economy voluntarily, or who enjoyed the luxury of being listed later as "dead" while receiving payments in restitution for charged wartime deprivations and impositions, will no doubt never be known.

In the department of "biologic genocide," we find Lemkin once more summoning up the propaganda *Black Book of Poland* (1942) which emphasized a nightmare they held in common with Lemkin, an outrageous concept of German potency, imagining, on the basis of the orders issued in Norway and Poland in 1941-42, a diabolic plot to breed millions of Germans to blot out and replace native populaces there, and eventually everywhere. No imaginative

Hollywood horror-movie fabricator had even come up with that
vision yet, but the *Black Book* and Lemkin (in *Axis Rule,* pp. 85-86)
were willing to entertain the solid possibility in the near future. What
German soldier fertility was likely to achieve in occupied Norway,
Holland and Poland, however, was what military occupations have
always produced through the millennia, tiny ethnic hybrid minorities, which Lemkin should have been thinking about as possible
candidates for protection from "genocide" in the future, as, for
instance, the part-white and part-black hybrid populations American
occupation forces bestowed on Japan, Korea and Southeast Asia.

In dealing with the concluding sub-divisions of his "genocide"
chapter, religious and moral, Lemkin again went to the well provided
by the *Polish Black Book,* with its inflammatory unsupported
charges of German occupation imposition of pornographic "publications and movies," as well as alcohol and gambling, upon the Polish
populace, (as if the Polish countryside were utterly innocent of these
diversions prior to German invasion), and the citing of a single decree
issued in Luxembourg which made it possible for its citizens who
wished to join German military or civilian activities to announce
their "resignation from a religious body" in the country, something
which may have been done by a small minority of Luxembourgers,
and hardly endangering the Catholic Church or its educational programs, which Lemkin's opportunistic employment of this legal
document sought to imply. (Lemkin averred that German plans in
Poland were all coordinated to concentrate popular attention on
"base instincts," thus substituting "the desire for cheap individual
pleasure" among the Poles as a replacement for their "collective
feelings and ideals based upon a higher morality." Again, the *Black
Book of Poland* (New York: G.P. Putnam's Sons, 1942) was his sole
supporting documentation for this divination, which actually had a
Leninist ring.

The Germans had company in Lemkin's appraisal of the state of
"genocide" in Central Europe, though rather subdued.The treatment
was however much the same: there was the usual emphasis on
economic analysis of the acts of the "genocidic" powers, especially
the new states of Slovakia and Croatia, with pro-German regimes and
also anti-Jewish policies: economic controls, property disposals,
labor, wage rates, finance, money systems and exchange rates,
exchange controls, industrial organization controls, regulation of
occupations, both professional and otherwise, agriculture, land
disposal, commercial procedures and marketing, all these are taken
up at some length and illustrated at least in part with appropriate
legal references in the documentation section. But, accompanying all
that were quiet allegations of physical "genocide," almost in the

nature of footnote citations. The following is the entry for Slovakia:

GENOCIDE LEGISLATION

As has been indicated, in accordance with the German pattern anti-Jewish legislation was introduced, involving deprivation of citizenship, confiscation of property, prohibition of the exercise of professions, forced labor, and deportations. From Slovakia, 130,000 Czechs were removed to Bohemia and Moravia, 60,000 Jews to Eastern Galicia in the Government General of Poland, and 10,000 Jews to Hungary. The new state considered its anti-Jewish policy to be of such importance that all anti-Jewish measures were codified in one Jewish Code consisting of as many as 270 articles. (*Axis Rule,* p. 143.)

It is worthwhile to observe that in this grab-bag of controls which he lumped together as "genocide legislation," in this new Slovakian state, Lemkin included nothing he had seen and nothing based on his special documentation. His sole support for all this came from a single secondary production of the International Labor Office, "The Displacement of Population in Europe," by one Eugene M. Kulischer, published in Montreal in 1943. In his own selection of laws and decrees from Slovakia, Lemkin confined himself to reproducing a swath from 1939-1940, covering 9 pages, which never even mentioned the word "Jew," and concerned only the establishment of the new state, while defining various monetary, property and political relationships. Again we see another example of the character of Lemkin's book, the inclusion of alarming charges virtually spliced to prosaic material largely inclined to produce somnolence, almost as though one were to see in a paragraph describing the futures market for frozen pork bellies a casual concluding sentence that a new world war had just broken out, and that half the world was incinerated. (One may note that the International Labor Office was a Stalinist-Comintern front for decades, and only recently did the political leadership of the USA shown the perspicacity to recognize this. Strangely enough, Kulischer had prepared a similar work to the one quoted by Lemkin, also published in 1943, *Jewish Migrations: Past Experiences and Post-War Prospects,* by the American Jewish Committee in New York, but it was not mentioned or utilized in *Axis Rule.*)

In the case of Croatia we have a similar example to the above on Slovakia: after listing as "genocide" in the latter of a few legal impositions relating to citizenship, economic regulation and the like, Lemkin concluded with the usual sensational *non-sequitur:* "It is reported that the Serbian population in Croatia is being subjected to massacres and tortures." Lemkin's sole reference for this savage note was a propaganda pamphlet published by a self-serving Serbian Eastern Orthodox Diocese located in *Canada* and the *USA*, titled *Martyrdom of the Serbs,* published in 1943. Lemkin's footnotes are heavily sprinkled with references to propaganda works of this kind, mainly printed in the USA and England, issued by adversaries of the Axis powers, of many different political and religious dispensations, which in court would have the validity of pure hearsay.

Lemkin also filed a "genocide" charge against Bulgaria (*Axis Rule,* p. 264), which consisted entirely of an alleged removal of 120,000 Serbs from Bulgaria back to Serbia, his source again being the ILO work by Kulischer, which more than once was cited to support some otherwise shaky or dubious claim. In dealing with Germany's wartime associates, Lemkin filed no charges of extermination or inducing mass deaths; in fact, he did not even refer to their concentration camps in his "genocide" chapter.

For that matter, the most curious lapse in *Axis Rule* is the general neglect of the whole concentration camp story. The reason for this near-omission is not made evident. Whether or not Lemkin wished to avoid any adverse remarks about the Stalinist camp system is not indicated anywhere, but even the domestic German camps escaped the voluminous elaboration one might have expected in this catalog of German political crimes, real or alleged. This is all the more strange, since one objective, in the arraignment of the Germans for their alleged barbarous bestialism, surely was their de-humanization as much as possible in the advance stages of preparing to descend upon them with vengeance. Lemkin seems to have passed by a top rank issue.

The only law in his compendium dealing with concentration camps is one promulgated by the new state of Croatia. In his text, Lemkin refers to concentration camps only in the context of being facilities administered by the German *Geheimstaatspolizei,* the Gestapo, for the disposal of "politically undesirable persons and of Jews," but mentions none by either name or location. (In his separate accusation of German extermination of Jews, he asserts that this was done, not in camps, but in special ghettoes, and in Polish, not German, towns, by the three methods mentioned above. Lemkin may have thought he was impressing his readers in the USA with a special sense of horror in accusing the Germans of killing by "gas in special chambers" or electrocution, but these were commonplace methods of execution for convicted criminals, usually murderers, in several American states.)

On page 105 of *Axis Rule* Lemkin mentioned the provision for concentration camps by the Italian criminal code for both Italy and

Albania; on page 138 he referred to a decree establishing a concentration camp by the "puppet" government of Czecho-Slovakia, and again on page 143 he mentioned the establishment of a concentration camp by the "puppet" government of Slovakia.

The Croatian law of July 20, 1942, which is reproduced in translation on page 615, is referred to a second time by Lemkin in his text, page 257, specifying that it was a camp intended to incarcerate violent criminals, for a period stretching from three months to a maximum of three years. Still another (page 263), this one a Hungarian camp set up in Yugoslavia, is mentioned, but not to be found is a general discussion of the camp system in Germany itself, nor the later so-called "death camps" created in Poland, one of the largest of which, Maidanek, had already been captured by the Red Army and given immense radio, magazine and newspaper exposure by the Soviet Union, three months before Lemkin's book was actually published. But the book undoubtedly was in page proofs by that time. Nevertheless, a wide range of publicity had been given this entire camp system, making all the stranger why Lemkin chose to neglect the very largest part of the entire topic.

Lemkin's "genocide" chapter ended in a *non-sequitur,* a short discourse on "occupation practices," mainly concerning the treatment of prisoners of war. It contained a broad hint that the Germans were guilty of "gruesome" atrocities, here, too, as charged by gossip and tales promoted by non-eye-witnesses of entirely German-enemy nature. Unmarked by Lemkin was any reference to the Soviet Union, not even a signatory to the 1929 Geneva Convention on the treatment of prisoners of war, let alone the Hague Conventions of 1899 and 1907, the Reds being revealed for several years after May, 1945 to have been wholesale violators of the most elementary considerations involving its prisoners, and all the "victors" being hit in turn with substantial charges of having abused and mistreated German soldiers in their hands. While content to suggest the Germans were flagrant violators of the Geneva Convention, Lemkin was prudent in avoiding any remarks which might have been construed as a complaint against the Reds for the same kind of behavior toward prisoners, or, for that matter, anything else that aroused his molten ire when charged to the Germans, 1939-1945. He appeared quite content to allow "genocide" to stand as an offense of which the Germans were the only significant perpetrators. And his formulation of their past offenses, real or alleged, into a "law" for the prevention of them in the future, had a basically false ring in it, despite the initial universal tendency to give it lip-service support.

In concluding this analysis and criticism of Raphael Lemkin's ninth chapter in *Axis Rule in Occupied Europe,* "Genocide," with a survey of his treatment of occupied Europe's Jews as a separate subject, attention is called to the very small amount of space he devoted to this as a related topic. Contrary to the assumptions and preconceptions of postwar commentators who were concerned primarily with Raphael Lemkin's enhanced reputation and meteoric rise, it is obvious to anyone who even just glances at his *Axis Rule* for a short time that it is not a *tour de force* concerned with the Jewish question, nor in any sense at all a lengthy and first-hand account published in advance of all others on the theme of the alleged mass-murder of European Jews during World War II. And it is nowhere a subterranean or camouflaged plea for recognition of Zionism or its territorial or political goals in Palestine.

Lemkin's chapter VIII, "The Legal Status of the Jews," takes up a mere *three pages* in a 712-page tome. And in the following Chapter IX, "Genocide," the subject of the alleged systematic massacre of occupied Europe's Jews is dealt with in just *twelve lines.* The confusing element, however, as has been seen in part, is due to Lemkin's bad organization, scattering pertinent bits of material related to these subjects all through the book. The index, and close reading, are, as has been seen, necessary if one wishes to be aware of all he had to say on these matters.

Perhaps the studied exploitation of Lemkin and his work by Zionist functionaries, starting around 1946, explains why his book was believed by those who did not bother to look at it to be a vast compendium of Zionist propaganda. One has to work hard at it to identify *any* of it in this light. Chapter VIII has little content of any kind of consequence and largely demonstrates Lemkin's repeated technique of switching abruptly from prosaic, dull matters of little significance to dramatic and abandoned propaganda fantasy having no evidence in support of it whatever. In the matter at hand, two of the three pages allotted to an examination of the wartime legal status of Europe's Jews are filled with dull aspects of occupation law, almost all of it pertaining, as we have seen before in a number of other places handled in the same way, and again showing the stigmata of a bad legal brief, to property and related economic matters and citizenship status, admittedly unfair and decidedly discriminatory, by American standards. But these laws nowhere indicate anyone's life was threatened as a result of their existence, and, as usual, lack any evidence one way or another that they had been enforced, obeyed, defied, ignored, allowed to lapse, or administered poorly, as a result of incompetent application by the Axis initiators. In the case of those laws involving money penalties, Lemkin chose, as did virtually every other person citing anti-Jewish laws, to omit mention of the class nature of the enforcement aspect. Those subject to these laws hardly were "the" Jews—too much was known of the affluent and the well-placed escaping the legal rigors of life in occupied Europe and in considerable numbers, to create the illusion that all suffered equally.

Having failed to demonstrate with evidence any lethal aspect of occupation law, Lemkin changed almost in mid-sentence to grave allegations of massacre and wholesale death suffered by Jews, on his last page devoted to the subject in Chapter VIII (p. 77). Here he spoke, as he did in other chapters, of a deliberate policy of liquidation of Jews "by massacres in ghettos," accompanied simultaneously by another calculated policy of mass starvation, "exposing them to mass death by creating unhealthy conditions in the ghettos and the forced labor camps." One of these two programs seemed superfluous, but no source in support of the charges was even alluded to at this point. Nowhere could Lemkin and his large contingent of assistants, with unlimited access to the largest and most prestigious law libraries, and the presumed resources of the famed and ceaselessly diligent Allied intelligence services, served by regiments of spies everywhere, come up with a law, decree or anything else of the kind dealing with the arbitrary putting to death of a single Jew, or anyone else.

An operation entirely devoted to the total extermination of European Jewry in the part of Europe occupied by Germany and its wartime allies and which was claimed even before Lemkin had finished his book, around mid-1943, to have already killed between two and four million of them, should have produced at least a little paper; the Germans reputed to being such meticulous record-keepers, one would have expected a vast amount of incriminating documentation to accompany such a mind-chilling program. Despite all this, Lemkin came up with exactly none.

Axis Europe was known to be crawling with Anglo-Russo-American spies, even in the German intelligence system; the very top-most secret code system of the Germans, "Ultra," had been cracked by Germany's enemies at about the time the war began in 1939. Highly-placed Nazi functionaries were Allied spies, and many Jewish espionage specialists were known to be at large all over Nazi-occupied Europe and even Germany itself, including half the membership of the famed "Red Orchestra." Zionist sources 35 years later were willing to admit that 1,000,000 Jews survived the war while living in war zones controlled by the Axis (though non-Zionists insisted the figure was far higher than that), and Communist spy rings of great sophistication worked out of the German concentration camps, and knew freely what was transpiring in all war theatres. All the above is but the skin surface of a situation that would take a set of ponderous

books to describe adequately. Nevertheless, despite all these avenues
to information and many others which there is not space to list, and
though Lemkin worked closely with a number of wartime Government agencies and administrative bodies in the USA, he still had no
more documentation to back up his charges of planned German
destruction, physically, of the entirety of European Jewry in their
area of control, than second-hand, third-hand or even fourth-hand
propaganda hand-outs from distantly-located emigre Polish politicians, and just as remotely-situated Zionists, supplying self-serving
works of the same kind.

In Chapter VIII Lemkin did not think it necessary to cite sources
for his charge of physical extermination of occupied Europe's Jews,
other than repeating gossip and the rhetoric of veteran anti-German
propaganda figures such as Rauschning, the Marxist liberal Yugoslav,
Louis Adamic, (a member of nearly all wartime Stalinist fronts),
quotations from Hitler's *Mein Kampf*, and the Polish *White Book* and
Black Book. In Chapter IX, after elaborating a bit on this theme in a
12-line sub-paragraph, Lemkin advanced other references in support
of the mass murder charge, a work titled *Hitler's Ten Year War on
the Jews*, prepared by the Institute of Jewish Affairs of the World
Jewish Congress, (1943) and the "Joint Declaration by Members of
the United Nations," issued in London and New York on December
17, 1942, and published a short time later in Vol. III, No. 1 (1943)
of the *United Nations Review*. This is all Lemkin could come up
with, and since they preceded his own book by some time, it can be
seen that despite his reputation in the matter, Lemkin really contributed nothing to the account concerning the alleged extermination
of occupied Europe's Jewry. That those at Nuremberg and in the
early years of the United Nations Organization in Paris and at Lake
Success, N.Y. should have regarded Lemkin as an authority on the
subject is neither understandable nor explainable.

The shortcomings of Lemkin's sources are really not at issue
here, and the assumption may be made that the publishers of these
propaganda works and Lemkin both knew of their significant failings
and serious omissions as dependable factual reports. However, since
nothing whatever was said about these, a brief summary of some of
the missing picture is in order here. One may argue from the point of
view of "balance" that the WJC's Institute of Jewish Affairs should
have published companion booklets on the Polish and Russian "war"
on the Jews, though these would obviously have had to go back far
beyond the ten years covered in the study of the conflict with Hitler
and the Germans. But this *was* wartime, a specially brutal one, and
dealing with the shortcomings of others who were now protagonists,
even if by chance, made mandatory the discussion of just part of reality.

As for the wartime United Nations' "joint declaration," perhaps its authors had a few qualms about claiming the Germans were perpetrating "mass executions" of "many hundreds of thousands" of *"entirely"* innocent men, women and children. Surely they were aware of the immense scope of the civilian warfare against the German occupation army, the several thousands of daily acts of sabotage, the gun-running, the ambushes and the assassinations, let alone the pitched battles where the terrain made such possible. And Lemkin, as a later admitted guerrilla in Poland himself at the start of the war, for six months, should have been the one least ignorant of it all. But other than his brief commentaries here and there which praised such civilian participation and tried to make out German laws and actions attempting to suppress this as reprehensible, if not "genocide," of a sort, there is no discussion that part of what was happening to Jews was a consequence of their own prior acts.

Even casual readers far from the scene in the USA were made aware of part of this story. Such works as *Story of a Secret State,* by the Polish-London-exile-government agent, Jan Karski, also published in 1944 (Boston: Houghton Mifflin), boasted of the three or four separate underground forces fighting the Germans in Poland, one of which appeared to be entirely Jewish, by his enthusiastic and favorable description. But the full picture was never shown any time, and latter-day efforts at filling in the missing sections have never been comprehensive. Lemkin's posture of portrayal of Occupied Europe's Jews as an innocent and harmless minority moving on, unresisting, to mass murder, was partially undermined by the boastful claims of belligerent Zionists in later years, but it escaped criticism in the fateful years of the remaining 1940s. It was all quite safe for the American Jewish Committee to publish Yehuda Bauer's booklet *They Chose Life,* on October 25, 1973, which went on at length about the extensive Jewish sabotage, smuggling and black market activity and the omnipresent armed guerrilla warfare, featured by the bristling armament of Jewish underground units in the ghettos of *forty* cities in Eastern Europe. Not a breath of such possibilities could be detected in Lemkin's work, the product of a lifelong resident of Eastern Europe, and surely one to know what was going on there.

If Lemkin and the protagonists of the extermination story were exceedingly tender about the matter of guerrilla warfare in the East, while advancing the claim of the massacres taking place in these armed-to-the-teeth ghettos, the twin claim accompanying this, that a deliberate policy of "mass starvation" was taking almost as many lives, must surely have been proposed with the knowledge that this situation was also debatable. Lemkin quoted from the Zionist propaganda book, *Starvation over Europe (Made in Germany)*, also issued by the Institute for Jewish Affairs in 1943, which declared for a fact that the Jews of occupied Europe were assigned an *absolute zero* meat ration; Lemkin dutifully reported this (*Axis Rule*, p. 87) and found no reason to question its veracity, or the similar claim that Jews were allotted zero fuel in winter, nor the other charges of planned starvation in this same publication.

The citing of rationing decrees was believed to be a correct way to estimate the situation, not the consulting of those who could report what was really going on. But even the daily press had long acquainted people with the existence of a continent-wide black market, which was known to make posted food rationing regulations a joke. The "liberators" of the Western European countries formerly under German control reported no universal starvation upon arriving on the scene, except in some concentration camps, and hardly among *all* of those there, for that matter. The scientific magazine *Human Biology* as early as 1955 published a series of articles summarizing statistics on height and weight of children during and after the war in various regions of Axis-occupied Europe, and concluded that there was virtually no difference, which they ascribed to the near-normal wartime nutrition, in turn resulting from the never-ceasing, omnipresent and perpetually active black market in food. Two interesting commentaries by Americans early in 1945, one shortly before the end of the war and another a month after the cessation of hostilities, are worth examining in the above context.

The first report is that by Frederick C. Crawford, former president of the National Association of Manufacturers, who was a "guest" of the U.S. War Department in France in the early winter of 1944-1945, and whose account delivered before the U.S. State Chamber of Commerce on conditions in France was summarized in *Newsweek* ("American in Paris," January 15, 1945, pp. 41-42):

> I saw fat horses drawing wagons equipped with rubber-tired wheels. I had been told that France was suffering, told that we must give the French 100,000 tractors to plow with or we should have to feed them for a year.
>
> We went to the Ritz Hotel. The big brass doorknobs and all the decorations were there. The hotel looked well-painted with new silk curtains hanging. Some of the rooms were modernistic.
>
> "French workers had been paid liberally by the Germans. There was every indication, I was told, that the Germans expected to stay in France and wanted prosperity there. Under deficit financing they built a consumer boom. A fine conservative Frenchman I had known for years told me that had it gone on for a year and a half more, he believed the French working people would have settled for things as they were.

The French and Belgian underground was composed largely of Communists, young people and ex-convicts, who robbed ten peaceful French families for every train that was blown up. A similar condition exists in Norway.

A collaborationist is one who expanded his business under the Germans or who has incurred the enmity of labor leaders.

It can be understood that challenges to the official propaganda in mass circulation in the U.S. such as Crawford's report on the relative prosperity in France and absence of people dropping in the streets from hunger, standard Communist and Zionist nightmare assertions, would be deeply resented here, and a not very convincing effort was made to discredit him. But even more directly bearing on the theme of starvation or the absence of it was a report published at the end of May, 1945, further undermining the official propaganda of German looting of Western Europe of food and allowing the Belgians, French and Dutch to starve, a yarn repeated in American circles for five years. This report was made by Major General Warren Draper, Deputy Surgeon General of the U.S. Public Health Service and Chief of the Supreme Headquarters' Military Government Public Health Branch. Gen. Draper flatly denied that they had encountered any famine in Western Europe, nor had the health of the people there been ruined during the war. He further stated that mortality tables had been lower for the entire area in 1944 than in 1943, including infant mortality. As for France, Gen. Draper said that they had found "very few cases of serious malnutrition—very few more cases of malnutritional disease than you would find anywhere." In Holland, Gen. Draper found that food concentrates made by the ton in England and America, for injection into the veins of Dutchmen claimed by Allied propagandists to be too weak even to eat, were simply unneeded. He said that few such starving people had been found outside concentration camps, and that as a consequence, Dutch warehouses were still filled with much of this food, sent there recently by both air and sea transport. ("Starvation, Limited," *Newsweek,* June 4, 1945, p. 65.)

It is quite likely that there is hardly a paragraph in Raphael Lemkin's *Axis Rule in Occupied Europe* which might not be ably confronted by counter-stories and statements such as the above undercut the nightmare line of Europe's Jewry, or others, being systematically starved to death, but perhaps enough has been advanced by now in dealing with the shortcomings of this massive book in portraying faithfully the real situation taking place in occupied Europe. The revelations from Western Europe might have been matched by similar ones from the East, had not the Stalinist Iron Curtain fallen upon the eastern two-thirds of Germany, Poland

and most of Central and South-Central Europe all the way to Vienna by the end of May, 1945. As a result, the conditions to elaborate upon and to magnify horror stories prevailed there in their best dimensions, and the combination of both Stalinist and Zionist political plans for the future made expert use of the situation to wire down for "history" the wartime propaganda, which also had the effect of substantiating such propaganda in the form in which it had been infused into Lemkin's book. Support from these influential areas of Europe partially explain the sudden rise of Lemkin as an authority in the circles attending the newly-created United Nations Organization, and the ultimate advancement of his wartime thesis into new international law. An examination of the promotion of Lemkin and his views and the drive to obtain UN adoption of his invention, "genocide," is now in order.

(1) Lemkin astutely avoided making the faintest allusion to historically verifi-
     able events of considerable horror in the annals of previous "genocide,"
such as the total massacre of the white French minority by the negroes on the Caribbean island of Saint Domingue (Haiti) by 1804, and then the mulattoes, leading thenceforth to the most degeneratively backward "nation" ever known in the Western Hemisphere. Lemkin could have made his thin, obscure and feeble catalog useful by remembering things like Haiti, but that did not seem to be part of the scheme. Nor had he any intention of directing any light upon "genocide" brought about by minorities upon majorities, which would have severely wounded the synthetic non-event he was busily pasting together. (For an assessment of the principal facts concerning the "Christian Assyrian" incident of 1933, which demonstrates the essential triviality and exaggeration of Lemkin's representation of it all, see the extended note following Chapter VI, below.)

Chapter Five

SUCCESS: THE UNITED NATIONS ORGANIZATION ADOPTS 'GENOCIDE' AS A NEW INTERNATIONAL CRIME

AS THE REVIEWS OF *Axis Rule in Occupied Europe* began to proliferate in the early months of 1945, the repetition of the name, and spread of the reputation, of Raphael Lemkin, grew with them. Head consultant of the Foreign Economic Administration by now, as well as a key lecturer before the School of Military Government at Charlottesville, Virginia, where the USA's commissariat for the future overlordship of their soon-to-be defeated enemy and coming satellite, Germany, were being trained, it was obvious that Lemkin was being consulted by the mighty, and was headed for even bigger things.

It was in full knowledge of his increasingly influential credentials that the main warrior voice of American liberalism, *The Nation,* ran a long two-part essay by him in February and March, 1945, which described a new area in which he would swing some weight, the coming trials of the defeated enemy for "war crimes." Titled "The Legal Case Against Hitler," Lemkin showed additional skill in elusive, slippery legal talk, the very largest part of these nearly twelve large columns of abstract verbiage seeking to put down the belief that the coming prosecution of Hitler would be *ex post facto.* Hitler was simply a "common criminal," said Lemkin, and neither he nor his subordinates should be allowed to enter such a plea or defense. Before long he was soon involved in promotion of his new word, which he already assumed was also a thing, or a "crime." But he was rather muddy in describing what the crime was. He seemed at one point to be willing that the indictment go back to the period even before Hitler had become political chief of Germany, and base it on the rhetoric in his early 1920s writings; "We should not overlook the fact that in the final analysis what Hitler was advocating in *Mein Kampf* was the destruction of whole nations and peoples." It seemed to Lemkin that this was as substantial material on which to base the prosecution as *evidence* of *acts* and *witnesses,* and approved by many who yelled to high heaven a few years later when the identical approach was taken toward their ideological favorites.

In the second part of his essay Lemkin stoutly maintained that of the numerous "war crimes" which the Germans had committed, the worst were those "committed against the inhabitants of the occupied countries," though he made it evident that he was not forgetting what had happened in Germany itself, since it was essential to his entire concept of "genocide" that what a State did to any of its own nationals within its boundaries was not an internal matter, but of international concern.

Lemkin also vociferously opposed any handling of indictments for "war crimes" before German courts and judges. The German judiciary were all "morally depraved," and should never be allowed to try their own accused. In fact, Lemkin wanted the entire prosecution to be conducted before strictly U.S. military courts.

On the rejection of the possible argument of subordinates of Hitler that they were "following superior orders," Lemkin really was not advancing any new thinking. This had already been set down definitively by such grim retributionists as Prof. Sheldon Glueck of the Harvard Law School and Lemkin's own guiding angel in the Carnegie Institution, and official launcher of his book, George Finch, Director of Carnegie's Division of International Law. Both had written grimly on the matter in essays published in the summer of 1943, though Finch's position went back to the aftermath of World War One, and was embalmed in an issue of another Carnegie front, *The American Journal of International Law,* as far back as 1921. From these two separate strains of cultivated and sophisticated Germanophobia, a generation apart, Lemkin concluded that "In the main, Anglo-Saxon doctrine and practice are opposed to the excuse of war crimes on the plea of superior orders." It would have helped in the comprehension of Lemkin's line if he had mentioned some *law,* to go along with his "doctrine" and "practice." It was the thesis of the opponents of such "trials" that there was no *law* to try the defendants *on;* no legal codes anywhere contained a category specifically called "war crimes."

Lemkin's "history" cited in support of some of his approach in this very influential *Nation* two-part essay was the usual hash of semifictions, tempered by just enough facts to mislead a hasty reader. He misrepresented the Evian conference of July, 1938 as being primarily concerned with refugees from Germany, when the majority of those seeking to leave had already found homes elsewhere by then, and totally ignored the concern of the conference with political, mainly Marxist, and related ideological cases, and far more from Poland, Hungary, Rumania and Austria than Germany. He was more concerned with the refugee status of the property of Germans, it seemed, taking space to mention specifically, "Wholesale confiscation of the property rights of entire groups of German citizens has been detrimental to their foreign creditors and undermined international trade." Lemkin did not discuss owners of property in Germany who were citizens of other countries and lived elsewhere. (In his book, Lemkin had designated property confiscation of this kind as economic "genocide," though the dual nature of the involvement suggested that one's creditors abroad who had not been paid might also sue as victims of "genocide.") Still another item Lemkin added to the fanciful total was a bellow about "pogroms" conducted against Jews in Germany in 1938, which carefully papered over attestations by residents in Germany, 1933-1939, who made a point of denying they had ever witnessed attacks on Jews by civilians in Germany during that time. (Lemkin would have been hard put to discuss pogroms against Jews in his native Poland during that same time without using up the entire space his *Nation* essay consumed.)

But the kernel of the essay concerned another announcement of his new word, "genocide," in language similar to that used in his preface to *Axis Rule* except that this time he spelled "homicide" correctly, though repeating his questionable tactic of comparing his vague and generalized would-be offense with such specific offenses as piracy and the slave and narcotics trades:

> The Nazis have destroyed whole nations, a crime for which the present writer has coined the word "genocide"—in analogy with homicide and fratricide. The world should feel and express its solidarity in the condemnation of so monstrous a crime. Expression of such solidarity might well take the form of an international treaty, to be signed by the United Nations and the neutrals, in which "genocide" would be placed on the list of international crimes, along with piracy and trade in women, slaves and narcotics. The crime of genocide should be made extraditable.

Lemkin's turgid discourse may have edified those with talents such as his among his American colleagues, but it did not charm all his technical readers. Two months later, with Allied "victory" achieved and with most of the enemy leaders in their jails, the *Nation* chose to run a long critique of Lemkin by a fellow Central European refugee, Rustem Vambery, former professor of criminal law at the University of Budapest, a sometime political refugee in the USA, and chairman of one of the many utterly hopeless refugee political-loser groups swarming in America, this one the Committee for a New Democratic Hungary. Vambery did not think very highly of Lemkin or his constructs. Though seeming to favor the view of anti-trial elements by pointing out that "No textbook of the criminal law of any country contains the term 'war crime' or 'war criminal'," and asserting in no hesitant way, "there is, indeed, no such thing as war crime, meaning a special class of crime," Vambery quickly demonstrated that he sided with the Stalinists in urging that the captured enemy leaders should simply be murdered, and promptly. Speaking of the past, when dogs and even chickens had been put on trial, Vambery observed, "there is no record of man-eating tigers, lions, or other wild animals being brought to trial," pointing out that they had always been killed "without legal formalities," to which he concluded, "There is no reason why wild beasts in human form like the Nazis should be dealt with differently." In Vambery's view, "Nazism and Fascism" were "revolutionary movements," and "law, the static force of society, is not an adequate means of dealing with these passing events." What Vambery urged at once was "swift and merciless retribution," uncluttered by legal niceties, as the only real and effective way of bringing about the counter-revolutionary obliteration of these unruly forces.

However, though some of the smaller fry of the enemy leadership were disposed of in the manner Vambery enthusiastically suggested, Mussolini being the only prominent personage a casualty of this Communist political biology, it became increasingly obvious as 1945 wore on that some kind of judicial proceeding would precede the extermination of the political leadership class of the defeated powers, both West and East. And it was not surprising that Raphael Lemkin showed up at Nuremberg as a political adviser to the U.S. Chief of Counsel for Prosecution of Criminality of the U.S. Prosecution headed by Supreme Court Justice Robert H. Jackson.

By October, 1945 Lemkin was in London, where an English edition of his *Axis Rule* appeared, published by Allen & Unwin, early in 1946. Copies of this circulated at Nuremberg, leading to the impression that Lemkin had been in London all along and that the book had been written and first published there. Just how much impact the book had is a matter of opinion, but some of it no doubt was used by the prosecution in preparing their case against the Nazi defendants. Not long before arriving overseas, Lemkin had published still another article on his obsession in *Free World,* "Genocide—A

Modern Crime." But the first general notice, reaching a large audience, which credited Lemkin with inventing this new word, was in the *New York Times* for October 22, 1945, even though the Washington *Post* had identified him as the coiner of the word in 1944. From that time on, Lemkin's press notices proliferated, and large papers known for their hyper-liberal leanings the world over all contributed to the publicity drum-fire in his behalf. Before the Nuremberg verdicts of October, 1946 "genocide" had become a global verbal reflex. And not long afterward, Lemkin acknowledged the crucial help the reiteration of the word in large newspapers around the world had been:

> An important factor in the comparatively quick reception of the concept of genocide in international law was the understanding and support of this idea by the press of the United States and other countries. Especially remarkable contributions were made by the *Washington Post* (since 1944), the *New York Times* (since 1945), the *New York Herald Tribune, Dagens Nyheter* in Stockholm, [and] *Sunday Times* of London.

And so, a global press campaign established the reputation for the new word and crime, "genocide," which its author in a book of over 700 pages failed to support with a single witness or verifiable piece of direct evidence insofar as it involved his principal accusation, the deliberate, planned, official mass murder of Jews and other minorities in Axis-occupied Europe, 1940-1943, which latter, as we have seen from his documentary acknowledgments in his book, was borrowed from prior propaganda handouts in the first place. Nevertheless, from this time on it became obvious even to those who did not devote too much study to the matter that Lemkin, his ideas and opinions were managed professionally from a public relations vantage point during the fifteen years between the launching of his neologism "genocide" until his demise.

When the New York *Times* credited Lemkin with coining the word "genocide," it did so indirectly, quoting from a London *Sunday Times* piece summarized by the Associated Press on October 21, 1945. This in turn was a summary of the indictment against the German defendants at Nuremberg the previous week, Count #3 of which charged all 24 defendants with having "conducted deliberate and systematic genocide, viz., the extermination of racial and national groups, against the civilian populations of certain occupied countries." This sounded as though Lemkin had actually prepared this legal verbiage for the International Military Tribunal sitting in judgment.

However, it was not until June 26, 1946 that major attention began to accrue to the word in the mass newspapers. On that day the word "genocide" was first employed by Sir David Maxwell-Fyfe, of the British prosecution, when he addressed the defendant Constantin von Neurath in this manner: "Now, defendant, you know in the indictment in this trial we are charging you and your fellow defendants, among many things, with genocide." This must have been quite gratifying to Lemkin, who had just published another article on the subject, in the prestigious *American Scholar,* and was at work on others for international consumption later in the year, or early 1947.

But Lemkin was already looking past Nuremberg, and at the coming first session of the United Nations Organization. His *American Scholar* piece made the familiar points already seen several other places, and actually had become so formalized that they appeared almost without a change in a piece in the *Christian Century* ten years later. The condemnation of expulsions and economic expropriation of minorities as "genocide", even though no deaths occurred, (Lemkin seemed to be more forceful here in declaring minorities were not to be disturbed anywhere for any reason), and his determination to see that the threatening or injuring of a minority *within* a national State be construed as an *international* offense, and prosecuted and punished outside that country, were declared here with vigorous emphasis. As he went on, concerning the latter:

> It would be impractical to treat genocide as a national crime, since by its very nature it is committed by the State or by powerful groups which have the backing of the State. A State would never prosecute a crime instigated or backed by itself. It must be considered an international crime.

Lemkin made one strange proposal in this essay, to the effect that "international law be changed so that in time of war the treatment of civilian populations will also be under supervisory control of an international body like the International Red Cross." The amusing innocence of this fades when one contemplates what an international supervisory body might have been able to do for the civilian population during the phosphorous bombing of Hamburg, the obliteration bombings of Berlin and Dresden, the incendiary demolition of Tokyo, and the atom bombing of Hiroshima and Nagasaki. Undoubtedly, those who study contemporary contingency plans involving the likely atomization of tens of millions of civilians in a few minutes may wonder if Lemkin's grasp on reality had momentarily slackened, in delivering himself of this astounding proposal.

But the importance of Lemkin's *American Scholar* essay was that it was concluded with his own first draft version of a genocide convention, such as he was shortly to bring before the UN. And it can be assumed that he was still wearing the same Germanophobic blinders while doing this, unaware that much of anything had gone on since the first week of May, 1945. For example, on July 4, 1946 a violent disturbance had broken out in Lemkin's homeland, Poland, described in the *Encyclopedia of World History* (Boston: Houghton, 1948, p. xlvi), as "an anti-Jewish pogrom," in Kielce, which *killed* 48 Jews. More outbreaks on July 12, also in Poland, killed 20 more Jews. Nothing like this had ever happened in Nazi Germany. But neither event attracted a glance from Lemkin; he was still busily at war with Hitler. Despite this and all the copious additional evidence of Poland and its neighbor Russia as being the centers of the most fierce repression of Jews in history, Lemkin could still have the effrontery to write in the *American Journal of International Law* a few months later, and remark, in still another weary recital of his "genocide" fable, of "Germany, the classical country of genocide practices," an ethnic slur which if said by a German of some other place, might have been grounds for an accusation of "genocide" by Lemkin.

With reference to the deaths of Jews in post-war Poland, some attention to its politics might have cleared up the mystery as to the cause of this. But Lemkin showed no interest in the clash among Polish factions created by the effort to establish the first Stalinist Communist regime there, headed nominally by Boleslaw Bierut. This actually raged until 1950 and many Poles were killed, both among the Communists and the partisans of other elements ranging from remnants of the Peasant Party to those loyal to the government-in-exile factions represented by such figures as Mikolajczyk. In the New York *Times* for March 2, 1946 the general secretary of the Canadian Jewish Congress, H.M. Caiserman, declared that he knew of 800 Jews who had already been killed by anti-Communist factions in the "underground" against the aspiring Bierut regime, and the conclusion would have suggested that many others he did not know about had also been slain in the post-May, 1945 civil war. Therefore the killings of scores of others as reported in the *Encyclopedia of World History* in the spring and summer of 1946 were far more to be related to internal politics and pro-Stalinist activities than as a result of what they termed to be "pogroms." It also suggested that many Communist Jews had returned to Poland from the Soviet Union to take part in this bloodletting in Poland.

Lemkin's appearance in London was no chance affair. He was already beginning his campaign to lobby "genocide" into existence as a new international crime via the infant United Nations Organization, and started right away when the first meeting of the General Assembly convened January 10, 1946. From that time on Lemkin was to become an increasingly familiar figure in the lounge, the corridors and meeting rooms and in the press section of the UN. A New York *Post* reporter, John Hohenberg, reminiscing about Lemkin over 20 years later, remarked about his tireless tramping from one place to another in the UN, collecting press notices about his drive for a genocide "treaty," growing "paler, thinner and shabbier," in Hohenberg's words, while continuously badgering reporters in the press section. There are various descriptions of Lemkin, some of which seem to be of different men, from the comments on his height, and contenance; even his published pictures seemed to be of different men, on occasion. But there was no doubt about his deter-mination concerning his brain-child, "genocide." Hohenberg remarked on being approached by Lemkin repeatedly, the latter whispering to him of the resistance he was encountering, and mutter-ing on occasion about the "plots" against him, which Hohenberg recalled he listened to genially, without sharing Lemkin's excitement or concern as to their substance.

The London meeting produced no results other than his initia-tion of his proposal, which moved no one to action right away. Lemkin's first big breakthrough was a talk with Panama's represen-tative, Ricardo J. Alfaro, who came away much impressed. This was followed by Lemkin's meeting with Warren R. Austin, the USA's first ambassador to the UN, which also ended on a positive note. In the meantime, the word "genocide" was getting additional and spec-tacular mileage at Nuremberg. Its use by both the principal British figures of the prosecution, Maxwell-Fyfe and Sir Hartley Shawcross, the Attorney General of Great Britain, to castigate the Nuremberg defendants collectively, was more than Lemkin expected. This led to a major New York *Times* editorial, "Genocide," on August 26, 1946, followed by two think-pieces on it, by the *Times*'s house expert on many things, Waldemar Kaempffert, which were separated by a long letter to the *Times* from Lemkin, who went into additional aspects of the subject, while also bringing readers and editors up to date on what the UN was doing on the matter.

The *Times* once more reminded readers that Lemkin had inven-ted the word later used at Nuremberg, identifying him as still a Duke University law professor and "an advisor on foreign affairs to our War Department." The editorial also made a point which later vulgarizers of Lemkin's term did not seem to understand, that he had no intention of posting a prohibition against ordinary mass murder:

> By "genocide" Professor Lemkin means the biological and cultural destruction of national, religious and other entities. "Mass Murder" is not enough, because it says nothing about motives . . . .

Again we see here Lemkin's determination to establish separate categories involving large-scale death; only that resulting to minorities from conscious and deliberate intent, which presumably could be proven with little difficulty, in his mind, would enjoy denunciation and proscription as "genocide."

In summarizing Lemkin's intention to push for UN establishment of "genocide" as an international crime, the *Times* editorial concluded,

> This new principle in international law is necessary, for no state would prosecute a crime instigated and committed by itself. The Eighth International Conference of American States, for example, provides that any persecution on account of racial or religious motives is international in character. By implication, "genocide" has already been recognized as a distinct crime, with a distinct technique and distinct consequences. It now remains to incorporate the term in international law, which is what Professor Lemkin has already half-accomplished. By charging the defendants in the Nuremberg trials with genocide, the United Nations place them in the position of world enemies. A justification of their motives and deeds on national or other grounds is impossible, and if it were possible, the war would have been fought in vain. It now remains to include the term in the sentence.

Kaempffert's piece on October 20, four days after the hangings of the major Nuremberg defendants, contained little new, summarizing the language of Count #3 of the indictment, which used the word "genocide," and mentioning some new historical examples Lemkin was now citing, as having inspired him, including the Turkish massacre of the Armenians after World War I started, the destruction of Carthage (his first citation from antiquity), as well as the Crusades, which Lemkin assessed as "largely wars of extermination." But whether any of these met Lemkin's standards in the intentions and motives department, and how, was not elaborated upon. Kaempffert was satisfied to summarize Lemkin's approach in this manner:

> In Professor Lemkin's formulation, genocide is the result of a conspiracy. It should be punishable not only by an international court but by the courts of any country to which a defendant might have escaped.

Here we see new confusion piled upon the old; Lemkin had begun with the definition of "genocide" as a *collective* crime committed by *a group upon another group,* hence, collective indictments and punishments. Something of this sort had already taken place at Nuremberg, even though "genocide" had not been one of the formal crimes for which the defendants had been convicted. Now, however, we are seeing, in Kaempffert's summary, attention to a single defendant who hypothetically has fled from the scene of a collective "genocidal" crime to some more distant place. Already one can see problems in the making for hypothetical future courts and prosecutors.

On November 8, 1946 the *Times* published as its lead letter to the editor a long communication from Lemkin himself, written from Washington the day before, in which first he called attention to the UN representatives from Cuba, India and Panama having introduced a resolution, calling on the UN "to study the problem of genocide and to prepare a report on the possibilities of declaring genocide an international crime and assuring international cooperation for its prevention and punishment and also recommending, among others, that genocide should be dealt with by national legislation, in the same way as other international crimes."

Noting that the US representative on the Steering Committee of the UN General Assembly had "moved for the inclusion of genocide in its agenda," Lemkin admitted that there was much concern in the UN about the definition of this new crime. But he firmly adhered to his view that it had to be considered as a collective crime. "Genocide" was always a crime "directed against a human group as an entity"; "the actions involved affect individuals not in their individual capacity but as members of the group." And, Lemkin emphasized, "A human group can be destroyed through different means ranging from mass killings to the disintegration of its spiritual resources."

Despite this group-victims and group-guilt concept, Lemkin agreed that "for purposes of international legislation the definition must be limited to more basic elements, such as killings, mayhem, and biological devices (sterilization)," and that "Only acts undertaken habitually and systematically and deriving from an organized plan or conspiracy should be included" in this master definition.

While once more boiling down his personal definition of "genocide" as "the physical and biological destruction of national, racial, ethnical and religious groups," Lemkin pointedly omitted *political* and *economic* categories from his select list, but he was far more concerned with continuing his fight against Hitler and the Nazis than he was in establishing an attack-and-critic-proof definition of his new crime, and omitting the above two was to contribute heavily to his defeat in the United States when the drive to obtain ratification was staged. Now, he was more obsessed with once more charging, indirectly, that the Germans had gassed millions to death and had also sterilized millions of women, as well as extending his drive to make the actions of a State responsible to persons in another State, and he was chagrined that nothing was in existence to assist in applying criminal sanctions against the Nuremberg defendants for what had happened in Germany between 1933 and 1939:

> Because of lack of adequate provisions and previous formulation of international law, the Nuremberg Tribunal had to dismiss the Nazi crimes committed in the period between the advent of Nazism to power and the beginning of the war . . . .

Lemkin seemed to have in mind a ponderous international political machine which would be scrutinizing the behavior of every national state in the world every minute of the day forever, searching for evidence of "genocide" and prepared to prosecute and punish every instance of it swiftly and severely, from the general tone of this first massive personal communique to the *Times.* No scourge of political sin in world history seemed to approach him in zealotry at this moment, when victory was plainly dawning for his campaign.

Things began to move fast now. On December 11, 1946, a month after Lemkin's long epistle to the *Times,* the first major fruit of his lobbying came in. The UN General Assembly, meeting in the Palais de Chaillot in Paris, adopted by unanimous vote a resolution which Lemkin was credited personally with drafting which was to become the Convention on the Prevention and Punishment of Genocide, two years later, almost to the day. The resolution defined "genocide" as "the denial of the right of existence of entire human groups," and included other pet Lemkin notions, such as the disallowance of any possible plea of having acted in behalf of the State, this being reinforced, presumably, by the "principle" introduced at Nuremberg of individual criminal responsibility for any such acts. The major barrier then, as now, appeared to be the problem of how this new crime was to be enforced. Two years were to be spent debating this issue, and when the 1946 resolution became the 1948 "Convention," it had still not been clearly ironed out, another loose end which contributed to its failure to secure U.S. Senate ratification. As Lemkin worded it in late 1946, there being no UN law or law-enforcing machinery, the UN member states endorsing this idea would each have to pass "appropriate" enabling legislation so that "genocide" cases could be prosecuted in their respective courts. In the process the collective vs. individual nature of the "crime" made its way to the fore again, with Lemkin now appearing to agree that those who were indicted for committing it would undoubtedly be individuals; the recently-terminated Nuremberg proceedings had found several individuals guilty, and it was these individuals who were hanged and imprisoned. It did not seem at that moment that there was a way out from this problem; though a group was specified as the only likely recognized victim of "genocide," it would have to be individuals who would have to submit to the legal proceedings resulting from indictment for its commission. But the matter was far from resolved, and it surfaced repeatedly thereafter. Kaempffert reviewed all this in a second *Times* essay on January 5, 1947, while ruminating on the consequences of this latest Lemkin-UN action of a month previous. Kaempffert indicated in his account that Lemkin had the same problem weighing on him since 1933, when he had presumably submitted his draft measure to the League of Nations' International Conference for Unification of Criminal Law. It was in this that he tried simultaneously to establish something he had not yet named would be construed as a *group* crime, while suggesting at the same time that an offender might be apprehended and tried in any country regardless of jurisdiction, "or the offender's nationality," as Kaempffert phrased it. So—though a single person might not be the *victim* of "genocide," a single individual now could certainly be prosecuted for committing it, according to Lemkin's tangled legal net, insofar as he had built it by the end of 1946.

"Genocide" became a subject entry in the New York *Times Index* in January, 1947. In that month also appeared still another summary of it all by Lemkin in the *American Journal of International Law,* "Genocide as a Crime under International Law," which probably was his clearest statement on the subject but added little but grace notes to a now-familiar refrain. His problem now was, clearly, that of *enforcement*: how were "genocidists" to be guaranteed certain punishment? The absence of numerous Germans charged with "war crimes" weighed heavily on his consciousness in worrying about this, and the strong possibility that persons sought for "genocide" in the future might make their apprehension difficult by fleeing elsewhere prompted Lemkin to bring up the subject repeatedly, no more sharply anywhere than in his *AJIL* article. Here he strongly insisted on extradition procedures being guaranteed, though he thought it would be even better if there existed an understanding that persons charged with "genocide" would be subject to punishment in any given country to which they had fled, regardless of where the "crime" had been committed.

It was in this piece also that Lemkin veered away from calm and measured legal sonorities to deliver yet another poisonous lecture to the occupied German state, which he thought was about to be revived as a member of the world community of nations, even if it was at that time barred from membership in the victors' new global club, the United Nations. Scolded Lemkin,

> Germany, the classical country of genocide practices, must not profit by the situation that the United Nations genocide resolution does not bind her as a state because she is not a member of the UN. Since

Germany's practices actually provided the basis for developing the concept of genocide, she should be the first country to include the crime of genocide in her criminal code.

Lemkin had finally dropped the disguises and subterfuge, and his diversionary tactics in crediting historical events over the centuries for motivating him in his "genocide" crusade, including those famous 600 "Assyrian Christians" massacred in Iraq in 1933; the real driving force had always been, from the beginning, Adolf Hitler and German National Socialism starting in 1933; all the rest was diversionary deception.

There was one other item of special interest in this latest expounding of the "genocide" doctrine: Lemkin's recognition of a threat to the primacy of his entity by the growing talk of "human rights," at this moment, especially, in the United States. Lemkin grumbled that here there was even developing a tendency for the two to become blended to the point that they tended to become identical in the popular mind. Lemkin lectured those with this erroneous tendency to this effect:

> Genocide deals with the life of peoples—the annhilation of existence. Human rights is concerned with different levels of existence, while genocide deals with non-existence.

In Lemkin's view, "human rights" was a very controversial subject still; "genocide" was not. It was to be the prime irony of this entire affair that the United Nations were to adopt the Universal Declaration of Human Rights the day after the Genocide Convention, and that the former was gradually to eclipse the latter in steady stages during the succeeding three decades, to the point where by 1977-1978, 30 years later, "human rights" had taken over almost the entire world stage, while "genocide" had slipped back into the obscure regions of indistinct terminology and had become virtually little but a spinal cord reflex used as a synonym for a massacre, as far away from Raphael Lemkin's original conception as it was almost possible to get.

But Raphael Lemkin had to experience arriving at the pinnacle of success with his legal baggage before sensing the coming eclipse of his political dream for the future. The year 1947 might be designated the occasion of the achievement of the first major time of heightened consciousness of "genocide," with a general inkling as to its possibilities as an exploited verbal reflex. It was being used more and more in every-day written and conversational traffic, and the momentum was carrying it through the halls of the mighty and the counsels of the influential at a good clip.

In the UN, after contemplating what they had accepted from Lemkin in December, 1946, it was decided that it needed additional work. So a committee of three, one of them being Lemkin, working with the UN secretarial staff, were authorized to prepare a "draft convention" on genocide, which was then circulated among the representatives of the various governments at the UN. The first draft of this "draft convention" was completed on June 10, 1947, it was announced at the newest meeting place, Lake Success, N.Y., though it appears that the press release incorporated a mistake, or else the editors of the New York *Times* were guilty of too generous editing, because the news story appearing in the *Times* the next day (June 11, 1947, p. 14) stated, "The first draft convention calling on UN members to punish individuals or governments who seek to destroy entire racial, religious, national or political [sic] groups was completed here today."

Prepared by the "three international law experts," it described three separate categories of "genocide": the first condemned not only mass killings but also the placing of people in such a condition of health "that their death becomes imminent, as well as those wilfully starved or maltreated in concentration camps" or "used for medical experiments." The second classification was "biological genocide," the sterilization of groups and the "forced separation of families." The third was "cultural genocide," "the deliberate obliteration of the spiritual or cultural life of a people," the stealing of children "for purposes of indoctrinating them in a different cultural pattern," destroying art works, museums, libraries and churches, "stamping out prevailing customs and ideas," "removing the spiritual and intellectual leaders of the community" (no one commented on the thorough job just achieved in this last category in a dozen countries after 1945 by the Stalinists and their "democratic Allies" alike.)

The press report concluded by noting that the draft convention also stipulated that "public propaganda that seeks to justify genocide is a crime," and that public officials and "individuals" would be held responsible for such. And it was concluded by expressing the belief that it presumably contained provisions for enforcing the convention and for punishing violators.

From the General Assembly the draft convention went to the UN committee on Codification and Development of International Law, and in July, 1947 to the UN Economic and Social Council, where the new class of bureaucrats mulled it over the rest of the summer and most of the fall. During this period the pressure groups began to build up the drumfire in its behalf, and submerged "groups" who were not expected to take advantage of the situation started to lodge long, loud, impassioned wails of anguish as fellow victims of "genocide," to the accompaniment of vast waves of silence from the top echelons ruminating over this new crime in the inner sanctums of the UN.

On July 29, 1947 the Consultative Council of Jewish Organizations strongly urged UNESCO to adopt the draft genocide convention Lemkin and his two fellow experts had prepared for them. But the American Jewish Committee, the Alliance Israelite Universelle of France and the Anglo-Jewish Association of Great Britain modified their support by urging that the preamble of the draft convention be rewritten to define "genocide" as "the intentional destruction of a group of human beings whether the crime is committed on religious, racial, political [sic] or any other grounds," a sweeping definition which suggested that the draft Lemkin's committee had prepared had *not* included the *political* category in its list of protected groups, after all. But the concluding phrase recommended by these Zionist groups, "or any other grounds," was, if included, sure to halt moves for its adoption, if not stop it dead in its tracks: the Stalinist politicians, if none other did, sensed in this verbiage a coup for minorities to such a degree that political action against them for any reasons whatever would be instantly blared to the world as "genocide," and they soon were to demonstrate that even if they were ready to condemn the dead Germans once again, they had no intention of submitting to having their hands tied forever when it came to controlling their own minorities (of which they had a plenitude) in time to come.

The following day the National Conference of Christians and Jews, and the World Jewish Congress, the latter considered a non-governmental organization having "consultative status" with the Economic and Social Council of the United Nations, also, in a memorandum, urged UNESCO to go about the "speedy adoption" of the draft genocide convention, to outlaw "this foul crime against humanity." The WJC claimed 57 countries had already responded favorably to their position. The discordant note in this concerto of political pressure was a series of charges by Ukrainians, Lithuanians, Latvians and Esthonians that they were currently victims of "genocide" on the part of Stalinist Russia, and wanted the UN to do something about it. As these began to reverberate around the world in the fall of 1947, it gave the great patrons of "genocide" something to think about, and surely induced an inkling as to the future possibilities involved in the posting of continuous charges of "genocide" before the august chambers of the UN potentates, who presumably were still thinking of the past, and probably of the mind that all they were engaged in doing was the preparation of another pretentious ritual condemnation of hanged Nazis and Fascists. But the "genocide" charge ploy had really not yet achieved the volume of a trickle; the premises of the UN were to be almost swamped by such in years to come. In just the next year, as world politics based on the artificial alliance of 1941-1945 began to disintegrate, and the fully developed Cold War began to spread across the sky, those so cheerily complacent about what they thought they were achieving with this new political dynamite word would begin to know the sober underside of its implications. A characteristic of the struggle to get the genocide convention adopted and then ratified by the national governments of the adopting countries, 1947-1951, was an almost total ignoring of world affairs while this was going on, and especially a studied avoidance of coping with the many global bellows of "genocide" aimed at one country or another, in those years. Lemkin and his most industrious cohorts were almost totally immersed in history, while this was going on, and began to develop an awareness that the world was still in motion at about the occasion of Stalin's death in 1953, following which Jewish organizations began their stentorian attack on him posthumously and his successors for their "genocidal" policies toward the Jews of the Soviet Union. In the meantime, as will be shown, the UN was deaf, dumb and blind to the contemporary accusations of "genocide" which poured in from the trouble-spots of the world. That the UN did nothing about any of them is partially of significance, though the UN has never done anything about any of the others which took place thereafter, either. Never being able to overcome the country accused of "genocide" in the manner which befell the Germans in 1945, it is quite understandable that nothing was ever done about a "genocide" charge. The fundamental hollowness and impotence of the whole "genocide" show was plainly discernible long before it became a paper taboo in the UN.

The "genocide" issue was moving on inexorably toward full UN acceptance by the end of 1947. On November 21 the General Assembly in still another resolution called on the Economic and Social Council to keep working on the subject, and to submit an acceptable draft convention at the third Assembly session, scheduled to take place at Lake Success, N.Y. And from this latter location, Lemkin, now referred to as "United Nations advisor on genocide," on December 19, declared that the UN resolution was "a real revolution in international law." In one of his few comments on the Nuremberg trials, Lemkin agreed that they had made "an advance of 10 or 20 per cent toward outlawing genocide," and thought that "a victor in war has the right to try war criminals in an occupied country for atrocities against their own citizens" had been established as a "principle" during those proceedings. The need now, Lemkin insisted, was that of getting passed a statute in international law under which *individuals* committing crimes of genocide might be tried in times of peace. Once more Lemkin's reasoning showed the tangling consequences of the collision between his group-crime concept of "genocide" and the sticky problem of deciding who would stand accused of it. His previous rationalizing had assumed the haling of a considerable number of persons before the bench simultaneously, a view probably influenced by his expectation that after victory in Europe in 1945, an immense collection of Germans would be brought before the court to answer for charges of committing "war crimes." Two dozen at Nuremberg had been a fair bag, but as time was going on, the tendency had been fairly strong for these "war crimes" courts to deal with specific individuals, more and more. His changed views on the problem perhaps reflected what was going on in the real world, in this case. This last statement in 1947 was notable for another reason, the admission for the first time that some resistance was being encountered in the lobbying at the UN, presumably the result of instructions getting back to the representatives in the General Assembly from their respective governments. Though agreement on outlawing "genocide" appeared to be a painless and largely costless verbal political commitment on their part, the possibilities of the consequences in the future, based on what had been advanced already, were not all that favorable in appearance. There were polite rumblings that the provisions being recommended for punishing "genocide" in the future suggested, at least to some of them, the likelihood of infringment on their particular national sovereignty. Lemkin thought he had effected a permanent and irreparable breach in the wall of nationalism everywhere, permitting a new era of unlimited elbow room, and domain for unrestrained movement, by minorities. But the sentiment of nationalism was apparently not as completely spent as he thought. That of the Germans and their wartime associated powers may have been nearly expunged, but elsewhere there was quite a different situation. It was to be brought to his attention soon, and rudely.

In the *United Nations Bulletin* for January 15, 1948 Lemkin prepared a much-abridged version of his "Genocide as a Crime Under International Law" which had appeared in the *American Journal of International Law* a year before. In this account he added some new examples of the world's best known cases of "genocide," the only one cited from the pre-Christian era being the destruction of Carthage. To this he appended "the destruction of the Albigenses and Waldenses, the Crusades, the March of the Teutonic Knights, the destruction of the Christians under the Ottoman Empire, the massacre of the Herreros in Africa, the extermination of the Armenians, the slaughter of the Christian Assyrians in 1933, [sic] the destruction of the Maronites, and the pogroms against the Jews in Czarist Russia and Rumania." Nowhere did he post the necessary evidence that any of these was planned, deliberate and intentional.

This list was more than an expansion of the scope of his new crime to demonstrate its ancient trappings (some of these had been included in *Axis Rule*, it will be remembered) for a new international audience in the shape of the United Nations Assembly: it also revealed Lemkin in a new light, at least moderately so. Eschewing his single-minded campaign, so far waged as though time were standing still at around October, 1946, he showed wary and perceptive political canniness in omitting any possible reference to Stalinist "genocide" whatever. The actions of the Leninist-Stalinist regime alone could have filled his article to overflowing, but not a critical word was to be found in Lemkin's new catalog of the doings of "genocide" in history. His attack on Stalin for conducting "genocide" on the Jews lay in the future; for the moment not a breath of complaint was to be seen in Lemkin's steamy prose here. In fact, with his native Poland now a firm Soviet puppet state, and his own hope of a further political career there (if indeed he ever contemplated this) as dead as the dinosaurs, he still could not bring himself to a critique of his homeland, the scene of the worst physical attacks on Jews in all of Eastern Europe. It goes without saying that Lemkin failed to hint even at the systematic murder of the entire Polish army officer corps by Stalin's henchmen, some 15,000 in all, over 4,000 of them having been discovered in a mass grave at Katyn in 1943, as has been seen. This made the "slaughter of the 600 'Assyrian Christians' in Iraq" look like a somewhat lesser event to be memorializing. But this was just one occasion of Lemkin's peculiarity in selectivity when it came to recalling the highlights of "genocide" in the past. And he seemed to have forgotten that he had already credited the Germans with being his sole inspiration in conceiving this "crime."

There were other aspects in this latest memoranda on "genocide" by Lemkin, this one also for international consumption. Becoming aware that the various Communist regimes were advancing their own stories of the Nazi massacres to enhance their own political status and future, as well as to embroider the plausibility of their own hanging bees of captured German and other Axis enemies, Lemkin had to expand the number claimed to be dead. Since it had been created as a conventional statistic at Nuremberg that 6,000,000 Jews had been put to death during the war by the Axis, though nothing faintly describing a scientific census had been conducted by anyone, and that all manner of meretricious claims had been made by almost everyone with access to a publisher of any kind, some as high as 40,000,000, the Communist claims made it necessary to expand the number declared as dead as the result of deliberate, planned Axis extermination. In this new brief on "genocide" Lemkin now charged the Nazis not only with "destroying six million Jews," but also "several million Slavs, and almost all the gypsies of Europe." (Lemkin was rewarded for this generous inclusion of non-Jewish dead in the Nazi record in the next three decades by several Communist works issued in Poland and the Soviet Union which almost removed the Jews entirely from the list of the honor roll of the massacred.)

Still another revealing item in this *UNB* article was Lemkin's latest definition of "genocide," in which the category "political" was once more added to this on-again, off-again continuing effort. This seemed to reflect also a temporary twist in the world political line on the part of the Soviet representative at the General Assembly, who momentarily had agreed to this inclusion, or at least seemed to have done so, if the later complaints of the American and British representatives were to be believed. But on the nature of the crime, Lemkin sounded as of yore, denouncing "genocide" as "the crime of crimes," that "to cause death to the above-mentioned groups [national, racial, religious, linguistic, *and* political], directly or indirectly," was indeed "the most heinous of all crimes." On the condemnation of this killing *directly* Lemkin had no trouble in mobilizing the United Nations majority. It was on the definition of what *indirectly* killing these minorities constituted that he was to come a cropper.

To be sure, the culminating aspects of the drive to sell "genocide" to the United Nations Organization ran into complications, partially due to the coming into existence of the State of Israel and the collapse of the Afro-Asian colonial systems of the "victorious" European powers in the war ending in 1945. But far more was due to the falling-out of the winning "Allies" after that same date, and the consequent Cold War among them, which already appeared to be a serious affair by the spring of 1948, when the final drive to elevate "genocide" to the prime position among international crimes began to take shape.

On April 14, 1948 the Assembly in session at Lake Success created a 7-nation committee of "international law experts" to whip into final shape a convention to outlaw "genocide," obviously working closely on the model Lemkin and his two confreres had already presented. An impasse occurred immediately—over the basis of the definition of "genocide" as an international crime. This new committee included a representative of the Soviet Union, P. D. Morozov, who wanted the definition to read, "an act directed toward the destruction of human groups for racial, religious or national motives."

France and Lebanon were willing to go along with this, but the Polish representative, Prof. Alexander Rudzinski, supported by the Chinese, called this an "erroneous" conception of it all. Morozov's wording, in their view, "confused the victims of the crime with the motives behind it." A sulfurous wrangling ensued, and arguments continued for months, further complicated by the opportunistic attractiveness of the entire concept. While this latest UN committee were laboring on a satisfactory verbalization of "genocide" the surroundings were rent by mighty wails from several points of the world compass charging this land or that with committing it. In mid-April the Pakistanis had accused India of "genocide," so had China charged Japan, and the Indonesians had a similar accusation naming the Dutch with similar action. We have seen that several had already been lodged by the Baltic peoples and Ukrainian nationalists against the Soviet Union. And there were many more to come.

The closing stages leading to the creation of the Jewish state in Palestine coincided with the terminal moves establishing "genocide" as international law, and the decorum of the UN was rudely disturbed several times by sensational acts of terrorism by Zionist desperadoes, though these latter events, no matter how lethal they were, actually did not make the agenda, but did manage to delay action on "genocide" by taking up time to discuss their significance, and what UN action might be taken about them.

The slowing down of action on "genocide" seems to have stimulated the coming into existence in the USA of a "United States Committee for United Nations Genocide Convention." presumably to step up the volume and the temperature of pro-"genocide" convention lobbying. Composed of "clerical, and lay leaders of the Protestant, Catholic and Jewish faiths," according to the New York *Times* of June 21, 1948, its function was supposedly to be purely "educational," in order to stimulate action leading to "adoption of legislation by all countries to prevent and punish genocide." The latter wording was significant: it was the language actually used in the final verbalization of the "genocide" convention. But the new pressure group was involved in a step beyond the UN's possible action. Anticipating that a very clumsy if not utterly unworkable contraption would come out of the UN when it came to enforcement machinery applying to this new international crime, this "committee" was already thinking ahead, and working for *ratification,* presumably by the United States, in particular, which had to take place before enabling legislation could be introduced and passed, which would provide for apprehension and punishment of committers of "genocide" on the *local, national* level. In this sense this new lobby, headed by the New York City attorney, James N. Rosenberg, and having for figurehead vice-chairmen the noted 1939-1941 pro-war activist, Clark M. Eichelberger, and such a polished establishment spokesman as Henry Noble MacCracken, was premature. It still had to be processed through the UN yet, let alone ratified by the U.S. Senate, before any action could be engineered to bring about the enabling legislation which was frankly announced as their real goal.

The *ad hoc* seven-nation committee set up by UNESCO finally got in gear by late summer, and submitted the desired revised draft of the original Lemkin draft to the Council, which turned it over for some time, and after something called "general debate," not unlike the ratification of the death of an aunt, sent the revision on to the General Assembly, which in the fall of 1948 was convened at the Palais de Chaillot in Paris once more.

The Cold War had already polarized the UN on the "genocide" question, as well as on many other matters separating the one-time warriors-in-arms fighting the Axis powers. In September and October, 1948 the wrangling reached a contumacious pitch, especially over two issues, whether there should be machinery for international apprehension and punishment of violators of the "genocide" convention, now conceded surely to be adopted, the question now remaining being simply *when* this was to take place. The other subject not yet settled was whether there would be agreement on the inclusion of a "political" category among the stipulated groups whose future killing or suppression as per the Lemkin recipe would merit condemnation as "genocide."

The Soviet bloc, and especially the Soviet Union and Poland, and Yugoslavia, expressed much unhappiness with the revised draft of the general convention even before UNESCO passed it on to the General Assembly because it contained no mention of their late adversaries; it "did not link genocide with fascism and nazism as its originators." This collided with Lemkin's new-found historical thesis on "genocide," which, as has been seen, went as far back as the obliteration of Carthage by Rome, 202 B.C. Perhaps Stalin's late "allies" should have conceded on this point: after all, the Roosevelt and Churchill regimes had spent hundreds of billions of dollars and expended hundreds of thousands of lives in a war whose only clear winner was their colleague Stalin, spreading the joys of Marxist-Leninist-Stalinist Communism to an additional twelve countries. But the realities of world politics now suggested that much future mileage might be made out of "genocide" simply as a global verbal reflex, one of the luxuries in this department lying in the possibilities of the political hay which might be made accusing an adversary of "genocide," along with any additional useful accusation which might be conjured up. So the chastened anti-or-non-Soviet bloc dragged their feet noticeably on this issue. Charges of "genocide" had already been launched in a most vociferous manner by Ukrainians and Balts; the two sides of the Cold War were obviously preparing to accuse one another of this one a wholesale basis as soon as it became propitious. At the very time the Assembly was discussing this aspect, the lines were already taking shape on the quarrel between Pakistan and India. As the debate over these above details in the revised draft convention was going on, the representative of Pakistan, Mrs. Shoista S. Ikra Mullah, had filed a bitter complaint that "whole races were still being persecuted in India." The Soviet Eastern European bloc casually ignored the Pakistani complaint, diverted attention to yet another chewing-over of the Nuremberg Trials, and glossed over the entire subject of India's behavior. But, strangely enough, India's representative supported the British position on the future provision of punishment for committing "genocide," that it be made international, and not depend on the legal machinery of the various national states to apprehend and punish violators within their own national states. In the course of taking this rather individualistic position, India's representative, K.V.K. Subdarans, blandly ignoring Pakistan, urged that the UN get on with an international draft convention without "further academic discussion."

Sir Hartley Shawcross, the United Kingdom prosecutor at Nuremberg, also insisted rather sharply before the General Assembly that any eventual tribune contemplated for future punishment of "genocide" had to be international. Sir Hartley reasoned that since "genocide" was generally perpetrated by States, the courts of these States would likely be most unreliable and would be most remiss to find their own national state figures guilty.

When it came to the subject of including "political" among the groups whose annihilation would be proscribed, the Cold War separation was represented by the combat between the Soviet bloc and the United States representative on the UN Legal Committee, Ernest A. Gross, which latter organization had the final say on the draft convention the UN membership would vote upon. Gross, on October 14, pointed out that the Soviet Union had originally supported the inclusion of a provision "outlawing the physical extermination of groups on the ground of the political opinion of their members," and he could not understand why they had recently made a "startling reversal" on this stand, and now firmly opposed it.

But the resistance to this clause extended well beyond the Soviet bloc. It was admitted that "several delegations outside the Soviet group" also had objected to the inclusion of the clause forbidding "political genocide." The arguments used included the assertion that political groups were not "cohesive" to begin with, very hard to identify, and that furthermore, the inclusion of an interdiction of this kind would prohibit any government anywhere from preventing a revolt, the assumption being apparently that the main beneficiaries of the "political" taboo in the "genocide" department would be revolutionaries, rendered immune from repression.

Gross was mainly concerned with answering the second of these objections. He said that in the history of the persecution of political minorities, in the case of the German and Italian dictatorships, these latter had experienced no difficulty in clearly identifying opposition political groups and in moving swiftly against them. In the case of the Soviet Union, said Gross, since there the Communist Party was the only political party, *anyone* acting outside this organization was so clearly identified that the subject did not have to be explored further. Others were concerned about the possibility of an ethnic minority becoming a political party or an organized political force; such a thing was already staring them in the face in the case of Zionism in Palestine.

As it turned out, "political" was left off the list of protected groups, and the matter of punishment was left in such a tangled state of confusion, involving the possibility of both national *and* international punishment apparatus, that it eventually contributed markedly to the ultimate refusal of the U.S. Senate to ratify the Convention.

On the afternoon of Thursday, December 9, 1948, the United Nations General Assembly adopted unanimously the Convention which designated "genocide" to be an international crime. Meeting in the Palais de Chaillot in Paris, the vote was 55-0. Originally the Soviet bloc and Great Britain abstained when the document was first presented by the UN Legal Committee, but all switched to an affirmative vote to make it unanimous, though the delegates from Costa Rica, El Salvador and South Africa were not present when the balloting took place.

Assembly President Herbert V. Evatt of Australia promptly loosed upon the representatives a torrent of spirited rhetoric, praising their action as "an epoch-making event in the development of international law," and urging them vehemently to work for the parliamentary ratification of the convention in each of their national homelands.

But even in this seemingly universal approval, there were threads of disagreement which had not all been worked into the fabric of the Convention. The Soviet Union had proposed five amendments to the document but they were all defeated prior to the balloting. The first called for the insertion of a reference to nazism and fascism in the preamble as the originators of "genocide"; the second would have added another proscribed "genocidic" crime, "cultural genocide";

the third would have deleted a reference to a possible international penal tribunal to try "genocide" cases; the fourth would have prohibited everywhere the existence of organizations "inciting to racial, national and religious hatred," and the fifth would have added a clause making the Convention applicable also to any colonies of any of the signatories, an obvious move calculated to embarrass the Western powers still occupying Afro-Asian real estate.

At the time these five were defeated, two additional resolutions were adopted: one of these virtually amounted to the provision originally advanced by the Soviet representation, in that it applied the Convention to the colonial possessions, or their "dependent territories," as the new euphemism for such of such signatories as had them. The second, however, made a muddy situation even more murky, in that it tried to solve the only real matter in all the turgid "genocide" verbiage from the time Raphael Lemkin began it, and that concerned how those found guilty, after Nuremberg, of committing "genocide" were to be punished. The new resolution adopted referring to this issue requested the International Law Commission to study both the possibility and the desirability of creating an "International Penal Tribunal," possibly a "criminal chamber" bolted to the International Court of Justice still sitting at The Hague, which would hear "genocide" cases. But there still remained the avenue of domestic prosecution of "genocide" within any given national state of a signatory, as well. Nevertheless, the possibility of the transfer of such a case was not only implied in this continued search for an international legal machine to handle it, but the latter was also made easier to conceive by the pledge of the contracting parties to the Convention to grant extradition of accused "genocidists," the assumption being that such persons might not only be extradited to stand before the courts of another country, but before this new international bench as well, should it come into existence. And here the legal giants of the UN planted in their new construct the seeds of its guaranteed sterility in the USA. If Senator Taft (and, later Justice Douglas) were to be the undoing of Lemkin's dream of a no-*ex post facto* verdict on Nuremberg, the tangled snarl in which the UN Legal Committee left the punishment section of the Genocide Convention created for Lemkin the undoing of this new invention, in the shape of the opposition of the senior statesmen of the American Bar Association, as will be seen.

In the meantime, however, it was triumph and rejoicing and extravagant compliments, all around. The New York *Times* hailed Lemkin and the final success of his "15-year fight" for the "ban" on "genocide", and published a picture of Lemkin while applauding his success in the following prose:

Today marked the climax in the career of Dr. Raphael Lemkin, member of the Yale Law Faculty, who has devoted more than fifteen years of his life trying to have a ban on the destruction of human groups written into international law. Even coining the word "genocide" to express the concept of killing entire groups is attributed to him.

The text of the Genocide Convention (the term "convention" in international law simply means an agreement among "sovereign nations") is to be found as the first appendix to this study, and need not be repeated here; its shortcoming and flaws will be dealt with subsequently as the struggle to get the Convention ratified is taken up. But one of its strange contradictions is worth nothing. In Article II "genocide" was defined as "acts committed with intent to destroy, in whole or in part, a national, ethnical, racial or religious groups" [sic], and the Article then went on to describe these acts. It will be seen that the *political* group was omitted, and in Article VII it stipulated that the commission of any "genocidal" act would not be considered a "political crime" "for the purpose of extradition". The Genocide Convention was not innocent of or unconcerned with politics, however; it simply was careful as to what would be considered "political." But for Lemkin, in his moment of victory, the "small cloud on the horizon" no larger than a man's fist showed up the next day; on December 10, 1948 the General Assembly adopted the Universal Declaration of Human Rights, the concept which vied with "genocide" for popular support thereafter. When the General Assembly's presiding officer, Australia's Herbert V. Evatt, expansively hailed the UN's submission to the governments of the world's national states of the International Convention to Prevent and Punish Genocide and the Universal Declaration of Human Rights (in *United Nations Bulletin,* January 1, 1949, p. 2), as the two outstanding achievements of the United Nations, he did not seem to realize that the august global politicians had fabricated, on two successive days, two quite different approaches to the problem, a matter Raphael Lemkin had already recognized and commented upon, and which were to collide increasingly even in the years immediately ahead. But it would take some time for the general awareness to evolve to recognize that there was a fundamental problem in trying to adjust Lemkin's conceptions of group injury, group guilt and group punishment to the individualized view of the matter as expressed in the "human rights" declaration. And, in a similar way, despite the plain language of Article II of the Genocide Convention, it would be a long while even for those who should have known what they were doing or saying, such as the compilers of dictionaries, to realize that there was no mention of *political* groups enjoying the paper

umbrella protection of the Convention on Genocide (even as late
as the 1979 printing of the immense and widely sold unabridged
Webster Third New International Dictionary [1976] it still included
"political" among the protected groups [p. 947]).

Chapter Six

THE BALANCE SHEET OF 'GENOCIDE' RATIFICATION: RAPHAEL LEMKIN'S VICTORY IN THE UN AND FAILURE IN THE USA

WHAT WERE THE political forces which had triumphed in the adoption by the United Nations of the Genocide Convention? To be sure, it was the coalition of anti-Nazi elements that had morally, financially and militarily propelled World War Two to the kind of interim settlement the world was then "enjoying," at the end of 1948. Among them in Europe were the several varieties of Marxism, and in particular the operational Stalinist and pro-Stalinist forces in about twenty countries. In addition there were the several varieties of pro-war liberalism abroad and in America, many of them long-time Stalinist transmission-belts, sharing the great victory. Essentially these two major impulses had joined hands in getting through the Genocide Convention as another anti-Nazi insurance policy, though very little may have been said of this while the UN maneuvering had transpired. Some 25 years later, the UN was far less circumspect, and, ignoring Raphael Lemkin's alligator tears and trembling memorials presumably commemorating distant past victims of "genocide," earned an award for honesty and frankness by declaring flatly that it was Nazi Germany which had been the only real inspiration behind the entire affair (*The Crime of Genocide* [1973], p. 1).

But joining them, obviously, were the architects of the "bi-partisan" world control system in the United States, fueled and spurred by the opulent and affluent pro-World War II Anglophile forces represented in the moneyed and aristocratic interventionist fronts of 1939-1941, if not earlier. The resulting global machine,

even after its failure to recruit Stalin and Mao Tse-tung into a *real*
"one world," a planetary spread-eagle which would have made any
dream of any previous world-mobilizer look exceedingly pale and
feeble by comparison, was still a ponderous and very formidable
construct, re-organizing and running the "free world" and laying the
foundation for the amassing of fortunes totalling in the many hundreds of billions of dollars in the generation after war's end.

Getting along with Communism, Stalinist or Maoist, was something which hardly tasked their powers. The English writer George
Orwell fully recognized the ability of the two Eurasian Red worlds to
"co-exist" with the non-Communist Western one, and the necessary
part all three played in propping up one another and providing each
in turn with excuses for their home populations when they adopted
one program or another, despite occasionally sounding as though
they were the most implacable of opponents. This is the core of
Orwell's famed novel *Nineteen Eighty-four,* originally titled *Nineteen
Forty-eight,* and published in 1949. This book was not a futuristic
science fiction tale; in novelized form it described the real world of
1948, and everything in it was either in existence or well along the
line of production. And his description of the heatings and coolings,
the hostilities and the detentes, among the three-fold world masters,
was anything but an imagination of things to come. As for the purely
Soviet vs. "Western world" confrontation, with all its spy scares and
provocative episodes, despite it all, they both managed, with great
solemnity, to exchange the job every month of guarding seven
German prisoners in the immense Spandau prison in Berlin, a ceremony of far more than passing interest and even greater significance
in revealing who their common enemy really was. The Cold War
neatly concealed their joint conduct of warfare on the Germans for
years after the formal termination of the shooting in May, 1945.

In the USA, the dominant forces of finance, industry, commerce
and agriculture must have gone to considerable effort to suppress a
continuous guffaw while trembling in public about the "menace of
Communism," and pursuing minor functionaries (but never anyone
of substantial prominence) for allegedly advancing the interests of
the other via some espionage caper. Though reenacted in many ways,
as Orwell correctly recognized, this was essentially a deception, and
intended to make easier the advancement of domestic policy, though
his effort to alert the English-speaking world about the nature of this
basically dishonest "cold war", via the devices of fiction, was short-
circuited. The clever conversion of his commentary in novel form on
the world of 1948 into a tale supposedly of things in the world to
come, some 35 years away, was a publisher's smart sales ploy as well
as a fundamental diversion of its readers from its real message. Had

Orwell lived, it would have been interesting to see if he would have commented on the basic alteration achieved in distorting his principal thesis.

The "West" faced about as much of a threat to their economic power from Communism as the world of the Industrial Revolution even in its early decades faced from a system no further along than stone hatchets. They had put down the *real* threats to their power in destroying the Italo-German-Japanese revolutionary upstarts, whose incredible energy and organizing genius, even considering their considerable handicaps, must have thrown a serious fright into many of their antagonists in the struggle of 1939-1945, especially when they thought about the future. The new world now in the hands of the "victors" had to be structured so as to keep them *down,* not so much as to keep the Communists *out,* though it had to appear as though the latter were the sole motivation. The last thing the "free world" feared was the spasmodic and sickly productivity and the outrageously poor quality of the output of the Red world; only the most desperately poor considered Communist products worth striving to possess, and 35 years after war's end, it was still unordinary to see Communist artifacts in the "West," with the exception of weapons. Only the gross distortions of central planning, which kept the Red civilian-consumption sector largely in the final quarter of the 19th century, made possible the lopsided allocation of resources resulting in good guns. There were few who feared a system which could not even feed itself, but its publicized ominousness, used as public policy, made the civilian population of its apparent adversary also amenable to control which they otherwise might not have endured at all. Even in the Far East, a totally battered and flattened Japan, by comparison with the victorious Reds of China, still were to be calculated at an advantage best measured in terms of a century of more, perhaps two, in some opinions, over a regime which even after a generation was best known for ping pong. For the "liberators," converting the vanquished into economically powerful political satellites was the main job lying ahead; the "free world" had learned the hard way what Lawrence Dennis had meant when he spoke of "the bloody futility of frustrating the strong."

In the meantime, however, the sham had to be carried on, since an enemy somewhere had become an operational necessity for the victorious regardless of location. Foreign policy was simply the major tool in controlling and directing domestic policy. In Orwell's book it was frankly endorsed and employed as basic dynamics; in the "real world" it was too, only that domestic manipulation via foreign policy simply had to be disguised and never admitted regardless of circumstances.

When Raphael Lemkin was engaged in preparing *Axis Rule in Occupied Europe,* the seminal work in which the entire concept of "genocide" was detonated, he had principally the backing of one of the influential fronts of this grand coalition of Insider forces which was to take back the world, after putting down the massive challenge of 1939-1945, with the support of the resources of the entire political regime ("bi-partisan") directing this recovery, called "liberation" for posterity. A subsidiary, and, at the start, minor, contributor to Lemkin's efforts, was the waxing strength of Zionism, to be mobilized later as a full partner in the "free world" master structure, and to receive in turn full support, as it went about its 19th century-style colonial invasion of the Arabic Middle East for the purposes of establishing the 19th century conception of the Jewish homeland, Israel.

So, though Zionist interest as such had little to do with the creation of the idea of "genocide," it was evident that after its endorsement by the United Nations as an international crime that Zionism would be a strong force seeking to get the idea planted around the world, and implemented as national policy in all countries that it could influence. Hence one sees, in the major offensive in behalf of "genocide" as US policy between 1949 and 1954 especially, an immense contribution in the form of money and political pressure from Zionist organizations. Pressuring for ratification of the Genocide Convention by the U.S. Senate came before everything else, because it was a treaty, and no legislation applying to the domestic definition of "genocide," with provisions for its prevention or punishment by law, could come up for consideration before this ratification took place. This was the general argument in 1949.

For Stalinist Communism, "genocide" had a basic function to perform, differing from the purposes it might serve for others, including Zionism and its affluent "free world" support system, particularly in the Anglo-American world. For Communism, "genocide" was an adjunct to their policy immediately next door, helping make easier the control of the vast region of Eastern and Central Europe overrun by the Red Army in 1944-1945, the sole basis for their claim to dominate the area still. "Genocide" was the cornerstone of the anti-German common front which the Soviet needed to keep their part of the New Dispensation intact and free from disintegration back to the situation prevailing between 1919 and 1939. Combining "genocide" and the tireless exploitation of the German wartime concentration camps, mainly those in Poland, were the indispensable ingredients to perpetuating a permanent regional Germanophobia.

It is no surprise, therefore, as one begins to examine the move to get the Genocide Convention ratified around the world, including the United States, that a variety of conflicting objectives lay behind the drive. Zionism's beachhead had already been established in Palestine when the ratification impulse began; the maneuvering between Soviet Communism and its bloc of new puppet Red regimes in Eastern and Central Europe, as against the Anglo-American-directed "free world" bloc, was an event taking place also at the same time, and dominating the headlines.

But there was no movement made to dispossess the Stalinist regime of its newly-acquired real estate, with the exception of the activities which got the Reds to withdraw from Austria, though the Communization of adjoining Czecho-Slovakia far more than made up for that. Elsewhere the Red wave did not recede, and despite the tactic of "containment" adopted by the "free world" from sometime in 1947 onward, no serious effort was made to dislodge Communist control anywhere in Europe, even if there was comfort taken in Western circles when Josip Broz Tito maneuvered Red Yugoslavia out of the immediate political grasp of Stalin, while remaining fully as Communist. Nor did any campaign to restrain the Communist saturation of Central Europe occur while the main effort to ratify the Genocide Convention took place. Though at tremendous expense the "free world" prevented the Reds from absorbing the entire city of Berlin, jointly-managed hundreds of kilometers behind the Red frontiers in "East" (read: Central) Germany, a political arrangement almost breathtaking in its stupidity on the part of the "free world," the only direction in which things proceeded, from a geo-political point of view, 1945-49, was the extension or consolidation of Communist territorial expansion.

The Genocide Convention at bottom was a useful device to institutionalize the new status quo and make future change in it very difficult, since it grew increasingly evident that in any future war, regardless of its basis, a "genocide" charge would be probably the first political act anyone would hear about. And with the memory of Nuremberg to guide all concerned, the contemplation of belligerence in the future would surely bring to mind even to professional military people the new look in international neckwear which had been introduced among the convicted Germans in October, 1946. (It has been especially interesting to note the behavior of losing leaders in the wars since 1945.) The map of Europe, 1983-1984, is almost identical to what it was, 1949-1950, when the worldwide drive to obtain universal ratification of the Genocide Convention began. It is undoubtedly the result of many factors that this is so, and that the emergence of the concept of "genocide" and its entrenchment as an "international crime" is a minor influence in all this. Surely, "genocide" fixations had no restraint upon the far more fluid circumstances which went into the changing of the maps of Africa and Asia, politically. But no one has ever assessed the psychic impact of the loosing of the "genocide" idea in the world, and what it contributed to the geopolitical realities which have featured the world since 1945.

Some understanding of the matters discussed in the foregoing memorandum on general world history just preceding, during and just after the first major drive to bring about world ratification of the Genocide Convention may help promote an insight into what will be a rather detailed examination of the highlights of this campaign, with the main emphasis on what took place in the USA.

Before an examination of the mixed fortunes of the ratification campaign in behalf of the Genocide Convention, a few aspects of it deserve a brief analysis. It was to be binding only on those countries which ratified it, and it was to become binding on all these ratifying member states of the UN as international law as soon as 20 states had ratified it according to the constitutional processes peculiar to each ratifying state. (It might also be worth keeping in mind that the Genocide Convention is not a one-way street; ratifying states may repudiate, or "denounce" the Genocide Convention, which is in force in renewable periods of five years among those participating. A state may withdraw from it by announcing the intention to do so six months before the expiration date of the most recent 5-year period in which it is committed to adhere to it. And if it ever happens that fewer than 16 countries remain under it, the Genocide Convention will expire.)

The drive to get it ratified universally by the UN membership began virtually with its adoption on December 9, 1948. From that time on, there were more representatives of states in the UN which signed it; this automatically passed it on to the legislative machinery of that state, and ratification then become possible, though in several cases ratification came long after that state's UN representation signed it; in the case of the USA, ratification never did occur after UN representation signature, and ratification has not occurred to this day.

It did not take long to see some of the reactions to UN adoption on December 9, 1948. In a matter of days the UN Film Board authorized the production of an official UN film strip, "Genocide, The Greater Crime," and simultaneously announced the sponsorship of a moving picture, a feature film by the new Polish Communist regime, "The Last Stop," produced and directed by Wanda Jakubowska, "on life in the Auschwitz concentration camp." (*United Nations Bulletin,* January 15, 1949, p. 102.) This was hardly the last such enterprise by an Eastern European Communist regime pushing the German concentration camp saga as an accompaniment to one or another seemingly unrelated program somewhere, and the obvious intent to push Communist fortunes instead of any other beneficiaries was transparent. The "genocide" ploy had already become an agency and device of Stalinist politics.

Raphael Lemkin's travels become numerous after December 9, 1948. A later biographical sketch remarked that he had "visited several European capitals" between that date and April, 1950, by which time twelve ratifications to the Genocide Convention had been received by the UN General Assembly. In the meantime, signs of things to come from the negative side slowly came into view. The first of substance came out of the annual meeting of the House of Delegates of the American Bar Association in Chicago on February 1, 1949. The talk of the desirability of United States ratification had begun as soon here as elsewhere, and ABA notables had been ruminating over it for some weeks before this occasion. Here the opposition was concentrated for some spell, and at this time it was reflected in the resolution offered by Frank E. Holman, of Seattle, the president of the ABA, which declared that the US Senate should not ratify the UN Genocide Convention "until and unless there has been accorded the time and opportunity for adequate public discussion and understanding of the convention." The day before, the ABA House of Delegates had taken similar action on the proposed UN international convention on human rights, claiming that in both these UN constructs, "important Constitutional and legal questions regarding the effect on our domestic laws" were involved.

Five weeks later, the Association of the Bar of the City of New York at its meeting of March 9, with former Secretary of War Robert P. Patterson presiding, by voice vote became the first important legal group in the USA to approve the ratification of the Genocide Convention. However, it was not entirely a matter without its conflicting strains. The possibilities in the GC for new political utility, now that the Nazis were extirpated, quickly showed themselves. The delegates were treated to a rousing statement by Adolf A. Berle, a prominent from the New Deal (and former assistant Secretary of State), who charged that the Soviet Union was perpetrating "genocide" upon the Baltic States and the Ukraine (it was to be four years before this became a general chorus insofar as Stalinist behavior was involved), while James N. Rosenberg, the executive chief of the most prominent pressure group urging USA ratification of the GC, also averred that "genocide" "possibly existed" in India, Pakistan and South Africa as well, with Berle concluding that "genocide of religious groups" had "already begun in Bulgaria." This was a salvo of the kind of charges which one was to see almost on a monthly basis in some of the succeeding decade and a half, and really has never ceased.

The delegates also listened to Judge Joseph M. Proskauer hail the Convention as "one of the most beneficial accords in the history of the world," while denouncing the negative action of the ABA delegates the previous month as "the most retrograde, retroactive,—I don't hesitate to say this—pusillanimous act that has ever happened in the history of the organized bar in this country." The good Judge was accusing the American Bar Association of cowardice, but who they were afraid of was never revealed.

But all was not sweet accord at this gathering of the New York City lawyers; critics insisted the Genocide Convention was unconstitutional and an invasion of the sovereignty of the US, and "not broad enough to take on political and economic discrimination in the Soviet bloc," maybe the most telling criticism of the GC in this country. This latter critique was especially severe from Murray C. Bernays, who thought the UN Genocide Convention should have been called a convention "against genocide as practiced by the Nazis but not genocide as practiced in the Soviet bloc." Others present were unhappy with the superficial level on which the Convention had been examined as a legal construct, and, as Dudley B. Bonsal observed," its impact on existing law." These dissidents insisted that the Convention had to be studied more closely with respect to the Constitution and other legal aspects, and a resolution was made that it be recommended that the Convention be reworded so as to accord protection to "political and economic groups" as well.

By now Lemkin had become a luminary, and received his first major periodical exposure in the New York *Times Magazine* on March 20, written by Gertrude Samuels, which revealed many facts of his Polish background, former employment in the Polish Foreign Office and early efforts in behalf of his invention, "genocide," though it was not called that in those days. The author also revealed Lemkin's part in the civilian warfare in Poland in 1939, "wounded in the Battle of Warsaw," and subsequent escape into the woods to fight for several more months as a guerrilla, where "he subsisted on potatoes and leaves for six months." The rest was devoted to his escape route to Sweden and then to the USA, his career at Duke University through the war until Nuremberg, about which he told his *Times* interviewer he was "bitterly disappointed" for the International Military Tribunal's failure to try the Germans for what they had done at home between 1933 and 1939. Samuels went on to discuss Lemkin's early and ineffective days at the UN, where he was referred to as a "dreamer" and "Polish fanatic," down through his eventual victory in December, 1948. Now in the Yale Law School and supposedly working on a vast historical study of "genocide," though from the context of his views he was still dealing with the German concentration camps, he could not subdue the impulse to make a remark about the ratification business, saying, "I think it would be an inspiration if the United States showed the way and ratified it first." Lemkin was to propagandize the ABA several times in 1949. It was ironic that over the next 35 years the USA gave every indication of becoming the land which would ratify the Convention last, if at all.

On June 16, 1949 President Harry S. Truman submitted the Genocide Convention to the U.S. Senate, urging prompt ratification. This country, said Mr. Truman, had to "maintain" the "belief" of "less favored peoples" "in our policies and our acts," and this was a primary way to do all that. The five-year-battle over ratification of the Genocide Convention was on. The pressure groups started to bloom that June as well. The following day the Church Peace Union, meeting in Atlantic City, and headed by Dr. Ralph Sockman, urged the Senate to ratify, and a delegation, representing half of all the womens' organizations in America, told the new UN head, Norway's Trygve Lie, that they were "joining the great humanitarian movement of universal conscience," and would "push strongly" for Genocide Convention ratification immediately. Included were Fannie Hurst, representing the Coordinating Group of Womens' Organizations, Mrs. Ruth Byron Rohde, former US Minister to Denmark, Mrs. William Dick Sporborg, member of the UN National Commission for UNESCO, and Mrs. Oswald B. Lord, of the UN Childrens' Emergency Fund.

In the meantime, obstreperous legal minds persisted in presenting stubborn objections to the Convention, including former New York State Governor Nathan L. Miller at the New York State Bar Association's June 24 meeting on the Convention and the Human Rights covenant. Like Holman of the ABA, Miller protested that barely anyone had read either of them and that they were being pushed on the country prematurely. He failed to see what the hurry was all about, remarking that no emergency of any kind requiring hasty ratification existed. Denying that the Nuremberg Trials were a proper analogy to and affording support for the Genocide Convention, Miller also suggested that the US Bill of Rights was a better model for the human rights covenant. Again, former N.Y. State Supreme Court Justice Proskauer, now head of the American Jewish Comittee, took up support of the Convention and denied Miller's charges, but got diverted into talking about human rights, which no one had yet recognized was quite the opposite of what Raphael Lemkin had sold the UN under the name "genocide."

As usual, showing up almost everywhere a discussion of "genocide" might occur, Lemkin addressed a big meeting of the Mt. Holyoke College Institute on the UN on June 29, urging Senate ratification, and declaring that it was already "overdue by 2,000 years". (One observer suggested 4,000 or 6,000 years, which might have had some effect on the hundreds of "genocidal" wars mentioned in the Old Testament, wherein all survivors of the defeated were frequently put to death, a form of "genocide" no one seemed able to remember in 1949.) Agreeing that the Convention did not "solve the mistreatment of minorities within nations," nevertheless Lemkin insisted that he was afraid Senate failure to ratify it would render his creation a "stillborn child."

In the United States the battle had barely been joined when the first Genocide Convention ratification came through, though there was a faintly humorous circumstance connected with it. On July 5, 1949 Norway claimed to be the first endorser of the GC which ratified it, a claim disallowed the following day, when it was discovered that the ratification documents of Ethiopia had been submitted five weeks earlier, and had "gone unnoticed on someone's desk" at the UN until July 6. But Norway still claimed to be the first to ratify by parliamentary action, the Norwegian parliament then authorizing King Haakon to issue the official decree. That of Ethiopia had been signed by Haile Selassie before June 1, and one did not need too much imagination to surmise what kind of 'parliamentary action' had taken place under that barbaric ruler, whatever his immense reputation as a result of the Anglo-French League of Nations exploitation of his pleas before that body at the time Ethiopia had been invaded by Mussolini's Italy in 1935-36.

Raphael Lemkin was immediately on the spot, vociferously hailing Norway's action as "a significant milestone" and a "challenge" to other parliamentary bodies to hurry up on action leading to universal ratification. Still teaching at Yale, Lemkin seemed to find time to be everywhere.

In the USA, however, the battle had hardly been joined. Late summer 1949 found the pro-GC pressure groups at prime heat, the constitutional theorists just as warmly engaged in analysis of the Convention, and the political exploiters of "genocide" just rising up to their opportunities. The ABA was back with new objections, and their critics were responding with sharp attacks on their objections.

The signal for the really heavy political traffic on the Genocide Convention was the announcement in August, 1949 that a subcommittee of the Senate Foreign Relations Committee would start hearings on the ratification question, chaired by Sen. Brien McMahon (D-Conn.) during the early weeks of the coming session of Congress. On August 28 a combined pressure move by 26 national organizations, all associated with the National Civil Liberties Clearing House, hailed this new development, and began their squeeze on the Senate for agreement on GC ratification. This band of groups included the American Veterans' Committee, the Americans for Democratic Action, B'nai B'rith, the American Jewish Committee, Hadassah, the Amalgamated Clothing Workers and the Evangelical and Reformed Church.

There seemed to be some relation between the news that a Senate subcommittee would hold hearings on ratification of the GC, and the annual American Bar Association meeting, in St. Louis, the first week of September. The highlight of the session was the address on September 6 of Harold Stassen, then president of the University of Pennsylvania, and, over the years to come, a perennial candidate for the presidency of the USA. Stassen took advantage of a steadily growing anti-Soviet propaganda throughout the Truman years in the White House by attacking what he called the Stalinist policy of "practicing genocide" behind their Iron Curtain barrier in Central Europe. Stassen denounced this as "the most hideous crime of human misconduct," though naming no victims. There were enough pro-ratification forces in the ABA to back a ratification resolution, made by the ABA's Section on International Law, but with *reservations.* The ABA's Special Committee on Law and Justice under the United Nations opposed this, while Stassen introduced still another element, favoring adoption of a new Constitutional amendment to permit treaties to be contracted by the Senate, but without their becoming *domestic* law automatically. This peculiarity, of ratified international treaties becoming binding on the home populace in their internal affairs as well, had already been the basis for a considerable resistance to the ratification of this particular UN convention, especially. As the New York *Times* writer William M. Blair summarized it,

> The constitutional provision that makes treaties a part of domestic law is the crux of the fight. Many lawyers maintain that Americans would sacrifice civil rights under United States law and that the fundamentals of this country's system of jurisprudence would be destroyed by the international agreement [on "genocide."]

The *Times* sought out Lemkin's opinion on Stassen's charge against the Soviet Union, and Lemkin agreed for the first time in public that the Reds were into "genocide" by his standards on what it constituted. His explanation was that "genocide had important security implications," and "That is why Russia is committing genocide today." What he meant by these remarks was as muddy as several of his previous observations. If Soviet-acquired minority populations via the Yalta and Potsdam agreements were causing Stalin trouble, and that they were being repressed or killed to lessen their nuisance effect on what the Reds considered law and order, was what was involved here, it would have helped if Lemkin flatly declared this to be the case. As later became known, massive transfer back to Stalin of millions of people who had fled the Soviet Union had taken place after Potsdam, and a vast number of them had been slain or removed to distant work camps under the most miserable circumstances. It was still too delicate a moment to discuss this widely, even though official relations between the USA and USSR, not to mention between the latter and Great Britain, had badly eroded by now. But neither Lemkin nor Stassen would present a bill of particulars concerning what Stassen's startling charge consisted of.

There was no doubt that the ABA's membership was mainly perturbed over the implications of ratification of the Genocide Convention upon domestic law, however. It was put into a minimum of words the day after Stassen's electric address by Carl B. Rix of Milawukee, former ABA president. Observing that in the world, only in France and the USA did a treaty also become the supreme law of the land internally, Rix agreed with the view that upon ratification of this UN Genocide Convention, its provisions would "supersede the statutory and common law in the United States." He also favored a constitutional amendment stipulating that ratification of a treaty did not strip the states "of their power of self-government."

Various sly insinuations leaked about the land that the ABA really did not oppose "genocide" led to a sensitivity on the subject which found the St. Louis meeting on September 8 condemning "the mass killing of innocent people" (though this was not really what Lemkin was talking about or what the UN convention at issue was about, except indirectly), but the delegates voted to reject the Genocide Convention in the form presented for ratification by the US Senate. This vote followed what was described as three hours of "hot debate," the only vote in support from a prominent participant being that from the Solicitor General for the United States, Philip B. Perlman, and separately from John Foster Dulles, now a Senator from New York. Rix, and Holman, the outgoing ABA president, issued sharp objections to the GC, Holman in particular being incensed at the thought of "international penal courts" having jurisdiction over Americans charged with "genocide," which possibility was plainly stated in Article VI. Holman also objected to other parts of the Convention's structure, calling them "catch phrases" and "loose language being sold under noble titles."

On September 10, 1949 the *Times* published the statement by Sen. Dulles "deploring" the ABA rejection of the GC, stating that he was "greatly disappointed," and commenting further, "It is hard to see how a beginning can ever be made in developing international law if the nations are not willing to ban effectively the crime of genocide," which he identified, but not correctly, by Lemkin prescriptions, as "the killing of masses of human beings merely because of their race or religion." The *Times* hailed Dulles in fulsome fashion, adding high praise of him as "one of the forgers of bi-partisan foreign policy," a reference to the stunning somersault he had performed, along with Senator Arthur Vandenberg of Michigan, between 1939 and 1949, a fundamental action in the forging of the post-1945 Insider Establishment, of course.

There was some doubt then, and later, as will be seen, just how deeply Dulles was involved ideologically and in any other way in the "genocide" idea and promotional campaign. In his book *War or Peace* (New York: Macmillan, 1950), issued just prior to the outbreak of war in Korea, Dulles referred only briefly, and far from clearly, to the "genocide" ratification affair. Since he was far more concerned with explaining the new "bi-partisan foreign policy" revolution which had taken shape after August, 1944, one of the fruits of which had been his appointment by President Truman on November 18, 1948 as Acting Chairman of the United States Delegation at the United Nations General Assembly, it may be that his energies and attention were diverted to what he considered more important things. Hence his book contained only a few lines on the subject, and were not very illuminating.

Dulles recognized the constitutional question raised in the controversy over U.S. ratification of the Genocide Convention. In his book he reprinted Article VI of the Constitution which specifically designated treaties made under the authority of the United States being also "the supreme law of the land," but went on to remark that "the United States is drifting away from that point of view"; "We do not seem to be willing to permit international law defining individual rights and duties to become the law of our land."

Actually, it was not a matter of new sentiment or thought on the subject. It was still a matter of black and white in the Constitution, and not capable of being altered simply by the registration of changed opinions or attitudes. Dulles did not face that aspect of it at all. He did express the view, in harmony with some pro-Genocide Convention forces, that the Convention had been "deliberately drawn" "so that it would not be 'the law of the land' " and would be valid in the USA only after "subsequent domestic legislation" (an admission of the crucial importance of the enabling legislation which ratification would call forth), though this too was really only an opinion, and sharply at variance with the views of Dulles' fellow lawyers and colleagues in the ABA. From Holman across the board, and on down through the '50s, they were anything but of the mind that the Genocide Convention had been intentionally fabricated so as not to be construed as coming in under the umbrella of Article VI; that is what they were arguing about at the very time Dulles seemed so sure that there was nothing for them to be perturbed about. And from internal evidence it appeared that his brief disquisition on the Genocide Convention in his book dated from the fall of 1949, at a time when he was also surfacing in the newspapers as a protagonist of ratification.

The *Times* on October 1 published a letter Dulles made public which he wrote to James N. Rosenberg, of the National Conference of Christians and Jews, reaffirming his support for the Genocide Convention. The other main critic of the ABA publicized by the *Times* was Rep. Emanuel Celler of New York, who professed to be "amazed" by the ABA action, and threw in the opinion that the ABA was "erroneous" in believing that "an international tribunal could override or supersede American courts," though this is not what the ABA critics were quoted as having declared; Holman believed the language of Article VI implied original jurisdiction in such cases by an international court, as well as possible appellate jurisdiction, as planned.

The American Bar Association was little more than a yet-uncaptured redoubt on the way toward the breaking down of all resistance to the ratification of the Genocide Treaty in the late summer of 1949, in the view of the dominant liberal opinion in the land. But it was a pesky and very annoying holdout in what looked otherwise as a clear and unobstructed sweep. During the acrimonious Bar Association debate, it became an unofficial liberal allegation that the real reason for the resistance to the GC in the USA was the feeling that Americans might end up in international courts growing out of "genocide" charges filed in behalf of a Negro in the South, and the definitions of "genocide" in Articles II and III in the Convention made possible a range of complaints which went a light year beyond lynching; as it stood in Part *b* of Article II, hurting someone's feelings could be construed as "genocide," since this identified even "mental harm" to a minority group member as such. This "mental harm" clause was to cause the proponents of the GC, and Raphael Lemkin himself, considerable heartburn before the matter had cooled off in defeat.

The *Times,* totally committed to the ratification, gave much space to pro-ratification spokesmen and voices. One, at the time of the maximum resentment at the ABA rejection, probably summed up the views of the liberal sentiment at its most florid. Reporting on the words of a prominent New York City rabbi, William F. Rosenblum, on September 18, the *Times* quoted him as stating before his congregation that "any" inclination on the part of Americans to "hold back" from ratifying the Genocide Convention was "moral suicide," and to allow the fear that some person might be charged with "genocide" in this country to dominate attitudes toward this would deeply prejudice people in other countries. Resistance to ratification Rabbi Rosenblum called "a filibuster against the national will," and having taken so prominent a part in its UN adoption, failure now to back ratification would make this country "the object of international suspicion and contempt."

The *Times* went back to legal theorist critics ten days later, publishing in its letters section a very lengthy dispatch from Robert S. Marcus, Political Director of the World Jewish Congress, criticizing Holman and the ABA for its rejection, and especially their objection to Article VI, which included the reference to the establishment of an international penal tribunal somewhere, and which might "supersede American courts," assuming that such was established and made operational. Marcus supplied the opposite view, that Article VI did not create such a court, nor establish that it would have "unequivocal jurisdiction," even if it were to come into being in the future. This long discourse may have soothed some apprehensions that the ratifiers of the Genocide Convention had a commitment to create such a tribunal, and that there was an obligation on anyone's part to accept its jurisdiction were that kind of court to come into existence. The following week the *Times* published the ABA's reply to Marcus, signed by C.W. Tillett, the Secretary of the ABA Section on International and Comparative Law. Here he revealed that the ABA had sent its proposals for re-wording parts of the Genocide Convention to the McMahon Senate Subcommittee.

In the meantime, additional support for ratification continued to be noted. On October 22, 1949 the board of directors of the General Federation of Women's Clubs passed a resolution endorsing the Genocide Convention. And in the UN, nations were still crowding forward at least to sign the adoption document. But there was an amusing selectivity on the part of the UN top management as to what countries might subscribe to this declaration of intention. Its overwhelmingly far left membership was appalled when the UN Legal Committee allowed a loophole which permitted the detested Spanish regime of Gen. Francisco Franco to sign the Convention, and hasty action was taken to exclude Spain; by rewording the 1948

resolution the alteration made Spain ineligible to receive an invitation to subscribe to the Genocide Convention from the Secretary
General of the UN. But to even things a little, the UN also rejected
the effort of the Soviet Union to get Mongolia and North Korea
included among the signatories.

In the case of other Stalinist "republics," there was less resistance. On December 16, 1949 the Soviet Union itself, flanked by
Byelorussia and the Ukraine, signed the resolution "with reservations." This raised this number by the end of 1949 to 37, but only 4
states had ratified the document by year's end: Ethiopia, Norway,
Iceland and Australia, the latter probably largely due to the prominence in the UN machinery of its own Herbert V. Evatt.

The Stalinist "reservations" were interesting: like the resistants
in the USA, it would not accede to the International Court of Justice
having a voice via a created subsidiary criminal court in future
"genocide" cases, insisted the Convention was to apply to the territories or colonies of contracting nations as well, and that agreement
of *all* the parties involved had to take place before a dispute dealing
with "genocide" could be submitted to the International Court of
Justice itself; the wording of the Convention allowed such to happen
if *any* party to a dispute of this nature cared to submit it.

The hearings before the McMahon Subcommittee on the Genocide Convention were scheduled to start on January 23, 1950 and
proceed through February 9. But the pressure began well before that,
including the New York *Times*'s first two major editorials strongly
urging Senate ratification, on January 2nd and 22nd, the latter on
the eve of the opening of the hearings. These appeals were slightly
seasoned with new "genocide" charges against the Soviet to give the
problem an immediate aspect, this time including allegations that
Greek children had been abducted to Russia four to five years earlier.
Praising the actions of US representation in the UN for leading in the
fight for UN adoption of the Genocide Convention, the editors were
now puzzled at hesitancy on US ratification. The criminalization of
"genocide" was "one of the greatest civilizing ideas of our century,"
they maintained, and were positive in their view that there was "little
justification for this indifference and delay," American ratification
being considered by them as "long overdue." This latter view in the
issue published the day before the hearings was accompanied by the
relation that there were now 7 ratifying states, Ecuador, Panama and
Guatemala having been added to the previous four since the last
count had been publicized.

Contributing to the "genocide" offensive mounted against Stalin
in relation to the *Times* editorial stand was Julius Epstein, Executive
Secretary of the American Committee for the Investigation of the

Katyn Massacre, whose long letter approving their charges was decoration on his review of the salient facts surrounding the mass murder and vast grave associated with the sensational 1940-1943 Polish officers case. This was still an embarrassment to most of the wartime establishment in the USA, having done their best at the time to assist the Reds in blaming the Germans, and now wishing to change horses and adopt the reverse position. There was more to be heard about this shortly, when the wartime liberal front chose to support the anti-Soviet view on this event publicly, in 1952. At the moment, however, Epstein's insistence on subscribing Katyn under the category of "genocidal" acts, as well as calling this extermination "the greatest military crime in history," mainly discommoded that sector of "genocide" opponents who preferred to identify only the Germans in the defendants' corner.

The pinpointing of pressure via telegrams, a separate campaign of public propaganda upon the elected officialdom, also got underway. On January 11 the Federation of Jewish Womens' Organizations, at their 30th annual convention in New York City, passed a resolution providing for separate wires to be sent to President Truman and each member of the Senate Foreign Relations Committee and its Genocide Sub-committee, urging ratification; "the world is waiting for our endorsement."

But it is unlikely the Truman Administration needed such spurring. The Administration timed a major drive for ratification with the Senate hearings, the principal testimony from this sector being provided by Under Secretary of State Dean Rusk. He reviewed the idea of "genocide" now becoming commonly repeated, and pointedly called attention to the real consequence of ratification, the passage of "adequate" laws by ratifying states "to punish genocide." But he thought there was only world moral pressure to bring this about; a state which did not do so only ran the risk of "moral condemnation of the International Court of Justice," in Mr. Rusk's view. An offending country which did not have punishment procedure in its domestic legal system might be haled before the General Assembly, and there "to suffer the force of world opinion," and the UN Security Council could consider "genocide" a threat to international peace, in which case Rusk was hinting at possible international military action against the offender.

Under questioning from Sen. Bourke B. Hickenlooper (R-Iowa), Rusk agreed that the Convention did not strike at things like the Stalinist concentration camps, a subject most of America's dominant pro-Soviet liberal establishment still did not want to talk about. And Rusk was not primarily concerned about amending the definition of "genocide" to include protection for "political or class groups"; he felt it was wiser to stress at the start a halting of "murders on an ethnical basis," as the *Times* reported him saying.

Two other Administration spokesmen shared top billing with Rusk, Solicitor General Perlman and former War Secretary Patterson. Perlman was still indignant with those critics who were of the mind that the GC ratification would alter relations of the federal government and that of the states on a constitutional basis. And, said the *Times*, Perlman "declared under questioning that there was 'no shadow of a basis for supposing that local crimes such as lynchings, racial or religious riots, could be brought under the penalties to be raised against genocide.' "

Patterson, representing the main pressure group for ratification, the United States Committee for the Genocide Convention, spent his time denouncing the "legalistic objections" of the critics, and ridiculed opposition views in general. The *Times* thought it worthy that the front former Sec. Patterson represented was of a general nature, and not identified with any specific business, labor, social or ethnic composition.

The mobilization of the prestigious protagonists of the Genocide Convention by the Administration seemed to have stiumulated the American Bar Association's critics to new heights of vehemence in advancing the ABA objections to Raphael Lemkin's unique invention. The most articulate was Alfred T. Schweppe, of Seattle, chairman of the ABA's Committee on Peace and Law Through the United Nations, who again countered Perlman's position that the GC's penalties could never be construed as being applied to individual crimes charged as "genocidal" in the USA. Schweppe insisted that these latter were liable to trial before putative international tribunals, not in the courts of the states in which they might have been committed. Schweppe again called attention to the first definition of "genocide" in Article II of the Convention, "acts committed with intent to destroy, in whole or in part, national, ethnical, racial or religious groups." As the *Times* reported his response to Perlman,

> A part of a group, Mr. Schweppe said, could be a single individual. Slayers of a Chinese on the Pacific Coast could be considered guilty of genocide, a crime under international law, instead of homicide.

Schweppe also objected to the wording of clause *c* of Article III, which found punishable "direct and public incitement to commit genocide," as a violation of US constitutional guarantees of free speech. And he held special objection to the famous clause *b* of Article II in which "genocide" was also stated to consist of "causing serious bodily or mental harm to members of the group." Here he once more pounced on the vulnerable "mental harm" item, one which had already caused Lemkin much perturbation. Schweppe maintained this was a catch-all "to cover almost any alleged misdoing." And he was joined by another previous critic, Rix, in a general warning about "this new doctrine" under which individual crimes were about to become part of the body of international law. Rix favored *two* new constitutional amendments, one removing the provision making a treaty the supreme law of the land, the other for providing for specific states' rights.

Leander Perez of Louisiana, chairman of the States Rights Committee, denounced the Genocide Convention as a "monstrosity" and a "dishonest subterfuge," but the others testifying before the McMahon subcommittee were all GC supporters: Thomas A. Dodd of Connecticut, an assistant prosecutor at the first Nuremberg trials ("the fiction of state responsibility is an empty one—it is people who make up governments"), Stanley Ruttenberg and James B. Carey of the CIO, Michael Straight, of the AVC and *New Republic* magazine, Mrs. Eunice Carter of the National Council of Negro Women, and again, Berle, chairman of the New York City Bar Association.

The following day (January 25) representatives of Catholic, Jewish, Greek Orthodox, Unitarian and Methodist organizations testified before the SFRC subcommittee, as well as Adrian S. Fisher, legal advisor to the US State Department. His attempt to rebut the ABA representatives was anything but convincing. After listening to several objections to the definition of "genocide" in the Convention for its omission of *political* from the list of protected groups, McMahon finally commented on this, and admitted that it was a severe weakness. Mass extermination for political reasons could easily be achieved without any conflict with the Convention under consideration, and he concluded, with a heavy-handed aside apparently aimed at Stalin, "Neither Hitler nor his counterpart in the world today would have been touched by this convention." (In saying this, Sen. McMahon indirectly admitted the Nazi policy toward the Jews was political, not racial.)

Still other friends of the Genocide Convention were heard that day, including Dr. Brendon F. Brown, dean of Catholic University Law School, and a former part of the US prosecution of the Japanese in the Tokyo war crimes process, and Mrs. Ruth Gage-Colby, representing the Women's International League for Peace and Freedom. But the emotional star of the session was Rev. Athenagoras Kokkinakis, of the Greek Orthodox Diocese of New York City, who repeated the earlier charge of "genocide" against Soviet Russia on the grounds of kidnapping Greek children for transportation into Red areas, the figure now being advanced as 28,000.

Less than a week after the hearings had begun, the New York State Bar Association announced their support for ratification of the GC with several reservations, which seemed to be a foretaste of things to come. One of their withholdings of agreement consisted of their refusal to go along with the count that held a country liable for injuries it might inflict on its own nationals, and the other major one was a refusal to support the acceptance of the jurisdiction of any international court to punish Americans "for acts of genocide." What seemed to be so natural for application to the Germans a few years earlier did not seem to be so appetizing if the prospective defendants were likely to be Americans.

As if to lend a current note of immediacy to the proceedings as a relief from the legal theorizing, the Executive Council of the American Federation of Labor, in urging the Senate to ratify the Convention, made public what they claimed was the just-discovered "fiendish plan" by the Soviet Union and its now-Red Satellite countries "to exterminate all their Jews under the guise of 'cosmopolitanism.' " It had already begun by rigid exclusion of them from many occupations, the Communist Party, and the government apparatus, while Soviet occupation troops in the new Red countries were conducting "cultural pogroms" against Jewish intellectuals. This sounded like Lemkin's rhetoric in *Axis Rule in Occupied Europe* all over again, though this time the accused was the most sacred of Lemkin's sacred cows in 1943-44, Stalinist Russia.

Before the hearings wound up there was time for one more hectic round of contest among the legal minds, Solicitor General Perlman coming forth with another turgid appeal to the Senate for ratification, to be countered, strangely enough, by George A. Finch, the original guiding angel of Lemkin in seeing his *Axis Rule* into existence, who now took up the ABA position that the Genocide Convention was gravely defective by failing to incorporate a ban on mass murder of "political and economic groups." Finch was quoted as declaring,

> This convention is no help because it is really a cloak for the commission of genocide by totalitarian nations. All they have to do is kill people, not as members of a selected group, but as a political group.

Finch had placed his finger on one of several extremely vulnerable spots in the Genocide Convention, and the one which seemed to be most understandable to those people not learned in the arcane aspects of legal theory.

The McMahon subcommittee wound up its hearings as planned on February 9, listening to Constantine R. Jurgela, representing the

Lithuanian-American Council, and Prof. Lev. E. Dobriansky of Georgetown University and president of the Ukrainian Congress Committee of America, who both accused the Russians of "systematic" annihilations of Liths and Ukrainians, while gathering a vast protective ring of non-Russians around the Soviet Union for geopolitical objectives.

With the hearings over, it was now time for the in-fighting, while waiting for the McMahon subcommittee to make its recommendations to the full Senate Foreign Relations Committee. Sen. McMahon made the wait almost unendurable for many, by delaying his report for almost 9 weeks. To keep interest from flagging, on March 9, 1950 the new state of Israel deposited its ratification papers with Trygve Lie, Secretary General of the UN, at Lake Success, N.Y., thus becoming the 8th to do so, though 43 had signed the December, 1948 adoption document by the UN, by now. A fourth major *Times* editorial complaining of the McMahon subcommittee's tardiness appeared in the issue for April 2, which was another ten days in coming.

The McMahon report finally was filed April 12, 1950, recommending ratification of the Genocide Convention, but with four "understandings": 1: it was to be understood that the crime of "genocide" would be defined in the USA as the commission of acts with intent to destroy an entire national, ethnical, racial or religious group within the territory of the United States; 2: the United States Government would understand and construe the words "mental harm" appearing in Article II to mean only permanent physical injury to mental faculties; 3: it would be understood and construed that the words "complicity in genocide" (clause *e* of Article III) were to mean only participation before and after the fact and aiding and abetting in the commission of the crime of genocide, and 4: in giving advice and consent to the ratification of the Genocide Convention, it was to be understood that it was being done in harmony with Article, I, Section 8, Clause 10 of the United States Constitution, with the result that the "traditional jurisdiction" of the states with respect to criminal charges and proceedings were not to be considered abridged in any way in so doing.

Sen. McMahon was of the view that these four stipulations took care of all the objections he and his subcommittee had heard. He made special reference to their care in seeing to it that no individual crimes were ever to construed as "genocide"; an offense in the USA to be so held would have to affect "a substantial portion of the group concerned."

A mixed reaction greeted this conditional approval of the Genocide Convention, on the part of its most vociferous and most critical supporters alike. The *Times*'s fifth major editorial published April 14 hailed it feverishly, and looked forward to speedy Senate passage and presidential signing by Truman. But there were still mutters of discontent, which Solicitor General Perlman thought could be traced to the "group in control" of the ABA, which he found not only hostile to the Genocide Convention, but antagonistic "to other proposals to protect minorities from discrimination on account of race or creed or color." Perlman delivered this opinion in a speech before the Federal Bar Association in Washington April 24. It was at the start of Senator Joseph R. McCarthy's charges of the Administration's sheltering of Communists in government jobs. The main address at this Washington convocation of federal lawyers, where Perlman continued his feud with the American Bar Association over the GC, was made by Pres. Truman himself, denouncing McCarthy and his accusations. The *Times* reported, "The Administration's assault on Communists in this country, the President argued, has eliminated them as a serious threat to our security without damaging individual rights and freedom." (A few subdued antagonists of the Genocide Convention had even been sensitized by observing that some of the stentorian champions of Raphael Lemkin's legal construct had Stalinist pedigrees as well, even though Soviet ratification seemed as problematical as that of the USA.)

A last-minute flurry of heavy pressure-group muscle occurred as the session of Congress was running out. The National Community Relations Advisory Council, the "policy-formulating body" of 6 national Jewish organizations and 28 local community councils, in their 3-day eighth annual meeting, on May 28 issued a "strong plea" for ratification, and adopted yet another resolution forwarded to the SFRC, calling upon the Senators involved to "report favorably and promptly" to the Senate as a whole, urging ratification prior to adjournment. It was their opinion that other nations were waiting on US action. But none was forthcoming from the US: the ratification group got Liberia instead, which become the 11th UN member to ratify, these latter now also including Jordan and Monaco.

The sixth major *Times* editorial in behalf of the Genocide Convention the day after Liberian ratification showed much anxiety that the Congress might go home before doing anything, and was much irked that despite all the organizations in the land for it, there still was no Senate action. And for emphasis the editorialists called out,

> As Prof. Raphael Lemkin, one of the pact's chief architects, puts it, "Humanity is our client. Every day of delay is concession to crime." The United States cannot be a party to that concession.

But become one it did. And in lieu of further emoting in behalf

of Lemkin's dream law, the *Times* ran a long two-part analysis of
what the struggle was all about by one of their more percipient
viewers of the current scene, Arthur Krock, titled "The Genocide
Treaty and the Constitution."

In this lengthy essay, Krock demonstrated that there really was
something to the basis for the resistance to the Convention, and that
it was not just stubborn obstreperousness after all. He called the
conflict "the most important constitutional issue in our recent
history." Krock actually found it to be two issues, not one. In
Krock's words, they were these questions: "What types of treaty
commitments are 'self-executing,' and therefore automatic replace-
ments of domestic law?" and "Is there a moral obligation on
Congress to legislate those commitments which are not 'self-executing'?" A problem had just come up recently, he noted: the recent
decision of the California Court of Appeal, that US adherence to the
UN Charter had automatically repealed that state's alien land law,
had been confronted by one of the "understandings" of the
McMahon subcommittee, which had removed the treaty foundation
on which the California appeals court had based its opinion. (Speaking of the 4 McMahon "understandings," Krock revealed that the
State Department was responsible for substituting this word instead
of using the word "reservations," generally applied to objections to
Genocide Convention wording or meanings by the Soviet bloc.)

Krock, in a long quote from Lemkin, tried to clarify the situation
but made it worse by doing so. Lemkin cited Article V of the GC,
which obligated signatories "in accordance with their respective
Constitutions," to supply the necessary legislation to carry out the
pledges before the UN and provide penalties for conviction of "genocide." And in trying to distinguish between the UN Charter and the
Genocide Convention, Lemkin described the former as simply a
"general law," as opposed to the GC, which was "a special criminal
law treaty." And he concluded that the Genocide Convention could
not come into force until and unless Congress provided legislation
for applying penalties.

Such ABA critics as Rix, Schweppe and Finch on the other hand
maintained that senatorial ratification *committed* the Government to
provide legislation to carry out the "genocide" treaty, therefore the
Genocide Convention *was* self-executing. Furthermore, the purpose
of Article V was not to allow the US the freedom of deciding
whether to legislate or not, but to obligate nations like Britain, where
treaties, unlike in the USA, did *not* become the law of the land
unless there was Parliamentary implementation.

Krock, summarizing Supreme Court decisions in the past, generalized that when the US had ratified treaties which dealt with

domestic matters, such as crime was, Congress was given powers to legislate that it did not possess under the Constitution, which reserves such powers to the states, and that, therefore, when such treaties were ratified, they really amounted in substance to a new constitutional amendment.

Calling the 4 McMahon "understandings" "reservations" once more, Krock said that they 1: sustained the traditional division of jurisdiction between the federal government and the states; 2: narrowed "genocide" down to something involving a "substantial portion" of an endangered group; 3: made it definite that "participation before and after the fact" would have to be established to make it an official crime in the USA as per the treaty, and 4: stipulated that the "mental harm" term used in Article II had to consist of "permanent physical injury to mental facilities" not just something in the nature of hurt feelings [the Subcommittee probably meant "faculties," not "facilities," in the above reservation].

As to critics of the verbiage in Article IX of the Convention, Krock was even surer that they had a strong point; even the New York City Bar Association, which was for the Genocide Convention, had done so with a reservation on Article IX, insisting that no state was to be held liable in damages for injuries inflicted by it on its own nationals (though this was precisely what the Germans were being held accountable for at that moment to Israeli subjects who were former German nationals.) And Krock concluded that Lemkin's attempt to clarify the situation just made it more confused than before. As to the Genocide Convention as a whole, Lemkin might define it as a "criminal law treaty," but, amended Krock, it was one "which requires one to bear in mind the element of intent." Krock thus indirectly gave evidence that he was aware that Lemkin's approach, even when it concerned a massacre, was not one which dwelled on the act itself, but the motivation for it, an approach which essentially found nothing wrong with an extermination if no evidence or proof could be determined that it was deliberately planned.

A lull in the "genocide" controversy which set in after the McMahon subcommittee filed its report continued through the rest of the spring of 1950, to end in the sensational events of late June when the actions occurred which led to the war in Korea. But the protagonists continued to pull on to the scene their biggest guns in the never-ending propaganda offensive. Speaking on June 20 before an audience of 1000 in New York City at a gathering sponsored by the National Conference of Christians and Jews, Brig. Gen. (ret.) Telford Taylor, one of the most prominent among the American prosecutors at the Nuremberg trials, declared that the USA would suffer "a devastating blow" to its prestige if the Senate failed to ratify the Genocide Convention. Now in private law practice in the city, Taylor flatly opposed the ABA reservations and criticisms of the Convention. Taylor added a not too appropriate story in illustration of what he was trying to say, a remark he attributed to a German official who had approached him after Nuremberg, and who asserted that the trials had done nothing but prove that "there was one law for Germans and another law for everybody else." With respect to the recently-concluded war Taylor's unidentified German observer was quite right; the whole war had been fought on that basis, the German adversaries never having been bound, in their own minds, by any rules applying to their foe. But it was hard to see what Taylor was trying to say by bringing this up in relation to the Genocide Convention, which ratification of was in question at that moment. Even if ratified by the US, it still was binding only on the ratifying states, so a two-law system would prevail anyway.

On the heels of the Taylor oration, the following day the *Times* featured in its letters section a long dispatch from still another Nuremberg prosecuting team member, Dodd, who had already joined the fray with the ABA by taking a public position close to that advocated by Taylor. After a bit of self-service and self-praise for his part as executive trial counsel at Nuremberg, he devoted most of his space to objections to the ABA criticisms of Schweppe and others, though the position he took was not very strong. He ended up by claiming that if the Genocide Convention had existed in 1933, Hitler's policies in Germany would have been stopped by the "world opinion" expressed by member states in the League of Nations for the equivalent of the Convention at that time. When he considered it all in the light of the moment, in 1950, insofar as it now might be used against the Soviet Union, Dodd felt comfortable in asserting that "Russia will not be able to push genocide too far once it becomes an international crime." What Dodd did not explain was how anything might be done about it if the Soviet *did* "push genocide" "too far."

Still another legal notable strongly favorable to the immediate ratification of the Convention, Berle, furnished the *Times* with a letter 1½ columns long, published July 2, attacking the ABA position, listing a collection of other establishment luminaries favoring his approach, making light of all objections, and especially showing concern over the need for early enabling legislation by Congress in the wake of ratification. There was no worry about simple criminal proceedings against those charged in the USA with "genocide," since all the acts listed in the Convention, Berle claimed, already were crimes "under the criminal codes of every state." But prosecution under these circumstances was not the same as pursuit under a different set of laws specifically intended to enforce the Genocide Convention, where the alleged crime would be complicated by charging the possession of the intent "to destroy a national or racial group."

But a big change in the entire picture related to the "genocide" affair had taken place three days before; President Truman's order around mid-day of June 27, 1950 to the armed forces to defend South Korea and Taiwan, and to take measures for the defense of the Philippines, Vietnam and the rest of Indo-China, took the subject out of the largely theoretical and into the practical political arena. For the rest of the time the subject was an intense issue, the "genocide" question was to be linked to affairs related to the Korean War, and it was to slip out of the center of attention only with the halting of that war. During the period of hostility, repeated charges of "genocide" were to issue from the Administration, its war allies, and a wide variety of private pressure groups against the North Koreans, Russians and Red Chinese, some of them as comprehensive as those Raphael Lemkin ever lodged against Germany and the Axis powers, but the inconclusive outcome of the war was to render them all quite ineffective; in the absence of another unconditional surrender, the total of all the Korean War "genocide" accusations amounted to little but empty and idle talk. Though the Genocide Convention was to be ratified by the necessary 20 countries and to go into effect January 12, 1951 the war was to go on for well over two more years after that, and the UN never did anything about any of the numerous "genocide" accusations in that time.

It was instructive to note that "genocide" was on Mr. Truman's mind the very day he sent the armed forces of the country into war in the Far East. A few hours after his famous order, he laid the cornerstone of a new $15,000,000 federal courthouse in Washington, and his speech accompanying that action did not dwell on the war but on the Genocide Convention, which he hoped the Senate would ratify before the sitting session of Congress adjourned. "We must do our part to outlaw forever the mass murder of innocent people," the President called out, though again we see a vulgar interpretation of what Lemkin had in mind. And a vast massacre of innocents in China was under way, which a U.S. Senate Judiciary Committee some years later was to estimate at well in excess of 30,000,000 murdered Chinese. But no one was talking "genocide" about that in late June, 1950, and when the charges of "genocide" *were* to be invoked against Red China, they were generally rarely for these reasons.

It did not take long for the new dispensation to catch on. The *Times,* in an editorial on July 8, paraphrased Truman's speech of the afternoon of June 27 mentioning "genocide," and the editors reiterated his argument, adding, "The Korean situation, where fratricide is being cruelly fomented by a United Nations member, the Soviet Union, dramatizes the necessity for the genocide law." One could not figure out whether the editors were suggesting that the struggle over this left-over piece of World War II in the Far East might have been inhibited by the ratification of the Genocide Convention, or whether the ratification would have made possible "genocide" proceedings against Stalin, once the war was under way. In either case the proposal hardly was convincing.

A few weeks later the connection of "genocide" to the war in Asia became clearer. On August 21, the Korean representative to the UN sent a note to the heads of 57 governments, warning of "imminent danger" of mass murder to 700,000 Christians in South Korea, from which contingent came many of the latter's leaders, and most of the opposition to Moscow. Blaming the Korean delay of ratification of the Genocide Convention on the disorder caused by the invasion of the Communist forces, he called for ratification by enough states to make the Convention operational in the month of the next General Assembly meeting, scheduled for Flushing Meadows September 19.

Mr. Truman quickly got the hint, and in a letter to Senator Tom Connally (D-Texas), chairman of the Senate Foreign Relations Committee, made public August 26, the President also added a veiled charge that the Reds were genociding South Korea. He supported this by sending Sen. Connally a copy of a letter of July 31 from the Korean ambassador, John Myun Chang, to the U.S. representative in the UN, Warren Austin, in which Amb. Chang charged the invading Reds with "trying to destroy the Korean people [in the South] in part by liquidating those who provide the national, cultural and religious leadership and who lent to the nation forces of cohesion." This was a description of what the Bolsheviks had actually achieved in Russia and its surrounding territories, 1917-1925, which Raphael Lemkin never even alluded to in his memorialization of acts of "genocide" which purportedly so galvanized him into his work leading to the development of his new international crime. For the moment, however, the charge that it was happening in South Korea under the same auspices a quarter of a century later had to rest.

In the meantime, the pressure groups were still busily pushing for US ratification of the Convention, and Sen. McMahon had increased his public visibility in continued promotion of the same. The World Baptist Congress, meeting in Cleveland late in July, 1950 with a reported 20,000 delegates present, passed a resolution urging speedy Senate ratification of the GC, in the midst of other resolutions

committing the membership to work in behalf of minorities all over
the world. But the most active at the time of the first few weeks of
the Korean War was the redoubtable womens' Zionist organization,
Hadassah. On June 19, its president, Mrs. Samuel W. Halprin, had
sent a telegram to the Foreign Relations Committee, urging prompt
ratification of the Convention. A public repeat of this plea for
immediate ratification by this same organization occurred August 22,
which was blended with a resolution backing the stand taken by Pres.
Truman and the United Nations in Korea.

In between these was their 36th annual convention in New York
City, at which the featured speaker was Sen. McMahon. Though his
address was largely an attack on the Soviet Union's atomic research
policies, the head of the SFRC subcommittee found time to enter a
plea also in behalf of early ratification of the GC; "It is high time
that the perpetrators of genocide be treated in the manner they
deserve," the Senator grimly declared, though he did not specify
whether he meant that they were to re-punish the Germans, or
whether he had other defendants in mind. Another invited speaker,
Arthur Lourie, consul general of the new state of Israel and its UN
deputy delegate, delivered an attack on the Arabs, which added
variety to the occasion.

Sen. McMahon by this time was very confident that decisive
Foreign Relations Committee action on the Genocide Convention
was imminent. On August 23 he announced that he would seek final
action by the full Committee at its next meeting, August 29, though
he thought this would be "hard to do," because the Senators were
busy as members of other important committees. Whatever took
place, he was pessimistic about the entire Senate voting for ratification prior to adjournment even if the full SFRC recommended
ratification. He also revealed that the letters, telegrams and editorial
press notices received by the Committee ran about 50-50 on the
merits or demerits of the Genocide Convention. Openly referring to
the subcommittee's "understandings," now, as "reservations," he
echoed the State Department in his conviction that ratification by
the USA with reservations would lead to re-negotiation of the entire
Convention, which was something those close to the Lemkin recipe
dreaded. There was some doubt among them that it might get
through the General Assembly a second time.

On September 1, 1950 the pro-Convention forces got a mild jolt:
the Senate Foreign Relations Committee voted to defer action on the
Genocide Convention. But Sen. McMahon was cheerful and hopeful
that the full Committee would get around to a recommendation
for ratification before the end of that session of Congress. And in
just a few days, he had got over his fear of the consequences of a

recommendation for ratification with reservations: he no longer thought this would lead to the re-negotiation of the entire Convention. Sources eager for US ratification of *some* kind of Genocide Convention undoubtedly had an influence in soft-pedaling this kind of talk; something here was preferable to nothing.

A stream of ratifications of the Genocide Convention came during the late summer of 1950, but they did not include the United States. They were from El Salvador, Haiti, Saudi Arabia, Costa Rica, Tito's Yugoslavia, then Cambodia, embattled Korea and France, rounding out the necessary ratifiers by October 14. Another major *Times* editorial occurred with the news of Yugoslavia, Saudi Arabia and France acceding, appalled that the Senate was still "quibbling." The editors concluded that it was "unthinkable" that the USA would not be among the first 20 ratifying states, at which point the Convention would go into effect, after a 90 day wait. (As of January 1, 1973 there were 76 nations which had ratified, and the United States was still among the non-ratifiers.)

In the meantime, the American Bar Association continued its diligent theoretical dissection of the Genocide pact, almost as if there was no real world, at times, and seeming to ignore what the day-to-day effect of world politics was upon the whole affair. And those who did recognize the latter were moving into the exploitation of "genocide" as an atrocity potential in the war now spreading rapidly in the Far East.

Stassen, the chairman of the ABA's Section of International and Comparative Law, was the organization's speaker at its 73rd annual convention in Washington on September 16. He spoke on the constitutional aspects of international agreements implementing the United Nations Charter, and his section was appointed to study the specific question, "whether our constitutional system can be overridden by, or should preclude, or is consistent with, ratification of such agreements as the Genocide Convention." His vice-chairman, Lyman M. Tondel, Jr., had a printing run off of the pros and cons within the ABA on the Convention, which was distributed to members of the federal government at this same time. Tondel was especially resentful of pro-Convention sub-rosa allegations that the ABA was hostile to the idea of condemning "genocide," retorting, "As far as the principle of opposition to genocide is concerned, there is no question but the American Bar Association is lined up against genocide with all right-thinking people, and it has so gone on record."

The Truman regime demonstrated some resourcefulness in the propaganda department by its exploitation of the Katyn Forest massacre of Polish officers, in lieu of something contemporary with which to belabor Stalin. This represented a profound turnabout from

1943, when the existing wartime alliance with the Soviet Union found American official opinion solidly behind the Reds in charging it to the Germans. But they had known at least since May 1945 that an American prisoner of the Germans, Lt. Col. John H. Van Vliet, Jr., had been taken to Smolensk by the Germans to witness the exhumations of the +4000 dead Polish officers shot and buried there. Lt. Col. Van Vliet was convinced by the evidence that it was indeed the Reds who had murdered them all, and when he was freed from a prisoner of war camp and reached US lines on May 5, 1945 he had been sent to Washington to report to Maj. Gen. Clayton Bissell, then Assistant Chief of Staff of Army Intelligence. After his interview with Gen. Bissell, Van Vliet dictated a full account of his experience, but was ordered to say nothing at all about the matter, to April 26, 1950. On that day he was asked to make a new statement for Maj. Gen. Floyd L. Parks, his earlier one having "disappeared." This he did, and it was finally released in Washington by the Department of Defense on September 18, 1950. The timing could not have been better, the news being added to contemporary "genocide" charges being lodged against the new enemy, this time involving the dear "ally" of five years back, Stalinist Russia.

This campaign also coincided with the closing stages of pressure for ratification of the Genocide Convention. In fact, when Korean ratification was announced at the UN meeting in Lake Success October 9, by the Korean foreign minister, Col. Ben C. Limb (the South Korean National Assembly, meeting in the "fugitive" capital of Taegu, had voted in approval, and the ratification documents had been signed by President Syngman Rhee), he accompanied this news by formally accusing North Korea of "genocide" before the UN, claiming the systematic extermination of South Korean professional men, Christians, as well as women and children indiscriminately, "to interrupt the biological continuity of our nation." The wording sounded as though he had consulted Raphael Lemkin on its style. Nothing came of this, of course.

To be sure, this was not the time to alter the majestic harmony of the moment with some harsh jangling of immediate political concern: the United Nations were about to put the Genocide Convention into worldwide effect as international law, the magic number of 20 ratifications being reached less than a week after Col. Limb's "genocide" charge against North Korea. In fact, with South Korea's accession, there was one more than required, the UN Ambassadors of France, Haiti and Costa Rica also indicating their countries' ratification of the "genocide" treaty.

On Sunday, October 15, 1950 the New York *Times* proudly announced the day of triumph in this manner:

> After nearly five years of painstaking effort in the United Nations, the international convention against genocide will go into effect Monday [October 16] Prof. Raphael Lemkin, father of the convention, announced today.

After the expiration of a 90-day period, the Genocide Convention was to become binding on its ratifiers, and become international law. The *Times* story went on to recite Lemkin's attainments (he was still with the Yale School of Law at the moment), as well as repeating the oft-told story of Lemkin's entire family presumably having been exterminated in Poland by the Germans (on some occasions he was known to blame the Russians for some of the family deaths.)

Two days later the *Times* printed a picture of the UN representatives involved in the general ceremony ratifying the Genocide Convention, Lemkin being seated at the far right of the group photograph, and witnessing the formality. It was the moment of grand triumph, and many thought that now for sure the momentum would propel the United States into the ratification column in very short order. Senator Herbert H. Lehman (D-New York) fired off a telegram to Sen. McMahon, urging prompt action on the Convention, and hoping the USA would not become "the last to ratify" it. Another rueful *Times* editorial complaining over non-ratification, admitted the Convention might not be a "perfect document," agreeing that, for instance, in the case of clause *b* of Article II, "it might be hard to bring home the offense of causing serious . . . mental harm to members of a recognizable group." Nevertheless, the editors insisted, the Genocide Convention was a badly needed addition to international law, as the problem persisted. Now, added to "Hitler's massacre of six million Europeans" there was "Soviet Russia's hideous treatment of its own dissenting minorities." Again, the lesson was being impressed that "genocide" promised to be useful in war propaganda for as far ahead as anyone might care to gaze; its applicability was limited only by the vision and imagination of those ready and willing to employ it. Its effectiveness as *law* was quite another matter, however. At the moment it was about to go into effect, it appeared totally unenforceable.

Three days after the UN announced its 20th ratifying member state, President Truman declared that he would again urge the Senate to ratify the "genocide" pact when it reconvened in November. And the propaganda agencies of the higher echelons began to play hard ball with a vengeance in the effort to break down and discredit the major pockets of resistance. In a front page story in the *Times* October 15 which seemed to be orchestrated with the news of impending victory in the UN, Joseph E. Johnson of the Carnegie Endowment for International Peace, accused the American Bar Association of using a Carnegie grant to the ABA to fight the "genocide" treaty. The Carnegie organization was reported to be especially offended by publications of the ABA's Special Committee on Peace and Law Through the United Nations, whose chairman was identified as William L. Ransom.

The ABA's then-current president, Cody Fowler of Montgomery, Alabama, promptly denied the ABA was misusing funds from a Carnegie grant, and looked on Johnson's letter as merely a request to learn how the money had been spent.

The news that Mr. Ransom had been deceased for over a year and a half, since February 19, 1949, and that the terms of the original grant had been exceedingly imprecise, did not make this Carnegie sally look too good. There was even some doubt that Johnson had accused the ABA of misusing these funds, but Schweppe, who had replaced Ransom, took off after Johnson anyway. Five days later, he denounced Johnson's contention as "utterly without foundation," and charged Johnson with being a long-time (since 1942) State Department employee, and, since 1947, a State Department Policy Planning Committee member. Schweppe further charged that it was the State Department which was the agency of the Administration really pressing for the ratification of the Genocide Convention, and that it was State which had presented it to President Truman, to, in turn, pass it on to the Senate. It was State's resentment over the ABA having been responsible for the Senate McMahon subcommittee preparing the four reservations to the Convention, which was behind all this, and that Johnson did not represent the Carnegie trustees in his complaint, but was speaking "at the instance" of Solicitor General Perlman, the latter disturbed that his views on the Convention had been voted down by the ABA. The feud between Perlman and the ABA apparently was still alive though conducted on what seemed to be a very distant front. It had more time to run, as will be seen, though no one thought at the moment to call attention to the fundamental part the Carnegie organization had played in launching Lemkin's book, in which the word "genocide" and the preparation for selling the idea as international crime were first laid out.

Despite the infighting which this incident revealed, there seemed to be every indication that US ratification of the Genocide Treaty was on its way, though the war between Perlman and the ABA persisted into the end of 1950. Perlman continued to charge the ABA with fighting the Convention, and on one occasion distributed to the Senate Foreign Relations Committee a letter from Dodd to Schweppe, complaining that the ABA was misrepresenting his position by identifying him with an anti-Convention ABA booklet, when he, Dodd, had already testified before the McMahon subcommittee that he backed the Genocide Convention as it stood.

The issue in the fall of 1950 however seemed to be that there was strong sentiment for ratification by the US with the reservations already made public for six months, but that there was apprehension that the Soviet Union, now that the Cold War, and the hot one in Korea, had hardened the attitude on all world political affairs, might torpedo US plans. It had been customary, under the League of Nations, for a power to ratify a treaty *with* reservations and become a party to that treaty if the others, which had ratified *without* reservations, did not object. It was now believed the Soviet would object to the American reservations, in which case the USA would be excluded from the Genocide Convention.

But the Soviet satellite Bulgaria had already ratified the GC with reservations in July, 1949, and the USA had not objected to the Red reservations then, though now ran the awkward risk of having its ratification rejected by a possible Soviet objection. If the matter was to be submitted to the UN's Legal Committee for an opinion, it was thought that this might lead possibly to years of debate, and pressure was on to move the USA into the ratification column at the earliest possible time. When the *Times* ran an urgent editorial on the matter on November 1, the editors urged the General Assembly to accept US ratification with the four reservations, which the paper thought was on the verge of passage in the Senate. Two days later Sen. McMahon wrote to the *Times* in support of this program, and deplored published reports that the UN had received a resolution proposal to debate the matter, while referring to the "thousands" of communications he was receiving from religious, labor and womens' groups strongly favoring ratification.

The following day, the US joined with 11 other countries in the UN in submitting a joint amendment under which terms the United Nations General Assembly would accept ratifications with reservations, thus officially changing the procedure, and making it impossible for any ratification to be blocked by another UN member.

This was seen as the prelude to a quick Senate ratification of the Genocide Convention. But the new, 81st, Congress was as dilatory as the "do-nothing" 80th, and drew a reproach from the *Times* on January 15, 1951 for still not having acted on the "genocide" treaty. This editorial closed with another weary entreaty addressed to the Senate to get on with the ratification.

By now, however, the Convention was running into heavy traffic in the attempt to gain first call on the attention of Congress. The war in Korea and the struggle with the Soviet bloc in the contest for Europe steadily moved the question of the Convention back down the agenda. There seemed to be nothing for its proponents to do but to dig in and spend an undetermined period of time in dreary, hard plugging for their desired objective. This involved a persistent publicity campaign, the continuation of a stream of messages from pressure groups, and the attempt to weave their campaign into the fabric of the Cold and Korean Wars. By trying to make it seem that there was mileage to be attained in these two struggles by using the "genocide" concept, the proponents of the latter hoped to succeed where the effort to get the Convention ratified simply on the basis of its presumed detached merits did not appear to be going anywhere.

One of the most revealing incidents in the new tactics of attracting support to the "genocide" question on the basis of its relevancy to the moment took place on January 18, 1951, and it involved the recruitment of Raphael Lemkin himself instead of just another invocation of his ideas. At a luncheon in his honor sponsored by the American Jewish Congress in New York City, at which he received their citation for his "inspired and historic achievements in initiating and bringing to a successful conclusion the enactment of the Genocide Convention into law," Lemkin, after making another plug for Senate ratification, launched into an extended analysis of the war in Korea as it related to "genocide," a discussion which brought him into a most unusual extension of the concept into geopolitics of the entire area.

Admitting that "history" was "changing fast," Lemkin told his gathered admirers that the world was "faced with the real possibility of genocide occurring in Asia in the wake of the Communist war." What he now termed "The Chinese war of aggression against the United Nations and South Koreans" was an obvious "planned totalitarian effort to eliminate democratic influence from Asia," and was plainly "an expression of genocide technique."

Elaborating further, Lemkin made several observations which if they had been made by anyone else would have promptly brought the charge of "racism" from his listeners; "The present gigantic struggle in Asia carries in itself the seeds of genocide and its victims will be nobody else but the white man." Lemkin went on to talk forebodingly about the "outposts of the Western world" in the South Pacific, by which he meant Australia and New Zealand, and predicted the coming of a time when they "might need the protection of the genocide law." After all, Lemkin said, calling attention once more to the war in Korea, since its fortunes had turned with the massive entry of Red China troops, "The orders of the Chinese generals now speak about annihilation"; "They don't call for victory as is usual in military commands, but for complete destruction and extermination."

This was new and trendy, and a change of some dimensions from his continuous dwelling upon the late war and the Nazis, though the latter were never forgotten, regardless of what the realities of the moment called for (Lemkin's sole remedial program in *Axis Rule*, mainly provisions for restitution courts, was being innovated in occupied Germany.) And he always had time for new appeals for ratification of the Convention; the day after his discussion of the war in the Far East as a new adventure in "genocide," Lemkin spoke before the heads of the National Federation of Business and Professional Women's Clubs, a meeting of representatives of 77 groups, set up in the form of a "United Nations Workshop," and urged them to press for ratification of the Convention in the Senate.

Other forces intensely interested in the ratification offensive also saw a considerable gain to be made in tying in "genocide" to current politics. Berle, present with Lemkin at a joint press conference at the offices of the Bar of the City of New York offices at 42 West 44th Street, complained that the failure to be a part of the Genocide Convention deprived the United States "of a powerful weapon in the struggle against Communism." Warning against "the delusion that the crime of mass extermination had died with the Hitler regime," Berle declared that there was evidence that the Soviet Union was engaged in "genocidal acts" against the populations of Esthonia, Lithuania and Latvia, and was deporting "thousands upon thousands" of their males to Siberia, and their women to Turkestan.

This all had a ring of the kind of continuous propaganda recently brought to such a high pitch and with such resounding success in the 1941-45 years against Germany, but somehow it now was on the flat side; the notion that another vast crusade be undertaken in still another effort along the lines of that recently concluded against the Germans was not very stimulating at that moment, with things not going very well in the Far East.

But there was still exploitable mileage in relating the persistence of tactics reminiscent of the previous war. If the Balts and Ukrainians seemed to be enjoying no success in the underside of the Cold War, it did not mean that no one was. When the Jewish Labor Committee's national executive board held their annual conference at Atlantic City on February 17, 1951, Jacob Pat, executive secretary of the New York section, told the other delegates that the JLC "underground" had recently rescued "1000 endangered Jews" from "behind the Iron Curtain." Furthermore, JLC agents were arranging for the escape of "many thousands more—all under the noses of the Soviet-dominated secret police," in five satellite countries. It was a repeat of what they had done a decade ago, he reminded them: "In 1940, just ten years ago, we set up an underground operation that rescued thousands of important fighters for freedom from Hitler's slave Europe." He described the use extensively of "misleading identification papers" to spirit them to non-Communist countries and then to "permanent freedom" in Israel. Pat said that it took about $100 per person to obtain for them illegal credentials on the black market, but that it got increasingly more expensive as the rescue operation approached the Soviet Union. Inside Stalinist Russia, the Jewish Labor Committee did not work, Pat concluded; there were too few "trustworthy" people there to help them.

In support of this sober conclusion, tied to still another plea for the recognition of the "genocide" pact, was a report from a different body of labor leaders a few weeks later, whose 17-page memorandum was supplied to the New York City press. Charging that "persons of the Jewish faith in the Soviet Union and its satellites" were being "subjected to cultural and spiritual genocide," and that the Soviet was executing a "pogrom" against them, the collaborating participants in this broadside, David Dubinsky of the ILGWU, Jacob Potofsky of the Amalgamated Clothing Workers, CIO, Joseph Boskin, general secretary of the Workmen's Circle, and Adolf Held, chairman of the Jewish Labor Committee, concluded by charging the USSR with violating the Genocide Convention, and pleading, "We appeal to the conscience of humanity to intervene in time and terminate this genocide." There were no interventions by anyone then or later, but pronunciamentos of this sort were to be seen almost on an annual basis thereafter, into the end of the 1970s, and early 1980s.

On February 23, 1951 the nominating committee for the Nobel Peace Prize meeting in Oslo, Norway nominated Raphael Lemkin as one of the 28 persons to be considered for the award of that honor. Among his fellow nominees were Justice Robert H. Jackson of the USA and Sir Hartley Shawcross of the United Kingdom, for their work at the Nuremberg trials of 1945-46, which had never struck much of anyone as an event having much to do with "peace," as well as Robert M. Hutchins of the new Ford Foundation, and Frank Buchman, of Moral Rearmament.

The year 1951 represented a period of drastically reduced expressions of enthusiasm for the Genocide Convention, generally speaking, laying aside the occasional attempt to stir indignation over world affairs as a device for providing a piggy-back assist for ratification sentiment. To begin with, some emotional fervor evaporated when the Convention became operable as international law, on January 12, and even the atrocity charges and the fulminations against the Soviet Union in the immediate period afterward lost some of their impact with the going into force of the Convention among the UN ratifiers.

As for Americans, 1951 was a bad year for them insofar as it concerned performance in the war in Korea. The concentrated attention devoted to the question of American ratification of the previous two years was lost as the community in general suffered the distractions which grew out of the often dismal and dreary news from the Far East. The subject of the Genocide Convention was definitely moved to the back burner, to come alive, again, as an issue in the presidential campaigning of 1952.

Though the Soviet Union was the target for repeated accusations of "genocide" by various Zionist and ethnic organizations in the USA which stemmed from the lands which had all become Soviet satellites from mid-1945 onward, it managed to ignore them, was faced by no action taken by anyone, and actually used 1951 as a time to push its own version of favored treatment as a ratifier with reservations, indirectly achieving what the Americans had also hoped to get done in this department.

This became a live issue in April, when the Soviet bloc again brought up their position before the International Court of Justice that they believed they had a right to sign the Genocide Convention but to retain, on the basis of national sovereignty, any reservations they wished. Though several lands challenged them on this, on May 28, the justices of the International Court ruled by a vote of 7-5 that the USSR and the other Soviet bloc states (Ukraine, Byelorussia, Poland, Czecho-Slovakia, Rumania and Bulgaria) might sign the Genocide Convention with reservations, as long as these latter were not incompatible with "the object and purpose of the Convention." The dissenting side had maintained that, to do this, the Soviet bloc would have had to obtain the consent of *all* the other ratifiers to date.

Though this actually advanced an American objective, and removed American apprehension over what might face *their* essay at ratification with reservations, the event led to nothing from the American side. By July 20, 1951, when Nationalist China ratified the GC, its papers being deposited with the UN by Dr. T.F. Tsiang, its permanent representative, 30 states had now ratified it, and American action of this sort seemed as remote from actuality as ever.

Only a smattering of resolutions by interest groups urging this action occurred, all the way through the summer, including a subdued gesture in this direction even by the ABA, whose New York City convention found Mr. Stassen speaking in behalf of ratification once more, but just as emphatically as in the past as to the necessity to hedge this action with reservations, "to protect domestic laws and the rights of the 48 states." And it was obvious that he had joined the ABA elements which did not believe the Convention was self-executing by his follow-up recommendation that Congress also "legislate on genocide," an action which could not take place until ratification had occurred.

Even Hadassah, at its 37th annual convention at Atlantic City, the following day, so preoccupied with voting for approval and funds for a large collection of Zionist projects, both for Israel and in the USA, spent far less time and emotion on the Genocide Convention than earlier, even if its 3500 delegates did find time to adopt unanimously a resolution calling for "prompt" ratification of the Genocide Convention. This news was buried on page 32 of the next day's New York *Times.*

Raphael Lemkin's numerous protagonists received a disappointment on November 5 when the Nobel Peace Prize Committee bypassed him and awarded the 1951 honor to the ancient French labor union bureaucrat and ILO functionary, Leon Jouhaux, an event which may have represented superior maneuvering on the part of the friends of the Soviet. Despite this, there had already seemed to exist a somewhat subdued support and publicity for the repeated charges of "genocide" being made against the USSR in the UN. There were a few still coming through toward the end of the year but only one of truly sensational quality in the manner of the previous few years. This one was included in a New York *Times* editorial on December 16, which, in view of its vociferous acclaim for Lemkin, for having invented the word "genocide," and the Genocide Convention, "one of the truly great and positive contributions" of the UN, sounded like a consolation prize of a kind for Lemkin in lieu of his failure to gain the Nobel Peace Prize. In its closing lament that the US was still not a ratifier of the Convention (there now were 31 who had), the editors once more unleashed a fierce attack on the USSR for its actions against "national groups behind the Iron Curtain," which were being "ruthlessly exterminated," especially in Poland, Czecho-Slovakia and the Baltic countries; "millions of their countrymen" had vanished, as well as 70,000 Hungarians, and the editors again threw in the Greek children, though they had cut down the number to 20,000 kidnapees. In any case, it was high time to ratify the Genocide Convention and to "condemn this outrage." Nothing was done, but even before the editors could sit back and luxuriate in emotions well-expressed, they got a prompt commentary from the ABA's Rix, who pointed out to them that Soviet meting out of punishment to people in the Soviet bloc was not being done to them as members of racial or religious groups, "as such," but for "political crimes or as enemies of the state." And Rix rubbed it in here, noting that the failure of Lemkin, and the others he worked with on the various drafts of the Genocide Convention, to include "political" in the categories which when harmed intentionally would be considered "genocide," amounted to a validation of these Soviet persecutions; furthermore, Rix warned, "If the [genocide] treaty is ratified the United States will have no grounds whatsoever for complaint" about any past or future Soviet action or behavior of this sort.

This did pose an awkward political dimension to this situation. Though it was the conservatives who were normally expected to be hostile to Stalinist Russia and its policies, it was the liberals, heatedly for the Genocide Convention, who were engaged in the most extreme and incendiary anti-Soviet charges, by far, during this pro-ratification contest. It was to become so even more markedly in the coming 1952 election, during which Raphael Lemkin maintained his high political visibility. There is little doubt, though, that criticism such as that leveled by Rix, that liberal hysteria for ratification of the "genocide" pact without amendment, such as the inclusion of "political" among the stipulated groups, was, in effect, placing the stamp of approval on "genocide" conducted in other and absolutely safe ways, was a telling annoyance and irritant.

As a presidential election year, 1952 promised to add unordinary elements of the "genocide" pact ratification question. Various additions to the general picture took place, some of them dramatic and arresting, though, as will be seen, no significant departure took place from the post-1947 foreign policy of the country, and the ratification problem remained unchanged as well.

But it did look for a time that this Korean war year #3 would be an ideal time to initiate some policy changes toward Soviet-held Europe at the same time, and urgings of this sort from what might be called the "Iron Curtain ethnics" in the USA led to their invoking the "genocide" pact, and to push somewhat harder and louder for its ratification by the USA, though the argument that it would be of assistance in bringing about changes in Eastern and Central Europe never did emerge very clearly, operationally speaking.

An early voice in February, 1952 for ratification was the Lithuanian-American Council, which, hailing the first anniversary of Voice of America propaganda broadcasts to their homeland, implored the Senate to ratify as the first step in a positive program beyond the already formalized establishment "containment" policy toward European Communism to break the Stalinist hold on Iron-Curtain Europe.

Those calls in late spring and early summer, as the national nominating convention time drew near, were somewhat stronger. The Polish-American Congress, whose 2000 delegates representing America's six million people of Polish extraction met in Atlantic City May 31, also urged immediate ratification of the Genocide Convention, so that the application of sanctions in the Convention "against the Soviet criminals" could be pushed early in the approaching next gathering of the UN General Assembly.

By far the most fiery and explosive of such remonstrations came a few weeks later, however, after a Democratic candidate for the Presidency had endorsed the Genocide Convention, and after the Republican national convention had failed to include in the party platform a pledge to pursue its ratification.

Lemkin vociferously acclaimed Averell Harriman on June 22 for being the first presidential candidate to come out for prompt ratification, and quoted Harriman as saying,

> Adoption of the Genocide Convention will serve as a warning and a deterrent to the Soviet leaders, who are quite capable of decimating and liquidating whole populations in an effort to maintain their control.

But when the Republicans avoided the subject in preparing their party platform in mid-July, despite an emotional plea for such promised action before the Republican National Committee by Professor Dobriansky (see pp. 272-3), a powerful letter signed by six heads of ethnic organizations in the USA protested this lapse in a lengthy *Times* dispatch. "The gruesome evidence of Soviet genocide is accumulating," it began; "Millions of our brethren and kin are dying in Siberia," "Hundreds of cattle trains are rolling eastward from Lithuania, Latvia, Esthonia, Poland, Czechoslovakia, Hungary, Rumania, Bulgaria, the Ukraine, and other countries." This was followed by still another claim of Greek children spirited off to the USSR, to which were added Polish children, Bishop Dibelius of East Berlin, and a contingent of East German kidnappees. And in deference to the American Chinese who also signed the statement, it concluded, "History will never forgive the staggering blood bath in Red China undertaken to destroy an ancient civilization." Though the signers thought the ratification of the Genocide Convention by the US Senate would stop all this, there was no indication how this would eventuate. With American hands quite full in Korea, the situation did not appear to be even faintly promising for anything to follow ratification of the Convention by much of anything other than more talk; there was an absolute lack of evidence that the USSR was about to become the scene of another Nuremberg; the latter was more likely to be a once-in-a-millennium event, not a repeatable extravaganza to prepare the dispatch of those who persisted in revolutionary political innovations. And for the ethnic minorities of the nations swallowed by Stalinism, there remained a painful dilemma in their simultaneous abhorrence of both the Germans and the Russians; their hope of something like 1919-1939 moving into the space between them and renewing that kind of world was the alternative they really were for, and the likelihood of that transpiring was exceedingly dim.

In the meantime the practical politicians took up the cry for the "genocide" pact, whetting the appetites of the smaller-nation ethnics of America, but offering them really little but sawdust, not any real political substance. A prime example was Adlai Stevenson's blistering speech in Buffalo, New York October 22, 1952, a major address which included a ferocious attack on Soviet "genocide," during which speech Stevenson again threw up to the Reds the Katyn massacre, and went on to accuse them, in 1952 in Poland and elsewhere, of "deporting whole populations for slave labor and a slower death." This sounded as though culled from Lemkin's similar rhetoric in *Axis Rule,* though charged to the Germans. However, Stevenson quickly covered his tracks by expressing unreceptivity to any talk about supporting any anti-Communist "liberation" movement in Poland, or anywhere else. His residual belligerence was saved for Sen. John W. Bricker (R-Ohio) for getting 45 of his Republican colleagues to back his proposal for a proposed constitutional amendment making it impossible to sign the UN Genocide Convention in its existing form. But how Stevenson or anyone else who favored American ratification might serve to inhibit Soviet behavior toward their minorities was never explained. Other than gaining votes from those sympathetically inclined there was nothing genuine involved in the 1952 political lip service to the Genocide Convention. The steadily-jelling Anglo-American Establishment had already opted for "containment" of the Soviet, in reality a formula for continuing the status quo in Europe indefinitely. Subscription to the notion that somehow adherence to the "genocide" pact might serve a political purpose in weakening Stalinism in Eastern and Central European lands engulfed by the Red Army might have been designated as cruel, unusual and unnecessary psychological self-punishment.

While the superficial political climate reflected the bogus hope that the "genocide" pact might soon be a ratified reality in the USA, Raphael Lemkin continued to be a global personality. He was nominated for the second year in a row for the Nobel Peace Prize, one of 27, by the Nobel committee in Oslo on March 6, 1952. His citation hailed him for inventing "genocide," and glowed at his "personal triumph" at the United Nations in 1948. But it sounded most unpeace-like in its clamorous acclaim of Lemkin for his part as a "veteran of the underground fight against the Nazi invaders of Warsaw." Assuming this was an expectable consequence of Norwegian

Germanophobia in this war-backwash year, still it was strange for an element presumably so concerned for a law-abiding world to nominate a guerrilla warrior for a global peace prize, in view of this kind of endeavor making one a violator of the Hague Rules of Land Warfare, while specifically depriving him of legal status as a war participant. But it was of no consequence, for, after mulling it over for seven months, the Oslo committee decided to suspend the award of a Nobel Prize in this category for 1952, the 11th time this had happened since 1901.

Whether Lemkin was dismayed by this second event was not revealed, though nothing invidious was involved since the award simply was not made. It would seem that he had far more on his mind than the ministrations in Oslo, because more disturbing things were in the air, and they directly concerned his famous construct. A proposed international covenant on political and civil rights was before the Human Rights Committee as of May 26, and Lemkin looked upon it very bleakly. Two days before he warned that the Genocide Convention was "in danger of destruction," not by its enemies and adversaries, but at the hands of the UN itself, if the latter was not careful. He selected out for criticism Article III of this proposed covenant, arguing that it was far too sweeping, and unless narrowed down, might swallow up the Genocide Convention. Though phrased to cover only individual instances or cases, Lemkin thought it might be interpreted as applying to mass murder, and that took it into the preserve already assigned to "genocide" considerations. So he was back at the UN doing the things he knew best how to do. As the reporter said in this same story, "Most of Professor Lemkin's work has been the behind-the-scenes and off-the-record kind – painstaking contact with delegates, jurists and anybody who could help him push the idea of a convention on genocide." Now he was looking for the same kind of help in trying to defend his "corner" from being impinged upon by something which might also divert attention and importance from it as well. As things were to develop, Lemkin from this point on was engaged in a losing contest with the rival convention dwelling upon "human rights," even though the enemies of one or the other did not discriminate: they were usually against both, as when the Daughters of the American Revolution committee meeting in Washington on April 15, 1952 entertained a resolution denouncing both, and the next day voted its formal opposition to the Genocide Convention (the "human rights"pact was still under construction) with only three dissenting votes. Their main objection was one already familiar to those who had followed the previous four years' debate: the fear that Americans would be spirited abroad under the terms of this pact, to be tried possibly by enemies of the USA, for crimes allegedly committed in the USA, in so doing depriving the defendants of the protection of the American Bill of Rights.

The next threat to Lemkin's intellectual baby came near the end of 1952, and was considerably more subtle, bringing back to the agenda the exquisite word-shaving so dear to the barrister-sodden UN General Assembly. On December 4 the Chinese delegation to the GA asked that body to revise the definition of "genocide" in the Chinese language, and wanted the wording to read, in English translation, "to cause harm or to destroy human groups in a ruthless manner." Lemkin, by now already on or still on the scene, was very displeased, and declared that the change would be a fundamental distortion, reducing the original concept to "simple homicide." The reporter interviewing Lemkin went on,

> The groups that Professor Lemkin had in mind when he first conceived of genocide were "such as have a definite place in history and the world community," he recalled. Genocide does not mean "killing three men on a street corner," he added.

The General Assembly voted the next day to refer the Chinese request to the GA's Legal Committee, and a minor tempest blew up thereafter which took up most of the month. A long letter to the *Times* signed by representatives of Hungarian, Czech, Lithuanian, Ukrainian and Albanian groups in America appeared on December 17, opposing the Chinese proposal and comparing their attempt to revise the "genocide" pact with the one proposed by the Soviet Union on November 20, 1947, which had been defeated. The Soviet had wanted the crime of "genocide" to be very general then, and were satisfied by the language in the Nuremberg indictment, "crimes against humanity." They preferred to have specific words such as national, racial, religious and the like not mentioned. Like the Soviet suggestion, these opponents declared, the Chinese recommendation would be a basic change in Article I of the Genocide Convention now ratified. "Crimes against humanity" were punishable only in case of an aggressive war, whereas "genocide" as now construed was punishable in wartime or peacetime. The generalizing of the definition would let the Soviet slide off the hook; it was not at war with its Iron Curtain satellites or their neighbors, and would thus evade criminal charges for what they were doing now to these people.

This drew a reply from the permanent delegate to the UN from China, Tingfu F. Tsiang, directed to the five Central-East-South Europe ethnic leaders, which said the Chinese recommendation was in no way intended to advance Soviet or any other goals; they were

just trying to get a Chinese text more in harmony with the other four
official texts. And Tingfu was very frank in explaining what it would
come to in Chinese:

> The promoters of the [Genocide] Convention have been mainly
> motivated by the desire to prevent a repetition of the tragic suffering of
> the Jews in Hitlerite Germany. If all should, in the Chinese text, use the
> term which would only cover racial groups, the Convention might not
> protect the Jews in the future because, in many circles, the Jews are not
> considered as a racial group but as a religious group.

By a vote of 24-16 the Legal Committee agreed with the Chinese
delegation on December 19, 1952 and permitted them to circulate
among the members their version for approval. And three days later
the Assembly approved a resolution favorable to the change in the
Chinese text but structured in such a way that it avoided re-sub-
mission of the entire Genocide Convention to the 40 countries that
had already ratified it. Lemkin's supporters claimed the change converted "genocide" into "homicide" in the Chinese text, which was
his original position to start with when it had first come up. Another
minor erosion had taken place in the "genocide" idea.

The issue did not drift off the agenda entirely, however. Seven
months later a substantial rejoinder from Herbert V. Evatt from
Australia took the Lemkin position, that the Chinese alteration
would replace the Genocide Convention with a "mere declaratory
restatement of the Nuremberg judgment," which, after all, Evatt was
now willing to agree, was not some scintillating piece of new galacti-
cally-important law-making, but simply "a military measure imposed
by a victor upon a vanquished nation." Evatt, the UN's presiding
officer when the original "genocide" adoption by that body had
occurred, also saw the change as one which would "confuse genocide
with war crimes punishable only as an incident to an aggressive war,"
and one which would "weaken" the "moral force" and "question"
the "legal force" of the Genocide Convention, which ratification, in
the view of Evatt, "was an epoch-making event in the history of
mankind."

The death of Josef Stalin on March 5, 1953 supposedly initiated
a wave of anti-Jewish repression in the Soviet Union. But Raphael
Lemkin made a world-wide charge of this latter nature seven weeks
before Stalin's demise. On January 17, Lemkin called upon the
United Nations Assembly "to find the Soviet Union and its satellites
guilty of violating the ["genocide"] pact by a determined campaign
to wipe out minorities behind the Iron Curtain," in which he specifically mentioned "Communist persecution of the Jews." In many
ways Lemkin's appeal blended for one of the few times the general

approach to the Genocide Convention by the Zionist organizations with the specific approach to this document taken by the non-Jewish minority ethnics of the submerged Soviet satellite states. Lemkin declared there was no question of Red guilt: the UN should indict the Soviet bloc and then "impose punishment," which he suggested could be a diplomatic break with them, and/or an economic boycott. (A Nuremberg hanging bee was obviously out of the question.)

The United States had a new president and new administration now, and Lemkin expressed the hope that President Dwight D. Eisenhower would afford the support of his Administration to any country which would initiate the case. Nothing of any substance followed, and it took the *Times* two months to produce editorial support for Lemkin with a strong sympathetic restatement of both the Iron Curtain ethnics' position, that they were going off in massive numbers to "Soviet slave-labor camps," and that it was being accompanied by a new "genocidal wave" which was concentrating on the 'extermination' of their "nationals of Jewish faith." Urging the UN to put Soviet Union "genocide" on its agenda, the editors insisted that "widening waves of genocide" were sweeping the world in 1953, and that the UN should start assembling evidence, hearing witnesses, and then act to "stop the atrocities." All this expostulation of the first three months of 1953 produced little but yawns, and a few more formal calls from minority organizations imploring the Administration to apply direct pressure upon the Senate to ratify the "genocide" pact. The Lithuanian American Council, the Polish-American Congress, and three other Polish organizations addressed telegrams to Pres. Eisenhower personally, urging him to prod the Senate into this action, so that promptly upon ratification the US delegation in the UN could invoke it against the USSR.

On April 6, 1953 there occurred an act of staggeringly negative effect upon the future hopes of Genocide Convention enthusiasts in the United States. John Foster Dulles, the new Secretary of State under Eisenhower, testifying before the Senate Judiciary Committee which was holding hearings pending acting on the new amendment proposal of Sen. Bricker, declared that the Eisenhower Administration would not "press for the ratification of the United Nations Genocide Convention." The impact of this upon the Lemkin forces in the land and elsewhere had the combined simultaneous effect of a major earthquake and volcanic eruption. It was also apparent why: the Administration was strenuously seeking for a way to de-rail the Bricker Amendment, which proposed that in the case of Executive Agreements, state legislatures would have to pass "appropriate" laws validating their terms before they became binding on the citizens of their states. Among those testifying in behalf of this were Bricker

himself, aided by fellow senators Everett M. Dirksen (R-Illinois) and
William E. Jenner (R-Indiana), plus former Notre Dame University
Law School Dean, Clarence Manion. All expressed great fear of
encroachments on the rights of individual citizens as a result of the
powers of the United Nations and its agencies, and also the new
North Atlantic Treaty Organization (NATO). Dulles was quoted in
the *Times* of admitting that there had already been 10,000 new
executive agreements just since the existence of NATO, and related
only to NATO. But the extension of the use of the executive agreement was the device most strategic to the extension of the world
power of the new Insider establishment, and it could not be given up.
So a trade-off was being advanced, and a standoff was likely to
result: abandoning the Genocide Convention amounted to a rejection
of the Lemkin and related pro-ratification forces, but at the same
time by resolutely opposing the Committee on Law and Peace of the
American Bar Association and the Bricker people, the Administration was seemingly holding out a faint breath of hope to the former.
It was obvious that the forces behind Eisenhower were frightened by
the Bricker apparition, which 63 senators said they favored in April,
1953, and more evidence of this was demonstrated by the testimony
of Attorney General Herbert Brownell before the Judiciary Committee the day after that of Dulles. But the situation only became
more pronounced, that a deal was being offered: the granting of firm
assurances that the Genocide Convention and other UN treaties of
the kind would not be pressed for senatorial action, in exchange for
abandonment of such heavy pressure on their part for the Bricker
Amendment. The residue of this promised disaster for the Lemkin
influence machine, and all related enthusiasts for the Genocide Convention. But it was all part of the effects of the narcotic politics of
1941-1948 starting to wear off, accompanied by the search for
something else more in harmony with the new realities.

That a general panic was permeating the Lemkin-pro-ratification
front was made evident very shortly after Dulles' electrifying
announcement of the policy reversal of the Eisenhower regime. When
the League for Industrial Democracy held their 48th annual luncheon at the Commodore Hotel in New York, an audience of 500 heard
Mrs. Eleanor Roosevelt, widow of the greatest of all liberal political
champions, express her "very grieved" state of mind on learning that
the new Administration would not be legally bound by the Genocide
Convention or three other pending UN covenants. Mrs. Roosevelt
also thought that the failure to ratify these four documents would be
a "disappointment" to the world's smaller nations. Why this would
not be also to the larger ones she did not expand upon.

Meanwhile the vying forces in the Genocide Convention impasse persisted in their customary gestures. Three weeks after the Dulles blow to the hopes of the ratifiers, the Union of American Hebrew Congregations, at their 80th biennial convention, undaunted by Administration withdrawal, imperturbably fired off to the Senate another resolution urging them to ratify the pact. On the heels of this came the 20th triennial convention of B'nai B'rith, billed as "the oldest and largest Jewish service organization in the country" by the *Times,* in Washington, where a resolution was offered by the Anti-Defamation League Committee deploring the Senate's failure to act, and crediting this dilatory record for providing "propaganda ammunition for the enemies of democracy abroad," along with having "withheld from the hands of those who wish to expose the evils of totalitarianism, as manifested by the upsurge of Red anti-Semitism, a most effective propaganda weapon." And in the same month of May, 1953 members of the Jewish Reform Congregations circulated among the members of the Senate Foreign Relations Committee copies of a pamphlet, *Genocide—A Call to Action Now,* issued under the joint auspices of the Union of Hebrew Congregations, the Central Conference of American Rabbis and the National Federation of Temple Sisterhoods.

On their part the opponents tended to blend their campaign in with the positive program they favored, the Bricker Amendment. One of the more effective displays of this joint sortie was put on during these same spring, 1953 days by the Daughters of the American Revolution in Washington, which managed to get Sen. Bricker himself as a speaker, along with the redoubtable anti-"genocide" pact veteran, the ABA's ex-president, Holman. Both made vigorous speeches asserting that the "greatest threat to American freedom" was "treaty law," and Holman went into a detailed examination of Dulles, entertaining deep suspicion that he had really undergone a change of heart on the Genocide Convention. Holman reminded his listeners that Dulles had been counted on as a strong supporter of the Convention down to the day before his April 6 bombdrop, that he had "intemperately" criticized the ABA in the past for opposing it, while noting that the Washington *Post,* the New York *Times* and the devoutly liberal radio commentator, Elmer Davis, World War Two head of the war regime's propaganda agency, the Office of War Information, had all expressed being deeply troubled by Dulles' somersault. But Holman was suspicious, and noted that Dulles had demonstrated flexibility and suppleness on another issue: in 1952 he had thought the federal government's treaty power was dangerous; in 1953 he no longer thought so. Holman was sure that Dulles secretly still was a partisan of the Genocide Convention.

Though the possibility of ratification of the Genocide Convention now seemed over the crest and on its way down the slippery slope, there seemed to be little to suggest that its proponents had given up and accepted this view; Dulles' announcement seemed to have stimulated even greater pressure on the Senate to get on with it. And accompanying this drive was a continuous coupling of the entreaties with scathing anti-Soviet denunciations, especially now from the Zionist and general Jewish interest groups, an approach they now seemed to share quite harmoniously with the Iron Curtain ethnics, whose spokesmen had initiated this aspect of the ratification-drive program.

On Sunday, May 24, 1953 the *Times* devoted still another major editorial to the "genocide" question, calling attention to the original draft convention having been introduced six years earlier, the finished product now enjoying 41 ratifications, including that of South Korea, "which is at the moment carrying the brunt of genocide as perpetrated by the Communist world." Lauding the Convention as the "most ratified" of all UN treaties, and weaving in a sharp critique of Dulles, there came the usual concluding fervid call for American ratification at once, using for their final emphasis an invocation of the religious issue: "Millions of Iron Curtain countries are religious victims of genocide—Protestants, Catholics, Jews, Muslims—in opposition to the [Communist] regime," while ringing in another potent emtional line for the clincher: "Entire national groups are disappearing—Estonians, Latvians, Poles, Czechs, Hungarians—in the master obliteration plan." No one bothered to recall Lemkin's similar sensational charges that this had been done by the Germans a decade before; one wondered if there might be anyone left to "obliterate," and where the Soviet Union was finding them. In any case, the hope to realize very much out of exploiting the Reds and Korea had to be achieved in a hurry, now, since the war in the Far East was rapidly wearing down, and actually had barely two more months to go. The Genocide Convention ratification front would soon need another major stimulus to help keep the entire enterprise alive, and none was forthcoming. Two coming events were just about to finish off this first great movement in the USA: 1) the ratification by the Soviet Union, and 2) the beginning of serious charges of "genocide" against Israel by various Arab lands. The momentum by the middle 1950s slowed down in a spectacular manner, and by the end of the decade had become barely a murmur.

But there seemed to be plenty of steam still in the pro-ratification camp in mid-1953, despite the growing adversities. When the Senate Judiciary Committee adopted a resolution June 3 proposing a constitutional amendment limiting the President's treaty-making powers it apparently stimulated a major statement by 34 Jewish organizations, nationwide, headed by the American Jewish Committee, which once more urged early ratification of the "genocide" pact, "deplored" Dulles' statement in April that they could expect no help in the course from the Administration, and closed by ringing in a Korean War "regular": a call for the US to take a position at this time, "When so many of the captive people of the world are threatened by Soviet tyranny."

To be sure, the problem caused by the objectionable phraseology in various Genocide Convention articles had not entirely been dissipated, even at this late date, a matter recalled by Arthur Krock in still another think-piece on the subject for the *Times,* in an essay, "The Present Status of the Genocide Treaty," in the issue for June 11. He reviewed the vulnerable parts of Articles III, IX and XII to the exclusion of the stir over parts of others, notable II and VI, commented on the Soviet bloc's objections in particular, while calling attention to others having trouble accepting parts of it: the Philippines, for example, had attached their reservations to *four* of the pact's articles. And Krock was sure that when the US got around to ratifying with their four reservations, it would further vitiate its impact, and "would leave even less of the machinery [of the Genocide Convention] to effect its grand design," whatever that may have been.

Krock's return to this aspect of the matter seemed to have inspired one more response from Lemkin, a nearly column-long letter to the *Times* and another weary recital of what he conceived "genocide" to be. But what made this response especially interesting was his finally responding to the criticism of the "mental harm" clause in Article II, which had been scorched and battered and ridiculed ever since the document had been spread about the world. Lemkin disavowed having anything to do with creating that, and identified this clause as a contribution of the Chinese UN delegation. He said it was based on their claim that the Japanese in their years of occupation of parts of North China (1931-1945) had brought about mental deterioration among "millions" of Chinese by "administering drugs" to them. Nothing was said that the Koreans, under Japanese occupation far longer than the Chinese, had lodged no such complaint, and left others to wonder who had "administered" the drugs used by the Chinese ever since the mid-nineteenth century Opium Wars with England. Lemkin's closing views were quite morose, fearing that the Convention was being gradually reduced to a "mere humanitarian proclamation," and that the very concept of "genocide" was being "deflated." But his main closing point was to divert attention to a part of the pact hitherto passed over: according to Lemkin, the heart of the Genocide Convention was Article VIII, not IX, or any other part. Article VIII read,

> Any Contracting Party may call upon the competent organs of the
> United Nations to take such action under the Charter of the United
> Nations as they consider appropriate for the prevention and suppression
> of acts of genocide or any of the other acts enumerated in Article III.

A pronounced if not spectacular change took place in the rationale of pro-ratification propaganda messages as the Korean War wore down in mid-summer, 1953. The whole war had found the calls for ratification tied in with deploring things happening in Korea and the Iron Curtain lands, creating the idea that there was political ground to be gained by the lodging of "genocide" complaints before the UN against Red China and the Soviet Union upon ratification. But the Dulles manifesto of April 6 started a drift to another position, one which was accelerated by the growth in formidability of the Bricker Amendment impulse, and such other internal American political tides of sentiment as could be found supporting the McCarran-Walter Act and the checking of immigration to the USA. These offended the same minorities, and one notes especially in the pro-"genocide" pact pronunciamentos from mid-1953 on a new element: the presence of a testy and sometimes belligerent side-attack on unliked domestic political activity, this markedly present in Zionist statements. By the time the shooting stopped in Korea on July 27, 1953 the changeover had become general, but the Iron Curtain ethnics continued their pro-ratification calls as before, adding complaints against the Soviet for the continued bad treatment of their fellow ethnics remaining in the homelands.

Some examples of the above might be considered. On June 14, 1953 George Arkin, grand master of B'rith Abraham, addressing 700 delegates representing 310 lodges of this group at its 66th annual convention, in Atlantic City, blamed the "same forces of bigotry" which launched the McCarran-Walter Immigration Act for "preventing the ratification by the Senate of the Genocide Convention," which position was broadly supported by a wire from Sen. Lehman, that the anti-"genocide" pact drive was "based on distortions and misrepresentation." When the Central Conference of American Rabbis met for their 64th annual convention in Estes Park, Colorado, their call for ratification of the Genocide Convention was directly linked to a denunciation of the McCarran-Walter Act and an especially hostile thrust at the Bricker Amendment. Even the World Jewish Congress, meeting in Geneva, Switzerland a few days after the Korean armistice, took a vague swipe at domestic American politics; Dr. Israel Goldstein of New York, addressing 300 Jewish leaders from 60 countries, declared the "sentiment" of the American people was being "ignored" by the still-unrealized ratification of the "genocide" pact. But the less national the exposure, the more extravagent the content of this kind of political in-fighting. One example from the inside pages of the *Times* illustrates the switch to purely internal factors in this new battleground of attempted opinion formation. On October 3, Rabbi Zev Zahavy's sermon before the synagogue of Congregation Zichron Ephraim at 163 East 67th Street turned into a hectic oration in behalf of immediate ratification of the Genocide Convention, which he insisted was need to aid in "annulling the perfidy of hatemongers" rapidly spreading all through the USA. He professed to see a violent hate campaign simmering in almost every large city in the USA, "spewing forth the brew of malicious racial slander." The "American wing of fanatical anti-Semites" were busily castigating "the defenseless minorities in America," and unless some "strong anti-genocide legislation" was "put into immediate effect," the "venomous fury of America's lunatic fringe" would soon imperil "many liberty-loving Americans." So we have here a novel plea in behalf of ratification, so that American minority people might have protection from other Americans, presumably "groups" representing the "majority," whose irascible misbehavior toward the unoffending and helpless minority might thus be checked and liquidated. This kind of outburst was not common, and undoubtedly most Americans were unaware of the existence of such sentiments, but on such unordinary moments they managed to surface.

Even the *Times* got around to sensing this profound change in emphasis and ultimately blamed the blocking of the Genocide Convention in the Congress on a band of "Southern and isolationist Senators," in November, on the same day that the American Jewish Congress held their 17th biennial convention at Hunter College (November 7, 1953), where the delegates made another plea for the ratification of the Genocide Convention, and listened to a bitter attack on Congress by their invited speaker, J.R. Wiggins, managing editor of the Washington *Post*.

In many ways there was not much else to do except proceed in this direction of internal advancement and entrenched domestic strength. The American ethnics, whether from the Soviet satellite bloc by origin, or descent, or the Zionist Jews, were steadily losing their impact in the United Nations. A new minority force was taking shape, known later as the Asian-African bloc, recognized even by Winston Churchill in a moment of ill-tempered growling in 1956 as a formidable presence. In addition to this, Zionism was well on the wane in the affections of increasingly larger numbers of the people represented in the UN, and losing ground to Arabic pressure on the other UN powers, a process which accelerated spectacularly, to the point where one day the state of Israel, once an utterly uncriticized sacred cow, was to be so isolated as to have almost no friend in the international organization except its welfare-remittance patron and protector, the United States, and such support as the latter was able to muster elsewhere on occasion. With this change in direction came Zionist emphasis on *local* and *national* establishment of "genocide" as a force, via enforcement of enabling legislation in one or another country which was determined to be favorable to such a policy. The drive to create the great international umbrella envisaged by Raphael Lemkin swiftly withered, and especially after the ratification of the pact by the Soviet Union. The stress thereafter was preponderantly upon establishing islands in the international community where "genocide" remained a viable entity primarily because local enabling legislation managed to be remarkably pointed, or extremely and diligently enforced, principally in subduing or smothering criticism of minorities as per the prescription in the Genocide Convention.

A flicker of hope that the Eisenhower Administration or Congress would take action on the Genocide Convention prevailed toward the end of 1953, encouraged by baffling and equivocal American statements which related to UN activities. The Senate Foreign Relations Committee's fourth anniversary of sitting on the Convention was noted sourly by its proponents in June, and later in the year they rejoiced in two more ratifications, by Uruguay and Lebanon. The encouraging development was the recommendation to the General Assembly by the UN Legal Committee on November 3 that the Secretary General urge those states which had not yet done so to "accelerate their ratification." The General Assembly went along with this by a vote of 50-0, the American delegate, Archibald J. Carey, voting with this majority support for the resolution. This vote led observers to believe that Carey had the support of Pres. Eisenhower and Sec. Dulles, who were believed to support the "genocide" pact in principle, even if political realities had led them to adopt the position taken in April. But on the heels of this vote came a statement from Henry Cabot Lodge, the U.S. representative to the General Assembly, which stated that though the American vote indicated that the USA abhorred the "crime" of "genocide," it was not to be taken as evidence of a commitment to ratify the Convention, nor was it to be an invitation for United Nations "propaganda" in the USA in behalf of ratification, since this was a matter pending before the U.S. Senate.

There was a burst of criticism from several sectors following this seemingly contradictory pair of statements. Sen. Lehman was deeply offended by the caution against UN propagandizing in behalf of ratification, but on the other hand, Senators hostile to ratification were made increasingly suspicious as to Dulles' real position on the matter, despite his April statement. The *Times* once more had Arthur Krock try to interpret the situation, and he saw Lodge's action as a part of the Eisenhower Administration's continuing effort to defeat the Bricker Amendment. Krock elaborated a bit, pointing out that the Soviet reservation on Article IX of the Convention and the "mental harm" clause of Article II had made it "deeply unpopular in the Senate," which still was of the mind that no treaty could become internal law in the USA unless Congress was empowered by the Constitution to make such law in the *absence* of a treaty. Later efforts by Lodge to explain what he meant mainly added to the mystification.

In January 1954 the transcript of the hearings before the McMahon subcommittee was published, a 600-page document. There were now 43 UN members which had ratified the Genocide Convention, and 39 which had not. This incident led to more calls for US ratification, not just expressions of "abhorrence," in the manner of Mr. Lodge. As if there had not been dissection of the "genocide" pact and its portent enough, the New York *Times* in one of its "Youth Forums" telecasts on the same day put together a panel of six high school students, assisted by Raphael Lemkin himself, in yet another tiring elaboration, from the Adelphi Television Theatre. The occasion amounted to little more than another platform for Lemkin, who took up much time discussing how the ratification of the Convention by the USA could be used in anti-Soviet politics, since his main argument rested on the conviction that the USSR was "extremely sensitive to world public opinion," which certainly must have been news to many students of world politics. He was confident that Soviet "genocide" would be deterred by a "widely accepted international convention outlawing mass crimes." No one asked Lemkin what he thought would be the impact on the USA of the Soviet Union ratifying the Genocide Convention, but the students got around to asking him if the Ku Klux Klan in America would be subject to "genocide" prosecution in the event of American ratification, to which Lemkin replied in the negative. Said Lemkin, "Only where the intent is to destroy a human group within a nation so as to deprive its "survivors" of an identity as a group would the law apply" here.

Lemkin was still fighting Hitler when the Korean war broke out in 1950, and was slow to catch on to the switch in villains in world affairs, though he finally got around to concentrating on Communist Russia as the "genocide" rogue state of the early 1950s. But his persistence in this after the 1953 Korean armistice when the other enthusiasts for the Genocide Convention were moving to still another point of attack was again made prominent in his January, 1954 telecast. Zionist spokesmen were gathering to the defense of Israel, and the spread of "genocide" talk to the Mideast was almost automatic.

A clear indication of the change in emphasis occurred the very day after Lemkin's TV appearance. Speaking in Boston at a testimonial dinner sponsored by the American Jewish Congress, Justice Justine Wise Polier, daughter of Rabbi Stephen S. Wise and herself national vice president of the AJC, was quoted as saying that "the threat of King Saud of Saudi Arabia to wipe out Israel" provided a test as to where the United Nations really stood by their support of the Genocide Convention, whether it was a "true commitment" or whether it was just a "pious wish." Describing this as "a revival of Hitlerism in the Near East," and "a challenge to every decent man," she failed to be specific as to what she thought the UN should do about this, or how it would go about prosecuting for "genocide" Saudi Arabia, a key ratifier of the Genocide Convention, as a time when it was needed for the pact to become recognized by the UN as international law, as has been seen.

Lemkin, keeping his eye on the UN in the spring of 1954, was of course more than an interested party to the workings of their 18-member Human Rights Committee, which was considering a new proposed Covenant on Political and Civil Rights. His memorandum to this committee, reminding them that they would be endangering the Genocide Convention by moving ahead with this new treaty, which dealt with individuals, as contrasted with "genocide," a group crime, indicated that he was not too aware of what was going on with respect to the principal object of his affections. Therefore, the news that the Soviet Union had ratified the Genocide Convention, on May 3, 1954, caught him by surprise as much as it did anybody.

In a ceremony from which the press was barred, the ratification documents were deposited with UN Secretary General Dag Hammarskjold by the veteran Red functionary and chief prosecutor of the 1936-1938 Moscow purge trials, Andrei Y. Vishinsky, these papers being accompanied by the already well-advertised Soviet reservation that the USSR would never permit a Soviet citizen to be called before the International Court of Justice on a "genocide" indictment unwillingly. Soviet Russia was the 44th ratification.

A few hours later, representatives of organizations in the USA of ethnic descent from 7 countries under Soviet domination circulated a memorandum before the UN charging the USSR with "genocide" by way of systematic deportations from the three Baltic countries, Czecho-Slovakia, Rumania and Hungary, as well as religious "genocide" against the Jews of Rumania, and the Eastern Orthodox congregations of Czecho-Slovakia, Poland, Rumania and Hungary. The Reds were called upon to make restitution for their acts by UN requirement, but of course nothing took place. The UN General Assembly was far too overwhelmed by the Soviet action even to consider the slightest sanction, and revealed their sentiments shortly after by exhibiting the Soviet GC ratification documents ostentatiously in a display case in the UN's public lobby in their new New York home.

The opponents of this wily political move could do little but sputter. A *Times* editorial shouted that an analogous act would have been "If Al Capone had jointed the Anti-Saloon League," and promptly ran off for its readers a review of "37 years of 'genocide' " attributable to the Soviet Union, including what had been visited during that time upon the Crimean Tatars, the Volga Germans, Chechens, Ingushi, the Ukrainians and the Balts. Calling the ratification "callous Soviet hypocrisy'" and a slick, cynical move, the editors frankly compared Stalin, now deceased a year, to Hitler, charged that the cause of freedom was now even more imperiled than before, and that the slave labor camps would become even more extensive, that now no one would be safe, and warned everyone that Soviet word was no better on agreements respecting nuclear weapons than they were on a subject such as "genocide."

The calls for US ratification of the Genocide Convention rapidly tailed off after Soviet ratification, and the decline of interest in this document was so precipitate from the spring of 1954 on that it was almost palpable. Even in the New York City region only an occasional plaintive call was registered in its behalf, in the closing years of the 1950s rarely more than two or three a year. Whether or not the Genocide Convention was a victim of the Cold War, as some viewed it, the near-fatal effect of Soviet ratification upon American interest in it was tangible, to all who cared to observe, within a year, at best. Were it not for a succession of periodic tremulous editorials in the New York *Times,* which sometimes read as though they came from a shop which fabricated them to expectable specifications, few would have been aware that this UN treaty was still an issue in American affairs.

In the meantime the adversaries of the "genocide" pact grew in determination to sink it indefinitely if not permanently. In June, 1954 Holman denounced the Genocide Convention as "fraudulent" while addressing attendants at a DAR tea in Washington. And the following week the pro-Convention forces suffered a bad blow when the prestigious National Federation of Business and Professional Women, for six straight years advocates of US ratification, withdrew their support from it at the final session of their national convention in St. Louis. In April, 1956 the DAR hit the "genocide" pact with a full salvo, while holding their 65th Congress in Washington, throwing in for good measure condemnation of other proposed international agreements as well.

A scattering of additional ratifications occurred at the end of 1954, including the newly sanitized state of West Germany, and Greece, but not the United States. A querulous voice was still occasionally heard in support of this; the *Times* early in 1955 now took the tack that US ratification was needed to give "moral inspiration"; "moral force is vital in a materialistic world," the editors assured everyone. Indeed, the prosperity and absence of international strife had made most Americans as indifferently distant to such a thing as the Genocide Convention as they may have been to a call to memorialize the Children's Crusade.

There were even dogged and stubborn supporters of ratification such as New York's Senator Lehman who could still assail the Soviet Union as he did in a pro-ratification speech in New York City's Town Hall on May 22, 1955 honoring the 37th anniversary of Armenia's short-lived independence. The *Times* said Senator Lehman "charged that Russia was practicing genocide on a vaster scale than Germany," undoubtedly referring to the Germany prior to 1946. This meeting bristled with anti-Red talk, as well as denunciations of those responsible for the USA's failure yet to ratify the "genocide" pact; Lehman called that a "shameful thing." His fellow speaker, Rep. (New York) Kenneth B. Keating, declared that the US was committed to the liberation of the "communist-enslaved peoples," but did not say when; "this position did not include the employment of armed forces at this time." But gunfire was not only the key to a successful "liberation" of the Iron Curtain satellite peoples; it was also fundamental to the enforcement of the Genocide Convention. That neither cause had any chance of seeing this happen was transparently obvious.

On September 30, 1955 Raphael Lemkin was back in the news momentarily after a substantial period of absence, when he was appointed a professor at the Newark campus of the Rutgers University Law School. Some of his past attainments were once more included in the brief stories on his new job, in a year marked by little concerning his most dearly prized project, though most of 1956 was even quieter. On the occasion of his award of the Cross of Merit from the West German government at the UN, Lemkin enjoyed the luxury of a lengthy interview which led to a substantial profile in the *Christian Century,* whose author declared that the German award had been made to Lemkin because it "sought to atone in a measure for the extermination of forty-nine members of his [Lemkin's] family."

When asked at this same time why the US had still not ratified the Genocide Convention, Lemkin replied with a long complaint that Americans did not understand the problem, and that Americans remained ignorant that "the Genocide Convention fits the American Constitution as a shoe fits a foot."

A roaring speech by Mayor Robert F. Wagner in New York before the Foreign Language Press shortly after echoed Lemkin, though Wagner added additional choice terms, including "criminal negligence" and "inexcusable cowardice" to characterize the Eisenhower Administration and Secretary Dulles for their failure to press for ratification. But this was about the last thing of this kind to be heard for some time thereafter.

The fall of 1956 found a number of remarkable things occurring, and most of them were not particularly palatable to the pro-Genocide Convention Establishment. To be sure, there were more ratifications, but not by the desired parties. Syria and Tunisia added their ratifications. But other things were not so welcome. France, engaged in wars trying to put down "liberation" movements in Vietnam and in Algeria, encounters in which she was to do most miserably, was hit by a "genocide" charge in behalf of Algeria filed at the UN by the new Asian-African bloc. Then there followed the English-French-Israeli war on Egypt. On October 29, 1956, the day Israeli troops invaded the Suez region, an Israeli patrol killed 48 Arabs for violating a curfew they never were aware of, at Kafr Kassem, near the Jordan border. This was denounced as "genocide" before the UN by the Iraqi minister, al Jamali, in December. And from that moment on, the passionate zeal for the Genocide Convention cooled markedly among Zionists everywhere. As continued charges of "genocide" came to be lodged by Arabs and others in the UN halls, over the next two decades or more, the pressure for ratification of the Genocide Convention became very specialized, and frequently tuned to the situation in one country or another. Especially as enabling legislation evolved in West Germany, Canada, France and England, the Genocide Convention came to be esteemed for its usefulness in suppressing criticism of specific minorities here or there, depending on their energy and diligence.

But one heard less and less of "genocide" being cited with respect to the inhibition or punishment of mass murder or in relation to the verbiage in the Genocide Convention. This latter enjoyed a very brief fashion once more with relation to the Soviet suppression of the revolt in Hungary, also in November, 1956, though sometimes this was a long time coming. The *Times* was a year in editorially denouncing the Khrushchev regime in the USSR for this, choosing to do so in commenting on the action of Pakistan as the Convention's

56th ratifier two days earlier (October 17, 1957), as well as hailing more effusively than ever before the inventor of "genocide." Congratulating him on his "fifty-sixth victory," the editors described Lemkin as "that exceedingly patient and totally unofficial man," to which hyperbole Lemkin replied with a column-long letter to the editors the next month.

Cheered by their accolade, and comforted that the Genocide Convention had exceeded by far the Nuremberg trials in getting across the nature and importance of the concept of group guilt, Lemkin was momentarily far more disturbed by two UN projects which he thought threatened to drive the "genocide" idea into near-total obscurity. The first of these was the Draft Code of Offenses Against Peace and Security of Mankind, which gave him the impression of being "an illegal attempt to revise the Genocide Convention," the other being the Draft Covenant on Civil and Political Rights, which he thought would lead to the destruction of the very idea of "genocide." He thought the writers of this were confusing "common murder" with "genocide," making it possible for "private individuals and hate groups" to go "practically unpunished," and, by making only the "authorities" responsible for what happened in the case of violations, diverting attention once more to specific individuals while "an entire nation or race is being put to death." Thinking in the UN was drifting away from his approach, and it obviously was not very pleasant for him to contemplate where they were going in doing so.

On Friday, August 28, 1959, the New York area and the United Nations entourage were shocked to learn that Raphael Lemkin had died of a heart attack that day, while in the Park Avenue offices of his public relations counsel, Milton H. Biow; he was just a few weeks past his 58th birthday. He had been spending the summer in Spring Valley, New York, working on his autobiography,* tentatively titled "Unofficial Man," which he had derived from a *Times* editorial two years before which had spoken of him as such. The *Times* the following day ran a column-long obituary of the inventor of "genocide," filled partially with facts and also a few mistakes and adding peripherally to what was known of him as published in various profiles in journals, newspapers and annual issues of *Current Biography.* The day after that, the *Times* published a parting tribute to Lemkin in the form of a first-column editorial, "Raphael Lemkin. Crusader," closing with still another brief recapitulation of his career, and a windup reproach to the U.S. Senate for never having ratified his Genocide Convention. As the editors concluded,

> Death in action was his final argument – a final word to our own State Department, which has feared that agreement not to kill would infringe our sovereignty.

The things that have happened to Raphael Lemkin's idea, "genocide," and the principal fruit of it, the United Nations Convention on Genocide, during the last 25 years is outside the purview of this study, though several references to the time following Lemkin's premature demise have been made throughout the account.

* Lemkin's obituary called attention only to his preparation of an autobiography, but previous sources had mentioned that he was at work on a massive world history of "genocide," from ancient times to Hitler. Attention has been once more directed to this latter work, apparently always only in vestigial shape. This has come about by the apparently recent discovery of Lemkin's public and private papers and correspondence, and put on exhibit at the main branch of the New York Public Library beginning December 9, 1983. The finding of these papers, according to the New York *Times* (December 4, 1983, p. 45) was credited to a journalist at the United Nations, Alexander Gabriel, who claimed he found them in a "coal bin," where this mass of papers allegedly had been discarded after Lemkin's death. (This story induces a credibility crisis.)

In ruminating upon what this pretentious history of "genocide" throughout the ages might be like, it is instructive to examine just one example of what Lemkin construed to be "genocide," and which he repeated in print several times, an alleged massacre of "Assyrian Christians" to the number of 600 in Iraq in 1933 (sometimes the number was 300 and it allegedly took place in 1930, but this may have been a transcription error.) The impression Lemkin gave was that these people had been obliterated just for being Christians, and presumably this had been the entire number of such persuasion.

How Lemkin became obsessed with this affair may have been due to his presence at the League of Nations in Geneva when the event and its ramifications were widely related and commented upon in the world press. A consideration of the main facts in the matter can give readers an inkling as to the disparity between the real situation and Lemkin's imagination, which probably existed in all the other things which he construed as "genocide," if the case of the "600 Assyrian Christians" is an example. That the affair came to the attention of the League of Nations while he was still associated with it may account for his remembering anything at all about it.

The people known fifty years ago as the "Assyrians" were a Nestorian Christian sect or tribe, approximately 30,000 in number, living mainly in eastern Turkey, originally. No one knew precisely how they had come within the British orbit during the first World War, but they had become affiliated with the British in Iraq, the latter creating the "Assyrian Levies" out of them, and inducing them to take part in hostilities. They had fought with ferocity against the Turks, their former hosts, and the latter, understandably resentful, expelled them from Turkey after the war.

In the hysteric atmosphere surrounding the early League of Nations, these Assyrian Christians longed for assistance in the creation of an independent state for themselves. But the League Council, despite its eagerness for hacking up and bolting Europe into new synthetic "states," frowned on this one, and in 1925 refused to act in their behalf toward this objective. In the disruption of Asia

Minor and the Middle East in general brought about at the conclusion of the war, the Assyrians ended up being scattered about in Syria and Iraq, in the latter case mainly among their hereditary enemies, the Kurds, another minority. And it was at the hands of the latter that they suffered most of the loss of life which Raphael Lemkin was to assess as "genocide."

However, the facts as they began to be revealed in the late summer of 1933 indicated that the Assyrian Christians were for the second time in fifteen years the victims of embroilment in big-power politics again, and that there was no intentional program on the part of anyone to exterminate them, or to integrate them forcibly into someone else's culture, the latter one of Lemkin's chief horror fantasies over the years.

Emerging from the shambles at the end of 1918 was a French presence in Syria which amounted to a full-blown colony. To the east the British further entrenched themselves in Iraq. The Assyrians were to be found in both and the border area between and the mountains were their primary concentration.

In 1932, however, the British complicated things immensely by departing from Iraq as a virtual British colony, and Iraq under King Faisal emerged as an independent state, while becoming a member of the League of Nations Council as well. It was unconcealed that the French considered Iraq a serious threat to their Syrian satellite as a result of this, and were bound to try to create trouble for the former. To complicate things further, the British were not exactly charmed with the ensuing situation, especially insofar as it involved the fate and future of the Assyrian Christians, whom the British still considered their protégés, a vestigial protectiveness engendered by memories of their assistance in the late war.

It was in the context of this tangled situation that a rebellious portion of the Assyrian Christians resident in Syria crossed over into Iraqi territory in the late days of July and into early August, 1933. They first encountered a small Iraqi police force, and, as one expert on the affair narrated, though unprovoked by the latter, massacred them to a man. Lemkin in his agonizing over the "Assyrian Christians" in later years, never mentioned that they had initiated the original bloodbath.

It became obvious in the following weeks that the French had inspired this action, and that it hardly could have been started without their at least tacit approval. But what confused other observers is that these Assyrian Christians were heavily armed with the very latest British rifles and other weapons. Furthermore they had the support of a foreign press, and were an obvious serious threat to the fledgling Iraqi state.

The subsequent dispatch of Iraqi soldiers to this troubled region led to considerable loss of life, though the casualties caused by the Assyrians were never totalled; only those they suffered received any attention, and Lemkin acted as though they were simply an inert and passive community set upon by vicious exterminators. There was an immense uproar in mid-August, 1933 about it all, especially in Britain, though there was copious attention in some sectors of the US press, the extent of American involvement (none, politically). It was never made too clear whether the majority of the Assyrian Christians killed subsequent to the foray across the Iraqi border were the victims of Iraqi troops or Kurdish tribesmen. There was reported a renewed assault upon Assyrian villages by the

Kurds, and in mid-August British sources claimed some 500 Assyrians had been killed, 200 of whom were claimed to be women and children not involved in the fighting. The British government of Ramsay MacDonald was reported to be "profoundly disturbed," and the Prime Minister himself hurried back to London, his agitation shared by Sir Francis Humphrey, British Ambassador to Iraq, and G.S. Ogilvie Forbes, British chargé d'affaires in Baghdad.

In a piece in the New York *Times* by their specialist on the spot, Ferdinand Kuhn, Jr., the British were once more reported to be in a state of great agitation over a homeland for their "ex-allies," and unhappy at what was happening to them at the hands of both the Iraqi armed forces, and the Kurds, who were now assessed to have "butchered them by the hundreds." There were some British views that excessive murderousness had been indulged in by pro-Turks in the Iraqi forces, still hostile because of the Assyrian fighting for the British against Turkey in the World War.

However, things were not that clear, nor was there any sign of agreement on the part of the Assyrian Christians themselves as to the nature of the conflict. Fourteen sectional leaders of the latter denounced the incursion from Syria into Iraq. In a pronouncement published in the *Times* August 25, 1933 they declared, "We, forming a majority of the Assyrian leaders, denounce the rebellious section of our race," and praised "the continued kindness of King Faisal and the Iraqi government." The British, torn between loyalty to past allies and the political realities of the new situation, seemed to agree that this sally from Syria had given the government of Iraq "great provocation," and showed it by arranging to have the principal leader of the Assyrian Christian insurrection, Mar Shimun, arrested and deported to the British-controlled island of Cyprus, in the Mediterranean, while engaging in further negotiation seeking to have the people involved resettled in "French Syria."

It was in the midst of this swirling confusion that the rebellious minority of the Assyrian Christian minority lodged a complaint of massacre against the Iraqi government, made in Geneva on the opening day of the 76th session of the League of Nations Council, September 22, 1933, reported to the world by the soon-to-be-famed Clarence K. Streit, founder of "Union Now" in 1939, in a by-lined piece to the *Times* the next day. It can be seen that Raphael Lemkin, in total disregard for the high mound of complicated and contradictory facts and opinions extant on this matter, simply took the Assyrian Christian allegation at face value as a proven matter, and built his case of "genocide" against them solely on that. What was obvious however was that the "Assyrian Christians" were neither in any danger of extermination as a people or of forced assimilation into hostile cultures surrounding them. In fact there was a woeful disparity between the conception of the affair in the imagination of Lemkin and the record as could be determined from many other points of view and vantage-points of observation. If Lemkin's subsequent history of "genocide" was built of stories such as his misconception of this one, then he must have been preparing one of the great pieces of fiction-fabrication of his time. (For a summary of the matters discussed in the above examination of the "Assyrian Christian" upheaval in the summer of 1933 and many additional illuminating factors a recourse to the pages of the New York *Times* is suggested, in particular the stories published in the summer of 1933 as follows: August 10, p. 11;

August 16, p. 10; August 17, p. 1; August 19, p. 9; August 20, Section 4, p. 3; August 25, p. 7; August 27, Section 1, p. 10 and Section 4, p. 5, and September 23, p. 32.)

Chapter Seven

POSTSCRIPT: THE 1970 U.S. SENATE FOREIGN RELATIONS SUB-COMMITTEE HEARINGS ON THE GENOCIDE CONVENTION AND ITS AFTERMATH

IT IS NOT THE purpose of this work to detail and document the story of the "genocide" impulse in its entirety to date but to concern itself with its relation to and during the career of Raphael Lemkin. The updating of the story is another topic, and likely to be a very mixed and strange bag, if the recent work by Leo Kuper, *Genocide* (London: Penguin Books, 1981), is any indication. But a way-station estimate of the situation midway between the death of Lemkin and the present was considered worthy of record, the hearings before the Senate Foreign Relations Committee's sub-committee headed by Senator Frank Church (D-Idaho) in April and May, 1970 pursuant to the urging by President Richard M. Nixon in February of that year that the Senate ratify the Genocide Convention. This was the first such presidential pressure to be applied to the Senate since the 1949 urging by Harry S. Truman over 20 years before, made even a little mysterious now, since Mr. Nixon had been the Vice President under Dwight D. Eisenhower in 1953 when it had been laid down as positive policy that no such urging would be forthcoming from the White House.

To be sure, a noticeable sag of interest in promoting the Genocide Convention after Lemkin's demise was a matter of record, internationally and domestically. In the ten years after that event there were only eleven new member states of the United Nations to submit ratifications, and they hardly included world powers, what with such lands as Jamaica, Mongolia, Upper Volta and Nepal characterizing the latest adherents.

The propaganda in behalf of ratification in the United States had also noticeably cooled, though it might have been construed that the publication in 1960 by the American Jewish Committee of Nehemiah Robinson's book, *The Genocide Convention,* was intended as an assistance in quite the opposite direction. However it did little more than repeat a much earlier United Nations publication, the over-five hundred pages-long U.N. General Assembly Official Records, 3rd Session 1948/49, Sixth Committee, a record of the debate which led to the creation of the document which became the Genocide Convention by adoption on December 9, 1948 (supplemented by the summary records of the meetings of the Sixth Committee dealing with legal questions related to the Genocide Convention debate, September 21-December 10, 1948.)

A better index to the cooling of zeal for the Convention that same year was the short commentary by Clark M. Eichelberger, in his book *UN: The First Fifteen Years* (New York: Harper, 1960). Eichelberger, mastermind in 1940-1941 of the famed pro-war Committee to Save America by Aiding the Allies, and a member of the just-as-famed committee of five who met in the State Department 1942-43 to draw up the first United States draft of a United Nations charter, lamented the sustained failure of the U.S.A. to ratify the document. He even managed to blame non-ratification by the United States for the failure of the UN General Assembly to condemn Red China for "genocide" for its action in Tibet in 1959, an alleged process containing more than the usual component of mystery for people of ordinary intelligence (Eichelberger, *UN,* p. 61); he neglected to assign responsibility for the UN failure to condemn all the other "genocide" charges prior to Tibet, however.

It was demonstrable that nothing had changed since 1948, regardless of Eichelberger's complaints, and the machinery for indictment of "genocide" accusations, on whatever level, was as lacking as it had been at the very start. What Eichelberger represented was the conventional employment of "genocide" charges simply as efforts to assist political embarrassment of adversaries here or there, in other words, the debasement of what was clearly an intended international criminal statute which was utterly unenforceable on the international level into a psychological warfare propaganda weapon. To this stage had Lemkin's glorious vision descended, with obvious indications that it would recede further.

By the mid-1960s, however, the blending of the drive for the ratification of the Genocide Convention and the greatly accelerated pressure for "human rights" partially reflected in the civil rights legislation in the United States, and the vast increase in public campaigns and demonstrations in behalf of same, had carried the initiative to a different plane. One could have imagined the anguished handwringing of Raphael Lemkin at all this, the realization of a development he had regularly deplored in the first decade of the coexistence of the Genocide Convention and the Universal Declaration of Human Rights. But even the UN itself had fostered this homogenization at the very beginning, as was evident from such of its publications as the portentous manifesto, *For Fundamental Human Rights,* the tenth chapter of which was devoted to the Genocide Convention. If few could now discriminate between something intended to advance and protect *groups* as well as pursue and punish *other groups,* as opposed to devices intended to do these functions for *individuals,* it represented the decay that had set in from the early days Lemkin had first formulated his sophisticated, complex and subtle crime down to the situation 20 to 25 years later, when it had all been reduced by propagandist vulgarians into a not too worthwhile or useful synonym for mass murder, which Lemkin had abhorred.

President Lyndon B. Johnson's designation of 1968 as "Human Rights Year" had considerably to do with bringing the Genocide Convention into substantial public view once more, partially correcting the slide into obscurity during the first ten years after Lemkin's death. Concern for the wondrously convoluted legal issues which had consumed millions of words in the 1949-53 years once more made itself felt as well, one of the principal fruits of which was the publication in October, 1969 by the President's Commission for the Observance of Human Rights Year of its "Report in Support of the Treaty-making Power of the United States in Human Rights Matters." This weighty document, in which former presidents of the American Bar Association among others, participated, sought through the ministration of remarkably astute pettifoggery to abate or neutralize arguments against American ratification of various international treaties, or "conventions," in the "human rights" arena, among which, of course, the Genocide Convention was specifically discussed and examined. It is a matter of opinion whether this new round of abstractions was superior or inferior to the level of quality in such discourse established during the original round of debate and dispute beginning in 1949. But it did represent a weakening in some circles of resistance to ratification, and an encouragement to the pro-ratification forces after several bleak years of mainly unconcern with and indifference to the entire thing.

By the time President Johnson's Human Rights Year Commission had got around to posting its hefty Report, however, some major changes had taken place politically on the national level. Johnson decided not to be a candidate for reelection in the spring of 1968 and the election that fall found Richard M. Nixon the victor, bringing in with him a new regime, one which did not necessarily inherit some of his predecessor's programs. There is no evidence Pres. Nixon was influenced by what had happened prior to his election when it came to the Genocide Treaty. But the renewal of pressure from the White House on the Senate to take up the matter of ratification again, about a year after his inaugural, can be more substantially related to an international event, and its impact upon and reflex-action by his State Department.

On January 30, 1970 the United Kingdom deposited its Genocide Convention ratification papers with the General Assembly of the United Nations. Other than the still-unsigned United States, it was the tardiest such ratification by a major world power, and the first of such in a dozen years, since that of India, having been submitted August 27, 1959. Followed swiftly by the passage by Parliament of enabling legislation, Britain and its associated lands about the globe were ready to start processing "genocide" cases in their various criminal courts, though, like all other signatories, they engaged in no such enterprise whatever. The significant response, though, was the almost-umbilical-cord reaction of Mr. Nixon's State Department, something which had not happened, let us say, in the case of Pres. John F. Kennedy's State Department following the ratification by the Democratic Republic of Congo (May 31, 1962).

On February 5, 1970, less than a week following United Kingdom ratification of the Genocide Convention, the new Secretary of State, William P. Rogers, addressed a letter to Pres. Nixon, urging him to request the Senate once more to proceed with the ratification of the Convention. His long dispatch went into superficial history of the evolution of the Convention, and included recommendations which were 20 years old, growing out of various reservations or 'understandings' arrived at when the Senate Foreign Relations Committee's McMahon Sub-committee had examined the document and made its recommendations in various of the foggy areas of this flower of United Nations legal byzantinism. If it was not too clear that it was the State Department once more which was the moving force behind ratification pressure it was far less occluded in this respect after the opening day of the next set of hearings, which became a certainty after the President's response to his Secretary of State.

On February 19, exactly two weeks later, Mr. Nixon addressed to the Senate his renewal of request for consent to ratification of the International Convention on the Prevention and Punishment of the

Crime of Genocide. It was a move which mystified many, particularly in view of Mr. Nixon's antecedents in the Eisenhower years, when that Administration skirted the matter entirely as a matter of policy, as has been seen in the previous chapter. There was no surge of popular pressure about the land for such action in these latter days, and try as they might, the seekers for motivation behind it all tended to conclude that it was mainly a State Department radar-signal-bounce reaction to what had just happened in Britain. The shallow roots of this newest essay in the endeavor to obtain ratification of the Genocide Convention were shortly to be demonstrated by the brevity and the halting conduct of the hearings which began pursuant to the President's request. (Both Sec. of State Rogers and Pres. Nixon in their communications reported Attorney General John Mitchell's opinion that there were no constitutional obstacles to United States ratification, a matter all were to learn once more was far from that clear after they had read the statement made on May 22, about which more later.)

Nine weeks after receiving Pres. Nixon's letter the Senate responded to him in the form of the initiation of hearings once more on the Genocide Convention. This time the Subcommittee of the Senate Foreign Relations Committee conducting these hearings was headed by Sen. Frank Church (D-Idaho) assisted by Sens. Claiborne Pell (D-Rhode Island), John Sherman Cooper (R-Kentucky) and Jacob K. Javits (R-New York); though Sen. Stuart Symington (D-Missouri) was listed as an additional member of this Subcommittee, he took no part in the hearings.

Originally it was planned to hold hearings on just two days, the 24th and 27th of April, though as will be seen another day was to be included later on as a consequence of matters not apparent when the original plans were made.

Eventually the verbatim minutes of the hearings, and documents and written statements submitted by persons and organizations which did not appear in person, were published as a 261-page official document, *Hearings Before A Subcommittee of the Committee on Foreign Relations, United States Senate, Ninety-first Congress, Second Session, on Executive 0, 81st Congress, 1st Session, The Convention on the Prevention and Punishment of the Crime of Genocide* (hereinafter referred to as *Hearings*), issued later in 1970 by the U.S. Government Printing Office.

The Church Subcommittee spent 7 hours and 40 minutes in session on the two days in April, listening to and questioning 11 protagonists of the Convention, and 5 antagonists. Approximately 7 hours were devoted to the proponents of ratification, several of whom were questioned at great length. The remainder of the time was devoted to opponents, who, strangely enough, were engaged in only a few minutes of perfunctory senatorial interrogation.

The morning session of April 24 (10 a.m. to 12:50 p.m.) was devoted entirely to advocates of ratification. In the order of their appearance they were Sen. William Proxmire (D-Wisconsin), probably the most vivacious and loquacious member of the U.S. Senate favoring the Genocide Convention, over the years (he was soon to have spoken in behalf of it over five thousand times); Charles W. Yost, U.S. Ambassador to the United Nations; Mrs. Rita Hauser, the U.S. Representative to the Human Rights Commission, and George Aldrich, Deputy Legal Adviser to the U.S. State Department.

The afternoon session (2:30 p.m.-3:50 p.m.) heard Laurence C. Smith, against, representing something called the U.S. Constitution Council, of Squires, Missouri; Bruno V. Bittker, for, an attorney from Milwaukee who had been very active in President Johnson's Human Rights Year activities; Warren S. Richardson, against, the General Counsel of the Washington, D.C.-based Liberty Lobby, and Dr. William L. Pierce, against, of Arlington, Virginia, who was identified upon senatorial questioning at the conclusion of his statement as a member of the National Socialist White Peoples Party located in that same community.

The session of April 27 was a single long and uninterrupted one (10 a.m.-1:30 p.m.) and heard in the following order Prof. Richard Gardner, for, representing the Ad Hoc Committee on the Human Rights and Genocide Treaties, of New York City; Harry Leroy Jones, against, a Washington attorney who had worked 25 years for the Department of Justice and who had served 20 years as a member of the Council of the Section of International and Comparative Law of the American Bar Association; William H. Rehnquist, for, Assistant Attorney General of the Office of Legal Counsel of the Department of Justice; Prof. Lev Dobriansky, for, president of the Ukrainian Congress Committee; Robert Layton, for, of the New York State Bar Association's Committee on International Law; Mrs. Ernest W. Howard, against, representing the American Coalition of Patriotic Societies, and Hope Eastman, for, the Assistant Director of the Washington Office of the American Civil Liberties Union.

Since it was the Administration which was applying almost all the pressure for ratification, the Subcommittee spent the largest part of their time listening to the statements of its representatives, they being the ones most likely to present any new ideas, if there were any, in behalf of this course of action, as well as the most ingenious reasoning or rationalizing in favor. Little time was devoted to opponents, most of whom took established positions and largely defended the trenches dug in 1949-1953; the Convention had been apprised a menace then and nothing that had happened since had enhanced its "image" in their view whatever. Despite the trickle of ratifications in the previous dozen years, what was occurring globally made the Genocide Convention appear to be more and more preposterous to its adversaries, and an irrelevant nuisance even in its best possible contemplation.

Indeed, rereading the testimony and replies to senatorial questioning in the 1970 hearings from some of those who appeared before them reflected an eerie feeling that time had been suspended for two decades. Hardly a new word was used and no new ideas were expressed. The same pro and con arguments used before the McMahon Subcommittee in 1950 surfaced again, the same attempts to allay the apprehension of the objectors came from the adherents, and as unconvincing as they had been 20 years earlier though through different spokesmen, and women, alike.

As the leadoff presentation before the Church Subcommittee, Sen. Proxmire more or less set the tone of the hearings, with his eager and enthusiastic approval of the move toward ratification of the Genocide Convention. He claimed he had spoken in behalf of ratification every day the Senate had been in session, January, 1967 to April, 1970. Blaming the objections of the American Bar Association before the MacMahon Subcommittee hearings in 1950 for the shelving of the Convention this long time, he quickly got into a familiar groove, sprinkled with dubious "history" and at one point an outright misconception in his urgency over the need for quick ratification. Sen. Proxmire, claiming it was the agitation over the Human Rights year that inspired the report by Supreme Court Justice Tom Clark in October 1969, smiling favorably on the Genocide Convention, which led to revived pressure for American ratification, soon showed the effect of 20 years of historical confusion by quickly misconstruing Lemkin's original doctrine in a statement which resulted in one more muddy blending of the Human Rights Declaration and the Genocide Convention, anathema to Lemkin in 1948-1959.

Sen. Proxmire put no new facts in the record in his emotional and spirited declamation, though he now found it safe to include Russian anti-Jewish *pogroms* (in the *Hearings* it was spelled "programs") and the Turkish actions against the Armenians in the World War One era as "genocide," something Lemkin had studiously avoided in 1943-44. But his mainstay as was that of everyone else was the legal proceedings against Hitler's regime at Nuremberg, without which "genocide" did not seem to have another single historical precedent which all proponents of the Genocide Convention agreed could be so interpreted. Sen. Proxmire managed to ignore the total absence of any legal proceeding against any alleged act of "genocide" anywhere worldwide during the preceding 20 years. Nor could he come up with a case involving a single soul in the world who might at that moment have benefited from American ratification of the Genocide Convention.

Upon questioning especially by Sens. Pell and Cooper, however, Sen. Proxmire showed signs of not too intensive understanding of several of the legal implications or even wordage of the Convention (see his remarks in *Hearings,* pp. 17-24), and at one point (*Hearings,* p. 23) in response to a question from Sen. Cooper did not seem to understand at all what was involved in the enabling legislation which would have to follow ratification in order to make "genocide" operative in the American criminal code:

> **Sen. COOPER:** "Is it your view that this Convention should it be approved by the Senate that legislation to implement it then ought to be adopted by the Congress?
>
> **Sen. PROXMIRE:** Yes. As I understand it, the principal legislation implemented would be the adoption by the Congress of the provisions required to establish an international penal tribunal."

Actually, this latter action rested upon the United Nations exclusively, and had nothing to do with specifically American enabling legislation, which had to deal solely with the definition of "genocide" in an American context, and the establishment of the specific penalties which would be incumbent upon anyone convicted in *American* courts for violation thereof. Americans were not committed to have anything whatever to do with an international criminal court, and Sen. Proxmire had inadvertently slipped into a serious mistake, assisting an important objection of his opposition that this was not just an apparition but a very real possibility, seriously endangering American civil rights. It was strange that no one at the hearings picked him up on this. Though the four participating members of the Subcommittee, all with proven liberal credentials regardless of party, were obviously sympathetic to ratification of the Genocide Convention, no other Senator favorable to this course appeared before them except Sen. Proxmire.

Now followed the heavy guns of the Administration, in succession, Amb. Yost, Mrs. Hauser, and Atty. Aldrich. Their uninterrupted performance was a high point of the entire hearings. What was to transpire thereafter in the April sessions was mainly decoration and addenda to a familiar and frequently-told tale. The most absorbing aspects of this part of the hearings were the pesky reiterated questions of the members of the Subcommittee, perhaps exceeding what they had wished to get into, in view of their basic favorable predisposition to ratification. But the rattled waffling and stumbling hesitancy of the Administration's experts probably encouraged Senators Church, Cooper and Pell to persist in interrogatories which only protracted the embarrassment of these notables. Subcommittee questioning was more or less at random, several things exciting their curiosity at different moments, and the three Administration dependables similarly replied when they thought their contribution might serve the Senatorial purposes, if not questioned directly by name. Some of the highlights of this part of the hearings, which lasted more than two hours, may now be taken up.

Sen. Church, sounding a little annoyed and baffled, half way through the question-and-answer time with his three star testifiers, got to the heart of the matter best in the following colloquy (*Hearings,* pp. 61-62) which found Amb. Yost on the receiving end:

Sen. CHURCH: "To what degree are we merely interested in becoming a party to this Convention for purely symbolic reasons. I do not discount the importance of symbolic acts, but the treaty is really pretty toothless. In fact, the Convention is about as toothless as one could be. It depends, does it not, on the self-execution of the parties. It has already been testified that the United Nations as such gathers no additional power [by U.S. ratification].

Can any of you cite a single instance where any one of the 70-odd countries that have in fact become members in this treaty have proceeded against any citizen within their jurisdiction, charged them with genocide, tried them, and convicted them? Has there been a single case where this treaty has actually been invoked on the part of any of the 75 countries that have ratified it?"

Mr. Yost took it upon himself to reply, and conceded that he was "not aware" of any such action either, while repeating his conviction that ratification was a worthwhile action. This simply provoked Sen. Church to re-emphasize his earlier reservation:

Sen. CHURCH: "But again, Mr. Ambassador, you are talking about the symbolism involved. I do not discount that. However, isn't this treaty really an effort to pound a few more nails into Hitler's coffin for the heinous acts that took place under his government during the war years and prior to the war years?

I find it hard to conceive that any government even though it might be a signatory to this Convention, which actually engages in such a practice in the future, is either going to confess to the crime or is going to take any action to punish itself. That exceeds the bounds of realism. Moreover, it is difficult to believe that any government, so inclined, would act against individual citizens within its jurisdiction who might be guilty of genocide."

Amb. Yost's response to this was similarly restrained as before, though doing his best to assert that there was something more than symbolism involved, suggesting that in some vague way it might be an assist to a registering of the "weight of public opinion." Sen. Church remained unimpressed and still was of the mind that it persisted in being something mainly of "moral importance," in Amb. Yost's words.

It is unlikely that any of the contingent bucking for ratification of the Genocide Treaty in 1970 knew or understood the Convention better than Amb. Yost. He was the only one to make a point before the Subcommittee, for instance, of the collectivist nature of the document, its primary if not sole emphasis on *groups,* not individuals, despite the bias in favor of the latter which was a consequence of the much heavier attention paid to that aspect in the 20 years' interlude. But throughout the session before Sen. Church's inquisitors he stubbornly held forth for ratification on abstract grounds. Close to the end (*Hearings,* p. 77) Mrs. Hauser supported his view, declaring that "as important a country as ours with its great moral leadership" should "be part of an effort in international rule building."

But in the history department and on the practical level there was lamentable backing and filling, by both Amb. Yost and Mrs. Hauser, when the Senators sought to eliminate their own ignorance on one matter or another by questioning these experts. (The historical preparation of the Subcommittee was not too profound; Sen. Cooper, for example, even thought it had been the U.S. Army which had taken the Auschwitz camp complex, not the Stalinist Red Army, many hundreds of miles from the American positions.)

On the tardy ratification of others, Sen. Church inquired of Amb. Yost why it had taken until January 30, 1970 for the British to do so, which the latter did not know. Mrs. Hauser volunteered hesitantly that it had taken them all that time to reconcile all their extradition treaties and get the consent of all their territories and possessions. It was at that point that Amb. Yost entered into the record the list of the 75 countries that had already ratified, but alphabetically, not chronologically. The latter would have been additionally embarrassing. Sen. Church was also intrigued that only two of the new states of black Africa had ratified the Convention, for which Amb. Yost advanced another vague and limping excuse (*Hearings,* p. 37).

Further subdued that no evidence was adduced that a "genocide" charge had ever even been submitted to the International Court of

Justice for an *opinion* in 20 years, let alone a criminal prosecution anywhere, the Senators were additionally discomfited by the results of further questioning on various specifics, and Amb. Yost and Mrs. Hauser were equally threadbare in the fact-supplying sector. Though neither the Senators on the Subcommittee nor the makers of statements before them managed to concern themselves with what had gone on in Red China the previous two decades, when the common traffic in international news had become convinced tens of millions had lost their lives there, the inquiries concerning other places were no more fruitful.

When Sen. Cooper wanted to know (*Hearings,* p. 38) why "genocide" in the Soviet Union had never been brought before the Security Council or the General Assembly "for action," Amb. Yost trailed off in reply, admitting the UN Charter provided no possibility of expecting "enforcement action." When the specific charge, repeated in world propaganda so frequently, 1948-1958, about the thousands of Greek children allegedly kidnapped to the USSR, an obvious and palpable act of "genocide" as per the Convention (*Hearings,* p. 66), there now was no general agreement that this *was* "genocide." The flustered silence of earlier years now was tempered by pleas that the children had not been killed, but raised as Soviet citizens to repopulate "a country that lost a lot of men in the war." (Lemkin had certainly not allowed such an excuse for the Germans when he was formulating "genocide" in 1943-45.) Bit by bit the Senators were beginning to realize that though political incitatory incendiarism seemed to be able to fashion "genocide" charges right and left, when it came to *legal* cases, it seemed to be an unusual crime, having been committed only once.

Mrs. Hauser, though she matched Amb. Yost in rhetorical declamatory eloquence in behalf of ratification, did not manage to comport herself any better when faced by Subcommittee questioning. In her historical recapitulation of the coming into existence of the Genocide Convention (*Hearings,* p. 39), she simplified things by asserting it was a "direct result" only of World War Two and the International Military Tribunal at Nuremberg, mentioning only "the mass murders of Jews" as its inspiration. After a tiresome rehearsal of the legal argumentation of 1949-52 she came down on the side of the "non-self-executing" view of the Convention, requiring implementing legislation, as "genocide" was not specified in the U.S. Criminal Code. Her closing discourse (*Hearings,* pp. 42-43) included a florid bit of bombast, identifying the Genocide Convention in the tradition of the great "human rights" documents of the past, in her opinion, *e. g.,* the Ten Commandments, the Magna Charta, the French Declaration of the Rights of Man, the U.S. Bill of Rights, and the United Nations Charter. One could almost imagine seeing the Raphael Lemkin of the 1950s cringe here, but she did not follow with the Universal Declaration of Human Rights.

Atty. Aldrich also came in for some lumps from the Subcommittee, and he, Mrs. Hauser and Amb. Yost on occasion all took a crack at answering some pesky question from the Senators *seriatim*, with imperceptible effect. After one long haggle between the Subcommittee and Aldrich on the effect ratification would have on American extradition treaties then outstanding with other ratifying countries, Aldrich inserted in the record a list of all these treaties. He and others had brought up that U.S. ratification of the Convention would require the renegotiation of all these extradition treaties prior to there ever being an American shipped out of the country to face a "genocide" accusation somewhere. The possibility of this happening seemed to entrance the Subcommittee, which returned to this subject over and over again, and never seeming to get an answer which they thought satisfactory from anyone. Other matters the Senators went back to repeatedly concerned the definition of the word "group" in the Convention, and how it might be interpreted in subsequent enforcement of a ratified Convention, and the possibilities involved which might come about from disagreements resulting from conflicting interpretations due to the byzantine incertitude of the East European verbiage in which Articles II, III and IX were couched. Raised in the Anglo-American tradition of plain and starkly-worded criminal statutes, such elusive and sinuous phrasing fundamentally irritated them, apparently. But they got chill aid and assistance here from their Administration ratification proponents.

Senator Church now went back to the questioning. When he expressed once more his mystification as to why no "genocide" action had been taken against anyone in 20 years (*Hearings*, p. 63), Mrs. Hauser's response was that the very existence of the Convention itself had effectively deterred the commission of "genocide" in that interval. (To some this sounded like an analogy to the apocryphal story of the demented man making believe shooting through the bars of his asylum with a wooden gun. When asked what he was doing, to which he replied that he was shooting tigers, and being told there were no tigers out there, he supposedly replied in triumph, "See? I've killed them all.")

When Sen. Church pressed her for an example of "genocide" any time in the 25 years since the obliteration of Hitler which the UN had suppressed, Mrs. Hauser could come up only with some influence which had been applied upon Venezuela for alleged treatment of some of their Indians "located far up the Amazon [River]." She claimed that this had led to a Venezuelan government investigation and then changing "various administrative practices." But upon further questioning about this incident she could not affirm that action had resulted from the invoking of the Genocide Convention, though this did not deter her from once more asseverating that "ratifying this Convention, we would advance the state of development of international law in the field of human rights."

When Sen. Pell (*Hearings,* pp. 64-65) tried to pin Mrs. Hauser down on what could be considered "genocide" in 1970, and whether the action of the Vietnamese in Cambodia, Indonesia's repressive behavior toward its Chinese, or the position of Jews in the USSR could be so construed, she evaded naming any, while volunteering the opinion that none of these latter could be interpreted as "genocide." While also denouncing charges that the U.S. was engaged in "genocide" in Vietnam, she admitted that the word was being "used very loosely" now, and wanted the world to get back once more to the specific legal definition in the Genocide Convention. But from what she advanced, she obviously did not know the meaning of the Latin and Greek derivations Lemkin had originally put together in making up the word.

Taking their cue from Sen. Church, Sens. Pell and Cooper started asking the same question. When Sen. Pell renewed his quest for an answer to his query as to why not a single case of even alleged "genocide" had ever come before the International Court of Justice in The Hague, which of course had only interpretational jurisdiction, Mrs. Hauser tried to remind the Senator that there was no international criminal court, and only *local* prosecution for committing the crime of "genocide" was possible.

Then, in a subsequent flurry (*Hearings,* pp. 76-77) Sen. Cooper chose to annoy Atty. Aldrich and Amb. Yost by asking once more why no legal charges of "genocide" had been made since the Genocide Convention became operational in January, 1951, ringing in the Biafra-Nigeria imbroglio, the Indonesian massacre of 200,000 "Communists," or the mutual killings in India and Pakistan, Amb. Yost replied that all had come before the UN but that "serious arguments" challenging them as "genocide" had stopped further action. So the entire business seemed to suffer terminally from the absence of what Mrs. Hauser had suggested might be called a "perpetual Nuremberg tribunal."

So nothing which had occurred worldwide since 1945 seemed to be clearly "genocidal," to the frustration of the Subcommittee, searching hard for almost anything which had ever happened anywhere since that year, in the hope of studying how it had been handled. Seemingly obsessed by their questioning at varying times about the possibility of an American, or more than one, being the defendant(s) in a "genocide" proceeding, especially abroad, they obviously wanted something of more recent vintage than Nuremberg to examine. But they had been reassured by Mrs. Hauser, who chimed in to offer her opinion that Americans would never be involved (she vigorously denied there was a "genocidal" component to the widely-trumpeted My Lai "massacre"), asserting, "I would find it a hard stretch of the imagination to conceive a situation in which the United States today or into the future would engage in acts of genocide." It must have been comforting to Mrs. Hauser and her partisans to have come upon a "crime" only non-Americans might, could or would commit.

It was obvious by now, surely, that Raphael Lemkin's diligent scurrying through history, seeking prior examples of his crime of "genocide," had been futile. The minuscule events he had culled from the past were pretentious, but now impressed no one. A quarter of a century after his invention they sounded like citations of ancient case law in a suit which neither the presiding judge nor the contending parties took seriously, and accepted only as window-dressing. All there was to "genocide" was Hitler Germany; everything before it was insignificant, and everything after it irrelevant, if anything of a "genocidal" nature had happened at all. The crux of the matter was the continuous refurbishing of the Hitler story and the endless buttressing of it all as solidly factual, about which no doubts could be allowed.

The Church Subcommittee had been foiled and baffled trying to find out what had happened in the field of "genocide" since the Senate had last held hearings on the Genocide Convention, 20 years before. But they also were vexed by several of the same kind of issues which had tied people up in 1950, and for the same reasons: the opaque and vague verbiage of certain parts of the Convention itself. Its critics had long attacked the phrase "members of the group" in the first two clauses of Article II. Lemkin himself had been maddeningly obscure on this, and as hard to pin down as trying to nail jelly to a post, as Theodore Roosevelt had described something in a much different context in the past. Lemkin had been willing to admit that it meant more than a few, and had been incensed at the Universal Declaration of Human Rights, with its emphasis on single persons. But by 1970 proponents of the Convention had already blended the two to the point where now persons could be found who spoke of "genocide" being committed against single individuals. This was complemented by previous and continuing controversy about a related phrase in Article II, where "genocide" was referred to as possibly being committed against "part" of a group. How big did this have to be? When she was asked about this by the Subcommittee

(*Hearings,* pp. 41-42), Mrs. Hauser admitted she was not sure when the crime against a people had reached the number qualifying it to be denounced as "genocide," in accord with the words in Article II. She plumped down on the side of a similar unmeasurable, the "reason-ableness" of such having at bottom to be worked out in the future by lawyers.

Sen. Cooper (*Hearings,* pp. 75-76) also wrung from the Administration representatives the concession that if two States disagreed as to what constituted "genocide" in a particular situation and could not agree on submitting the matter to the International Court of Justice for an opinion, then the matter never could reach trial as long as State No. 1 barred extradition of the accused to State No. 2, while refusing to try the matter itself, not recognizing the act involved as genocidal. This had grown out of prior exchange between Sen. Pell and the pro-Convention testifiers (*Hearings,* p. 68) on another thing which bothered the Subcommittee, the reservation by the USSR on Article IX of the Convention on this very matter.

Still another item of long standing dating from two decades earlier was the unfortunate insertion in clause *b* of Article II of the stipulation "mental harm." The Subcommittee wanted to know what it consisted of, and did one have only to subject a single person to it, or could "mental harm" be inflicted upon an entire *group.* And if this could be done, the Senators were especially eager to find out *how* this could be achieved. No one seemed to have the expertise on this point to give them much comfort; in general the newer genera-tion of pro-ratification protagonists fell back on the understanding the McMahon Subcommittee had construed in the past, "permanent impairment of mental facilities." (How this could be done to a *group* was left unanswered.)

Still another long-argued-over item, brought up in discourse over Article IX and earlier ones, concerned the possibility of a State being held liable in damages for injury inflicted *on its own nationals* as well as on nationals of another State, construed as "genocide." Americans had always bristled at this possible conception or constru-ing of the Convention, and it was another area where Lemkin had never been very lucid (though something of the sort had been forced *ex post facto* upon the Germans after 1945.)

In the last hour of the opening session the Subcommittee got into one of the exotic byways possible to those involved in the kind of ruminating they were doing and the repeated hypothetical situa-tions they posed for the Administration representatives before them. This was related to the "mental harm" issue once more. Senators Pell, Cooper and Church all jumped into this one (*Hearings,* p. 68) as to whether it could be possible to construe a dual school system in

which one part was "somewhat better than the other" as a "genocidal" instrument. Here they were getting into another of the vast
number of possibilities Lemkin had originally set up in putting the
idea of "genocide" together to start with. That such a situation
might cause "mental harm" to those in the poorer of the two sectors
was the issue. But Atty. Aldrich stemmed the discussion by bringing
up the point that "in order to be genocide [it] has to be done with
the intent to destroy in whole or in part the group." This quieted
down the Senatorial apprehensions on this matter, but at the same
time exposed what was the fundamental and unavoidable foundation
of *all* "genocide" speculations or allegations or charges; they all
called for demonstrable proof of *intent*. This was missing from most
of the hearings and from the very largest part of all the talk the
subject of "genocide" had ever stimulated in the past, and on down
into the present, for that matter.

The afternoon session of the Subcommittee hearings April 24
was largely a review of twenty-year-old arguments pro and con concerning the desirability or undesirability of ratification, and as such
represented almost an anti-climax to what had transpired in the
morning. Laurence Smith (*Hearings*, pp. 80-84), sounded more like a
protagonist of the Black Muslims than anything else, and set the tone
of his remarks by claiming American blacks were "the largest victims
of genocide in the world," and added a backup statement quoted
from Thomas Drake, President of the United Alliance of African
Organizations made Feb. 8, 1970, just a bare six weeks before, "It
can be proven without a doubt that the act of genocide is being used
at this present time against my people here in America." The Senators got a brief glimpse of what was in store domestically in the
American courts from this sector of the public upon ratification.

This kind of wild charge was precisely what Clarence Manion had
predicted nearly two decades earlier would be commonplace, and
repeated in a powerful written statement of a single page which
ultimately was included in the record (*Hearings*, pp. 235-236.) A
professor of constitutional law at Notre Dame University for 27
years, and Dean of its Law School for 12, Mr. Manion scolded Pres.
Nixon for his part in the renewed drive for ratification, reminding
him of his presence in a previous Administration which refused to
have anything to do with such a procedure. This was part of his
testimony:

> On April 6, 1953, Secretary of State John Foster Dulles and I were
> the only witnesses heard on the closing day of the hearings on the pro-
> posed Bricker Amendment by the Senate Judiciary Committee. I
> supported the Bricker Amendment and Secretary Dulles opposed it. He

maintained that no such amendment was needed at that time to protect the constitutional rights of Americans because the Eisenhower Administration did not intend to submit or press for ratification of any of the United Nations Conventions which were used as examples of treaties which would affect the domestic jurisdiction of the United States and/ or the constitutional rights of American citizens. He cited, as examples of such threatening multilateral treaties, the Convention for Political Rights of Women and Covenant for Human Rights *and the Genocide Convention,* the last of which had already been submitted to the Senate by President Truman.

Mr. Dulles' public promise not to sign or submit such treaties, nor to press for ratification of those of them that had already been signed and submitted was the controlling reason why the United States Senate did not subsequently ratify the proposed Bricker Amendment which ultimately failed ratification in the Senate by one vote short of the necessary two-thirds majority . . . President Eisenhower's submission of the Genocide Convention to the Senate for ratification in 1953 would have guaranteed the speedy passage and ratification of the Bricker Amendment which was designed by Senator Bricker and the American Bar Association specifically to prevent such treaties from superseding the Constitution as the Supreme Law of the Land. (Emphasized four words above italicized in Mr. Manion's statement.)

The contribution of the Milwaukee attorney, Bittker (*Hearings,* pp. 84-96) was largely devoted in the manner of 1949-53 to deflating the assertions of anti-ratification forces, and trying to demonstrate that their fears and objections were groundless. Nearly half of the space devoted to his presence among those making statements in the published record consisted of written materials submitted to the Subcommittee.

Richardson, general counsel for the Liberty Lobby (*Hearings,* pp. 96-101) presented a brief and succinct position-statement which adhered to that of the classic objectors to American ratification associated with the American Bar Association of two decades earlier. He did give the Subcommittee a few previously neglected matters to ponder, however, pointing out that if ratification took place with reservations or "understandings," achieved via a two-thirds Senate vote, it might be possible for a subsequent Senate to disavow these reservations by a simply majority vote. And in the same manner, following ratification, the enabling legislation stipulating what "genocide" would construe in an American context would also be the result not of a two-thirds but a simple majority, possibly by a single vote. Richardson presented the position of the Liberty Lobby as that of being willing to admit that such a thing as "genocide" existed, but that the organization preferred that it be handled as a matter to be further defined in the U.S. Criminal Code.

The final statement of the afternoon of the first day was that of Dr. Pierce (*Hearings*, pp. 102-105), a firm rejection of ratification action, while calling attention to the "fine print" of the Convention, which dealt with the non-lethal aspects, along with the relatively non-effective aspects of "genocide," attempts, advocacy and conspiracy to commit same, all to be construed as felonies, which he thought had "frightening" implications. His further assertion that the previous 20 years of congressional legislation accelerating racial integration harbored great ills for the white race and could also be construed as "genocide" of a sort, was imperturbably ignored by the Subcommittee members, who were interested only in where Dr. Pierce lived and the nature of his political affiliation.

Refreshed by a two-day rest, the Church Subcommittee reconvened in mid-morning of April 27 and held a single unbroken session of 3½ hours, which appeared to be all the time they were going to spend listening to statements concerning the Genocide Convention. The first statement before them was that of a quasi-government spokesman, though at the moment he was not in direct federal employ. Prof. Richard M. Gardner, professor of international law at Columbia (and a future U.S. Ambassador to Italy), came forward as the representative of an ad hoc committee speaking for 53 pro-ratification organizations; "Their membership runs in the tens of millions," Prof. Gardner assured the Subcommittee. A former Deputy Assistant Secretary of State for International Organization Affairs, 1961-1965, he had of late been involved outside his academic job in a series of UN bureaucratic matters.

Though one might have expected another brief for the State Department, of which they had already heard three, the Subcommittee got a number of other angles on the Convention, and they were perturbed by some of them. Originally Senator Church allocated Gardner only 10 minutes; he ended up on the stand for over an hour. One of his views was that enemies of ratification who feared such would violate states' rights must have realized that their position had been "rendered largely obsolete by the passage of the Civil Rights Acts of 1957 and 1964 and the Voting Rights Acts of 1965."

Prof. Gardner's opinions were sometimes novel and not commonly heard. One of his main points, probably made to mollify the people hostile to the Convention, was that nothing could be construed as "genocide" unless it was determined that there was present "an intent to destroy a people as a whole," (*Hearings*, p. 111) which directly contradicted a modifying clause in the very first sentence of Article II of the Convention. When he insisted that acts of "genocide" were already "punishable under Federal as well as State law"

(*Hearings,* p. 113), his hearers thought that this made his eagerness for the ratification of the Convention unexplainable.

However, he shortly became bogged down in the morass of detail related to the subject of extradition, a matter very dear to the hearts of the Senators, and a long and tedious exchange with them on this ensued, leading to the insertion in the record of all American extradition treaties (*Hearings,* pp. 118-127).

As questioning continued, Prof. Gardner returned to previous flights of eloquence, when he announced, in a statement which stood Lemkin on his head, that ratification of the Genocide Convention would be "a modest but important part of a total program to build an edifice of international law protecting individuals." Since Lemkin had always maintained the reverse, that the Convention was for the protection of *groups,* which the document plainly stated, it represented the decay that had set in during twenty years and how thoroughly the Human Rights Declaration and "genocide" concepts had been scrambled and blended. Indeed, Raphael Lemkin would have squirmed and perspired through all of Prof. Gardner's statement, a confused hash of both the above issues. With the inversion of the two UN documents of December 9 and 10, 1948 now so commonplace, undoubtedly the labor of the UN committee headed by René Cassin in assembling the "human rights" catalog, one which tumbled with ease over the tongue like nothing else, had achieved far more than they ever expected. (For a reference to Cassin's membership in, and from 1946 on, president of the UN Commission on Human Rights, and as the principal editor of the Universal Declaration of Human Rights adopted by the General Assembly 12-10-48, see his sketch in *Who's Who in World Jewry 1965* (New York: David McKay, 1965, p. 142.)

Prof. Gardner eventually was confronted by the Senators with the same questions they had perplexed the three Administration spokespeople with the first day they had met. And he responded much the same way they had. When Sen. Cooper again brought up the cases of alleged "genocide" on which no action whatever had been taken by the General Assembly or the Security Council, Prof. Gardner admitted nothing had been done because no power existed to coerce any action, and that even if these "genocide" charges had been cloaked under the umbrella of "threats to international peace," there still was no hope of action, as he was sure the USSR would veto any such move. Nevertheless he still had great faith in some mystical or magic power in this direction that would be unleashed by U.S. ratification (Sen. Church had gone to the trouble of soliciting from the Administration people three days before that no new power whatever would accrue to the UN upon American ratification of the Convention.)

Like Mrs. Hauser before him, Prof. Gardner (*Hearings*, p. 131) remarked that "We are in a period of history in which very loose and politically motivated charges of genocide are being thrown around," going on to specify, "There has been loose talk of genocide in Vietnam," even "loose talk of genocide within this country with respect to the Black Panthers and so on." He then astonished his listeners by asserting that he hoped that ratification would take place soon, and then such issues could be adjudicated before the 15-judge International Court of Justice in The Hague. They could be expected to be "objective" about it, and rule on it with "detachment." He expressed his trust in their "judicial and professional detachment," and looked forward to the USA being brought before the International Court by another country if such was wanted.

At the conclusion of Prof. Gardner's extended exposure on the stand, Sen. Church responded in much the same way he had after Amb. Yost and Mrs. Hauser had concluded, admitting that there were "good political reasons for the United States to ratify the Genocide Treaty," but qualifying this in the following manner:

> From the testimony that has been presented so far, the most glaring characteristic of this Convention is its weakness. The Convention is important chiefly for its symbolic value. I have no objection to window dressing . . . . Yet I question that this Treaty has much more to offer than symbolic value. Until now, even though 75 nations have signed the Convention, not a single action has been brought under it. I doubt very much that this will become an effective instrument in dealing with the crime of genocide. (*Hearings*, p. 135.)

From the tenor of the remarks above, it seemed that Sen. Church was growing tired of the proceedings, in many ways a wearying recycling of the same views and issues of 1949-51 and sometimes even more stultifying. But there were still seven more witnesses to appear, five of them favorable to ratification. The one immediately following Prof. Gardner, however, was not. Despite far more impressive experience and credentials in international law than Prof. Gardner, the Subcommittee implored Harry Leroy Jones to confine himself to the originally allotted ten minutes, which he largely did, though placing a vigorously worded statement in the record at the same time.

Jones more or less amounted to the American Bar Association's representative, though the ABA sent no official spokesman, for reasons Jones explained, despite specific encouragement to do so from Sen. Church, both for and against. (Sen. Church's communications to likely ABA representatives were included in the *Hearings*, p. 15.) Jones told the Subcommittee that at the February meeting of the House of Delegates of the ABA in Atlanta, these persons had voted by the slim margin of 126 to 130 refusing to reverse their 1949 position on the Genocide Convention. Their position of 1970 therefore was still that of 1949, even though there had been some major changes in the ABA between the presidencies of Frank E. Holman and the 1970 incumbent, Bernard Segal, a strong advocate of ratification (Segal's interesting letter on the subject to Subcommittee member Sen. Jacob K. Javits of April 15, 1970 was included in the *Hearings,* pp. 179-180.)

Jones concentrated not on the Convention but on the implementing criminal statute the Congress would have to enact *after* ratification. Having already seen a draft of this amendment to the U.S. Criminal Code (the Subcommittee members had not) which the Nixon Administration intended to propose, Jones went into a sharp analysis of this proposed legislation and the wordage of the Convention, especially Articles II and III. It was Jones's conclusion that "a Federal statute in the words of Articles II and II [of the Genocide Convention] would be unconstitutional as a violation of the due process clause of the fifth amendment" of the U.S. Constitution. Stressing that any criminal statute written in the language of these two Articles would be so ambiguous, indefinite and imprecise that they could easily be challenged on such grounds alone, his was an undeclared prediction that the courts could expect to be filled with cases involving confrontation of this part of such a statute, for sure. "The language of a criminal statute must stand on its own feet," Jones declared, recalling that the absurdly vague language of the Convention had been repeatedly pointed out many times before, and was convinced a statute written in its form would tie up the U.S. in appeals procedures for years in hopeless confusion and contradiction. Jones reemphasized his point with the following: "A statute which either forbids or requires the doing of an act in terms so vague that men of common intelligence must necessarily guess as to its meaning and differ as to its application violates the first essential of due process of law." The Subcommittee was dutifully impressed by this short but incisive lesson, and Sen. Church soberly remarked, "Mr. Jones, you have raised a question that the Subcommittee will want to look into very carefully." (Jones's oral statement and expert written statement follow one another in *Hearings,* pp. 135-147.)

Sen. Church then announced that the Subcommittee was going to "depart from the agenda" to allow an Administration pro-ratification spokesman to "sum up" its position. For this purpose they asked to "come forward" Assistant Attorney General William H. Rehnquist, shortly to become exceedingly better known as a new Supreme Court Justice. Sen. Church announced that Mr. Rehnquist

had done something "unprecedented," in fact, "slightly unbelievable," in presenting a written statement of only *one* page. In
substance it simply confirmed what Atty. Gen. John Mitchell had
told Sec. of State Rogers in his letter of January 26, 1970 (reproduced in *Hearings,* p. 165), that the Office of Legal Counsel of the
Attorney General's Office was of the opinion that there were "no
constitutional obstacles to United States ratification" of the Genocide Convention. (The field of battle was already switching to
something else, however: the likely constitutional ambushes and
traps in the enabling legislation which Congress would pass *after*
ratification.)

Mr. Rehnquist after submitting his statement on this subject then
announced he was ready to answer Subcommittee questions, and a
pettifogger's dream then ensued, in which members threw at Mr.
Rehnquist a long succession of the most unlikely consequences of
ratification that could possibly have been imagined, many of them
the result of correspondence the Subcommittee had received from
the citizenry at large. Some of them even Mr. Rehnquist, along with
a member of his staff, Jack Goldklang, could not answer. But he
promised to have them researched, and the expert opinion of the
Attorney General's Office on these matters were added to the record
in written form subsequently (Rehnquist's statement, transcript of
his replies to Subcommittee questions and the extension in print,
submitted May 8, 1970, are in the *Hearings,* pp. 147-165.)

The Subcommittee's next witness was a breath from the past,
and the only repeater from the 1950 hearings to make a presentation
also before that of 1970. Prof. Lev Dobriansky, the eloquent spokesman and leader of the American Ukrainian ethnic community, was
much more restrained than he had been two decades before, though
given to occasional thrusts of hyperbole so dear to the East European
mode of thinking on the subject. (They were not in the class with his
long and alarming declamation of the earlier time, which had charged
Stalin with being in the process of "wiping out" the forty million
Ukrainians in the USSR, a speech which Senator Herbert H. Lehman
(D-New York) had included in the *Congressional Record* (81 Cong.,
2 sess.), on Tuesday, July 25, 1950.)

In his florid discourse, interrupted by two emotional tributes to
the work and memory of Raphael Lemkin, Prof. Dobriansky scorned
all the discussion of the fine legal points during the two days as
"chaff," and little more than sophisticated evasion of the real task at
hand, the necessary and prompt ratification of the Genocide Convention. Sen. Cooper chided him mildly for his depreciation and
deprecation of the previous attention to legal points, reminding him
that the real tests were ahead before the whole Foreign Relations

Committee and then the Senate as a whole, and if these legal points in what was, after all, a matter of international law, were not ironed out now, the situation in the future discussion would be much worse. This sobered Prof. Dobriansky a bit.

Prof. Dobriansky had a new theory of "genocide." Now it was something only "totalitarian" regimes committed, never democracies. At the moment, with the Hitler time behind them, the only "genocide" powers were the USSR and Red China. He never mentioned the scores of futile charges of "genocide" made before the UN since 1948 and the utter ineffectiveness of everything done along these lines. His appeal was almost entirely rhetorical, and contained nothing substantive, nor any hint as to how American ratification would alter the existing world situation with respect to "genocide" in the slightest. He was much annoyed that there were charges of "genocide" taking place in the U.S., and like other witnesses before him, also deplored "the loose and indiscriminate bandying about" of the term "genocide" over the previous 20 years, to the effect that there was a massive misconception of what the term really meant. But for the most part Prof. Dobriansky's performance this time around was but an outline of his bravura exhibition of 1950, when his total contribution had taken almost 100 pages to reproduce in the published 1950 *Hearings.* (Prof. Dobriansky's contribution before the Church Subcommittee in 1970 *Hearings,* pp. 165-174.)

Putting in a very brief appearance on the heels of Prof. Dobriansky was Robert Layton, an attorney representing the Committee on International Law of the New York State Bar Association, largely to file a long written report on that organization's favorable recommendation on ratifying the Genocide Convention, which sounded almost exactly like that filed two decades earlier. This was something it had in common with most of the other statements submitted for the record by organizations which did not make personal appearances and which were published in the Appendix of the *Hearings* (pp. 225-261). Mr. Layton did make a special point of underscoring the New York organization's opinion that there was "no valid basis for concern over possible trial of Americans in foreign courts as the result of ratification of this Convention," a long standing irritant in the camp of enemies of ratification, and more so at that moment as a result of what was happening in the raging Vietnam war, where this had become an issue but on another and possibly related ground, namely, the likelihood of American prisoners of war being tried in North Vietnam as "war criminals." Mr. Layton said there was nothing Americans could do about something like this, but could effectively bar extradition of Americans concerned in some subsequent "genocide" controversy with a foreign power. (Statement and written position paper of NYBA, *Hearings,* pp. 174-182.)

Two women of most dissimilar views and positions were the last witnesses before the Church Subcommittee on April 27, 1970. Their presentations were brief and to the point. The first, Mrs. Ernest W. Howard, represented the American Coalition of Patriotic Societies, some 120 civic, fraternal and patriotic organizations, which somewhat upstaged Prof. Gardner's 53, though the former's three million members were obviously outnumbered by the "tens of millions" Prof. Gardner professed to represent. Mrs. Howard started out with a blunt no-nonsense prologue, "Almost 20 years ago, the American people fought the Genocide Convention to a standstill under the leadership of the American Bar Association. So great was their fear of the Genocide Convention the American people demanded a constitutional amendment to protect them from the dangers of treaty law," and reinforcing this with the logical conclusion, "The Genocide Convention or treaty was opposed then, and should be opposed now, on constitutional grounds." It was a remarkable condensation of all the main points emphasized in 1950 which took less than three pages to print in the record, and the Subcommittee either was so weary, or so subdued by her all-attack approach, that at the conclusion no one asked even the pretense of a question.

In one respect Mrs. Howard's statement differed from that of other opponents of ratification. It has been seen that though the very largest part of what went on the record in the hearings of 1970 was very similar to the experience in 1950 there was one propaganda variation which was novel in the later event. In 1950 the ratification process was just being contemplated worldwide, while in 1970 there were 75 countries which had ratified the Genocide Convention by the time the Senate hearings began. Supporters of American ratification added another weapon to their collection of persuasive arguments as a result. One advocate after another either in a direct or veiled manner suggested that the United States was losing out in some vague way in the field of international influence by failing to become a party to the Convention. Though no proof was advanced whatever, superficially this view had an appeal of sorts, and convinced an increasing number of its validity. This point had been made over and over in the 1970 hearings by the Convention's protagonists, and no one inimical to ratification came to grips with it until Mrs. Howard. She was especially repelled by the notion that the U.S.A. was losing ground particularly to the USSR and the Soviet bloc countries which had already ratified, and that they were exploiting "world opinion" to the detriment of American influence elsewhere as a result of American non-ratification.

Mrs. Howard met this head-on and called it "folly of the greatest magnitude" to suggest that the U.S. cave in and ratify the Genocide Convention because of the alleged pressure of "world opinion" and any pretensions of the Soviet Union and its satellites to moral superiority in this regard. (*Hearings*, p. 182.) In her view things were exactly the reverse. It was the Soviet bloc which was in trouble in this department, not America. Though signators, the bellows of "genocide" renting the planetary air were being aimed at *them* from the descendants and ethnic relations of a dozen of these countries living here and elsewhere. The U.S.A., on the other hand, was unblemished in this affair, and charges of "genocide" against Americans were being made *internally*, not by residents of distant lands. It was a point others should have made, and over all it might have discounted considerably from Sen. Church's repeated assertion that there were "good political reasons" for American ratification. As for the vaunted "Third World," the paucity of ratifications from black African states and the repeated massacres in and "genocide" charges emanating from these areas suggested that pretensions of moral superiority had better be very restrained from these centers of "world opinion."

The last statement, by Mrs. Hope Eastman, of the local office of the American Civil Liberties Union, was just as brief, and was concerned almost entirely with the charges by opponents of ratification that the phrasing of clauses *b, c, d* and *e* of Article III of the Convention was defective in American law. To be sure, when the document was in construction in the hands of the Sixth Committee of the United Nations in 1948, especially clause *c* had been fought bitterly by the American representative as a plain infringement of freedom of speech and freedom of the press. Mrs. Eastman asserted now that if the ACLU believed that the First Amendment of the U.S. Bill of Rights was being violated by Article III it would be the first to be complaining, but it was their considered opinion that it did not do so, and for that reason the organization was supporting ratification. Her answers to a few brief questions by Sen. Cooper were not too convincing, and there remained an irreducible remnant of lawmakers around the land that were convinced that if Article III were ever invoked following a putative American ratification, a veritable cascade of interminable appeals would be the most expectable result.

Senator Cooper, in the absence of the Chairman, Sen. Church, adjourned the meeting, with a further notice that the record of the hearing would remain open through Friday, May 8, presumably only for the placing of written statements for inclusion in the published *Hearings.*

At the start of the hearings on April 27, Sen. Church had announced that it would be the last day of such (*Hearings*, p. 107).

Those following the proceedings were therefore somewhat surprised to see the Subcommittee reconvened the afternoon of May 22, when it listened for nearly an hour and a half to a statement, testimony and response to questions concerning the Genocide Convention from Sen. Sam J. Ervin, Jr. (D-North Carolina), a veritable *tour de force* in opposition to ratification. The combination of eloquence and persuasiveness, bristling with constitutional law history, was heard with considerable restraint by the members of the Subcommittee. Sen. Pell was not present but Sen. Javits was, and it was the latter who was most annoyed by Sen. Ervin's presentation, which probably better than anyone since Holman in the 1949-1953 era best illuminated the operational impossibilities built into the Genocide Convention (the entire minutes of May 22 are reproduced in the appendix.) Sen. Ervin especially dwelled on its muddy imprecisions and its grave deficiencies by U.S. standards as an international criminal statute, which it obviously pretended to be. Sen. Javits was hardly impressive in his efforts to controvert Sen. Ervin during the session, and requested permission to file subsequently a list of written objections to and claimed refutations of the many points made by Sen. Ervin, who obviously arrived on the scene primed with an understanding and backup material which made him a most formidable adversary. The only matter which remained mysterious was the procedure whereby Sen. Ervin had managed to get the Subcommittee to reconvene to listen to his statement 3½ weeks after the announced closing of oral testimony.

At the close of his statement April 27, 1970 Prof. Gardner had implored and cautioned the Subcommittee, "I think the failure to act [on ratification] would be particularly unfortunate." It was verbiage spoken in the manner of the hectic pressure-people of 1950 such as Telford Taylor, who envisioned all manner of horrid national consequences for Americans by neglecting this affair. But there was no grave emergency importuning the U.S. Senate in 1970 any more than there had been in 1950. A very brief capsule account of the Genocide Convention's fate, 1970-1982, can serve to emphasize that.

The reaction to pre-and-post-hearings pressure was not notable in its intensity. Though the New York *Times* as usual had coordinated the publicity following the State Department's initiation of heat on Pres. Nixon early in February with its long-practiced editorial expertise twice (February 7, 1970, p. 28 and February 20, 1970, p. 40), response had not been exactly stirring. And such events as the ABA's support of its 1949 stand on non-ratification on February 23 had a further depressing effect.

Action by the full Senate Foreign Relations Committee was six months in coming, which may have been further conditioned by the

American Legion's national convention on September 3 approving
a resolution once more in opposition to the Genocide Convention.
Finally on November 23 the SFRC voted 10-2 to submit the Con-
vention to the full Senate for debate, recommending approval.
Nothing happened. And on March 30, 1971 the Foreign Relations
Committee once more voted favorably, this time 10-4. (New York
Times, November 24, 1970, p. 20; March 31, 1971, p. 11.) Why a
second vote had to be taken on this subject was never explained.

During all this time Sen. Proxmire continued to implore daily
for ratification every day the Senate was in session. Betty Kaye
Taylor, executive secretary of the Ad Hoc Committee on the Human
Rights and Genocide Treaties, hailed him for having spoken in its
behalf, as of May, 1971, a total of 5,520 times, surely a landmark
record of sorts in political failure (New York *Times,* May 2, 1971,
sec. VI, p. 98 for Taylor letter.)

At the time of the second favorable vote on ratification by the
Senate Foreign Relations Committee, its chairman, J. William
Fulbright, cautioned enthusiasts that action by the full Senate might
be delayed pending the drafting of enabling legislation setting the
definition and penalties for conviction of committing "genocide" in
the U.S.A. Sen. Fulbright emphasized that Pres. Nixon had insisted
on this procedure, and that ratification was not to be completed
prior to passage of this legislation. Now, it had been testified a year
before at the time of the Church Subcommittee hearings that the
Administration already had a draft of such legislation in existence,
though it was not made public then nor did it become part of the
record. Why this still seemed to be in the process of creation this late
was also not explained. (Some idea of what it must have been like
can be discerned from an examination of S. 3155, introduced in the
Senate on March 17, 1976 by Sens. Hugh Scott (R-Pennsylvania) and
Jacob Javits (R-New York), reproduced in the Appendix of this
book.) This seemed to be contrary to the procedure in many other
countries, where ratification of the Genocide Convention took place
in advance and sometimes some considerable spell *before* enabling
legislation followed. Nevertheless, nothing ensued relating to this
mandated procedure, and no enabling bill came to anyone's attention
resulting in comment in the interim.

A full year elapsed following the second vote of the Foreign
Relations Committee favoring ratification with nothing done, and
about all there was to show indicating there was still life in it at all
was a vigorous piece by Prof. Gardner and Arthur J. Goldberg (New
York *Times,* March 28, 1972, p. 43), an expectable rehash of the
Convention's history plus the usual exhortations to ratify, with the
same claims alleged that it was a "national disgrace" to persist in its

neglect. Accompanying this rhetoric was also the time-worn launching of rumors that sustained non-ratification here was posing "disturbing questions" abroad, though there was the expectable absence of what these "questions" were, and, especially, precisely *who* was asking them, and *where* these persons lived; this was as before left a total mystery. Another writhing editorial in the *Times* (May 8, 1972, p. 36) apparently had no effect, either.

Between May and October, 1972 there was some talk of a coalition of Sens. Javits, Church, Scott and Proxmire trying to unclog and unstall Senate action on the Convention. But action was at an enervatingly slow pace. Finally the unceasing efforts of the pro-ratification Senators paid off, as Senate Majority leader Mike Mansfield (D-Montana) agreed to schedule floor action on it in the first week of October. The sitting session of Congress was about to adjourn, and the hurry-up effort to squeeze it in prior to that time turned out to be a calamity.

On October 5, 1972, as New York *Times* stringer John W. Finney was to disclose in a special dispatch to his paper, it took the U.S. Senate only 12 minutes "to bury the Genocide Convention again" (New York *Times,* October 6, 1972, p. 30.) The maneuver to try to get an agreement to limit debate on the Convention to four hours was immediately objected to by Sen. Ervin, and, Finney related, "with that Mr. Mansfield laid the Convention aside." Following this Sen. Javits expressed the hope that it could be brought up "at a more propitious time" in 1973.

But nothing happened the entire year of 1973, other than the introduction in the House of Representatives in the first session of the 93rd. Congress of still another bill which would have served as the enabling legislation prior to the ratification of the Convention. As usual it involved a stipulation defining what "genocide" would be, sticking very close to the Convention's verbiage, but adding what the penalties would be for conviction of having committed "genocide," in order to make it a part of the U.S. Criminal Code (the UN Convention obviously omitted any reference to this operational necessity). Introduced by Reps. Peter Rodino (D-New Jersey) and Robert R. McClory (R-Illinois), on May 9, 1973 as H.R. 7662, it was referred to the House Committee on the Judiciary, as was to be the fate of the parallel Scott-Javits bill in the Senate three years later. It was strange that there was almost no attention devoted to the Rodino-McClory bill at the time it was introduced, even on the part of the forces favoring ratification of the "genocide" treaty. (One of the few appearances of the bill was the facsimile reproduction of the actual document on pages 31-32 of the Liberty Lobby's *White Paper on the Genocide Convention* [Washington, D.C., 1981]).

It will be noted that the Rodino-McClory bill was introduced at the height of the furor over Watergate, and both its authors were deeply involved in the actions being taken against the Nixon regime, Rep. McClory ultimately being the author of the third impeachment article against Pres. Nixon. That Reps. McClory and Rodino were two of the four highest ranking members of the House Judiciary Committee should not be neglected in trying to assess the political aspect of this latest sally in behalf of "genocide" action of some kind. That it all coincided with Watergate may be advanced as the reason it all escaped the argus-eyed defenders of the public in the press and failed even to be noticed by the most prominent of all bird dogs sniffing out any and all news and action related to the Genocide Convention, the New York *Times* itself. The ironic part of it however was that the two men responsible for drafting this enabling legislation, repeatedly averred to be Pres. Nixon's most insistently declared "must" since he had initiated the newest impulse toward ratification of the Genocide Convention in early 1970, were simultaneously involved at the very top of the proceedings which were to lead to Pres. Nixon's departure from the White House.

Later a letter to the *Times* from a B'nai B'rith aide, William Korey, published as a sort of commemoration of the 25th anniversary of the UN adoption of the Genocide Convention (New York *Times*, December 8, 1973, p. 35), served to call attention to the feeble pulse of the entire matter. Korey deplored the main terminal disease of the Convention, the worldwide sustained neglect, and the total lack of resort to it, even for presentation before the International Court of Justice, despite the continuous flow of "genocide" charges globally. Nevertheless he urged the Senate to ratify it.

Sen. Javits' "propitious time" was to come up at the very beginning of the following session of Congress. Starting right out with the opening on January 21, 1974 the speeches for and against ratification resumed, and by the end of two weeks of this an attempt was made to obtain cloture on debate and a vote in the Senate (New York *Times*, February 4, 1974, p. 11.) The *Times*'s stringer, Richard L. Madden, mentioned only the ABA and the Liberty Lobby as adversaries of ratification among organizations, along with some "conservative" senators who remained nameless here. On Tuesday, February 5 the first attempt at effecting cloture took place, a filibuster having been going on for some days. But in the balloting the supporters failed to get the necessary two-thirds vote, 55-36. (New York *Times*, February 6, 1974, p. 11.) Despite hectic promotional oratory in which World War Two and the Hitler era in Germany were recycled before the Upper House, with only the fate of European Jews memorialized as "genocide's" inspiration, the effort ran aground

on the determined opposition of Sen. Ervin, who subsequently was
singled out as the Convention's most redoubtable enemy. The *Times*
story repeated previous efforts at enrolling Sens. Church, Javits and
Proxmire as supporters and their belief that it "would be a symbolic
declaration against genocide." No mention was made of the legal and
non-inflammatory political front, where proceedings were non-existent, let alone not mentioning the scores of accusations of "genocide"
then going on and for the previous 25 years, mainly of signatory
nations to the Genocide Convention against one another, with the
usual zero results. Though it was customary to believe there had
been just one motion to close debate there actually were two. The
second took place the following day, and it was defeated 55-38, the
forces against gaining two votes of Senators not present at rollcall the
previous day. (New York *Times* note on Senate calendar, February
9, 1974, p. 32.)

Sen. Ervin and Sen. James B. Allen (D-Alabama) were mentioned
as specially destructive to the cloture motion and for effective fili-
bustering via "lengthy speeches" followed by another handwringing
editorial, "Burden of Guilt" (New York *Times,* February 7, 1974,
p. 36), concluding with the charge that non-ratification left "a cloud
over the nation," which no one seemed to see or report, however.
As consolation, five members of the Yale University Law School,
including Prof. Eugene V. Rostow, sent in an agitated letter urging
reconsideration, making the usual gesture of mixing up the human
rights and genocide matters, while declaring that the objections to
ratification had been "systematically refuted." This must surely have
been exciting news to such as Sen. Ervin and a majority of the
American Bar Association.

For all practical purposes this was the last gasp of the impulse
toward ratification of the Genocide Convention initiated in 1970
by Pres. Nixon, the State Department, and the Church Foreign Relations Committee Subcommittee. There was no mention of the
subject of "genocide" in the New York *Times Index* for 1975, and
a single comment, a *Times* editorial, in the year 1976 (February 26,
p. 30.) Apparently the *Times* did not consider newsworthy the
flurry of pro-ratification activity in the Senate that spring and early
summer, even if it was conducted with a large measure of camouflage
and absence of publicity. Those involved were the same Senators who
had been stopped in their tracks in February, 1970 and they abruptly
abandoned their efforts this time as well, but not before Sens. Javits
and Scott had actually prepared a bill defining "genocide" as it
would be considered as an amendment to the U.S. Criminal Code in
anticipation of ratification, though it may have been a bit presumptuous of them in so doing. But this bill was printed (S. 3155, 94th

Congress, Second Session), read twice and referred to the Committee on the Judiciary March 17, 1976 (see Appendix).

Following the inaugural of Pres. Carter early in 1977, the subject returned when he made a speech before the United Nations on March 17, in which he declared he would once more ask the Senate to ratify the Convention (New York *Times,* March 18, 1977, p. 10.) But nothing happened that year nor in 1978, the *Times* documenting a sole reference in the form of a letter from Sen. Proxmire, in which he claimed he was re-inspired to move for ratification once more after witnessing the television show "Holocaust." (New York *Times,* April 25, 1978.)

Though Pres. Carter was twice to recommend ratification to the Senate again in 1979, the sole reference to the subject in the *Times* was a letter to the paper from the executive vice chairman of the Zionist Organization of America, Leon Ilutovich, on the 30th anniversary of Pres. Truman's having submitted the Convention to the Senate in 1949 (New York *Times,* August 10, 1979, p. 24.)

And the Genocide Convention remained utterly unmentioned or unreferred to in the *Times* in 1980, 1981 and 1982 (even the subject failed to be mentioned in the *Index* for 1981). In 1982, the only occasion for the reference to the subject of "genocide" itself was a succession of stories about an abortive international conference on it scheduled in June of that year in Israel. When it became known that papers would be presented about Turkish actions against the Armenians in the World War One era, it touched off a fiery incident, leading to vast pressure on the conference organizers by the Israeli government to cancel it. Upon further Turkish protest all Israeli official and non-official agencies withdrew from any and all association with it. This affair raged all the month of June, 1982.

In the light of the history of spinal-cord-reflex politics in America, with substantial programs and policies in the past having been adopted impulsively and, occasionally, on a weekend basis, it remains quite possible for the Genocide Convention to be ratified by any given Senate in the same manner, providing a proper galvanization occurs, if fueled by something sensational. But, looked at from the perspective of the 40 years the concept of "genocide" has been in existence, it will be profoundly anti-climactic. The groundswell of its influence and impact long ago was scattered and dispersed. And its substance as international law has been so vitiated by a full generation of calculated avoidance and total non-enforcement among its signators that to claim even symbolic significance for adherence to it now is most questionable. As international law its future, like its past, is utterly dismal, but as a propaganda adjunct to guttersnipe politics its potential remains as high as ever. In the political climate prevailing internationally in 1983-84 the chances of being burned at the stake for witchcraft are probably as high as conviction for "genocide."

In Raphael Lemkin's catalog, *Axis Rule in Occupied Europe*, it was established that in any demographic relationship involving two peoples in disproportionate numbers to one another, whether living mixed or adjoining, at war or at peace, anything done or allegedly done by the larger to the smaller number could be construed by the latter as "genocide." All the latter had to do was utter the charge, upon estimating themselves the injured party. This wide range of possibilities, not just merely accusations of systematic mass murder, remains to this day in the Genocide Convention, though only sporadically exploited thus far.

But the more omnibus the "crime" the greater the likelihood of accelerating non-enforcement, very reduced respect, and ultimately indifferent dismissal. So the matter of ratification, one way or another, has steadily receded toward the horizon in importance, with the passage of time. It took a special kind of myopia in the 1940s to view Lemkin's work somehow as non-political. In its manifestation as the Genocide Convention over the last generation it is hard to conceive of it as anything else but political. The steady dissipation and evaporation of its presumed moral content stands in partial evidence of this. Its near-invisibility globally except as a doubtful tool, on occasion, in the promotion of incendiary statecraft is the present situation.

CONCLUSION

TODAY, OVER 40 YEARS after Raphael Lemkin invented the word "genocide," most people who have heard it think they know what it means. The overwhelming majority of them are mistaken; they do not. Few have the faintest idea of the variety of things Lemkin and others gathered in under the cloak of this word. If any impression at all is retained, it is the superficial belief that "genocide" is a synonym for a massacre, and this is dead wrong. Lemkin never constructed a brief against massacre. He was concerned with the disappearance or serious interference with the survival of just *groups* of a racial, ethnic, religious or nationalistic nature. The presumption by many is that he was thinking only of Jews, though his work does not show this, and was adduced to him on the basis of how his work was used in the program against the apprehended German leaders from mid-1945 on, and because the campaign to establish "genocide" as an international crime was so heavily subscribed to by organized Zionism and Jewry in general, though this zeal noticeably abated after Israel became a repeated target for "genocide" charges from the Arab world.

Lemkin's work nowhere displayed the faintest concern for majorities anywhere, regardless of what kind of "group" they may have been, and he never scolded a minority for having at any time in history attempted, or succeeded, in annihilating a majority. So one concluded that he always meant a minority when he used the word "group." In looking past his seminal wartime work in which he developed the entire "genocide" concept, one notices that he is not known to have uttered a word in condemnation of the frightful mass killings of Germans and anti-Soviet Russians after April, 1945, the expulsions back to Germany's western rump from Poland and Czecho-Slovakia, and the forced "repatriation" of Soviet nationals who had managed to escape westward from the nightmare of Stalin's Soviet Union, 1941-1945. Nor did Lemkin issue any notable unhappy commentary about the tens of millions of Chinese murdered by the Red regime of Mao Tse-tung during the decade he, Lemkin, was laboring so agitatedly for the Genocide Convention in the United Nations. No one ever made a point of his never supporting a single charge of "genocide" made before the UN General Assembly between 1948 and 1959, other than made by Jews, against the Soviet Union from 1950 onward.

From the examples advanced by him as the inspiration for his invention of "genocide," in every case we are made aware of his alleged sentiment in behalf of some tiny minority somewhere. But these condemnations of "genocide" in history are few, sometimes contradictory, and very selective, showing especial unconcern for the modern era and the Western world. Furthermore, most if not all of his examples fail to meet his own stipulation making them "genocide," namely, the requirement of *deliberate, organized, planned oppression or extermination as a matter of public policy.* In structuring "genocide," he reiterated and emphasized that *intent* had to be *proved*, and this is plainly spelled out in Article II of the United Nations Genocide Convention, of which he was the principal author. Therefore, a massacre, no matter how many millions might be involved, did not come under the heading of "genocide" without prior establishment of calculated intentional annihilation, along with the similar planning of a large number of harassments and vexatious interferences with the survival of such groups short of killing them. These are all enumerated in the Genocide Convention, have not been changed, and can be read by anyone in a copy of this document which is available to anyone with the price of a postage stamp, yet is ignored today by most of those who love to turn Lemkin's word over their tongues.

However, one must examine from the start how the whole concept of "genocide" was put together, as has been done in this book. Lemkin's launching pad, his book *Axis Rule in Occupied Europe,* finished late in 1943, published late in 1944, was prepared in a form resembling a legal brief, with historical decorations. Over 60% of this massive tome consists of reproductions in English language translation of more than 330 decrees, orders, promulgations, proclamations and emergency legislation by Germany and its allies, about 80% of them from the years 1940-1941, concerning various aspects of the organization and administration of such portions of Europe as their armed forces occupied during that time. Somewhere in this 400 pages of print one is supposed to find evidence for the existence of "genocide," as a conscious, planned policy. But, taking up first the most astounding aspect of this complex "crime," if a planned massacre of European Jewry in Axis-occupied Europe, 1941-1945, took place as Communist, Zionist and other spokesmen have alleged and propounded for over forty years, they have no business using Lemkin's book as evidence in support of that assertion, since it does not contain any, and whatever it has to say about the subject of planned mass murder is merely repetition of prior hearsay, all published well before Lemkin's reiteration.

In view of the gravity of the accusation, on which in the final analysis Lemkin's entire charge of "genocide" relied, one should have expected a solid, extended chapter on the matter involving allegations that by sometime early in 1943 the Germans had already murdered, systematically and deliberately as a matter of intentional policy, 2,000,000 Jews in German-occupied Europe. Instead, the heart of his case rested on an obscurely-placed footnote so brief that against the volume of material in his 712-page book, it was palpable only with special assistance, and perhaps involving scientific equipment.

The essence of the legal process, like historical writing, is the presentation in support of the thesis of *evidence,* principally of a *documentary* sort. After that comes *testimony* (even eye-witnesses have their limitations) and *opinion,* and the latter two are of somewhat inferior nature compared to the first-listed, and dramatically and pronouncedly so in the case of history. Lemkin was engaged in an attempt to produce both history and law, but managed to fall far short of the demands of both.

A large part of the indignation expressed by the legatees of Lemkin and the rest of the upholders of the "holocaust" status quo results from the insistence of the skeptics and critics on *some credible documentary evidence,* as a change from the tiresome and dreary emotional and sentimental *testimony* and *opinion* (and the citation of "confessions" extracted from captives not given the opportunity to engage defense counsel to cross-examine the extractors of the "confessions" on which the very heaviest portion of the official holocaust contention is lodged.)

It is increasingly evident also to a new generation uninfluenced by the Stalinist and Zionist politics of the 1945-50 period in particular, that "war crimes" proceedings involving charges of intentional massacres of millions, if conducted under the rules of evidence required in American courts, with defendants allowed procedural opportunity consisting in part of the verification of documentary evidence and cross-examination of witnesses which are commonplace in even the most prosaic circumstances, let alone in those processes where people are on trial for their lives, would never have lasted long enough to go to a jury, if not dismissed long before that. Eugene Lyons described Nuremberg as an "impious farce," but few if any of the "trials" which have followed it to this day have been any different.

Since the emphasis in Lemkin's *Axis Rule* was upon law, and the entire treatise intended as a prolegomenon contributing to a program involving the making of new international law, the book should be examined and criticized in this light. And on the basis of legal evidence presented by the author for the existence of "genocide" and his discovery of it, the entire thesis fails to hold water. Those who explore his massive tome looking for it will emerge with a barely perceptible catch, even using his standards. The total bag of such which can even by the most tenuous threads be even imagined as "genocidal" is alarmingly minuscule. From the regulations in occupied France which forbid escaped Jews from returning to the German-controlled area, to the decree in Serbia forbidding Jews and gypsies from operating vaudeville houses, cabarets, and carnivals and the like, Lemkin has presented legal support for evidence of "genocide" the strangest and sparsest assortment of legal impositions imaginable. There is a vast difference between having one's property confiscated or one's citizenship revoked, and being put to death arbitrarily.

With the exception of decrees of an emergency nature providing the possibility of a violator being subject to the death penalty, Lemkin nowhere reproduces a law or order of any kind which simply condemns people to die. The primary import of such as he does include under the heading in his book as "genocide legislation" has nothing to do with killing. And his reasoning in respect to some of Axis occupation policy approaches imaginative apprehension rarely seen outside science fiction.

One element of Lemkin's "genocide" obsessions concerned the conviction that the Germans intended to overwhelm various peoples by incredible mass-breeding by German soldiers and the women of occupied regions. Why these hybrid Germans were supposed to appeal to the racial sensitivities of the Hitler regime was never explained very well. Surely the latter would have preferred 100% ethnic Germans; Lemkin seemed to think they had in mind simply a populace with German fathers. So his pages tremble in places with synthetic horror of the alleged consequences of these biological policies for the Norwegians, Dutch, Poles and others.

In support of such long range intentions, Lemkin, almost in

catatonic shock, cited two emergency orders by the Germans which made the German government partially responsible for the maintenance and material subsidy of mothers of children by German soldiers in two occupied countries. That this was a sensible and practical solution to a social problem which has occurred in wartime for thousands of years was not even remotely considered by Lemkin. He not only designated such a policy as "genocide," but also denounced it as a calculated and deliberate program of "moral debasement" of the women and designed to produce illegitimate children. By default he favored the program of the "Allies," which historically has callously neglected the mothers of their soldiers' children in one land after another, and made to fend for themselves or to depend upon private charitable organizations which may on occasion have stepped in to try to remedy the situation.

It might be advanced just as easily that Lemkin's fear of the breeding capacities of the German armies in occupation and the availability of sufficient local women to make the likelihood of the submergence of the native stock with half-German hybrids seems grossly misconceived and a reversal of the real situation. Given a modest number of such births as he saw guaranteed by the German decrees in Norway and Holland (and the similar order in Poland providing small child subsidies for German ethnics resident there), though he never cited a statistic on this matter, and never was able even to determine if the program had been continued or abandoned, normal demographic expectations related to the activities of occupying troops as noted in previous generations in many other wars suggested that it would be these German hybrids who would be the minority, not the native stock, and that therefore Lemkin should have been expressing concern for *their* survival, and making a general demonstration in behalf of their minority group status. This of course he never even grazed. But Hitler's hopes aside, insofar as Lemkin tried to divine these in this case, he should have had more to substantiate his charge of "genocide" here than the expected behavior of German troops in the future, which is what he was really talking about, not any tangible evidence of any kind.

It is almost entirely of things of this sort that Lemkin's "genocide" case is built, not evidence of legal or other nature providing for the random putting to death of large numbers of people, or even one person. And it would appear that neither Lemkin, nor his battery of diligent assistants and researchers provided by the Carnegie Foundation, nor the resources of the Roosevelt Administration departments and bureaus for which Lemkin worked on the side, in addition to his labors in the Duke University Law School, and all the published sources provided by the Library of Congress, let alone the burgeoning files of the immense "Allied" espionage and intelligence apparatus, were ever able to come up with anything whatever even faintly of this order, otherwise it would have likely been reproduced in *Axis Rule* in dramatic bold type, and repeated no one knows how many times in succeeding years. In later times a lengthy string of boastful works claiming that the most intimate information about the Germans and their allies was fully possessed by their adversary via cracking their secret codes and infiltrating them with spies of all kinds, but strangely enough, this mountain of information contained not a word of solid worth verifying the incredible story of "genocide" Raphael Lemkin spread out.

A feature of this account was the peppering of his chapters with a repelling narrative of a program of deliberate mass exterminations beginning in 1941, the supporting bolster for such being culled from sources distantly related to what purported to be taking place. Surely something as vast and as gripping as the murder of several millions, in as concentrated a region as was claimed to be the area where it was taking place, would have produced some kind of literature or written record. Since he located a large number of German and other occupation laws, orders and decrees, mainly of an insignificant nature, surely there should have been one such piece of paper verifying the existence of a program putting into effect a mass murder program of such calculated proportions as to have no equal ever before, which might have formed the foundation of his case in this department. But one searches the length and breadth of *Axis Rule* without success here, finding only distant rumors and allegations by second, third or fourth hand commentaries. It does not speak well for the quality of the intelligence services of all the agencies which worked with Lemkin on his historic project.

The more one examines *Axis Rule in Occupied Europe* the more it takes shape, not as a study of the administration of German-controlled Europe between 1939 and 1945 (it contains almost nothing about this subject for the last three years prior to its publication) but as a brief for "Allied" propaganda emphasizing atrocities. Since he did not witness anything he included in his book, Lemkin essentially is passing on the substance of sources hostile to the Germans, much of it inflammatory rhetoric from various conduits of anti-Axis opinion-making, incapable of confirmation then and little of it since, with more than a dollop of ordinary mendacity.

In the matter of claims of deaths attributable to German action, there was no real limit to the imagination of Lemkin's sources, and it was his function to consider all of it as proven. A wartime adversary organization, be it Anglo-American, Soviet, or Zionist, had only to allege an immolation perpetrated by the Germans anywhere in the war zones to find prompt acceptance as fact by Lemkin. And the chance of being challenged or disproven in the USA or in England, where his book was jointly published, was virtually non-existent. No reviewer quarreled with a line of it, and anyone so brave or so reckless as to have done so in 1944-45 might have been even in danger of his life, given the climate of opinion in the closing months of the war.

The year 1944 was a time when atrocity propaganda exceeded by many magnitudes anything the world had seen, and probably surpassing anything of the kind since, as well. Stalin's armies had captured the first German concentration camp to fall in their hands in July of that year, and sensational accounts grew like bacterial spore colonies in all of the press of the Soviet's "allies" as well as in the USSR itself. The numbers of the dead allegedly exterminated by the Germans as deliberate policy escalated monthly, to be topped many times in the next two years, as the invention of such unverifiable statistical raw material for the propaganda mill became a veritable industry. A parallel atrocity propaganda was taking shape in the Pacific, with the Japanese the accused there, though Lemkin's study never ventured beyond the confines of Europe in the hands of the Axis powers. In view of the high state of emotion prevailing, Lemkin's book had unobstructed clear sailing upon its publication late in November, 1944, even though an almost invisible fraction of one per cent of the English-reading populace ever saw it.

What he had to say in *Axis Rule* reached individuals in a wide circle eventually, but this was the result of a ceaseless promotional and publicity campaign, eventually making him known all over the world. Many things he declared in his book become articles of faith everywhere, and his new word "genocide" ultimately acquired planetary use, and as more than one part of speech. And, thanks to this neologism of Lemkin, a substantial number of policy actions by various national states, particularly in the ten to twenty years after the first appearance of this word, came to be identified as "genocide" by whatever minority which felt itself to be a victim of this or that policy, even if that minority did not even live where the so-called "genocide" had been put into effect.

As has been seen, during the first and very hectic period of efforts to get the "genocide" convention adopted and then ratified universally, the major pressure applied politically in the United States came from organized Zionism, whose spokesmen were hardly all Jews. But the usefulness of the word "genocide" was gradually recognized during this time by ethnic groups which were largely non-Jewish, as well. Accusations before a global audience of "genocidal" policies flowed freely between 1948 and 1958. While Lemkin between

1944 and 1947 *may* have thought that his fellow Jews would be the primary beneficiaries of the establishment of a planetary prohibition of "genocide," it should have become obvious that immense complications lay in store, as his ideas spread throughout the world thanks to United Nations efforts, leading to many unexpected mutations. These in turn suggested evolutionary consequences Lemkin had never considered in first launching the term, especially after his legal contemporaries began to work on the future of it as international law. What lay within their grasp was the construction of a world-reaching protocol which not only might be the permanent protection device for minorities of special kinds everywhere, but a device which might even provide a prescription for something beyond guaranteed survival of minorities: a vehicle which might be employed here or there to be-devil majorities. Some hazy understanding of this began to seep through public consciousness, especially in the USA during the ratification contest. That the "genocide" convention got no farther than it did in America may be attributable to this gradual awareness of where the chefs of "genocide" intended to take their confection in the first place. And for many it brought them face to face with what the components of a social order consist of for the first time.

Ratification of the United Nations Genocide Convention by a sufficient number of states to make it operable worldwide as "international law" was the realization of a minority dream. What went into effect worldwide, through presumably binding only on the ratifiers, came as the result of action by 20 national communities, but amounting to the establishment of the will of a very tiny fraction of the world's population. That its moral weight would far exceed its political authority in terms of conventional representation was to be taken for granted. Now any offended minority had a global platform from which to air its grievance and to loose the most incendiary charges, with a guaranteed listening audience. There is no other comparable example of a minority so small making policy for so many which compares with the maneuvering which ended up in the UN ratification of the Genocide Convention.

Nevertheless, the more one ponders the word "genocide," and contemplates the current definition of it, as embodied in the UN Genocide Convention, the more its essence slips away from comprehension, and gets lost in vague verbiage. As the catchall definition of this synthetic crime was expanded clause by clause, its likely prosecution became less and less possible, let alone probable. As can be seen by a careful examination of Article II of the Genocide Convention, Lemkin and the ingenious men with whom he worked were concerned with far more than just physical extermination of some people. The new "crime" they created was aimed not only at those who might engage in action intending to reduce the numbers of a minority or to inhibit their growth. It also included acts which might interfere with or obstruct their maintaining their distinctive identity, well-being, and influence, regardless of any reasons for so doing. By the time Raphael Lemkin and his co-workers were through, assembling in their work of genius almost everything they could conceive as might discommode a minority somewhere sometime, they had fabricated an empty verbal balloon, seemingly constructed of something of substance, but actually as illusory a device as the spinners of legal abstractions had ever stitched together in history. Its unworkability was to be demonstrated repeatedly thereafter.

Though there have been many accusations of "genocide" made against a variety of countries in the last 35 years in the United Nations, there has never been a single international indictment, trial or conviction for such a "crime" before that body in all that time, or anywhere else. As an emotional verbal reflex, "genocide" has been sprayed on the world like a garden hose, but tangible responses have been imperceptible. In the eyes of some it never was intended to be anything but noise and smoke, though it took the appearance of a kind of insurance policy against anything happening again such as has long been claimed happened to the Jews of most of Europe during the Second World War. But even repeated claims of "genocide" filed by Jews against the Soviet Union in the last 35 years have been inconsequential, let alone the fate of "genocide" charges made by other and different religious and ethnic groups, which have all failed to get the political or moral support necessary to bring about desired action, or, for that matter, any kind of action at all.

A good case can be advanced to demonstrate that, thanks to the labors of Raphael Lemkin, primarily, the minorities of the world were placed in far worse predicaments, if not more actual danger, than they ever were in before, and that those devoted to a policy of actual extermination of this one or that one were given invaluable assistance in proceeding along such lines. The mass slaughters that took place in the last ten or twelve years of Lemkin's life went unpunished, and even largely unnoticed, even by Lemkin himself, as far as his public statements were concerned.

The sustained failure to include "political" among the category of putative threatened minority "groups" in Article II robbed the Genocide Convention of most of its possible value, and created a loophole by default, from which situation it simply remained for any land interested in eliminating a minority to identify or construe the latter as a *political* adversary of the State. The stupefying and almost unbelievable massacres of Communist China, Cambodia and Vietnam and those of several parts of Africa, as well as such events as the fierce bloodletting between India and Pakistan, and the overwhelming of Tibet by Red China, all escaped analysis as "genocide" in the final deliberations of the UN, despite the flaming rhetoric to the contrary elsewhere. What we have witnessed since the end of World War II has been a succession of real mass murders taking place in many parts of the world as a follow-up to the charges of this happening during that war which presumably inspired the whole idea of "genocide" to begin with, if we are to believe the language in the very first paragraph of the preliminary material accompanying the UN's own printing of the Genocide Convention.

Can it be said that, after all of Raphael Lemkin's efforts in inventing "genocide," and his decade and a half of ceaseless toil in seeking to get the world to look upon it as the crime of the ages, the safety and security and future of minorities has really been enhanced at all? Superficially this appears to be the case, and the righteous mouthing of the cliches the "genocide" crusade ennobled and engendered goes on every time a particularly repelling outbreak of minority persecution or massacre takes place. But there is also strong evidence that the situation likely to be assumed by protagonists of the original assertion here is anything but favorable.

On the continents of Asia and Africa the facts back up the view that minorities are probably more precariously perched than ever before. Elsewhere there is the sentiment that things are better, and in North America and Western Europe, much better. But Jews continue to complain bitterly about their status in the Arab world and in the Soviet Union, two vast stretches of the world. Other minorities similarly enter their laments concerning their situation in other places, and, overall, one gets the feeling that a wrong turn or two in world affairs might provoke as much trouble for this or that minority as ever happened or was believed to have taken place in the past. In 1979-1980 it was obvious that people with a strain of Chinese blood living in Vietnam were as endangered a minority as has ever graced the face of the planet. In Africa, in a dozen countries, various tribal groups are in grave circumstances, and their predicament promises to stay as bad if not get worse for a long time to come. In the meantime, racial hybrids in many parts of the world, especially in Asia, face incredible if not unsurmountable handicaps.

As already seen, the generous lapses in the wording of the Genocide Convention provide those seeking to impose on minorities with glowing opportunities. The absence of *political* and *economic* group categories from the protected, according to this Convention, is of primary importance in weakening its defensive shield. The opportunity beckons all interested in expunging an unwanted minority from the national scene and presence to designate such as *political* opponents, or the *economic* supporters of international enemies via the funding of subversion and treason. They have as a result the perfect excuse to advance whatever means may be construed as necessary to eliminate that minority, and all within the framework of UN legal guidelines; any signatory to the Genocide Convention has by default passed up any reason to object to such a process taking place.

Therefore, the enforcement of the Genocide Convention comes down to a local affair, in one state or another. The creation of international machinery for the processing of "genocide" cases has gone no further than it had at the time the Convention was ratified by the requisite number of UN member states early in 1951. Without a domestic support system for the prosecution of "genocide," in the form not only of enabling legislation implementing the local ratification of the Genocide Convention, but also the will to go ahead with such legal action, on the part of an operationally significant portion of the remaining part of that national populace not belonging to the protesting minority in question, then one may say that for all practical purposes the words in the UN Genocide Convention are nothing. The drive to make the Genocide Convention an international universality turned inward over 25 years ago; those who persist in urging its ratification here or there are thinking of its utility on their own domestic level now, against elements within their own national populace. The coming into existence of an international arena for the consideration of "genocide" cases, as Raphael Lemkin and his supporters dreamed of and talked of for so long, and still considered a possibility in the language of the Genocide Convention itself, appears to be utterly out of the question today.

Raphael Lemkin's principal legacy to the world is not only an ugly neologism which is deteriorating in meaning because of its steadily defective employment (even well-regarded dictionaries prefer their own imaginations instead of consulting the Genocide Convention.) It is also a promise of possible endless contumacy growing out of any possible attempt to make his concept work as operational international law. But as a ritual word, "genocide" may be around a long time, invoked by a succession of wily blatherskites hoping to make a little political hay, or used as a charge and counter-charge by all manner of unconscionable rogues and mountebanks in an effort to defame one another.

The chances of an actual legal event occurring in which a formal indictment is followed by a trial, conviction and punishment on the international level of someone charged with "genocide," let alone an entire *group* of "genocidists," as envisaged by Lemkin (one should keep in mind that as originally conceived by Lemkin, both the

victims *and* the offenders were *groups*), is exceedingly remote, unless
there is another war which is brought to a conclusion similar to that
ending in 1945. Few able to gain a propaganda or other psychic
advantage by bellowing accusations of "genocide" will ever pass up
such an opportunity, but, like counterfeit money, the validity of this
maneuver is sure to decline steadily, and the invocation of this word
some day may have all the weight of a prayer to the idols of pharao-
nic Egypt.

The more a word is intoned as a political accusation, the more
numb and unresponsive becomes public reaction. The most frightful
massacres of minorities (whether planned and intentional is not
established) decorated the 1960s and 1970s, increasingly responded
to by distracted yawns. The more often one heard the loud charge of
"genocide," the less there seemed to be done about it on all levels.
So what the world seems to be stuck with in this instance is a messy
legacy of World War II, and is not the gracious beneficiary of some
ageless and towering principle of right which will extend onward for
millennia.

"Genocide" long ago served its purpose in providing auxiliary
verbal support and dynamism for the procedure leading to the trial
and killing of the defeated enemy leaders at the end of World War
Two. Since that time its invocation has degenerated to a political
swear word, used shamelessly as a device for stirring up emotions
and for shoring up political courses of action here or there throughout the world, but it has been largely depleted of whatever substance
it ever originally possessed. Though still a redoubtable verbal reflex,
one must work hard to see any tangible value in its continuous and
mechanical invocation in modern world politics and statecraft.

The goal of all this work by Raphael Lemkin, however, was the
creation of international law applying to a new international crime,
and obviously he was thinking of a global machine which would deal
with it as part of international politics. This is plain to anyone reading Article VI of the Genocide Convention. But in over 30 years
there has yet to be a single case of such international punishment, or
even an unquestionable and unanimous condemnation even as a
declaration of intent. It goes without saying that there is nothing in
the shape of a created tribunal, court or judging body empowered
to listen to "genocide" charges, and issue pronouncements of innocence or guilt. If such a legal agency, other than those which exist in
individual states to take up such matters locally, provided for by
enabling legislation passed after ratification of the Genocide Convention, did exist, the problem of enforcing its judgment would be even
more formidable than bringing in the indictment. It would require
the substance of warmaking potential to make its will heard and

obeyed, as it is nearly unthinkable that a sovereign state would submit tamely to an international juridical invasion of its borders by the agents of foreigners to spirit off to jail or execution its citizens in the name of an agency alien to it, resulting from a charge stemming from the movement of legal machinery in some distant place.

However, Article VI begins, "Persons charged with genocide or any of the other acts enumerated in Article III shall be tried by a competent tribunal of the State in the territory of which the act was committed," and this is what "genocide," in view of its dismal record as an international matter, has descended to. It is also the reason for the continued agitation in one country or another for that nation's ratification of the UN Genocide Convention. The contemporary feebleness of the "genocide" impulse as a worldwide concern has sparked as compensation its utilization in domestic politics, but resting on the peculiar nature of minority relations and power structures, which vary from country to country. This is reflected in the enabling legislation which follows parliamentary ratification by this or that country of the Genocide Convention. The definition of "genocide" in the latter is so sweeping that it encourages a strategically-placed minority to lobby for passage of a law or laws that may render themselves virtually immune even from superficial criticism, on the grounds of constituting "mental harm" to them as incorporated in the Convention's Article II. Great Britain's Race Relations Acts are sometimes cited as examples of zealous national enabling legislation respecting "genocide" which is increasingly invoked to suppress spoken or written criticism of the behavior or beliefs of minorities in that country. This has been one of the few demonstrably successful operational tactics inspired by the "genocide" concept, a degeneration of its announced noble international goal into a questionable local political ploy. Structured in this way to redound to the comfort and welfare of minorities in that state, it still imposes a difficulty upon minorities employing this device to render themselves immune to public criticism, however. The pushing of such positions by law may provoke a constitutional question relating to free speech and related civil liberties, which, like the right to think, apply to majorities too. And too zealous enforcement can result in a socio-political situation with somewhat more grim and unwanted complications. It then depends upon the political wisdom of the minorities involved, and how far they are willing to employ minority parliamentary strength to ensure what may be an entirely illusory security. Any minority or any other "racial, ethnic, national or religious group" living in any national state on the planet which think they are safe to do what they please, always relying on the ultimate shelter of the umbrella of the Genocide Convention, are undoubtedly engaging in the same kind of illusion those who make use of fifty-year-old bomb shelters are indulging in, in a world about to mass-employ laser and particle beam weapons. The paper and words of the United Nations Genocide Convention are no more likely to provide the freedom from pressure that minority groups have been led to rest their faith in since Raphael Lemkin, than classical civilizations were able to muster protection from their adversaries by way of reciting the incantations of the priests of Baal.

Between 1943 and 1951, Lemkin and his co-workers in the United Nations provided minorities everywhere with a strategem, in the shape of the Genocide Convention, which invited the overplaying of their hand in a grave manner. In the decade roughly comprising the years 1963-1973 the world was treated to an explosion of reckless, violent hooliganism with lethal complications, instigated and carried out by minorities in several countries, notably in the United States and France. The assumption seemed to be that a new era had arrived in which minorities might engaged in whatever behavior they might choose, without fear of a reaction or reprisal, the notion apparently having got at large that psychologically and morally, majorities had been so cowed by the previous decade of minority pressure that there no longer was any need to have this in mind.

However, this same decade and that which followed were also featured by frightful reactions against minorities in several different countries on three continents. The minorities of the former cut which rejoiced in the hysteric delusions accompanying a victorious laying waste of the majority world about them, and which descended from others who were stentorian in denunciation of atrocities of this sort which they claimed to have sustained in the 1940s, were virtually inaudible this time around, the victims being someone other than themselves. But the lesson involved in this incredible interlude in the USA, in particular, was not lost on all. America's famous longshoreman philosopher, the late Eric Hoffer, appalled and deeply disturbed by the events in the USA, was convinced that the "violent minorities" were heading straight for a hecatomb if they did not modify their behavior sharply, and soon. In his book *First Things, Last Things* (Harper and Row, 1971), Hoffer was convinced that "a day of wrath" was "waiting around the corner," when he expected that "the saturated resentment of the long-suffering majority" would "crystallize in retaliation."

This never happened, of course. Hoffer miscalculated the capacity of the American majority for absorbing outrage. But the potential was there and Hoffer correctly sensed it, even if his time table was off. Perhaps this entire minority gout of pointless destruction, accompanied fortunately by a minimum of lethal consequences, had a deep philosophical tie-in with the immense impulse toward pro-minority protectiveness inherent in the accompanying sentiments played upon by organized minority politics, while the "genocide" subject washed across the world in the '40s and early '50s.

But the game was up now. Having served its immediate political purpose in the closing years of World War Two and those immediately afterward, it may be that, other than advancing minority advantages in one country or another, the "genocide" impulse had peaked, and now was on its way to becoming a verbal totem, a flimsy piece of paper incapable of protecting any minority anywhere, other than in those regions where cultural and civilizational levels were sufficiently elevated to preclude the intentional annihilation of minorities, not because some members of the United Nations had declared this to be a crime, but because it was something the psychically-human simply did not do.

In the trade-off, minorities of all kinds in such favored circumstances have to come to terms with the constant temptation to succumb to the beckonings of megalomania and temper their dreams of exclusive privileged status and/or overlordship, or run the risk of eventual reaction, as has been seen over the millennia, but which, in the modern world, and in the likely future, given the state of the art in the contrivances of violence, "genocide" or no "genocide," promises to make the inconveniences or the disasters suffered by minorities in the past little more than superficial irritations, by comparison.

THE CRIME OF GENOCIDE

a United Nations Convention Aimed at Preventing Destruction of Groups and at Punishing Those Responsible

UNITED NATIONS

GENOCIDE is a modern word for an old crime. It means the deliberate destruction of national, racial, religious or ethnic groups.

History had long been a grim witness to such acts, but it remained for the twentieth century to see those acts carried out on the largest and most inhuman scale known when the Nazi Government of Germany systematically annihilated millions of people because of their religion or ethnic origin. A shocked world then rejected any contention that such crimes were the exclusive concern of the State perpetrating them, and punishment of the guilty became one of the principal war aims of the Allied nations. The charter of the International Military Tribunal at Nuremberg, approved by the Allies in 1945, recognized that war criminals were not only those who had committed crimes against peace, and violations of the laws or customs of war, but those who had carried out "crimes against humanity" whether or not such crimes violated the domestic law of the country in which they took place.

During its first session in 1946, the United Nations General Assembly approved two resolutions. In the first, the Assembly affirmed the principles of the charter of the Nuremberg Tribunal. In the second—the basic resolution on genocide—the Assembly affirmed that genocide was a crime under international law and that those guilty of it, whoever they were and for whatever reason they committed it, were punishable. It asked for international co-operation in preventing and punishing genocide and it invited Member States to enact the necessary national legislation. In a final provision, the Assembly called for studies aimed at creating an international legal instrument to deal with the crime. That was the origin of the Convention on the Prevention and Punishment of the Crime of Genocide unanimously adopted by the Assembly on 9 December 1948.

The term convention in international law means an agreement among sovereign nations. It is a legal compact which pledges every Contracting Party to accept certain obligations.

1

How the Convention was Prepared

In 1946 the General Assembly requested the Economic and Social Council to undertake the necessary studies for drawing up a draft Convention on the crime of genocide. In 1947 the Secretary-General, at the request of the Economic and Social Council, prepared a first draft of the Convention and circulated it to Member States for comments. At that stage, the Secretary-General was assisted by a group of international law experts, among them the late Dr. Raphael Lemkin, who in 1944 had coined the term "genocide". In 1948 the Economic and Social Council appointed an *ad hoc* Committee of seven members to submit to it a revised draft. That the Committee did, and after a general debate, the Council decided on 26 August to transmit the draft to the General Assembly. At the Paris session of the General Assembly the draft was debated by the Legal Committee and adopted by the Assembly on 9 December 1948.

The Definition of Genocide in the Convention

Genocide, the Convention declares, is the committing of certain acts with intent to destroy—wholly or in part—a national, ethnic, racial or religious group as such.

What are the acts? First, actual killing. But it is possible to destroy a group of human beings without direct physical extermination. So the Convention includes in the definition of genocide the acts of causing serious bodily or mental harm; deliberate infliction of conditions of life "calculated to bring about" physical destruction; imposing measures to prevent birth and, finally, forcibly transferring children of one group to another group. Those acts, the Convention states, constitute "genocide". In accordance with the Convention, related acts are also punishable: conspiracy to commit genocide, direct and public incitement to commit genocide, an attempt to commit the crime and complicity in its commission.

To Prevent and to Punish

The Convention first declares that genocide "whether committed in time of peace or in time of war" is a crime under international law which the contracting States "undertake to prevent and to punish".

Main principles established by the Convention are:

(1) Contracting States are bound to enact the laws needed to give effect to the provisions of the Convention, in particular to provide effective penalties.

(2) States undertake to try persons charged with those offences in their competent national courts.

(3) Parties to the Convention agree that the acts listed shall not be considered as political crimes. Therefore, they pledge to grant extradition in accordance with their laws and treaties.

All those pledges are for national action. The Convention also envisages trial by an international penal tribunal should one be set up and should the

2

Contracting Parties accept its jurisdiction. Furthermore, it provides that any of the contracting States may bring a charge of genocide, or of any of the related acts, before the competent organs of the United Nations and ask for appropriate action under the Charter.

If there is any dispute between one country and another on the interpretation, application or fulfilment of the Convention, the dispute must be submitted to the International Court of Justice at the request of any of the Parties.

Who may be Punished?

Article IV of the Convention declares that those guilty of genocide and the other acts listed shall be punished "whether they are constitutionally responsible rulers, public officials or private individuals". That clause makes it impossible for a person to plead immunity because he was the head of a State or a public official.

Question of International Penal Jurisdiction

During discussion by the Legal Committee in 1948, international penal jurisdiction was considered carefully. As a result, the idea is envisaged and provided for in Article VI of the Convention. Further, in addition to the Convention, the Assembly adopted a resolution which made three provisions.

First, it recognized that "in the course of development of the international community there will be an *increasing need* of an international judicial organ for the trial of certain crimes under international law".

Second, it invited the International Law Commission to study both the desirability and the possibility of establishing such an international judicial organ "for the trial of persons charged with genocide, or other crimes over which jurisdiction will be conferred upon that organ by international Conventions".

Third, it requested the International Law Commission, in carrying out its task, to give attention to the possibility of establishing a Criminal Chamber of the International Court of Justice.

After studying that question, the International Law Commission concluded that an international criminal court was both possible and desirable but recommended it be a separate institution rather than a Criminal Chamber of the International Court. Assembly committees submitted draft statutes for such a separate court. By consensus, however, the General Assembly agreed that the problems raised by that matter are closely related to defining aggression and to the draft code of offences against the peace and security of mankind. It postponed consideration of an international criminal jurisdiction until it could consider reports on those related questions.

Parties to the Convention

All Member States of the United Nations are entitled to become Parties to the Convention. Some of them signed the Convention in Paris immediately after its passage by the Assembly on 9 December 1948. By 31 December 1949, the date set for closing the Convention for signature, 40 States had signed. Non-Member States, invited by the General Assembly, have signed as well as Member States.

3

A legal compact like the Convention does not become binding on mere signature. It has to be ratified by each signatory country according to its constitutional processes. The "instrument of ratification", a communication formally signifying ratification, is then deposited with the Secretary-General.

The Convention provided that, after 31 December 1949, no more signatures would be accepted. However, Member States, as well as non-members invited by the Assembly, may accede to the Convention by depositing "instruments of accession" with the Secretary-General.

The Convention came into force on 12 January 1951, 90 days after 20 States had ratified or acceded to it. Under its provisions, the Convention is renewable in successive periods of five years for countries that have not denounced it.

"Denunciation" is the term for the procedure of withdrawing from the Convention. Any country can give notice of such withdrawal six months before the expiration of the current period for which it is bound. If, as a result of such denunciations, there are fewer than 16 nations bound by it, the Convention will cease to be in force.

Ratifications and Accessions

As of 1 January 1973, instruments of ratification or accession to the Convention had been deposited by 76 Governments: Afghanistan, Albania, Algeria, Argentina, Australia, Austria, Belgium, Brazil, Bulgaria, Burma, Byelorussian SSR, Canada, Chile, China,* Colombia, Costa Rica, Cuba, Czechoslovakia, Denmark, Ecuador, Egypt, El Salvador, Ethiopia, Finland, France, Federal Republic of Germany, Ghana, Greece, Guatemala, Haiti, Honduras, Hungary, Iceland, India, Iran, Iraq, Israel, Italy, Jamaica, Jordan, Khmer Republic, Republic of Korea, Laos, Lebanon, Liberia, Mexico, Monaco, Mongolia, Morroco, Nepal, Netherlands, Nicaragua, Norway, Pakistan, Panama, Peru, Philippines, Poland, Romania, Saudi Arabia, Spain, Sri Lanka, Sweden, Syrian Arab Republic, Tunisia, Tonga, Turkey, United Kingdom, Ukrainian SSR, USSR, Upper Volta, Uruguay, Venezuela, Republic of Viet-Nam, Yugoslavia and Zaire.

Recognizing the importance of the Convention, the General Assembly and the Economic and Social Council appealed several times to States entitled to become Parties to the Convention to ratify it or to accede to it as soon as possible. While the response has been gratifying, a number of eligible States have not yet done so.

The General Assembly has also recommended that Parties to the Convention should take all possible measures to extend the application of the Convention to the Territories for the conduct of whose foreign relations they are responsible. Australia and the United Kingdom, the only Parties to the Convention in that situation, have done so.

---

*The reference to China is to be understood in accordance with General Assembly resolution 2758 (XXVI) of 25 October 1971. By that resolution, the General Assembly decided: "to restore all its rights to the People's Republic of China and to recognize the representatives of its Government as the only legitimate representatives of China to the United Nations, and to expel forthwith the representatives of Chiang Kai-shek from the place which they unlawfully occupy at the United Nations and in all the organizations related to it."

Question of Time-Limit for Prosecution and Punishment of War Crimes and Crimes against Humanity

In 1965, the question arose in some countries of applying the statute of limitations provided for in their national laws to the prosecution of war crimes and of crimes against humanity. The Commission on Human Rights requested the Secretary-General to undertake a study of the problems raised in international law by war crimes and crimes against humanity and a study of legal procedures to ensure that no period of limitation should apply to such crimes. On the basis of that study, the Commission began, in 1966, to prepare a draft Convention.

The matter was taken up in 1967 by the General Assembly, which in 1968 completed and adopted the Convention on the Non-Applicability of Statutory Limitations to War Crimes and Crimes against Humanity. The Convention entered into force on 11 November 1970. Article I of the Convention, which defines crimes to which no statutory limitation shall apply, irrespective of the date of commission, lists among those crimes "the crime of genocide as defined in the 1948 Convention on the Prevention and Punishment of the Crime of Genocide".

Other Activities of the United Nations related to the Genocide Convention

Various subjects debated by United Nations bodies, such as the preparation of a draft Code of Offences against the Peace and Security of Mankind; the punishment of war criminals and of persons guilty of crimes against humanity; *apartheid* and measures to be taken against nazism and other totalitarian ideologies, and practices based on incitement to hatred and racial intolerance, have also raised questions connected with the Genocide Convention.

In 1969, the Economic and Social Council approved the decision of the Sub-Commission on Prevention of Discrimination and Protection of Minorities of the Commission on Human Rights to undertake a study on the prevention and punishment of the crime of genocide. That study is in progress.

Prospects for the Genocide Convention

Throughout the world people aware of the importance and vital necessity of the Genocide Convention are working for its general acceptance and for its observance. The basis of their support transcends religious beliefs and crosses political lines.

Perhaps the best expression of the Convention's appeal was made by the late Gabriela Mistral, the famous Chilean poet who won the Nobel Prize for Literature in 1945.

"With amazing regularity genocide has repeated itself throughout history", she wrote. "Despite all advances in our civilization the twentieth century must unfortunately be considered as one of those most guilty of the crime of genocide. Losses in life and culture have been staggering. But deep in his heart man cherishes a fervent yearning for justice and love; among small nations and minorities the craving for security is particularly alive. The success of the

5

Genocide Convention today and its greater success tomorrow can be traced to the fact that it responds to necessities and desires of a universal nature. The word genocide carries in itself a moral judgement over an evil in which every feeling man and woman concurs."

TEXT OF THE CONVENTION

THE CONTRACTING PARTIES,

HAVING CONSIDERED the declaration made by the General Assembly of the United Nations in its resolution 96 (I) dated 11 December 1946 that genocide is a crime under international law, contrary to the spirit and aims of the United Nations and condemned by the civilized world;

RECOGNIZING that at all periods of history genocide has inflicted great losses on humanity; and

BEING CONVINCED that, in order to liberate mankind from such an odious scourge, international co-operation is required:

HEREBY AGREE AS HEREINAFTER PROVIDED:

Article I

The Contracting Parties confirm that genocide, whether committed in time of peace or in time of war, is a crime under international law which they undertake to prevent and to punish.

Article II

In the present Convention, genocide means any of the following acts committed with intent to destroy, in whole or in part, a national, ethnical, racial or religious groups, as such:

(*a*) Killing members of the group;

(*b*) Causing serious bodily or mental harm to members of the group;

(*c*) Deliberately inflicting on the group conditions of life calculated to bring about its physical destruction in whole or in part;

(*d*) Imposing measures intended to prevent births within the group;

(*e*) Forcibly transferring children of the group to another group.

6

Article III

The following acts shall be punishable:

(a) Genocide;

(b) Conspiracy to commit genocide;

(c) Direct and public incitement to commit genocide;

(d) Attempt to commit genocide;

(e) Complicity in genocide.

Article IV

Persons committing genocide or any of the other acts enumerated in Article III shall be punished, whether they are constitutionally responsible rulers, public officials or private individuals.

Article V

The Contracting Parties undertake to enact, in accordance with their respective Constitutions, the necessary legislation to give effect to the provisions of the present Convention and, in particular, to provide effective penalties for persons guilty of genocide or of any of the other acts enumerated in Article III.

Article VI

Persons charged with genocide or any of the other acts enumerated in Article III shall be tried by a competent tribunal of the State in the territory of which the act was committed, or by such international penal tribunal as may have jurisdiction with respect to those Contracting Parties which shall have accepted its jurisdiction.

Article VII

Genocide and the other acts enumerated in Article III shall not be considered as political crimes for the purpose of extradition.

The Contracting Parties pledge themselves in such cases to grant extradition in accordance with their laws and treaties in force.

Article VIII

Any Contracting Party may call upon the competent organs of the United Nations to take such action under the Charter of the United Nations as they consider appropriate for the prevention and suppression of acts of genocide or any of the other acts enumerated in Article III.

Article IX

Disputes between the Contracting Parties relating to the interpretation, application or fulfilment of the present Convention, including those relating to the responsibility of a State for genocide or for any of the other acts enumerated in Article III, shall be submitted to the International Court of Justice at the request of any of the parties to the dispute.

Article X

The present Convention, of which the Chinese, English, French, Russian and Spanish texts are equally authentic, shall bear the date of 9 December 1948.

Article XI

The present Convention shall be open until 31 December 1949 for signature on behalf of any Member of the United Nations and of any non-member State to which an invitation to sign has been addressed by the General Assembly.

The present Convention shall be ratified, and the instruments of ratification shall be deposited with the Secretary-General of the United Nations.

After 1 January 1950 the present Convention may be acceded to on behalf of any Member of the United Nations and of any non-member State which has received an invitation as aforesaid.

Instruments of accession shall be deposited with the Secretary-General of the United Nations.

Article XII

Any Contracting Party may at any time, by notification addressed to the Secretary-General of the United Nations, extend the application of the present Convention to all or any of the territories for the conduct of whose foreign relations that Contracting Party is responsible.

Article XIII

On the day when the first twenty instruments of ratification or accession have been deposited, the Secretary-General shall draw up a *procès-verbal* and transmit a copy thereof to each Member of the United Nations and to each of the non-member States contemplated in Article XI.

The present Convention shall come into force on the ninetieth day following the date of deposit of the twentieth instrument of ratification or accession.

Any ratification or accession effected subsequent to the latter date shall become effective on the ninetieth day following the deposit of the instrument of ratification or accession.

Article XIV

The present Convention shall remain in effect for a period of ten years as from the date of its coming into force.

It shall thereafter remain in force for successive periods of five years for such Contracting Parties as have not denounced it at least six months before the expiration of the current period.

Denunciation shall be effected by a written notification addressed to the Secretary-General of the United Nations.

Article XV

If, as a result of denunciations, the number of Parties to the present Convention should become less than sixteen, the Convention shall cease to be in force as from the date on which the last of these denunciations shall become effective.

Article XVI

A request for the revision of the present Convention may be made at any time by any Contracting Party by means of a notification in writing addressed to the Secretary-General.

The General Assembly shall decide upon the steps, if any, to be taken in respect of such request.

Article XVII

The Secretary-General of the United Nations shall notify all Members of the United Nations and the non-member States contemplated in Article XI of the following:

(a) Signatures, ratifications and accessions received in accordance with Article XI;

(b) Notifications received in accordance with Article XII;

(c) The date upon which the present Convention comes into force in accordance with Article XIII;

(d) Denunciations received in accordance with Article XIV;

(e) The abrogation of the Convention in accordance with Article XV;

(f) Notifications received in accordance with Article XVI.

Article XVIII

The original of the present Convention shall be deposited in the archives of the United Nations.

A certified copy of the Convention shall be transmitted to each Member of the United Nations and to each of the non-member States contemplated in Article XI.

Article XIX

The present Convention shall be registered by the Secretary-General of the United Nations on the date of its coming into force.

APPENDIX II

GENOCIDE CONVENTION

FRIDAY, MAY 22, 1970

UNITED STATES SENATE,
SUBCOMMITTEE ON GENOCIDE CONVENTION
OF THE COMMITTEE ON FOREIGN RELATIONS,
Washington, D.C.

The subcommittee met, pursuant to recess, at 2 p.m., in room S-116, the Capitol Building, Senator Frank Church (chairman of the subcommittee) presiding.

Present: Senator Church, Cooper, and Javits.

Senator COOPER. I will call the subcommittee to order now. I understand that the chairman, Senator Church, will be here in a short time. The witness today is Senator Ervin. The Senator would like for us to proceed.

STATEMENT OF HON. SAM J. ERVIN, JR., A U.S. SENATOR FROM THE STATE OF NORTH CAROLINA

Senator ERVIN. I am deeply grateful to have such a large turnout, because often committees only have one.

Senator JAVITS. Mr. Chairman, the chairman of the subcommittee is necessarily stationed on the Senate floor in connection with the Church-Cooper amendment and he asked us to proceed.

Senator ERVIN. Gentlemen, I welcome this opportunity to appear before the subcommittee and to urge the subcommittee to recommend to the full committee that the so-called Genocide Convention not be reported to the Senate for consideration.

Senator JAVITS. I didn't get that. Not be reported?

Senator ERVIN. Yes. It would be extremely unwise for the Senate of the United States to ratify the Genocide Convention. This is particularly true at a time when it is manifest that a substantial part of the American people wish to contract rather than expand their international obligations.

194

HISTORY OF THE GENOCIDE CONVENTION

During the 1940's activists connected with the United Nations engaged in a strenuous effort to establish by treaties laws to supersede domestic laws of nations throughout the earth. The Genocide Convention represent one of these efforts. It originated in a resolution of the United Nations condemning genocide as a crime whether "committed on religious, racial, political, or any other grounds." When reduced to its final form it excluded genocide committed on "political" grounds because some of the parties to it did not wish to surrender even nominally their right to exterminate political groups hostile to their rulers.

Under its provisions, individuals as well as persons exercising governmental power would be subject to trial and punishment for offenses which have always been regarded as matters falling within the domestic jurisdiction of the various nations.

The Genocide Convention was adopted by the General Assembly of the United Nations on December 10, 1948, and was submitted by President Harry S. Truman to the Senate for its consideration on June 16, 1949. The Senate Foreign Relations Committee appointed a subcommittee composed of very able Senators, who conducted hearings in January and February 1950, and reported to the full committee that the United States should not ratify the convention in any event unless the Senate adopted four substantial understandings and one substantial declaration. Since this report was made, the Senate Foreign Relations Committee and the Senate itself by inaction have refused to ratify this convention.

In contrast to the attitude represented by this inaction during the preceding 20 years, the Senate Foreign Relations Committee has apparently revived the question of ratification during the past few months, notwithstanding the fact that there has been no change of circumstances which would make what was unwise in 1950 wise in 1970.

The only arguments now advanced for ratification of this convention is that it would improve the image of the United States in the eyes of Russia and other totalitarian parties to the convention, which strange to say have repudiated by understanding and reservations many of the provisions of the convention.

For example, these nations refused to be bound by article IX which subjects their actions under it to the jurisdiction of the International Court of Justice. Some of the proponents of ratification by the Senate advance the rather strange argument that the United States can safey ratify the convention because there is no effective way to enforce its provisions against the United States if the United States refuses to abide by them. I cannot buy this argument because I think that any nation which makes a contract in the form of a treaty should accept its obligations even in the event such obligations prove to be contrary to its own interest. Otherwise, why make treaties.

Before discussing the obligations which the United States would assume as the result of Senate ratification of the Genocide Convention, I wish to call attention to its salient provisions.

195

PROVISIONS OF THE GENOCIDE CONVENTION

By the Genocide Convention or treaty the contracting parties affirm in article I "that genocide, whether committed in time of peace or in time of war, is a crime under international law which they undertake to prevent and to punish."

Articles II and III of the Convention read:

ARTICLE II

In the present convention, genocide means any of the following acts committed with intent to destroy, in whole or in part, a national, ethnical, racial or religious group, as such:

(a) Killing members of the group;
(b) Causing serious bodily or mental harm to members of the group:
(c) Deliberately inflicting on the group conditions of life calculated to bring about its physical destruction in whole or in part;
(d) Imposing measures intended to prevent births within the group;
(e) Forcibly transferring children of the group to another group.

ARTICLE III

The following acts shall be punishable:

(a) Genocide;
(b) Conspiracy to commit genocide;
(c) Direct and public incitement to commit genocide;
(d) Attempt to commit genocide;
(e) Complicity in genocide.

Article V obligates the contracting parties to enact the necessary legislation to give effect to the provisions of the convention and to provide effective penalties "for persons guilty of genocide or of any of the other acts enumerated in Article III."

Article VI provides that "persons charged with genocide or any of the other acts enumerated in Article III shall be tried by a competent tribunal of the nation in the territory in which the act was committed or by such international penal tribunal as may have jurisdiction with respect to those Contracting Parties which shall have accepted its jurisdiction."

Article VII provides that the parties to the treaty pledge themselves in genocide cases to grant extradition in accordance with their laws and treaties. Article VIII provides that "any Contracting Party may call upon the competent organs of the United Nations to take such action under the Charter of the United Nations as they consider appropriate for the prevention and suppression of acts of genocide or any of the other acts enumerated in Article III."

Article IX provides that "disputes between the Contracting Parties relating to the interpretaion, application, or fulfillment of the present convention * * * shall be submitted to the International Court of Justice at the request of any of the parties to the dispute."

This brings me to the considerations which ought to deter the Senate from ratifying the Genocide Convention. Time and space compel me to limit my statement to only the most substantial of them.

196

CONVENTION DISTORTS CONCEPT OF GENOCIDE

1. If the Senate should ratify the Genocide Convention, the United States would be obligated by it to prosecute and punish public officials and private citizens of our country for acts alien to the concept embodied in the term "genocide."

The definition of genocide appears in article II which states that the term "genocide" embraces five specified acts "committed with intent to destroy, in whole or in part, a national, ethnical, racial, or religious group, as such." The Convention definition of "genocide" is inconsistent with the real meaning of the term, which is "the systematic, planned annihilation of a racial, political, or cultural group." The word "annihilation" clearly contemplates the complete destruction or the complete wiping out of the designated group.

Yet, the convention definition covers the destruction either in whole or in part of members of a group embraced by it. This means that a public official or a private individual is to be subject to prosecution and punishment for genocide if he intentionally destroys a single member of one of the specified groups.

When it considered this convention in 1950, the subcommittee of the Senate Foreign Relations Committee took note of the fact that the convention distorts and perverts the entire concept embraced in the word "genocide," and for that reason stated that the Senate ought not to consider ratification of the convention unless it announced this understanding of its meaning:

* * * that the United States Government understands and construes the crime of genocide, which it undertakes to punish in accordance with this convention, to mean the commission of any of the acts enumerated in article II of the convention, with the intent to destroy any entire national, ethnical, racial, or religious group within the territory of the United States, in such manner as to effect a substantial portion of the group concerned.

This distortion and perversion of the plain concept embraced in the word "genocide" represents an effort on the part of the drafters of the convention to make punishable either in the courts of an adherent to the treaty or in an international tribunal to be established under the terms of the treaty, all of the acts enumerated in article II and III of the convention.

Since an intent to destroy a single person belonging to one of the four designated groups would subject an official or individual to punishment, the treaty would make virtually every person in any nation adhering to it a potential victim of "genocide" as the meaning of that term is distorted and perverted by the convention. This is true simply because virtually every person on earth belongs to one or more of the four groups designated.

This observation is made exceedingly plain by the fact that an ethnical group is a "social group within a cultural and social system that claims or is accorded special status on the basis of complex, often variable traits including religious, linguistic, ancestral, or physical characteristics."

197

DRASTIC IMPACT OF CONVENTION ON OUR SYSTEM OF GOVERNMENT

2. Article II, section 2 of the Constitution provides that "the President shall have power, by and with the advice and consent of the Senate, to make treaties, provided two-thirds of the Senators present concur." Article VI of the Constitution provides that "the Constitution and the laws of the United States, which shall be made in pursuance thereof, and all treaties made or which shall be made under the authority of the United States, shall be the supreme law of the land; and the judges in every state shall be bound thereby, anything in the Constitution or laws of any state to the contrary notwithstanding."

If the Senate should ratify the Genocide Convention, these constitutional provisions would automatically make the convention the law of the land, put all of its self-executing provisions into immediate effect as such, and impose upon the United States the obligation to take whatever steps are necessary to make its non-self-executing provisions effective. This means that the provisions of the Genocide Convention would immediately supersede all State laws and practices inconsistent with them, and would nullify all provisions of all acts of Congress and prior treaties of the United States inconsistent with them.

While Congress could repeal provisions of the Genocide Convention by future legislation, the States would be bound by them as long as the convention remained in effect. Moreover, the Genocide Convention would immediately require and authorize the Congress to enact legislation implementing its provisions, even though such legislation were beyond the power of Congress in the absence of the convention, and even though such legislation would deprive the States of the power to prosecute and punish in their courts acts condemned by articles II and III of the convention.

POWER OF CONGRESS TO DEFINE FEDERAL CRIMES

Senator CHURCH. I would like to ask a question at this point.

Is it your position that, in the absence of a Genocide Convention, Congress would be without the power under the Constitution to outlaw genocide as a Federal crime if it chose to?

Senator ERVIN. Absolutely.

Senator CHURCH. Do you think that it would require the convention to give Congress the power to define "genocide" as a Federal crime?

Senator ERVIN. Yes, undoubtedly; because Congress has no power generally to punish homicide as a Federal crime.

Senator CHURCH. Thank you.

Senator JAVITS. Could I ask one other question? Does the Senator contend, therefore, the convention could convey upon the Congress a power which it does not have under the Constitution of the United States?

198

Senator ERVIN. Yes; that is well established. It has been established in a multitude of decisions of the Supreme Court that a treaty, since it is the supreme law of the land, operates to override the powers reserved to the States by the fifth amendment.

Senator JAVITS. To draw that to its logical conclusion, the Senator concedes that a vote of two-thirds of the Senate concurred in by a President proposing the treaty can change the Constitution of the United States by giving a body organized under the Constitution other or additional power.

Senator ERVIN. No, I don't claim that it changes the Constitution of the United States because the Constitution of the United States says the treaty shall be the supreme law of the land; and by reason of that provision of the Constitution it takes precedence over any State law to the contrary and any prior act of the Congress to the contrary. That has been established by a multitude of cases.

Senator JAVITS. I know that. But we are talking now about constitutional authority. The Senator claims that even if such legislation were to go beyond the power of the Congress, as fixed by the Constitution, the Senator would have us believe that the treaty ratified by two-thirds of the Senate could extend Congress' power beyond the power it has under the Constitution.

Senator ERVIN. Yes: that is held in a multitude of cases. For example, under the Constitution of the United States the Congress has no power to legislate with respect to land titles within borders of the State. That is power reserved to the States by the 10th amendment.

It has been held in, I would surmise, 15 or 20 cases that a treaty of the United States, where the United States enters in a treaty which gives people who are denied the right to own land by State law, that this treaty provision outlaws the State law. It was also held in the *Holland* v. *Missouri* case, that the Congress has no power under the Constitution to regulate hunting within the borders of the State. That was so held by the Supreme Court of the United States. Then Congress made a treaty with Canada under which the United States and Canada agree to protect migratory birds. Then Congress passed a law and held that the law of Congress outlawing the killing of these birds was binding, that since a treaty is the supreme law of the land that the treaty supersedes powers of the States. So there is no question about that.

CAN TREATIES ENLARGE THE POWERS OF THE FEDERAL GOVERNMENT?

Senator JAVITS. I don't find myself in agreement with the Senator on the concept that the Congress does not, under the Constitution, have authority to pass a law respecting genocide. It would have that authority by virtue of this treaty, and I know about the migratory bird case. It has been often argued as the Senator argues, but it has often been argued precisely the other way. It came up in respect of the Bricker amendment. The same argument was made and the Senate turned it down. I agree that a legal question like that, of a highly controversial kind brought up in this regard, brings us into a very complex legal

199

argument: but I think we have to face it. I cannot accept the Senator's conclusion, and let it stand unchallenged, that the constitutional authority of the Congress is enlarged by a treaty.

As to a clear intent to supersede any inconsistent laws, that is another matter, because there is provision for it in the Constitution. But as to enlarging the powers of the Congress, I can't accept that.

Senator ERVIN. Well, I would say to the Senator from New York history shows that is the very reason a provision was made in the Constitution that treaties should be the supreme law of the land. That provision was placed in there as history shows because we had the treaty which ended the war of the revolution between the United States and England, and it secured certain prompted rights of people who had been loyal to the British Crown. The States ignored those things. For example, they had statutes confiscating property of people who were disloyal to the colonists and the State courts upheld the validity of these laws and then they wrote the Constitution to get around the same thing.

They also had a provision barring suits by laws of the States, and the State courts upheld the validity of these statutes of limitations which barred suits by British subjects and the State court denied their claims. And so that was one of the reasons they put this very provision in there.

So in some of the early cases, like a case that arose in the State of Virginia where the British property which had formerly belonged to the British subjects had been confiscated and sold to people who were loyal to Virginia, and claims that the British subjects had held against Virginians were held barred by State law by statute of limitations, and the Supreme Court of the United States held that the treaty with England had the effect of nullifying these laws with the State of Virginia, that British subjects could recover the land that they had lost under these laws and they could bring suit on these claims notwithstanding the fact they were barred by the statute of limitations in the State of Virginia.

And if the distinguished Senator from New York will look at the annotations under the Constitution of the United States, annotations being made by Prof. Edwin S. Corwin, he will find a multitude of cases of this character.

Senator JAVITS. I don't think we should get in a legal argument here but I think the Congress does have the power to deal with offenses against the law of nations, article I, section 8, clause 10 of the Constitution; and, therefore, it could make genocide a crime. Therefore, this treaty does not and would not extend its constitutional power nor could it do so.

Senator COOPER. You are saying, first, that if we do not ratify this convention and the Congress attempted to enact legislation defining "genocide" in the terms that appear in the convention, that, in your view, the Congress would be acting beyond its authority.

Senator ERVIN. Yes.

200

Senator COOPER. The crime would be a State offense with State jurisdiction.

Senator ERVIN. Yes.

Senator COOPER. But then you are saying that if we ratify the convention, then the convention becomes the law of the land.

Senator ERVIN. Yes, sir.

Senator COOPER. And it would convey upon Congress Federal jurisdiction.

Senator ERVIN. That is right.

Surely, the Senate should pause and ponder what the impact of the ratification of the Genocide Convention would have on our system of government.

IMPACT ON CRIMINAL JURISDICTION

3. One of the most drastic impacts of the ratification of the Genocide Convention would have upon our system of government is in the criminal field. To make this transfer of jurisdiction workable, Congress would be required to enact new laws laying down rules of procedure to govern the trial of these newly created Federal and international crimes. Pending the passage of such laws, our country would experience utter confusion in the administration of criminal justice in respect to homicides, assaults and batteries, and kidnapings.

Proponents of ratification may argue that many homicides, assaults and batteries, and kidnapings would not fall within the definition of "genocide." This contention accentuates rather than minimizes the folly of ratifying the Genocide Convention.

As has been pointed out, virtually every person in America falls within one or more of the four groups designated in the Genocide Convention, and any offense denounced by the Genocide Convention against any one of them would ostensibly fall within the scope of the convention. The jurisdiction of the Federal courts under the Genocide Convention would not depend upon what the jury found in particular cases. It would depend upon the allegations made in the indictments or informations charging the offenses.

Consequently, we can reasonably expect that demands will be made that every homicide, every assault and battery inflicting serious injury, and every kidnaping shall be tried in a Federal court, or in an International Court to be established pursuant to the convention. What this will do to increase the congestion in the already overburdened Federal courts of our land beggars description.

In the absence of ratification of the convention, demands have already been made that the United Nations investigate the slaying of Black Panthers by police officers on the ground that their slaying constituted genocide under article II(a) and that the United Nations investigate the action of the legislature of one State in respect to welfare benefits on the ground that the legislative action constituted genocide under article II(c).

201

I respectfully suggest that the Senate should pause and ponder whether it is desirable to ratify a convention which would necessitate a fundamental alteration in the way in which criminal justice has been administered in the United States ever since our country came into existence as a free republic.

When the subcommittee of the Senate Foreign Relations Committee considered the Genocide Convention in 1950, it clearly recognized that ratification of the convention would play havoc with our system of administering criminal justice in respect to domestic crimes made Federal and international crimes by articles II and III, and for this reason decided that the Senate should not ratify the convention in any event without making this declaration:

In giving its advice and consent to the ratification of the Convention on the prevention and punishment of the crime of genocide, the Senate of the United States of America does so considering this to be an exercise of the authority of the Federal Government to define and punish offenses against the law of nations, expressly conferred by article I, section 8, clause 10 of the United States Constitution, and consequently the traditional jurisdiction of the several States of the Union with regard to crime is in no way abridged.

Confusion in the administration of criminal justice in respect to domestic crimes made Federal or international crimes by the Genocide Convention would not disappear with the enactment of legislation by Congress implementing the convention. The validity of this observation may be illustrated by taking a single crime, that of unlawful homicide. Under the Constitution of the United States, Congress does not have the power to make unlawful homicides generally Federal or international crimes. If ratified by the Senate, the Genocide Convention would give Congress this power in respect to homicides constituting genocide under the definition contained in the convention. Jurisdiction to prosecute and punish other unlawful homicides would remain in the State.

CONCURRENT OR EXCLUSIVE JURISDICTION

Senator CHURCH. May I ask at this point another question? If this were to happen and Congress were to pass implementing legislation defining the crime of genocide, would that preempt State jurisdiction? We have many cases where there is Federal jurisdiction and co-existent State jurisdiction in the State courts. In your judgment, would this be a situation where both would exercise concurrent jurisdiction, or would it be a situation in which the Federal jurisdiction would be exclusive?

Senator ERVIN. I think the Federal jurisdiction would clearly be exclusive because the convention places upon Congress the duty to pass laws which will implement the treaty and provide for the punishment or suitable punishment for genocide.

Senator CHURCH. Could Congress confer the jurisdiction jointly to State courts as well as Federal courts?

Senator ERVIN. I do not believe it could, because Congress assumes the word state used in the genocide treaty refers to the United States,

refers to nations, not States. The U.S. Congress, rather the United
States under this genocide treaty would assume the duty as a nation
to punish these offenses which are defined as genocide in this convention, and clearly it would be the duty of the United States to take over
from the States under this the prosecution of these cases.

Senator COOPER. The convention would become the supreme law of
the land.

Senator ERVIN. Yes, sir.

The only distinction between unlawful homicides remaining in the
jurisdiction of the States and unlawful homicides transferred by the
Genocide Convention and acts of Congress implementing it to the
Federal Government would depend upon whether the homicide is
committed with genocidal intent. As a consequence, every unlawful
homicide would apparently be within the jurisdiction of both the Federal and the State Government insofar as the external circumstances
of the slaying are concerned.

Hence, either State or Federal courts could assert jurisdiction in
respect to virtually all homicides, and an acquittal of the charge in one
court would not bar a second prosecution based on the same facts in
the other court. This being true, a person could be twice placed in
jeopardy for the same offense.

The power of a Federal court to try a person for a homicide on the
ground that it constitutes genocide depends upon the allegations of
the indictment and not upon the ultimate finding of the jury. On a trial
in the Federal court, the jury would be compelled to acquit the accused
of genocide unless it found that he acted with the requisite genocidal
intent, no matter how atrocious the circumstances attending the homicide otherwise might be. In such a case, the accused would go un-
whipped of justice unless he was placed upon trial in a State court.

The Senate should be slow to ratify any convention which would
make such confusion in the administration of criminal justice in cases
of this kind.

MEANING OF CONVENTION SHROUDED IN UNCERTAINTY

4. If the Senate should ratify the Genocide Convention, it would
place obligations upon the United States to prosecute and punish as
genocide acts whose nature the convention fails to dispose and to take
steps whose nature the convention fails to reveal.

If the convention is ratified, article II(b) would impose upon the
United States the duty to prevent and to prosecute and punish public
officials and individuals who cause "mental harm to members" of
any one of the four groups named in the convention. What mental
harm means in this context is totally incomprehensible, and what psychological acts or omissions are made punishable in this context are
left in obscurity. When the subcommittee of the Senate Foreign Relations Committee considered the Genocide Convention in 1950, it
reached the conclusion that the Senate ought not to ratify the Genocide
Convention in any event unless it expressed this understanding "that

203

the U.S. Government understands and construes the words 'mental harm' appearing in article II of this convention to mean permanent physical injury to mental faculties."

Senator CHURCH. May I ask if you approved of the wording of that understanding?

Senator ERVIN. Yes, I think the United States would be very foolish to ratify it without putting in this understanding. In fact, I think the United States would be very foolish to ratify it even with this understanding.

If the convention is ratified, article II(c) would impose upon the United States the duty to prevent and to prosecute and punish anyone who deliberately inflicts "on the group conditions of life calculated to bring about its physical destruction in whole or in part." What this means, no mind can fathom. Does it mean that a State or county official who refuses to give to a member of one of the four groups designated in the convention the amount of welfare benefits deemed desirable is to be punished or prosecuted for genocide? Does it mean that the Court of International Justice shall have power under article IX to adjudge that Congress or a State legislature which does not make available to members of one of the four groups what the court deems to be adequate welfare benefits has violated the convention?

If the convention is ratified, article III(c) makes any official or individual in our land punishable for "direct and public incitement to commit genocide." What does this mean? Does it mean that the convention undertakes to make a Senator or a Congressman punishable for genocide if he makes a speech outside of the chamber of his respective House in which he justifies the action of Arabs in killing Jews, or the action of Jews in killing Arabs? Does it undertake to deprive public officials and citizens of America of the right to freedom of speech with respect to matters falling within the terms of the genocide convention?

TREATIES CANNOT TAKE AWAY RIGHTS GUARANTEED BY CONSTITUTION

Senator CHURCH. Could any provision in this convention, any convention, or treaty operate to deny a citizen of the United States rights guaranteed to him under the Constitution?

Senator ERVIN. I would give a negative answer to that question were it not for a case that originated in the city of Chicago. The case was *Terminiello* v. *Chicago*, 337 U.S. 1 and it dealt with an ordinance of the city which made it unlawful for any person to make speeches or issue any literature which made reflections upon any race of men. The defendants were convicted in the courts of Illinois under the ordinance and the case was heard by the U.S. Supreme Court. By a vote of 5 to 4 the Supreme Court declared the ordinance invalid: however, both the majority and the minority indicated that when such speeches present a clear and present danger to incite others, they are not protected by the first amendment. The four dissenting Justices pointed out many cases in this area.

Senator CHURCH. That seems a very strange decision.

Senator ERVIN. It is when you consider the language that might create a precedent declaring the present danger of riots.

Senator CHURCH. That really is not in response to my question. In the decision, you raise a question as to the decision of the court passing upon the first amendment. No treaty was involved in the Chicago case. It was a city ordinance. The question was whether or not the ordinance conflicted with the free speech guaranteed by the first amendment.

Senator ERVIN. That is right.

Senator CHURCH. My question was, no treaty, whether it is this treaty or any other treaty, or no statute of any kind, that undertakes to deny a citizen of the United States rights guaranteed under the Constitution, can do that unless the Supreme Court of the United States decides that the statute is constitutional? In other words, the Constitution stands above both treaties and statutes.

Senator ERVIN. Well, I would say if the Constitution is interpreted correctly that would be my interpretation. But the Supreme Court has indicated particular situations dealing with racial speeches which could be prohibited by an ordinance that denied people the right of freedom of speech. Of course, this is in a field that involves racial questions just like the genocide treaty involves racial questions. If the Court can envision such an ordinance dealing with racial questions, that is can uphold, then the Court can certainly uphold similar legislation enacted by Congress under treaty, or the treaty itself, which is the supreme law of the land.

Senator CHURCH. You are criticizing a decision the Court made rather than the principle that is involved, and the principle is that both treaties and statutes are subject to the Constitution.

Senator ERVIN. Yes. There is only one case that I know that lays down that thing, and I think is sound and that is in the *Reid* case. But there are some other strange decisions that hold under treaties we can provide for the trial of an American service man in a Japanese court where he is denied the right to be indicted by a grand jury, a trial by jury, and that is the *Girard* case which was handed down a few years ago. In other words, I think the Constitution itself says you can't take away a basic right, but the Supreme Court has held to the contrary.

"COMPLICITY IN GENOCIDE"

If the convention is ratified, public officials and private citizens in our land will be subject to punishment in Federal courts or possibly in international penal tribunals to be established under article VI if they are guilty of the undefined offense designate as "complicity in genocide." What is complicity in genocide? The convention does not say.

When the subcommittee of the Senate Foreign Relations Committee considered the convention in 1950, it recognized the vagueness and uncertainty of this proposed Federal and international crime, and rec-

205

ommended that the Senate should not ratify this convention in any event without stating the following reservation "that the U.S. Government understands and construes the words 'complicity in genocide' appearing in article II of this convention to mean participation before and after the fact and aiding and abetting in the commission of the crime of genocide."

If the convention is ratified, article II would impose upon the United States the obligation to prevent and to punish as a crime under international law any act of genocide "whether committed in time of peace or in time of war," and article VIII would permit any party to the convention to call on the United Nations to take such action against the United States under the charter of the United Nations it considers "appropriate for the prevention and suppression of acts of genocide, or any of the other acts enumerated in article III" occurring or likely to occur anywhere in the United States.

What actual obligation does article I impose upon the United States with respect to events occurring either in peace or in war in lands beyond the seas? Does it require the United States to go to war to prevent one nation from killing the nationals of another nation? The convention does not say, but article IX places the power to determine this question in the International Court of Justice.

Does article VIII imply that the United States agrees that the United Nations is to investigate or take action concerning the acts of public officials and individuals occurring within the borders of the United States? The convention does not say, but article IX leaves this determination to the International Court of Justice.

Able lawyers have expressed the fear that article VI imposes upon the Congress an implied commitment to support the creation of an international court for trials of American citizen for genocide. I find myself in complete harmony with their opposition to subjecting our citizens and other persons within our territorial jurisdiction to trial, conviction, and sentence for acts of genocide committed in the United States by an international penal tribunal where they would not be surrounded by the constitutional safeguards and legal rights accorded persons charged with domestic crime.

CONVENTION MAKES SOLDIERS PUNISHABLE FOR SERVING THEIR COUNTRY IN COMBAT

5. If the Senate should ratify the Genocide Convention, it would make American soldiers fighting under the flag of their country in foreign lands triable and punishable in foreign courts—even in courts in our warring enemy—for killing and seriously wounding members of the military forces of our warring enemy.

This is made indisputable by article I which provides that genocide is punishable under the convention whether it is committed in time of peace or in time of war, and by the fact that it contains no provision exempting soldiers engaged in combat from the coverage of the provisions of the convention. When soldiers kill or seriously wound members of a detachment of the military forces of a hostile nation, they certainly do so with intent to destroy, in whole or in part, a national group as such. Hence, their acts in combat fall clearly within the purview of the convention. In such cases, they are triable and punishable under article VI in the courts of the nation in whose territory their acts are committed, or in such an international penal tribunal "as may have jurisdiction with respect to those contracting parties which shall have accepted its jurisdiction."

These things being true, American soldiers killing or seriously wounding North Vietnamese soldiers or members of the Vietcong, or South Vietnamese civilians in South Vietnam, are triable and punishable in courts sitting in South Vietnam, and American aviators who kill North Vietnamese soldiers or civilians in bombing raids upon targets in North Vietnam, and who fall into the hands of the North Vietnamese, are triable and punishable in the courts of North Vietnam. No sophistry can erase this obvious interpretation of the Genocide Convention.

CONVENTION SUBORDINATES THE AMERICAN GOVERNMENT TO THE WORLD COURT

6. If the Senate should ratify the Genocide Convention, article I would impose upon the President, as the Chief Executive of the United States, the duty to enforce both the provisions of the convention and any acts of Congress in implementing them as the supreme law of the land.

Article V would obligate the Congress to enact legislation to give effect to all the provisions of the convention, and to provide effective penalties for persons guilty of genocide or of any of the other acts enumerated in article III, and article VI would obligate the Supreme Court of the United States and all inferior Federal courts created by Congress to interpret and apply all of the provisions of the convention and of the acts of Congress implementing it to cases coming before them under the terms of the convention and the acts of Congress implementing such terms.

7. If the Senate should ratify the Genocide Convention, it would bring into play article IX which provides that disputes between the parties to the convention relating to the "interpretation, application, or fulfillment" of the convention "shall be submitted to the International Court of Justice at the request of any of the parties to the dispute."

Under this article the International Court of Justice would be empowered to decree that the President of the United States, as chief executive officer of the United States, had interpreted and applied the provisions of the convention incorrectly and by so doing impose upon the President of the United States its notions as to how the convention should be interpreted and enforced; the power to adjudge that legislation enacted by Congress to give effect to the provisions of the

207

convention was insufficient to fulfill the obligations imposed upon it by the convention; and the power to adjudge that the Supreme Court of the United States and Federal courts inferior to it had interpreted and applied the provisions of the convention incorrectly and by so doing require these tribunals to apply its notions as to how such provisions should be interpreted and applied to future cases coming before them.

When their attention is called to the drastic powers which the ratification of the Genocide Convention would bestow upon the International Court of Justice in respect to the President, the Congress, and the Supreme Court and other inferior Federal courts, the proponents of ratification assert that these agencies of the Government of the United States do not have to obey the rulings of the International Court of Justice if they deem that such rulings infringe upon the fundamental sovereignty of the United States. In so doing they ignore the solemn obligation assumed by the United States under article 94 of the charter of the United Nations which reads as follows: "Each member of the United Nations undertakes to comply with the decision of the International Court of Justice in any case to which it is a party."

The Charter of the United Nations clearly contemplates that the United Nations will not interfere in the domestic affairs of any nation. The Genocide Convention goes a bow shot beyond the charter of the United Nations.

It undertakes to regulate certain domestic affairs of the parties to it by converting what have always been domestic crimes into international crimes, and confers upon the International Court of Justice the vast powers set forth in article IX.

Consequently, if the Senate should ratify it, the Genocide Convention would render the Connally Reservation, which was designed to prevent the International Court of Justice from exercising jurisdiction over any domestic affair of the United States, inapplicable to any of the matters covered by the convention, and would nullify the Vandenberg Reservation to the jurisdiction of the International Court of Justice which stipulates that American acceptance of compulsory jurisdiction of the Court shall not apply to "disputes arising under a multilateral treaty, unless all parties to the treaty affected by the decision are also parties to the case before the Court, or the United States specially agrees to jurisdiction."

CONCLUDING COMMENTS

What I have said does not militate against the good intentions of those who drafted the Genocide Convention, or those who favor its ratification. All of us are opposed to the systematic, planned annihilation of any national, ethnical, racial, or religious group. The existing laws of the United States and its several States are adequate to punish all of the physical acts of violence denounced by the Genocide Convention. Hence the Senate does not need to ratify the Genocide Convention

208

in order to make these acts punishable as crimes if committed within the borders of our land.

But the Senate should not permit itself to be persuaded by the good intentions of the proponents of ratification to ratify a convention which would have such a tragic impact upon the system of government which has always existed in our land, and which for the first time in our history undertakes to make undefined psychological harms inflicted in some undefined manner Federal and international crimes.

The American Bar Association has twice urged the Senate to reject the Genocide Convention—once in 1949 and again in 1970.

In closing, I urge every member of the Senate to read the booklet entitled "the Convention on the Prevention and Punishment of the Crime of Genocide" prepared by 36 of the most distinguished and patriotic lawyers of America.

When this convention was originally submitted to the Senate for ratification or rejection, one of America's ablest jurists, Orie L. Phillips, Chief Judge of the U.S. Court of Appeals for the Tenth Circuit, wrote an article entitled "The Genocide Convention: Its Effect on our Legal System," which appeared in the American Bar Association Journal for August 1949. I attach a copy of this article to this statement and commend its reading to all of the Members of the Senate.

I would not in the interest of time read his article. I ask that it be printed in the record as a part of my statement.

(The statement follows:)

[From American Bar Association Journal, August 1949]

THE GENOCIDE CONVENTION: ITS EFFECT ON OUR LEGAL SYSTEM

(By Orie L. Phillips, Chief Judge, United States Court of Appeals for the Tenth Circuit)

In this article, Judge Phillips makes a concise, precise, analysis of the terms of the proposed Convention on the Prevention and Punishment of Genocide, and then discusses the effect of the Convention should it be consented to by the Senate. He points out that under the Constitution, a treaty is the supreme law of the land, superior to any state constitution or statute, and any existing federal statute, and that once a treaty has been approved by the Senate no further action is necessary to make it part of the municipal law of every state, binding upon individuals. While recognizing our international responsibilities, Judge Phillips questions the wisdom of this Convention and offers a suggestion that will carry out our international obligations without subjecting individual Americans to trial and conviction by a court that may not operate under the safeguards to an accused accorded by our legal system.

On June 16, 1949, the President transmitted to the Senate the Convention on Genocide with the request that the Senate give is advice and consent to its ratification.

By this Treaty the contracting parties confirm that genocide is, "A crime under international law which they undertake to prevent and punish."

Articles II and III of the Convention read:

209

ARTICLE II

In the present Convention, genocide means any of the following acts committed with intent to destroy, in whole or in part, a national, ethnical, racial or religious group, as such:

(a) Killing members of the group;

(b) Causing serious bodily or mental harm to members of the group;

(c) Deliberately inflicting on the group conditions of life calculated to bring about its physical destruction in whole or in part;

(d) Imposing measures intended to prevent births within the group;

(e) Forcibly transferring children of the group to another group.

ARTICLE III

The following acts shall be punishable:

(a) Genocide;

(b) Conspiracy to commit genocide;

(c) Direct and public incitement to commit genocide;

(d) Attempt to commit genocide;

(e) Complicity in genocide.

Article V obligates the contracting parties to enact the necessary legislation to give effect to the provisions of the Convention and to provide effective penalties "for persons guilty of genocide or any of the other acts enumerated in Article III."

Article VI provides that "persons charged with genocide or any of the other acts enumerated in Article III shall be tried by a competent tribunal of the state" in which the act was committed, or by "such international penal tribunal as may have jurisdiction with respect to such contracting parties which shall have accepted its jurisdiction."

Article IX provides that disputes between the contracting parties relating to the "interpretation, application or fulfillment of the present convention," shall be submitted to the International Court of Justice at the request of any party to the dispute.

Thus, it will be seen that it is proposed by the action of the President, consented to by two-thirds of the Senators present [1] when Senate action is taken, to define certain acts, which have traditionally been regarded as domestic crimes, as international crimes and to obligate the United States to provide for their punishment and for the trial of persons accused thereof either in our domestic courts or in an international tribunal.

Treaty-making power is reviewed

It would seem appropriate, therefore, to review the treaty-making power.

Section 2 of Article II of the United States Constitution authorizes the President by and with the advice and consent of the Senate to make treaties, provided two-thirds of the Senators present concur.

The power is not one granted by the states. Neither did the powers of external sovereignty depend on the affirmative grants of the Constitution. If they had not been mentioned in the Constitution, they would have vested in the Federal Government as necessary concomitants of nationality. They embrace all the powers of government necessary to maintain an effective control of international relations.[2]

". . . the external powers of the United States are to be exercised without regard to state laws or policies."[3]

". . . the field which affects international relations is 'the one aspect of our government that from the first has been most generally conceed imperatively to demand broad national authority.' "[4]

The treaty-making power is not limited by any express provision in the Constitution. But it does not authorize what the Constitution forbids and its exercise must not be inconsistent with the nature of our Government and the relation between the states and the United States.[5]

The treaty-making power is not subject to the limitations imposed by the Constitution on the power of Congress to enact legislation, and treaties may be made which affect rights under the control of the states.[6]

210

Treaty is equivalent to statute

A treaty, entered into in accordance with constitutional requirements, to the extent that it is self-executing, has the force and effect of a legislative enactment and to all intents and purposes is the equivalent of an Act of Congress. In addition to being an international contract, it becomes municipal law of the United States and of each of the states, and the judges of every state are bound thereby, anything in the constitution or laws of any state to the contrary nowithstanding.[7]

In the event of a conflict between a treaty made in accordance with constitutional requirements and the provisions of a state constitution or a state statute, whether enacted prior or subsequently to the making of the treaty, the treaty will control.[8]

But, a treaty may be abrogated by the enactment of a subsequent federal statute which is clearly inconsistent therewith.[9]

Thus, it will be seen that it is proposed that we set out on a course, under a power without express limitation and of broad scope, to enact domestic criminal law, without any concurrence by the House of Representatives, the body traditionally regarded as closest to the people.

Moreover, if the offenses involved should be regarded as international in character by Section 8 of Article I of the United States Constitution, Congress has the power "to define and punish . . . offenses against the law of nations."

Convention would become supreme law of land

Since the Convention in most respects is self-executing, in those respects, on ratification, it would become the supreme law of the land. That would not be true as to any other contracting party except France and a few other states. Even if non-self-executing, the obligation to implement the Treaty by legislation is as binding as the Treaty itself.

It is one of our fundamental concepts that a legislative body, in the exercise of its power to declare what constitutes a crime, must define it so as to inform persons subject thereto, with reasonable precision, what it intends to prohibit so they may have a certain and understandable rule of conduct and know what it is their duty to avoid. "A statute which either forbids or requires the doing of an act in terms so vague that men of common intelligence must necessarily guess at its meaning and differ as to its application, violates the first essential of due process of law."[10]

Do the definitions in Articles II and III of the Convention meet that test?

What is a part of a national, ethnical, racial or religious group—one member, two members, how many?

If an act was done with intent to destroy two members of a group, although actuated by no malice toward the group as such, would that be genocide?

Would it not be more accurate and desirable if the perequisite intent was defined as an act committed with intent to injure one of the enumerated groups as such, so as to make it clear the act must be directed toward the group as such and not merely at an individual member or members thereof?

What is meant by mental harm?

Does not complicity mean the act of an accessory, or to aid, abet, assist, or incite genocide?

A person accused of an offense defined by the Convention, if tried by an international penal tribunal, would not be surrounded by the safeguards we accord persons charged with domestic crimes.

---

1 See Art. II. § 2, United States Constitution.
2 *United States* v. *Curtiss-Wright Corp.*, 299 U.S. 304, 315–318.
3 *United States* v. *Belmont*, 301 U.S. 324, 331.
4 *United States* v. *Pink*, 315 U.S. 203, 232.
5 *Asakura* v. *Seattle*, 265 U.S. 332, 341; *Holden* v. *Joy*, 84 U.S. 211, 243; *Geofroy* v. *Riggs*, 133 U.S. 258, 267.
6 *Missouri* v. *Holland*, 252 U.S. 416, 432.
7 See *Valentine* v. *Neidecker*, 299 U.S. 5, 10; *Whitney* v. *Robertson*, 124 U.S. 190, 194.
8 *Santovincenzo* v. *Egan*, 284 U.S. 30, 40; *Nielsen* v. *Johnson*, 279 U.S. 47, 52.
9 *Whitney* v. *Robertson*, 124 U.S. 190, 195; *Botiller* v. *Dominguez*, 130 U.S. 238, 247; 52 *Am. Jur. Treaties*, 818, § 21; Note, 134 *A.L.R.* 885.
10 *Connally* v. *General Const. Co.*, 269 U.S. 385, 391.

211

Should we ratify convention with reservations?

In the event we ratify the Convention, should we, by reservation, expressly provide that citizens of the United States and persons within the territorial jurisdiction of the United States, charged with an offense defined in the Convention, will be subject to trial and sentence only by a competent judicial tribunal of, and sitting within, the United States, vested with jurisdiction over such offense by federal legislation; that a citizen or other person so charged shall be presumed to be innocent until his guilt has been established by lawful evidence beyond a reasonable doubt; that a citizen or other person so charged shall be protected by all the safeguards embraced within the Constitution of the United States, including the rights guaranteed by the Fourth, Fifth, Sixth, and Eighth Amendments to the Constitution of the United States, to an accused charged with a domestic crime; and that such citizen or other person shall not be subject to be charged, tried, or sentenced by any international penal tribunal? Of course, no international penal tribunal has yet been created, and the advice and consent of the Senate would be necessary to subject our citizens to the jurisdiction of such a tribunal should it be created. But should we not endeavor to close the door to the giving of that advice and consent in the future?

Although the United Nations Charter provides that nothing therein contained shall authorize the United Nations to intervene in matters which are essentially within the domestic jurisdiction of any state, since our representatives have participated in the drafting and approving of the Genocide Convention, if it should thereafter be ratified by the United States, would the matters embraced in such Convention be thereby withdrawn from our domestic jurisdiction?

Should we agree to submit to the International Court of Justice a dispute as to the interpretation, application, or fulfillment of the Convention by us? Suppose a citizen of the United States was charged with one of the offenses defined in the Convention—the group involved being an alien racial group—and tried in a competent tribunal in the United States, and our domestic courts, including the Supreme Court of the United States, should hold the act did not constitute an offense under the Convention. Could the state, of which the alien group were subjects, seek a review as to the interpretation of the treaty in the International Court of Justice? If it could not seek a direct review, could it seek an interpretation by the International Court which would be binding on our domestic courts in the future?

Should we obligate the United States to undertake to prevent and punish genocide in other states? Such seems to be the import of Article I of the Convention.

I assume that no one will deny that the acts defined in the Convention as offenses are abhorrent and the purpose to prevent them wholly commendable. The question is as to the method and means to attain that end.

If genocide and kindred offenses defined in the treaty are in fact international crimes, would not the wise course be to enact domestic legislation under Section 8, Clause 10, Article I of the Constitution of the United States, defining such offenses, and providing for the trial and punishment of persons committing such offenses, in our own domestic courts, where the accused will be guaranteed his constitutional rights and accorded due process under our concept of that phrase? We would thus set our own house in order, would offer the same protection to the accused as one charged with any domestic crime, and would reserve to our own courts the final determination of questions as to the interpretation of the penal statute. To agree, by international convention, to so define, try, and punish persons who commit the offenses which the treaty undertakes to define, would seem to me to wholly fulfill our international obligation, and would avoid many serious questions with respect to the incipient effects of ratification of the Convention on our constitutional and legal system and questions of policy which will arise on a consideration of concurrence by the Senate in the proposed Convention.

Senator CHURCH. Thank you for your statement. I want to apologize for having been a little late, but I was held up on the floor.

212

Senator Ervin. Those things are understandable to us because each of us has 10 times more things to do than we can get around to.

"IN WHOLE OR IN PART"

Senator Cooper. I think the Senator has always provided very helpful comments. I note that your definition of what the crime of genocide would be is, "the annihilation of a whole group."

Now, the convention itself, in article II, says "genocide means any of the following acts committed with intent to destroy in whole or in part."

How would you draw a distinction between destruction of a group "in whole or in part." How would we define it?

Senator Ervin. That is why I think they have distorted the plain meaning of the concept of genocide. In other words, when you undertake to exterminate a group or destroy a group in whole or part, if you destroy one member of it you are destroying it in part. And that is one which makes it go far beyond what true genocide is. If you destroy one member of either one of these four designated groups, because he is a member of one of those four designated groups, you have destroyed the group in part.

Senator Cooper. The question would be determined upon the basis of the intent?

Senator Ervin. Yes.

Senator Cooper. Or the ability to prove intent.

Senator Ervin. Yes.

IMPLEMENTATION OF TREATY

Senator Cooper. Under this convention, if it should be ratified, Congress would have an obligation to enact legislation to make it effective, wouldn't it?

Senator Ervin. Yes, the President assumes that obligation.

Senator Cooper. Now for article V. If the treaty should be ratified, it would be our duty to follow its provisions, not to evade them, is not that so?

Senator Ervin. That is correct.

Senator Cooper. Article V provides that the contracting parties undertake to enact, in accordance with their respective constitutions, the necessary legislation to give effect to the provision of the present convention.

What would occur if the Congress did not enact legislation?

Senator Ervin. Any party to the treaty could go before the International Court of Justice and obtain a decision from that court that the United States had not performed its obligation under the treaty.

Senator Cooper. Article VI provides that "persons charged with genocide or any other acts enumerated in Article II shall be tried by a competent tribunal of the state in the territory of which the act was committed or by such international penal tribunal as may have juris-

213

diction with respect to those contracting parties which shall have accepted its jurisdiction."

There is no such international tribunal. If an American national commits a crime of genocide, as is interpreted in the country where the act is committed, and the American returns to the United States before he is tried, would the United States be under the duty, under the treaty, to return our national to the country where the act was committed?

Senator ERVIN. Yes, because it assumes a duty under the treaty to enact such legislation or to take such action as will be necessary to carry out the terms of the treaty.

Senator COOPER. We had testimony from the State Department. It said in effect, as I understood it, that the Department would not be bound by Article VI, but that extradition would be determined by the terms of an extradition treaty.

Senator ERVIN. Well, Article VI provides that the parties to the treaty pledge themselves in genocide cases to grant extradition in accordance with their laws and treaties. That obligation would rest on the United States, if it had a treaty, for extradition to the particular country which was asking for the custody of these people. But if it didn't have a treaty, Article V would come into play.

Article V obligates the contracting parties to enact the necessary legislation to give effect to the provisions of the convention and to provide—I can stop right there—"to give effect to the provisions of the convention."

One of the provisions of this convention is that a case is going to be tried, a case arising under the convention is going to be tried in the competent court of the territory of the country in whose territory the act was allegedly committed. The State Department to the contrary notwithstanding, I would say, if there is not an extradition treaty in existence that would require us to extradite, it would be the duty of the Congress to pass one for the particular instance because that would be necessary to give effect to the provisions of the convention to the effect that a person committing an act of genocide was to be tried in the court of the nation in whose territory the act of genocide occurred.

In other words, the State Department baffles me why it wants to get a treaty like this ratified and then tries to devise dubious ways to show that you don't have to do what it obligates us to do is something I can't comprehend.

Senator COOPER. One of the problems that concerns me in ratifying the treaty relates to the obligations we undertake in carrying it out. But the arguments we heard concerned methods for evading it.

Senator ERVIN. The convention clearly provides in Article VIII that if you have an extradition treaty it will be carried out, and it provides in Article V if you don't have such a treaty we will enact laws to that effect.

214

OBLIGATION TO EXTRADITE

Senator Church. As I recall, both the State Department witnesses and the Justice Department witnesses were in agreement that our obligation to extradite under the treaty is limited by the treaty's terms only to those countries with which we have established extradition treaties.

Senator Ervin. That is true about the immediate extradition. But under Article V we have contracted to enact the necessary legislation to give effect to the provisions of the convention, and the convention provides that a man is to be tried in the court of the nation in whose territory the alleged act of genocide occurred. So if we don't have a treaty now we are obligated to pass a law to provide for delivering him over to that nation. And neither the State Department with assistance of the Department of Justice can erase that provision in the treaty or destroy its plain meaning.

Senator Cooper. It was suggested by the Department of Justice and the State Department that before an American national could be returned to the state for trial where the alleged offense was committed, that first, as Senator Church said, we must have an extradition treaty with that state, that it must provide that the accused receive the type of due process in the trial in that state as in the United States. Also there would be recourse to habeas corpus in this country for determination whether or not there was probable cause that the crime had been committed.

Senator Ervin. There is not a syllable in the convention that guarantees any American who may be tried in a court of a foreign nation for genocide that he will have any of the safeguards that surround him here. Not a word.

Senator Cooper. Do you think the American national whose extradition was requested by another country could have available to him a writ of habeas corpus.

Senator Ervin. I do not. I do not. Because it would be denied on the ground here the supreme law of the land provides for trial in courts of a foreign country.

Senator Church. Is it not true, Senator, that we presently have extradition treaties with a number of countries? We have promised or assumed the obligations to extradite an American citizen, for instance, for the crime of murder if it were committed in London. We do have treaties by which the American citizen, in conformity with the treaty, would be turned over to the English authorities for trial.

Senator Ervin. That is right.

Senator Church. This, then, doesn't establish a new precedent in that regard?

Senator Ervin. Oh, no, except it puts an obligation on us to provide either by treaty or law for the extradition of people to countries for trial in the courts of a country for genocide where we have no treaty and have no law that would require it or permit it at this time. You can't try a man in a court of a foreign nation without his being there and we say we will do everything necessary to carry out this treaty.

215

So that makes it very clear to me we are obligated to make treaties or enact statutes that accomplish that purpose in cases where we now have no extradition treaties.

Senator COOPER. In what respect would the procedure be different if Congress should enact legislation defining genocide, and a case arose where another state requested extradition of a U.S. national for that crime, and our national went into court for a writ of habeas corpus. Would we still have that same remedy available to an individual to have a determination made by a court of this country whether or not there is a prima facie case before the writ would be honored in cases of extradition?

Senator ERVIN. I believe most extradition treaties provide the only question that can be litigated is the question of whether a man is a fugitive from justice. You might raise it on that question if there is not some prima facie case that doesn't exist that he is not a fugitive from justice. But this treaty does obligate and provides the man is going to be tried in the courts of the nation in whose territory the crime was committed, that we are going to do everything to effect the treaty, and naturally we would have to honor requests for extradition. And if we didn't have a treaty that covers extradition in that country we would have to make a treaty or pass a law.

INTERPRETATION OF TREATY OBLIGATION

Senator COOPER. The argument was made that this provision requiring trial in the state where the crime is committed was not expected to be observed in every case because in the debates in the U.N., as I recall, exceptions were provided for. Would the debate have any effect upon the convention?

Senator ERVIN. I wouldn't think so because here is the trouble. We can't interpret this treaty ourselves, give the firm interpretation to it. The Supreme Court of the United States can't do it. The President or the Congress can't do it. Because the power is given especially to the International Court of Justice, and whatever they say we have to follow.

Senator COOPER. The International Court of Justice cannot enforce it.

Senator ERVIN. No, but it can make decisions and we have promised in the United Nations to abide by any decision they hand down in any case we are a party to.

Senator CHURCH. In view of your own interpretation of the obligation we assume under the treaty goes far beyond the interpretation that the State Department and the Justice Department have given in their testimony, do you think it would be helpful, if this treaty is recommended for ratification, that there be an understanding that the obligation we assume, insofar as extradition is concerned, is limited to those countries with which the United States has established extradition treaties?

Senator ERVIN. No, I don't think so because I think that would nullify the clear intent of the convention. The best thing to do is to not assume the obligation that the convention puts on us in that respect.

Senator CHURCH. You don't think that an understanding then as to the extent of the obligation that is assumed would be helpful, since there is clearly a division of opinion between the Justice Department and State Department and their witnesses and your own opinion?

Senator ERVIN. But article IX says that neither my opinion nor the opinion of the State Department nor the opinion of the Justice Department is controlling, that the opinion of the International Court of Justice is what controls. And that is the danger of the treaty. In other words, we give an international tribunal the power to tell the President of the United States and the Congress of the United States and the courts of the United States what they have to do.

In other words, under article IX it says, the International Court of Justice has supreme and final authority to make all decisions with respect to the interpretation and the application and the fulfillment of the treaty. The International Court of Justice coud say an act of Congress we passed to implement the treaty doesn't fulfill our obligation.

Senator JAVITS. Senator Ervin, is it your contention that this is the first time the United States will have granted this type of jurisdiction to the International Court of Justice.

CONNALLY AND VANDENBERG RESERVATIONS TO WORLD COURT JURISDICTION

Senator ERVIN. I think it is in a treaty with terminology as vague as the Genocide Convention. In the first place, what would be made international crimes under this convention are now domestic crimes in the United States. As you know, the Senate adopted the Connally reservation which was designed to let the United States be the judge of what falls within the domestic jurisdiction of the United States. This would bypass and render the Connally reservation inapplicable because it takes and gives jurisdiction to the World Court over things which are within the domestic jurisdiction of the United States. So the Connally reservation would be rendered inapplicable and the Vandenberg reservation as I understand it, means we do not consent to the compulsory jurisdiction of the Court except in one or two instances, and the first is that all of the nations that are parties to a multilateral treaty must be parties to the case. This expressly says any party out of the 50 or 60 or 70 parties to the convention can take us before the International Court of Justice. The Vandenberg resolution says that requirement about all of the parties to the treaty being parties to the case can be waived by the United States by specially agreeing, but this would nullify the Vandenberg reservation, it would render the Connally reservation inapplicable.

Senator JAVITS. Wouldn't you agree that we have already accepted jurisdiction of a court—even if we dissented in the treaty—on Antarctica and the treaty regarding slavery, and that the Congress has an

217

absolute right, just as it has a right to make the Vandenberg reservation, to agree to whatever jurisdiction it wishes in a new treaty? If this is desirable in the interests of restraining others as well as ourselves, there is no inherent authority which dictates that we can't do it, is there?

Senator ERVIN. I don't know the treaty you are talking about, either one of the treaties. I am not familiar with the terms. I was under the impression that the treaty about forced labor and slavery had not been ratified by the United States.

Senator JAVITS. I believe it has and, Mr. Chairman, I ask unanimous consent that I may introduce at this point in the record provisions of other treaties accepting the jurisdiction of the International Court of Justice.

Senator ERVIN. I would venture to suggest that those treaties say what they are about. They tell us what acts are covered by them. Certainly slavery is a very well understood term.

Senator CHURCH. Without objection, the list of treaties containing the provisions which the Senator has referred will be incorporated.

(The information follows:)

TREATIES AND OTHER INTERNATIONAL AGREEMENTS OF THE UNITED STATES CONTAINING PROVISIONS FOR SUBMISSION OF DISPUTES TO THE INTERNATIONAL COURT OF JUSTICE, AS OF MAY 22, 1970

I. MULTILATERAL

Protocol on military obligations in certain cases of double nationality, concluded at The Hague, April 12, 1930: 50 Stat. 1317; TS 913.[1]

Convention for limiting the manufacture and regulation of narcotic drugs, concluded at Geneva, July 13, 1931: 48 Stat. 1543; TS 863.[1]

Convention on international civil aviation (ICAO), opened for signature at Chicago December 7, 1944: 61 Stat. 1180; TIAS 1591.[1][2]

Constitution of the Food and Agriculture Organization of the United Nations (FAO), signed at Quebec October 16, 1945 as amended (1950): 60 Stat. 1886; TIAS 1554, 12 UST 980; TIAS 4803.

Constitution of the United Nations Educational, Scientific, and Cultural Organization (UNESCO), concluded at London November 16, 1945: 61 Stat. 2495; TIAS 1580.

Convention on the Privileges and Immunities of the United Nations, dated February 13, 1946: 1 UNTS 16.

Constitution of the World Health Organization (WHO), opened for signature at New York July 22, 1946: 62 Stat. (3) 2679; TIAS 1808.

Instrument for the amendment of the constitution of the International Labor Organization (ILO), dated at Montreal October 9, 1946: 62 Stat. 3485; TIAS 1868.

Convention on Road Traffic, dated at Geneva September 19, 1949: 3 UST 3008; TIAS 2487.

International Sanitary Regulations (WHO Regulations No. 2), adopted by the Fourth World Assembly at Geneva May 25, 1951: 7 UST 2255; TIAS 3625.

Treaty of Peace with Japan, signed at San Francisco September 8, 1951: 3 UST 3169; TIAS 2490.

Universal copyright convention, dated at Geneva September 6, 1952: 6 UST 2731; TIAS 3324.

---

[1] By reference to the PCIJ. (References to the ICJ in place of the PCIJ in these cases is provided for by Article 37 of the Statute of the ICJ.).
[2] Appeals procedure from decision of the Council permits reference to the PCIJ (ICJ) if parties to dispute have accepted the Statute of the PCIJ (ICJ).

218

Constitution of the Intergovernmental Committee for European Migration (ICEM) : 6 UST 603; TIAS 3197.

Protocol amending the slavery convention of September 25, 1926 (46 Stat. 2183; TS 778), opened for signature at New York December 7, 1953: UST 479; TIAS 3532.

Protocol limiting and regulating the cultivation of the poppy plant and the production of, and international and wholesale trade in, and use of opium, open for signature at New York from June 23 to December 31, 1953: 14 UST 10; TIAS 5273.

International convention for the prevention of pollution of the sea by oil, signed at London May 12, 1954: 12 UST 2989; TIAS 4900.

Supplementary convention on the abolition of slavery, the slave trade, and institutions and practices similar to slavery. Done at Geneva September 7, 1956: 18 UST 3201; TIAS 6418.

Statute of the International Atomic Energy Agency, done at New York October 26, 1956: 8 UST 1093; TIAS 3873.

The Antarctic Treaty, signed at Washington December 1, 1969:[3] 12 UST 794; TIAS 4780.

Constitution of the International Rice Commission as amended at Saigon. November 19, 1960: 13 UST 2403; TIAS 5204.

Agreement for establishment of the Indo-Pacific Fisheries Council as amended at Karachi January 6–23, 1961: 13 UST 2511; TIAS 5218.

Agreement for facilitating the international circulation of visual and auditory materials of an educational, scientific and cultural character, done at Lake Success July 15, 1949: TIAS 6116; 17 UST 1578.

Convention on the settlement of investment disputes between states and nationals of other states, done at Washington March 18, 1965: 17 UST 1270; TIAS 6090.

Single convention on narcotics drugs, 1961, done at New York March 30, 1961: TIAS 6298; 18 UST 1407.

Protocol relating to the status of refugees. Done at New York January 31, 1967: TIAS 6577; 19 UST 6223.

Optional protocol to the Vienna convention on consular relations concerning the compulsory settlement of disputes. Done at Vienna April 24, 1963: TIAS 6820; 21 UST.

Convention on offenses and certain other acts committed on board aircraft. Done at Tokyo September 14, 1963: 20 UST 2941; TIAS 6768.

APPENDIX I.—A

The agreement of Paris, on reparation from Germany, on the establishment of an inter-Allied reparation agency and on restitution of monetary gold, opened for signature at Paris January 14, 1946 (61 Stat. (3) 3157; TIAS 1655), was signed on behalf of the United States on that date. It is followed by a *Resolution No. 8 on recourse to the International Court of Justice:* "The Delegates of Albania, Australia, Belgium, Denmark, France, Luxembourg, the Netherlands, Norway, Czechoslovakia and Yugoslavia recommend that: 'Subject to the provisions of Article 3 of Part I of the foregoing Agreement, the Signatory Governments agree to have recourse to the International Court of Justice for the solution of every conflict of law or competence arising out of the provisions of the foregoing Agreement which has not been submitted to the Parties concerned to amicable solution or arbitration.' " (*Department of State Bulletin*, January 27, 1946, p. 124).

All the other signatories to the Paris agreement had advised of their accession to this Resolution, as of July 22, 1948.

---

[3] Reference to the ICJ is subject to consent, in each case, of all parties to the dispute.

219

APPENDIX I.—B

With respect to the four Geneva conventions of August 12, 1949, for the protection of war victims, relating to: Condition of wounded and sick of the armed forces in the field (6 UST 3114; TIAS 3362); condition of wounded, sick or shipwrecked members of the armed forces at sea (6 UST 3217; TIAS 3363); treatment of prisoners of war (6 UST 3316; TIAS 3364); and protection of civilian persons in time of war (6 UST 3516; TIAS 3365). The following resolution was adopted on August 12, 1949, by the Conference of Geneva:

Resolution I.—The Conference recommends that, in the case of a dispute relating to the interpretation or application of the present Conventions which cannot be settled by other means, the High Contracting Parties concerned endeavor to agree between themselves to refer such dispute to the International Court of Justice.

II. BILATERAL

A. Commercial treaties with:

Country and date	*Treaty*
Belgium, Feb. 21, 1961	14 UST 1284; TIAS 5432
China, Nov. 4, 1946	63 Stat. (2) 1299; TIAS 1871
Denmark, Oct. 1, 1951	12 UST 908; TIAS 4797
Ethiopia, Sept. 7, 1951	4 UST 2134; TIAS 2864
France, Nov. 25, 1959	11 UST 2398; TIAS 4625
Germany, F.R., Oct. 29, 1954	7 UST 1839; TIAS 3593
Greece, Aug. 3, 1951	5 UST (2) 1829; TIAS 3057
Iran, Aug. 15, 1955	8 UST 899; TIAS 3853
Ireland, Jan. 21, 1950	1 UST 785; TIAS 2155
Israel, Aug. 23, 1951	5 UST 550; TIAS 2948
Italy, Feb. 2, 1948	63 Stat. (2) 2255; TIAS 1965
Japan, Apr. 2, 1953	4 UST 2063; TIAS 2863
Korea, Nov. 28, 1956	8 UST 2217; TIAS 3947
Luxembourg, Feb. 23, 1962	14 UST 261; TIAS 5306
Netherlands, Mar. 27, 1956	8 UST 2043; TIAS 3942
Nicaragua, Jan. 21, 1956	9 UST 449; TIAS 4024
Pakistan, Nov. 12, 1959	12 UST 110; TIAS 4683
Togo, Feb. 8, 1966	TIAS 6193; 18 UST 1
Viet-Nam, Apr. 3, 1961	12 UST 1703; TIAS 4890

B. Other bilateral agreements: [4]
Treaty with Canada relating to cooperative development of water resources of the Columbia River
Basin, Jan. 17, 1961 _____ 15 UST 1555; TIAS 5638
Consular Convention with Korea, Jan. 8, 1963____ 14 UST 1637; TIAS 5469

ANALYSIS OF TESTIMONY

Senator JAVITS. I would like to point out that I think the statement made by Senator Ervin gives us the most extreme interpretation of every aspect of this convention, as I will demonstrate in a moment; therefore, I wonder whether or not—and I will demonstrate this—I wonder whether Senator Ervin might be good enough to consider

---

[4] In addition, the United States concluded economic cooperation and aid agreements with 17 countries in 1948 which contain provisions for referral of disputes to the International Court of Justice subject, however, to the self-judging domestic jurisdiction reservation of the United States.

Source: Stat.—United States Statutes at Large. UST—United States Treaties and Other International Agreements (volumes published on a yearly basis beginning January 1, 1950). TIAS—Treaties and Other International Acts Series, issued singly in pamphlets by the Department of State.

the opportunity to analyze his testimony which makes a lot of charges of a most drastic kind.

Perhaps he would be good enough to come back after we have had a chance to study and to perhaps prepare some law, just as he has obviously prepared very closely on these very drastic charges.

Among these charges, for example, Mr. Chairman, is the statement on page 7 of Senator Ervin's statement about article II of the convention, that "if the Senate should ratify the genocide convention, the duty and the power to prosecute and punish criminal homicides, assaults and batteries, and kidnapings covered by categories (a), (b), an d(e) of article II of the convention would be forthwith transferred from the States which have always had such duty and power in respect to these crimes to the Federal Government."

In short, the Senator asks us to believe we would thereby be depriving every State court of a power to try cases involving homicides, assaults, batteries, and kidnaping because he himself argues——

Senator ERVIN. Wait a minute. I said it came within those three definitions, that would be genocide.

Senator JAVITS. I am coming to that—because he himself argues that the question of intent can only be tried in the Federal court and, therefore, that you wouldn't know whether or not a case came within those categories until you first tried every one of those prisoners in the Federal court; so it is argued that the word "forthwith" means literally that every State court would be immediately deprived of jurisdiction.

Second, on page 9, the Senator says, "Under the Constitution of the United States, Congress does not have the power to make unlawful homicides generally Federal or international crimes."

Now I would like to find out how it is that we already have so many crimes for killing under the Federal laws: and I don't know what the Senator means by homicides generally. Perhaps he would explain that. As I understand it, many kinds of killings are punished under the Federal laws; and we pass laws quite regularly which deal with killings as the result of Federal law. What is so unusual about that?

The third point is the statement on page 12. This is but a sample. "Does it require the United States to go to war to prevent one nation from killing the nationals of another nation? The convention does not say, but article IX places the power to determine this question," to wit, whether the United States shall go to war, in the International Court of Justice.

With all respect these statements are so extreme, as a sample, that I think we ought to have an opportunity—if this is the heinous thing we are going to do to our country—to analyze this statement, to check up on the law as carefully as Senator Ervin has done, and then, if the Senator would then be good enough, after we have both had an even chance, to respond to questions on this subject. I think the charge is so strong and so extreme it puts the questioners at a great disadvantage. You make a big charge and in 2 minutes we are supposed to think

221

up the whole body of law which represents the negation of that charge.
So I think we ought to have another chance.

Senator ERVIN. I would welcome a chance to come back and quote
to the committee.

I would say just in replying to part in your statement, I challenge
you to find any Federal statute that makes the crime of killing a Federal crime that is not related, confined to a killing that has some relation to a Federal purpose, to the thought of Federal purpose or on
Federal territory or to prohibit a killing on account of some constitutional right under the Federal Constitution.

Senator JAVITS. I am glad the Senator has refined somewhat his
very general statement, to wit, homicide generally; but I think it still
leaves us with the need for a rather through scrutiny of his statement, as I say, which makes such condign broad charges and conclusions, so that we may really deal with the questioning in an intelligent
way.

Senator CHURCH. It is best not to pass on the question of whether
or not the subcommittee will convene again until the members confer.
This meeting was held in order to oblige the Senator from North
Carolina who has had a long standing interest in the treaty and we
wanted to give him an opportunity to testify.

If it is decided that another meeting should be held, we will get
back in touch with you, Senator, and make an arrangement. In any
case, the charges you have raised against the treaty would be very,
very carefully considered prior to the time that any action is taken
by the subcommittee or the full committee.

Senator ERVIN. I just want to thank the chairman and other members of the subcommittee for making it possible for me to be here and
present my views on the subject.

POSSIBLE RESERVATIONS OR UNDERSTANDINGS

Senator JAVITS. Could I ask one thing. Would you think that you
could draft a set of reservations or understandings, in view of the fact
that you join in the universal humanitarian condemnation of what is
essentially proposed as the objective of this treaty, and you say "all of
us are opposed to the systemtic, planned annihilation of any national,
ethnical, racial or religious group"? That is on page 16.

Would you feel that you might be able to draft what you would consider to be an appropriate set of understandings and/or reservations
so that the Senate, if it thought it advisable, could ratify this highly
desirable humanitarian covenant?

Senator ERVIN. It would be difficult to draw as many reservations
that would protect the sovereignty of the United States against this
treaty. I have seven or eight in mind but the easy way to handle this
treaty is reject the treaty entirely.

Senator JAVITS. Wouldn't that run down the drain the great humanitarian objective which you yourself think is a very fine thing?

Senator ERVIN. I think that most civilized nations have got laws.

222

against what is true genocide. Not only that, they have laws against murdering anybody.

Senator JAVITS. Well I have little doubt, Senator, that Germany before and after Hitler had laws which dealt with the subject, but it didn't seem to prevent the greatest holocaust known to man.

Senator ERVIN. Yes, sir; I agree, I don't think if they had a genocide treaty it would have kept it down.

Senator JAVITS. At least there would have been some recognition of the fact that the world learns from experience, and is not sentenced, as those who refused to learn from experience, are sentenced to relive it.

Mr. Chairman, I must say that Senator Ervin is one of our finest lawyers, and I would hope very much also that we might enlist him after the give and take. Both he and I are experienced trial lawyers, and anything I have said would not one wit detract from my respect for Senator Ervin and his ability. I would hope perhaps we could, by this very process of attrition, come to some conclusion and get some clear idea as to what a man like the Senator would consider necessary, in his judgment, to enable us not to turn down such a longstanding and decently human effort, but to approve it.

(The following point-by-point rebuttal was subsequently submitted by Senator Javits:)

POINT-BY-POINT REBUTTAL

1. Senator Ervin argued that it would be particularly unwise for the United States to ratify the Genocide Convention at a time "when it is manifest that a substantial part of the American people wish to contract rather than expand their international obligations."

Answer: One must distinguish between different kinds of international obligations. It is true that many people have argued that American military commitments should be contracted. This view, however, does not entail the further argument that the development of international law should be halted. Treaties of a great variety of kinds not involving military commitments have been negotiated and have provided for more ordered relations among nations. It is hard to imagine that one would argue against the Genocide Convention on the grounds that it expands American international obligations.

2. Senator Ervin argues that under the Genocide Convention "individuals as well as persons exercising governmental power would be subject to trial and punishment for offenses which have always been regarded as matters falling within the domestic jurisdiction of the various nations."

Answer: The protection of human rights is indeed a matter of international concern. The United States has shown that it agrees with this view by ratifying the World War II peace treaties, the United Nations Charter, the Slavery Convention of 1926, and more recently the Supplementary Convention on Slavery (1967) and the Supplementary Convention on Refugees (1968).

3. Senator Ervin argues that the only reason for ratifying the Genocide Convention now is that "it would improve the image of the United States in the eyes of Russia and other totalitarian parties to the Convention, which, strange to say, have repudiated by understandings and reservations many of the provisions of the Convention."

Answer: The Convention should be ratified because the United States is unequivocally opposed to genocide. As the President in his message pointed out, U.S. ratification would be the "final convincing step that would reaffirm that the United States remains as strongly opposed to the crime of genocide as ever." U.S. ratification is long overdue.

In addition, many of the arguments against ratification have since 1950 been shown clearly to be invalid. For example, it is now clearly established that

223

the crime of genocide is a legitimate subject for an international treaty. Seventy-five nations have already become parties to the Genocide Convention.

It is not clear which reservations Senator Ervin makes reference to when he argues Russia and others have repudiated many of the treaty's provisions. The only reservation which the Eastern bloc countries have made that cuts down a provision of the treaty has the effect of requiring agreement of all parties to a dispute before that dispute is submitted to the International Court of Justice under article IX of the Convention. This does not affect the substantive provisions of the treaty. The bloc countries have made similar reservations to numerous other treaties to which the United States is a party.

4. Senator Ervin argues that the treaty is deficient in that it does not embody the real meaning of the term "genocide." He believes the term contemplates the complete wiping out of a designated group.

Answer: It is entirely legitimate that the term "genocide" be defined in the convention for the purposes of the Convention. "Genocide" was a new term and the definition in the Convention represented the international consensus on its meaning. It seems futile to look beyond that for the "true" meaning of the term.

Does Senator Ervin really believe that an entire group must be wiped out before it is fair to say genocide has occurred? This view would seem extreme.

5. Senator Ervin argues that, whether or not the provisions of the convention are self-executing, they would immediately supersede all State laws and practices inconsistent with them and thereby deprive the States of the power to prosecute and punish in their courts acts condemned by articles II and III of the Convention.

Answer: The Convention is clearly non-self-executing in view of the requirement of article V to enact the necessary implementing legislation. The administration intends to await enactment of such legislation by the Congress before depositing our ratification and thus becoming a party to the Convention. If there is supersession of any inconsistent State laws, it will be by the Federal legislation, not by the convention. It is difficult to imagine in what way any existing State law or practice could be inconsistent with the Convention.

The enactment of implementing legislation for the Genocide Convention by the Congress need not automatically preclude the States from prosecuting the acts proscribed by the Convention. Whether or not a congressional act preempts an area of law depends on the intent of Congress. If, as could be reasonably argued, Congress did not intend completely to fill this area of law, States would be free to continue to act in this area. To ensure that States would still have such freedom, the Congress could provide in its implementing legislation that nothing in that legislation should be construed as indicating an intent on the part of Congress to occupy, to the exclusion of State or local laws on the same subject matter, the field in which the provisions of the legislation operate.

6. Senator Ervin argues that the Convention could somehow alter the powers of the Congress under the Federal Constitution.

Answer: The Congress has the power under the necessary and proper clause of the Constitution to enact legislation necessary to implement a valid treaty. *Missouri* v. *Holland*, 252 U.S. 416, 432 (1920). The Genocide Convention would not, however, provide an example of a case where Congress would lack the power to enact the required implementing legislation absent the treaty. Genocide is a crime against the laws of nations. Congress is explicitly given the power to define such crimes under article I, section 8, clause 10, of the Constitution. The Genocide Convention would, although entered into under the treaty power (art. II, sec. 2, clause 2), require implementing legislation. The fact that Congress enacts a statute pursuant to a treaty, instead of under its otherwise delegated powers, does not alter its competence.

7. Senator Ervin argues that ratification of the Genocide Convention would have a drastic effect on our whole system of criminal justice because many crimes which are now crimes under State law could, with the addition of an allegation with respect to intent, be made Federal crimes. This, he argues, would create a situation where it would be uncertain whether it was appropriate to go to a Federal or State court, and would allow for dual prosecution of defendants.

Answer: The intent requirements for the crime of genocide are set forth in article II. In order for genocide to be committed, an act must be directed against the individuals involved qua members of a particular group, and there must be a specific intent to destroy the group as such in whole or in part. It would be reasonably difficult to prove this intent element in ordinary homicide cases, and it would seem far-fetched that United States attorneys would institute a large number of unfounded prosecutions. If an unfounded prosecution were instituted, Federal criminal procedure provides many safeguards to ensure that the prosecution would be dismissed. Since the standard is so stringent. It is not reasonable to argue that a major incursion into areas of State law would occur.

8. Senator Ervin suggests that, under article II(c) of the Genocide Convention, State or county officials, who refuse to give a member of one of the four designated groups the amount of welfare benefits deemed desirable, may be prosecuted for genocide.

Answer: Article II(c) of the Convention provides that one of the ways of committing genocide is by "deliberately inflicting on the group conditions of life calculated to bring about its physical destruction in whole or in part." This provision is aimed at conditions of life inflicted upon the group which are meant to cause death or grave bodily injury. Generally speaking, the provision covers "slow death" measures. See P. Drost, The Crime of State—Genocide, pp. 86–87 (1959). Denial of adequate welfare benefits is of a completely different magnitude than measures calculated to bring about slow death. In addition, the requisite intent to destroy in whole or in part the members of a group (see answer 7) would be lacking.

9. Senator Ervin argues that the provision of article III(c), which makes direct and public incitement to commit genocide punishable, might deprive public officials and citizens of America of the right of free speech.

Answer: Under current law, while mere advocacy of illegal activities may well be protected by the first amendment, direct and public incitement to commit illegal activity is surely not protected. See, e.g., *Brandenburg* v. *Ohio*, 395 U.S. 444, 447 (1969). Incitement crosses the bounds between protected and unprotected speech. The provision of the Genocide Convention therefore does not violate the Constitution. Moreover, were there any conflict, the first amendment clearly would control. *Reid* v. *Covert*, 354 U.S. 1 (1957) ; *Geofroy* v. *Riggs*, 133 U.S. 258 (1890).

10. Senator Ervin asks what is meant in article III(e) by "complicity in genocide."

Answer: The prohibition against the complicity is clearly aimed at accessoryship in crime of genocide, as defined in article II (not the other genocide acts listed in article III). When Congress enacts implementing legislation for the Genocide Convention, it will not be necessary to enact a special provision implementing article III(e) because accessoryship in Federal crimes is already outlawed by the United States Code. 18 U.S.C. §§ 2, 3 (1964).

11. Senator Ervin believes that the term "mental harm" in article II(b) of the convention is totally incomprehensible.

Answer: "Mental harm" means—and the administration has proposed an understanding to make this clear—permanent impairment of mental faculties. Thus, before a charge can be sustained, it must be proved that permanent impairment of mental faculties in fact occurred and that the defendant brought about this injury with the specific intent of destroying one of the protected groups. Thus, the standard is rigid enough to protect against frivolous allegations of genocide.

12. Senator Ervin seems troubled that article VIII of the convention would allow any contracting party to call upon the competent organs of the United Nations to take appropriate action for the prevention and suppression of genocide.

Answer: Article VIII does not, and indeed could not, change the jurisdiction of the United Nations. It merely confirmed the existing situation: members of the United Nations may already go to competent organs in appropriate cases.

13. Senator Ervin fears that article I of the Genocide Convention could require the United States to go to war to prevent the crime of genocide.

Answer: Article I confirms the principle expressed in Resolution 96(1) of the

United Nations General Assembly that genocide is a crime under international law in time of peace or in time of war. The parties to the convention undertake to prevent and punish this crime in the manner set forth in subsequent articles of the convention. Aside from this declaration, the article has no substantive effect, the main operative provisions being contained in articles II–VII.

14. Senator Ervin argues that article VI imposes upon the Congress an implied commitment to support the creation of an international penal tribunal.

Answer: In the more than 20 years since the Convention was adopted no international penal tribunal has been created. While one was proposed at the time of the drafting of the convention, this proposal has long been dormant and there is no reason to suspect that it will be revived. If such a court were proposed in the future, Senate advice and consent would at that time be necessary for the United States to adhere to the treaty establishing the court and accept its jurisdiction. The Convention clearly would not require the United States to accept the jurisdiction of such a court.

15. Senator Ervin argues that the Genocide Convention would make American soldiers fighting abroad triable in the courts of our enemies for killing or seriously wounding members of the enemies' military forces.

Answer: First, it should be pointed out that combat actions of American troops against enemies do not constitute genocide. For example, it is difficult to conceive that acts committed by U.S. troops in Vietnam could fall within the definition of genocide in article II. The article requires an "intent to destroy, in whole or in part, national, ethnical, racial, or religious groups, as such." Our soldiers are fighting to help the South Vietnamese defend themselves and therefore acts committed against other Vietnamese would not constitute genocide.

Of course, American soldiers who are captive in the country of an enemy of the United States could be subjected to prosecution by the enemy country for the crime of genocide regardless of whether the United States has ratified the Genocide Convention. Although we would feel such treatment entirely unjustified, we would be powerless to do anything about it other than to protest to the country or to the U.N. The action of the Senate, in giving its advice and consent to ratification, would therefore have no relevance to this question.

16. Senator Ervin dislikes the fact that the Genocide Convention provides in article IX that disputes between parties relating to the Convention's "interpretation, application, or fulfillment" shall be submitted to the International Court of Justice. He believes this provision nullifies the Connally and Vandenberg reservations to the jurisdiction of the Court.

Answer: Article IX is an entirely appropriate provision. The United States has, in many cases in its treaties, provided that disputes relating to interpretation, application, and fulfillment of a treaty shall be referred to the ICJ. Recent examples where the Senate approved similar provisions are the Convention on the Privileges and Immunities of the United Nations (1970), the Refugee Protocol (1968), and the Supplementary Slavery Convention (1967). A list of treaties with similar provisions has been included in the record of these hearings.

Article IX does not nullify the Connally or Vandenberg reservations. The Connally amendment, or self-judging aspect of our domestic jurisdiction reservation, could be employed to prevent the International Court of Justice from deciding a case brought against the United States based on our 1946 across-the-board acceptance of compulsory jurisdiction to any international legal dispute under paragraph 2 of article 36 of the Court's statute. The Vandenberg reservation, or multilateral treaty reservation, could prevent jurisdiction under the same paragraph of the statute in cases arising out of a multilateral treaty where all the parties affected by the decision are not parties to the case or the United States has not specifically agreed to jurisdiction. These reservations could not, however, be invoked under article IX of the Genocide Convention since the basis for the Court's jurisdiction would be paragraph 1 of article 36 of the statute, which gives the Court jurisdiction to decide legal disputes "specifically provided for . . . in treaties and conventions in force." Article IX of the convention thus has the effect of avoiding the application of the reservations in the extremely small class of potential cases that may arise from unresolved differences over the interpretation, application, or fulfillment of the convention.

Senator ERVIN. I would be pleased to draw the same reservations that the subcommittee of the Foreign Relations Committee suggested in 1950. I would be glad to draw a reservation such as Judge Phillips said: No American is going to be tried for any act of genocide in this country except in Federal courts where he would have the right secured to him by the Bill of Rights. I would be glad to do like the Russians and a large percentage of the other nations of the world, draw a reservation to the effect that article IX doesn't apply to us.

Senator CHURCH. Some of the understandings to which you have referred are in your testimony and, of course, they are available to this subcommittee.

It has the full record of the previous hearings and all of them will be taken under advisement.

Senator ERVIN. I will be glad to draw the other two and submit them to the committee. I am available to the committee.

Senator CHURCH. Thank you very much. We will be in touch with you.

(Whereupon, at 3:25 p.m., the committee was adjourned.)

APPENDIX III

94TH CONGRESS
2D SESSION

S. 3155

IN THE SENATE OF THE UNITED STATES

MARCH 17, 1976

Mr. HUGH SCOTT (for himself and Mr. JAVITS) introduced the following bill;
which was read twice and referred to the Committee on the Judiciary

---

A BILL

To implement the Convention on the Prevention and Punishment of the Crime of Genocide.

1   *Be it enacted by the Senate and House of Representa-*

2 *tives of the United States of America in Congress assembled,*

3 That (a) title 18, United States Code, is amended by adding

4 after chapter 50 the following new chapter:

5   "Chapter 50A.—GENOCIDE

"Sec.
"1091. Definitions.
"1092. Genocide.

6 "§ 1091. Definitions

7   "As used in this chapter—

8   "(1) 'National group' means a set of persons whose

9 identity as such is distinctive in terms of nationality or

II

2

1   national origins from the other groups or sets of persons

2   forming the population of the nation of which it is a part

3   or from the groups or sets of persons forming the interna-

4   tional community of nations.

5   "(2) 'Ethnic group' means a set of persons whose

6   identity as such is distinctive in terms of its common cultural

7   traditions or heritage from the other groups or sets of persons

8   forming the population of the nation of which it is a part or

9   from the groups or sets of persons forming the international

10 community of nations.

11   "(3) 'Racial group' means a set of persons whose iden-

12 tity as such is distinctive in terms of race, color of skin, or

13 other physical characteristics from the other groups or sets

14 of persons forming the population of the nation of which

15 it is a part or from the groups or sets of persons forming

16 the international community of nations.

17   "(4) 'Religious group' means a set of persons whose

18 identity as such is distinctive in terms of its common reli-

19 gious creed, beliefs, doctrines, or rituals from the other

20 groups or sets of persons forming the population of the na-

21 tion of which it is a part or from the groups or sets of

22 persons forming the international community of nations.

23   "(5) 'Substantial part' means a part of the group of

24 such numerical significance that the destruction or loss of

3

1 that part would cause the destruction of the group as a

2 viable entity.

3 "(6) 'Children' means persons who have not attained

4 the age of eighteen and who are legally subject to the care,

5 custody, and control of their parents or of an adult of the

6 group standing in loco parentis.

7 "§ 1092. Genocide

8 "(a) Whoever, being a national of the United States

9 or otherwise under or within the jurisdiction of the United

10 States, willfully without justifiable cause, commits, within

11 or without the territory of the United States in time of

12 peace or in time of war, any of the following acts with the

13 intent to destroy by means of the commission of that act,

14 or with the intent to carry out a plan to destroy, the whole

15 or a substantial part of a national, ethnic, racial, or religious

16 group shall be guilty of genocide:

17   "(1) kills members of the group;

18   "(2) causes serious bodily injury to members of the

19   group;

20   "(3) causes the permanent impairment of the men-

21   tal faculties of members of the group by means of tor-

22   ture, deprivation of physical or physiological needs, sur-

23   gical operation, introduction of drugs or other foreign

24   substances into the bodies of such members, or subjec-

4

1   tion to psychological or psychiatric treatment calculated

2   to permanently impair the mental processes, or nervous

3   system, or motor functions of such members;

4   "(4) subjects the group to cruel, unusual, or inhu-

5   mane conditions of life calculated to bring about the

6   physical destruction of the group or a substantial part

7   thereof;

8   "(5) imposes measures calculated to prevent birth

9   within the group as a means of effecting the destruction

10   of the group as such; or

11   "(6) transfers by force the children of the group

12   to another group, as a means of effecting the destruction

13   of the group as such.

14   "(b) Whoever is guilty of genocide or of an attempt to

15   commit genocide shall be fined not more than $20,000, or

16   imprisoned for not more than twenty years, or both; and if

17   death results shall be subject to imprisonment for any term

18   of years or life imprisonment. Whoever directly and publicly

19   incites another to commit genocide shall be fined not more

20   than $10,000 or imprisoned not more than five years, or both.

21   "(c) The intent described in subsection (a) of this

22   section is a separate element of the offense of genocide. It

23   shall not be presumed solely from the commission of the act

24   charged.

25   "(d) If two or more persons conspire to violate this

5

1 section, and one or more of such persons does any act to

2 effect the object of the conspiracy, each of the parties to such

3 conspiracy shall be fined not more than $10,000 or impris-

4 oned not more than five years or both.

5   "(c) The offenses defined in this section, wherever

6 committed, shall be deemed to be offenses against the United

7 States.".

8   (b) The analysis of title 18, United States Code, is

9 amended by adding after the item for chapter 50 the follow-

10 ing new item:

"50A. Genocide _____ 1091".

11   SEC. 2. The remedies provided in this Act shall be the

12 exclusive means of enforcing the rights based on it, but

13 nothing in the Act shall be construed as indicating an intent

14 on the part of the Congress to occupy, to the exclusion of

15 State or local laws on the same subject matter, the field in

16 which the provisions of the Act operate nor shall those pro-

17 visions be construed to invalidate a provision of State law

18 unless it is inconsistent with the purposes of the Act or the

19 provisions of it.

20   SEC. 3. It is the sense of the Congress that the Secretary

21 of State in negotiating extradition treaties or conventions

22 shall reserve for the United States the right to refuse extra-

23 dition of a United States national to a foreign country for an

24 offense defined in chapter 50A of title 18, United States

6

1 Code, when the offense has been committed outside the

2 United States, and

3   (a) where the United States is competent to prose-

4   cute the person whose surrender is sought, and intends

5   to exercise its jurisdiction, or

6   (b) where the person whose surrender is sought has

7   already been or is at the time of the request being prose-

8   cuted for such offense.

INDEX

A

Adamic, Louis, 164
Ad Hoc Committee on the Human Rights and Genocide Treaties, 260, 281
Agee, James, 110
Agudath Harabonim, 41
Alfaro, Ricardo J., 174
Aldrich, George, 260, 262, 266-7, 269
al-Jamali, 249
Allen, Albert, 35
Allen, Sen. James B., 284
Alliance Israelite Universelle, 181
Alter, Victor, 65
Amalgamated Clothing Workers, 203, 228
American Bar Association, 199-200, 202-207, 210, 214, 217, 221, 224, 238, 260-1, 274-5, 278, 283-4
American Civil Liberties Union, 279
American Committee for the Investigation of the Katyn Massacre, 209
American Federation of Labor, 212
American Jewish Committee, 41, 157, 181, 201, 203, 240-1, 256
American Jewish Congress, 41, 44, 74, 99, 226, 243
American Journal of International Law, 168, 173, 178
American Legion, 281
American Magazine, 36
American Scholar, 172
American Veterans' Committee, 203
Americans for Democratic Action, 203
Angell, Sir Norman, 47
Anglo-Jewish Association of Great Britain, 181

Arkin, George, 242
Assyrian Christians, 145-6, 251-4
Atrocity propaganda and stories, 47-51, 64-5, 72-3, 77; reactions to, 61-2
Austin, Amb. Warren R., 174, 219
Auschwitz, 52, 112-3, 198, 264
Australia, 208
Axelsson, George, 35
Axis Rule in Occupied Europe, 1, 4-5, 27; analysis of, 115-136; British edition of, 170

B

Babi Yar, 78-9, 105-6
Ball, George W., 124
Barnes, Harry Elmer, 63
Barnes, Joseph, 89
Baron, Prof. Salo, 106
Bauck, Erling, 112-3
Bauer, Yehuda, 163
Begin, Menachem, 30, 38, 99-100, 104
Belzec, 41
Benes, Edouard, 59
Berle, Adolf A., 199, 211, 217, 227
Berman, Sam, 90
Bernays, Murray C., 200
Bierut, Boleslaw, 173
Bingham, Alfred M., 102
Biow, Milton H., 250
Birchall, Frederick T., 20
Bissell, Maj. Gen. Clayton, 222
Bittker, Bruno, 260, 271
Black Book of Poland (1942), 155-6, 162

Blair, William M., 203
Blum, Leon, 53
B'nai Br'ith, 41, 203, 239
Boisson, Governor General, 107
Bonaparte, Napoleon, 125-6
Bonsal, Dudley B., 200
Borisovich, Abraham, 66
Boskin, Joseph, 228
Bourke-White, Margaret, 109
Bouton, Miles, 20, 102
Braginsky, Prof. Joseph, 130
Bricker Amendment, 237-9, 242
Bricker, Sen. John W., 233, 238-9, 271
Brickner, Dr. Richard, 63-4
B'rith Abraham, 242
British Ministry of Economic Warfare,
    62, 154
Brodninsky, Pavel, 66
Brown Book of the Hitler Terror, 20
Brown, Dr. Brendon F., 211
Brown, Cecil, 63
Brownell, Atty. Gen. Herbert, 238
Buchenwald, 53, 108
Buchman, Frank, 228
Bullitt, William C., 17
Business Week, 154-5

C

Caiserman, H. M., 173
Callender, Harold, 58
Calley, Lt. William, 134
Cambodia, 221
Carey, Archibald J., 244
Carey, James B., 211
Carnegie Endowment for International
    Peace, 1
Carnegie Foundation, 116-8
Carretta, Donato, 96
Carter, Mrs. Eunice, 211
Carter, Pres. James, 13, 285
Cassin, René, 273
Celler, Rep. Emanuel, 60-1, 206
Central Conference of American Rabbis,
    239, 242
Central Eastern European Planning
    Board, 42
Central Organization of German Jewry,
    102
Central Palestine Office, 99
Chang, John Myun, 219
Christian Century, 46, 172
Christian Science Monitor, 2
Church Peace Union, 201
Church, Sen. Frank, 255, 259, 263-4,
    266, 269, 272-5, 279-80, 282, 284
Churchill, Winston, 75-6, 82, 86, 88
Clark, Justice Tom, 261
Collier's, 47

Commager, Prof. Henry S., 63
Comintern, 102
Comite des Forges, 95
Committee of Jewish Writers and Artists,
    42
Concentration camps, Axis, 158-9
Connally, Sen. Tom, 219
Conservative Peers and Members of
    Parliament, 88
Consultative Council of Jewish Organi-
    zations, 181
Cooper, Sen. John Sherman, 259, 261,
    263, 265, 267, 269, 273, 276-7, 279
Coordinating Group of Womens' Organi-
    zations, 201
Costa Rica, 221
Council for a Democratic Germany,
    83
Court of International Justice, 229
Cousins, Norman, 63
Cowley, Malcolm, 37, 85
Crawford, Frederick C., 164-5
Creel, George, 89-90
Crossman, R.H.S., 107
Curie, Eve, 48
Current Biography, 17
Czecho-Slovakia, 3

D

Dachau, 20, 102, 108, 110
Dagens Nyheter, 171
Daniels, Howard, 38
Daughters of the American Revolution,
    234-5, 248
Davies, Joseph E., 59-60
Davis, Elmer, 66, 240
Davis, Jerome, 78
Deborin, Grigory, 131
de Gaulle, Charles, 95-6, 107
Dennis, Lawrence, 195
Debelius, Bishop, 232
Dieppe, 57
Dirksen, Sen. Everett M., 238
Displacement of Population in Europe
    (1943), 43
Dobriansky, Prof. Lev, 213, 232, 260,
    276-7
Dodd, Thomas A., 211, 217, 224-5
Dora-Mittelbau, 109
Douglas, Justice William O., 7, 190
Downs, Bill, 76
Drake, Thomas, 270
Draper, Maj. Gen. Warren, 165
Dreier, Alex, 35-6
Dubinsky, David, 228
Dulles, John Foster, 88, 204-6, 237-40,
    271
Dunkirk, 57

E

Eastman, Hope, 260, 279
Ecuador, 208
Eden, Anthony, 62
Ehrenburg, Ilya, 91
Ehrlich, Henryk, 65
Eichelberger, Clark M., 187, 256
Eichmann, Adolf, 10, 12-3
Einstein, Albert, 20
Einzig, Paul, 71
Eisenhower, Pres. Dwight D., 83, 255
Eliot, Maj. George Fielding, 85
El Salvador, 208
Emergency Committee to Save the Jewish People of Europe, 75
Encyclopedia of World History, 173
Epstein, Julius, 208-9
Ervin, Sen. Sam J., Jr., 280, 282, 284, Appendix II
Ethiopia, 202
Europe, coming Soviet expansion in (1943-44), 81-4
Evangelical and Reformed Church, 203
Evatt, Herbert V., 189-91, 208, 236

F

Fadiman, Clifton, 59-60, 72
Fainsod, Merle, 2
Federal Council of Churches, 88
Federation of Jewish Womens' Organizations, 209
Feilchenfeld, Ernst, 155
Feinberg, Chaim, 66
Feuchtwanger, Lion, 20, 75, 102-3
Finance, international, post-1919, 22-3
Finch, George A., 118-9, 168, 212, 215
Finland, 77-8
Finney, John W., 282
Fischer, Louis, 92
Fisher, Adrian S., 211
FitzGibbon, Louis, 104-5
Flandin, Pierre-Étienne, 107
Foreign Affairs, 4
For Fundamental Human Rights, 257
Forrestal, James, 99
Fortune, 54
Foster, Freling, 47
Fowler, Cody, 224
France, 221
Franco, Gen. Francisco, 207
Frank, Anne, 47
Frank, Hans, 141
Free World, 170
Frick, Wilhelm, 102
Fulbright, Sen. J. William, 281
Fuller, Gen. J.F.C., 88-9, 126

G

Gabriel, Alexander, 251

Gage-Colby, Mrs. Ruth, 211
Gardner, Prof. Richard, 260, 272-4, 281
General Federation of Womens' Clubs, 207
Geneva Convention (1929), 60
"genocide," 3, 7-9, 12-14; analysis of, in *Axis Rule in Occupied Europe*, 137-66;
Genocide Convention, 12-15; analysis of, 287-301; first draft of, 180; ratification of, 201-250, 258
Geraud, Gen. Henri, 96
Germany, Communists of, and Babi Yar, 78-9; planned postwar retaliation against, 62-3, 70, 85-92; postwar plans for, 93-5
Gerstein, Kurt, 7
Gibson, Hugh, 87-8
Glueck, Sheldon, 71, 168
Goebbels, Joseph, 66
Goldberg, Arthur J., 281
Goldklang, Jack, 276
Goldstein, Israel, 242-3
Gollancz, Victor, 80
Golovanivski, Savva, 106
Green, William, 65
Gross, Ernest A., 188-9
Grossman, Kurt R., 73
Grynszpan, Herschel, 37
Guatemala, 208
guerrilla warefare, 53-4, 57-60

H

Hadassah, 30, 39, 203, 220, 230
Haganah, 63
Hague Conventions (1899 and 1907), 54, 119, 125-9, 135-6
Haile Selassie, 202
Haiti, 166, 221
Halprin, Mrs. Samuel W., 220
Hammarskjold, Dag, 246
Harriman, W. Averell, 232
Harvard Law Review, 2
Hauser, Mrs. Rita, 260, 262, 264-9
Hecht, Ben, 54, 75
Held, Adolf, 228
Hemingway, Ernest, 72
Hess, Rudolf, 60
Heydrich, Gen. Reinhard, 59-60
Hickenlooper, Sen. Bourke B., 209
Hindus, Maurice, 49-50
Hitler, Adolf, 3, 34, 40, 61, 140, 152, 217, 261
Hitler's Ten-Year War on the Jews (1943), 44, 46-7, 99-101
Hoffer, Eric, 300-1
Hohenberg, John, 174
Holman, Frank E., 199, 201, 204, 206, 239-40, 247, 275

Hoover, Pres. Herbert C., 87-8
Hopkins, Harry, 87
Hornbeck, Stanley K., 84
Howard, Mrs. Ernest W., 260, 278-9
Huddleston, Sisley, 98
Hull, Cordell, 73
Human Biology, 164
Human Rights Committee, 234
Humphrey, Sir Francis, 253
Hurst, Fannie, 201
Hutchins, Robert M., 228

I

Iceland, 208
Ikra Mullah, Mrs. Shoistra S., 188
Ilutovich, Leon, 285
International Court of Justice, 190, 208
International Labor Office, 43
International Ladies' Garment Workers Union, 228
Institute of Jewish Affairs, 44, 46, 56, 99-101, 162-4
Iraq, 251-3
Irgun Zvai Leumi, 20, 31-2
Israel, 213, 285

J

Jabotinsky, Vladimir, 31
Jackson, Justice Robert H., 6, 170, 228
Jakubowska, Wanda, 198
Japan, postwar retaliation plans against, 84-5
Javits, Sen. Jacob K., 259, 275, 280-4, Appendix II
Jenner, Sen. William E., 238
Jewish Agency, 100
"Jewish Book Month," 1
Jewish Joint Distribution Committee, 43, 100
Jewish Labor Committee, 227-8
Jewish refugees, statistics on, 1941, 56
Jewish Reform Congregations, 239
Jews, allegations of extermination of in Europe, 1942, 44
Jews, escape from Europe of, 80
Johnson, Pres. Lyndon B., 257-8
Johnson, Joseph E., 223-4
Jones, Harry Leroy, 260, 274-5
Jordan, 214
Jouhaux, Leon, 230
Jurgela, Constantine R., 212-3

K

Kaempffert, Waldemar, 174-8
Kafr Kassem, 249
Karmen, Roman, 49
Karski, Jan, 163
Kasztner Report, 7

Katyn, 65-9, 103-6, 221-2, 233
Kaufman, Theodore N., 54-5, 72
Kaunas, 41
Keating, Sen. Kenneth B., 248
Kennedy, Pres. John F., 258
Kervyn, Prof. Albert, 110
Kessel, Sim, 112
Kharkov trials, 76-7, 90
King Faisal (Iraq), 252-3
King Haakon, 202
King Saud, 246
Kirchwey, Freda, 93, 98
Klein, Catherine, 80
Knauth, Percy, 97
Knieriem, August von, 129-130, 136
Koestler, Arthur, 153
Kokkinakis, Rev. Athenagoras, 211
Korea, South, 221
Korean War, 218-221, 229, 231, 242
Korey, William, 283
Korneichuk, Alexander, 68
Kraus, René, 58-9
Krock, Arthur, 215-6, 241, 245
Krüger, W.F., 154
Kuhn, Ferdinand, Jr., 253
Kulischer, Eugene M., 157-8
Kuper, Leo, 255
Kurds, 252-3

L

Lammers, Hans, 140
Land warfare, U.S. and British manuals of laws on, 127-9, 133-6
Lauterbach, Richard E., 51, 76, 79
Laval, Pierre, 106-7
Lawrence, David, 61, 87
Lawrence, W. H., 49-50
Layton, Robert, 260, 277-8
League for Industrial Democracy, 238
League of Nations, 251, 253
Lehman, Sen. Herbert H., 223, 242, 244, 248, 276
Lemkin, Elias, 24
Lemkin, Raphael, 1-8, 10-12, 17-22, 25-7, 32-4, 44-5, 52, 58, 83, 86, 96, 98-9, 101, 115-193, 196, 199-212, 214-6, 218-9, 222-3, 226-8, 230, 232-4, 236-7, 240-2, 245-6, 248-253, 255-7, 268, 276, 286-301
Levin, Meyer, 47
Liberia, 214
Liberty Lobby, 260, 271, 282-3
Lidice, 59-62
Lie, Trygve, 201, 213
Liebman, Rabbi Joshua Loth, 39
Limb, Col. Ben C., 222
Lindley, Ernest K., 85
List, Abraham, 103

Lithuanian-American Council, 231, 237
Litvinov, Maxim, 65
Lodge, Henry Cabot, 244-5
London Polish Government-in-Exile, 65-9
London *Sunday Times*, 171
Long, Breckinridge, 73
Lord, Mrs. Oswald B., 201
Lourie, Arthur, 220
Lozovsky, S.A., 62
Luce, Henry, publications, 68, 96
Ludwig, Emil, 70

M

Ma'ariv, 104-5
MacCracken, Henry Noble, 187
MacDonald, Dwight, 102
MacDonald, Ramsay, 253
Madden, Richard L., 283
Maidanek, 47-8, 51
Mallon, Paul, 6
Manion, Dean Clarence, 238, 270-1
Mansfield, Sen. Mike, 282
Marcus, Robert S., 207
Markham, R.H., 97
Mar Shimun, 253
Masaryk, Jan, 81-2
Matteotti, Giacomo, 65
Maxwell-Fyfe, Sir David, 172, 174
McCarran-Walter Act, 242
McCarthy, Sen. Joseph R., 214
McClory, Rep. Robert R., 282-3
McCormick, Anne O'Hare, 97
McDermott, Malcolm, 22, 26
McDonald, James G., 20, 108
McMahon, Sen. Brien, 203, 211, 220-1, 223, 225
Mikolajczyk, Stanislav, 42, 173
Miller, Nathan L., 201
Millis, Walter, 2
Mitchell, Atty. Gen. John, 259, 276
Moats, Alice Leone, 65
Moley, Raymond, 85-6
Mollo, Andrew, 111
Molotov, V.M., 48
Morand, Paul, 106
Monaco, 214
Morgenthau, Henry, Plan, 50-1, 83, 88-91, 119
Morozov, P.D., 185-6
Morrison, Charles Clayton, 88
Moscow "purge" trials, 10
Mosley, Leonard, 31
Mount Holyoke College Institute on the United Nations, 202
Mowrer, Edgar Ansel, 21
Muenzenberg, Willi, 20
Mussolini, Benito, 65

N

Nasz Przejlad, 24
"nation," definition of, 3
The Nation, 2-3
National Civil Liberties Clearing House, 204
National Community Relations Advisory Council, 214
National Conference of Christians and Jews, 181, 206, 216
National Council for the Social Studies, 55
National Federation of Business and Professional Women, 227, 247-8
National Federation of Temple Sisterhoods, 239
National Socialist White Peoples Party, 260
Neilson, Francis, 64
Neurath, Constantin von, 172
New Masses, 43, 45
New York Herald Tribune, 171
New York Herald Tribune Weekly Book Review, 1-2
New York City Bar Association, 199-200, 216, 227
New York State Bar Association, 201, 212, 260
New York Times, 2; definition of "genocide" in, 8; promotion of word "genocide" by, 171; editorials urging adoption of Genocide Convention in, 174-5, 208, 213-4, 218-9, 223, 225, 240, 243, 247-50, 282, 284
Newsweek, 164-6
Niebuhr, Reinhold, 71-2, 83, 103
Nixon, Pres. Richard M., 255, 258-9, 270, 281-2, 284
Nizer, Louis, 89
N.K.V.D., 99
Nobel Committee, 228, 230, 233-4
Norway, 202
Nuremberg, 7

O

Ogilvie Forbes, G. S., 253
Order of the Sons of Zion, 30
Orwell, George, 194-6
Ottawa conference on refugees, 73

P

"Pacificus," 84
Panama, 208
Parks, Maj. Gen. Floyd L., 222
Pat, Jacob, 227-8
Patterson, Sec. Robert P., 199, 210
Pavelic, Ante, 141
Peffer, Nathaniel, 85
Pegler, Westbrook, 72

Pell, Sen. Claiborne, 259, 261, 263, 267, 269
Pepper, Sen. Claude, 89
Perez, Leander, 211
Perlman, Philip B., 204, 210, 212, 214, 224
Petain, Gen. Philippe, 107
Peyrouton, Marcel, 107
Pierce, Dr. William L., 260, 272
Pilcewicz, Isydor, 103
Pol, Heinz, 71-2
Polier, Justine Wise, 246
Poland, 3; politics in, 1919-39, 18; Jewish affairs in, 1930s, 19; political affairs in 1930s, 23-4; anti-Jewish repressions in, 34-5; situation of Jews in, 1939-41, 37-9; Jews in, 1941-4, 39-40; Jews in, 1942-3, 43-4
Polish-American Congress, 237
Polish-American Council, 231-2;
Polish Committee of National Liberation, 49
Polish Fortnightly Review, 154
Polish National Council, 40, 42
Polish Penal Code of 1932, 22
Polish White Book, 38-9, 153, 162
Ponomarenko, Pantaleimon K., 130
Portalis, Jean Etienne Marie de, 125-6
Potofsky, Jacob, 228
Prawo karne skarbowe, 22
President's Commission for the Observance of Human Rights Year (1968-69), 257
Proskauer, Judge Joseph M., 200-1
Proxmire, Sen. William, 260-2, 281-2, 284-5
Publishers Weekly, 1
Pucheu, Pierre, 95-6

R

Radin, Max, 70-1
Ransom, William L., 224
Rassinier, Paul, 7, 107-8
Rauschning, Hermann, 152, 162
Refugees, 53, 73-5
Rehnquist, William H., 260, 275-6
"Resistance" action in Europe, 1944-45, 96-8
Reynolds, Quentin, 72
Rhee, Pres. Syngman, 222
Richardson, Warren S., 260, 271
Rix, Carl B., 204, 211, 215, 230-1
Robinson, Col. Donald B., 108-11
Robinson, Nehemiah, 256
Rodino, Rep. Peter, 282-3
Rodman, Selden, 102
Rogers, Sec. William P., 258-9, 276
Rohde, Ruth Byron, 201

Roosevelt, Mrs. Eleanor, 238
Rose, Billy, 73
Rosenberg, Alfred, 152
Rosenberg, James N., 43, 186-7, 199, 206
Rosenblum, William F., 207
Rostow, Eugene V., 284
Rousseau, J.J., 125-6
Roy Publishers, 79
Rudzinski, Alexander, 186
Rumana, Judge Thomas R., 103
Runes, Dagobert D., 130
Rusk, Dean, 209-10
Ruttenberg, Stanley, 211
Rybak, Lev, 66

S

Samuels, Gertrude, 200-1
Saturday Evening Post, 50
Saudi Arabia, 221
Saurin, Paul, 107
Schmitt, Prof. Bernadotte, 55-6, 70
Schwarzbart, Ignacy, 40-2
Schweppe, Alfred T., 210-11, 215, 217, 224
Scott, Sen. Hugh, 281-2, 284
Segal, Bernard, 275
Seyss-Inquart, Arthur, 7
Shawcross, Sir Hartley, 174, 187, 228
Shercliff, José, 53
Shirer, William L., 63, 66-7, 92-3
Shub, Boris, 99-101
Shub, David, 101
Sikorski, Gen Wladyislaw, 49, 66-9
Simon, Lord, 60
Smith, Fred, 83
Smith, Howard K., 36
Smith, Laurence C., 260, 270
Smuts, Jan Christiaan, 81
Snow, Edgar, 49-50, 94-5
Sockman, Dr. Ralph, 201
Sorokin, Joshua, 104-5
Sorokowski, Andrew, 106
Soviet Polish Atrocities Investigation Commission, 49
Spackman, Ellis E., 110-11
Spivak, Lawrence E., 108
Sporborg, Mrs. William Dick, 201
Stalin, Josef, 66, 69, 72, 81, 84, 92, 94-5, 197, 204, 236
Starvation over Europe (Made in Germany), 99-101
Stassen, Harold, 203-4, 221, 229-30
States Rights Committee, 211
Stevenson, Adlai, 233
Stone, I.F., 79-80
Stout, Rex Todhunter, 63, 83
Straight, Michael, 211

Strasburger, Henryk, 41, 46
Streit, Clarence K., 253
Subdarans, K. V. K., 186
Suslov, Alexander, 105
Swartz, Mary, 99-100
Symington, Sen. Stuart, 259
Synagogue Council of America, 41
Syria, 251-3
Szyk, Arthur, 90

T

Taft, Sen. Robert A., 6, 190
Taylor, Betty Kaye, 281
Taylor, Telford, 129, 136, 216-7
Teheran conference, 75
They Chose Life, 44
Thomas, Norman, 65, 84
Thompson, Dorothy, 91
Thorez, Maurice, 82
Tichonov, Samyun, 105
Tillett, C. W., 207
Times Literary Supplement (London), 2
Tito, Josip Broz, 197
Togliatti, Palmiro, 82
Tokayer, Rabbi Marvin, 99-100
Tolischus, Otto D., 2
Tondel, Lyman M., Jr., 221
Treblinka, 50
Truman, Pres. Harry S., 89, 201, 205, 209, 214, 218-220, 223-4, 255, 271, 285
Tsiang, Dr. Tingfu F., 229, 235-6

U

Ukrainian Congress Committee of America, 213, 260
Union of Hebrew Congregations, 239
Union of Orthodox Rabbis, 100
United Committee for the Struggle Against Pogroms in Poland, 20
United Nations (World War Two), and atrocity stories, 62; Commission for the Investigation of War Crimes, 75; Joint Declaration, 44; *United Nations Review* (1943), 44, 162
United Nations Organization, 8, 10, 205; *Bulletin* of, 183-5, 191; Childrens' Emergency Fund of, 201; and Genocide Convention, 14; and deliberations on Genocide Convention, 177-191; Legal Committee of, 207; Sixth Committee of, 256; and National Commission for UNESCO, 201
United States, Dept. of Army Field Manual FM 27-10, 90; Office of War Information, 66; Senate Foreign Relations Committee Subcommittee (McMahon, 1950), 202-9, 212-3, 215-6, 219-20;

224-5, 245; Senate Foreign Relations Committee Subcommittee (Church, 1970), 255-281; Senate Judiciary Committee, 218; State Department, 41, 224
United States Committee for the Genocide Convention, 181, 210
United States Constitution Council, 260
United States News, postwar plans for Germany, comments in, 86-7
Universal Declaration of Human Rights, 179, 191
USSR, reservations on Genocide Convention by, 208

V

Valutareglering och Clearing, 2, 26
Vambery, Rustem, 5-6, 170
Vandenberg, Sen. Arthur, 205
van Doren, Carl, 63
Vansittart, Sir Robert, 71, 91-2
Van Vliet, Lt. Col. John H., 222
Vassilevskaya, Wanda, 68
Verin, Judge, 96
Versailles, 3
Vichy, 96
Vidra, Abraham, 104-5
Vishinsky, Andrei Y., 246
vom Rath, Ernst, 37

W

Wagner, Mayor Robert F., 249
Wallace, Vice Pres. Henry A., 89
"War crimes," 52, 60-1
"War criminals," 10
Warhaftig, Zorach, 99-101
War Refugee Board, 51-2
Warsaw uprising, 50
Watergate, 282
Weigert, Hans W., 72
Weinreich, Max, 103
Weiss, Maj. Gen. Pierre, 96
Weizmann, Chaim, 43
Welles, Sumner, 30, 84
Werner, Max, 90-1
Wertenbaker, Charles Christian, 97
Werth, Alexander, 61
Whitcomb, Philip W., 106-7
Wiggins, J. R., 243
Wilson, Edmund, 102
Wise, Rabbi Stephen, 40-1, 45
Workmen's Circle, 228
World Baptist Congress, 219-20
World Jewish Congress, 40, 44, 60, 99-100, 181, 207, 242-3
World Zionist Organization, 43
Writers Committee to Aid Polish Jews, 35

Writers War Board, 83

Y

Yellow Spot, The (Der Gelbe Fleck), 102
Yiddish Scientific Institute, 103
Yost, Amb. Charles W., 260, 262-7
Yugoslavia, 3, 221

Z

Zahavy, Rabbi Zev, 243
Zapp, Manfred, 36
Ziff, William B., 78-9, 89, 130
Zilboorg, Dr. Gregory, 63-4
Zionist Organization of America, 30, 285
Zukerman, William, 35-6
Zygielboim, Szmul, 42